Intercultural Communication and Language Education

Series Editors

Stephanie Ann Houghton, Saga University, Saga, Japan
Melina Porto, La Plata, Argentina

This book series publishes top quality monographs and edited volumes containing empirical research that prioritises the development of intercultural communicative competence in foreign language education as part of intercultural citizenship. It explores the development of critical cultural awareness broadly aimed at triggering and managing personal and social transformation through intercultural dialogue. Citizenship education and interculturally-oriented language education share an interest in fostering learner exploration, critical analysis and evaluation of other cultures within dynamic socio-political environments.

To complement existing research on the development of intercultural communicative competence, this book series explores the techniques, processes and outcomes of intercultural language pedagogy and intercultural citizenship inside and outside the classroom. It also explores the nature, dynamics and impact of intercultural dialogue outside the classroom in real-world settings where various language codes are in use, including World Englishes and English as a Lingua Franca.

Further, this book series recognizes and explicitly attempts to overcome wide-ranging real-world barriers to intercultural dialogue and intercultural citizenship. This is especially important in the field of English language education considering the status of English as a global language and associated problems connected to linguistic imperialism, ideology and native-speakerism among others. To promote the development of deeper understandings of how such social problems connect to the use of foreign languages in general, contributions are also sought from disciplines outside foreign language education such as citizenship education, social justice, moral education, language policy and social psychology that shed light upon influential external social factors and internal psychological factors that need to be taken into account.

More information about this series at http://www.springer.com/series/13631

María Dolores López-Jiménez •
Jorge Sánchez-Torres

Editors

Intercultural Competence Past, Present and Future

Respecting the Past, Problems in the Present and Forging the Future

 Springer

Editors
María Dolores López-Jiménez
Universidad Pablo de Olavide
Sevilla, Spain

Jorge Sánchez-Torres
Centro Internacional de Estudios Culturales
Sevilla, Spain

ISSN 2520-1735   ISSN 2520-1743   (electronic)
Intercultural Communication and Language Education
ISBN 978-981-15-8244-8   ISBN 978-981-15-8245-5   (eBook)
https://doi.org/10.1007/978-981-15-8245-5

This Springer imprint is published by the registered company Springer Nature Singapore Pte Ltd.
The registered company address is: 152 Beach Road, #21-01/04 Gateway East, Singapore 189721, Singapore

Contents

Part II   Forging the Future

Chapter 1
Introduction and Overview

María Dolores López-Jiménez and Jorge Sánchez-Torres

1.1 Introduction

References to "culture" have become more and more prominent in applied linguistics, especially since the 1980s, to highlight the intimate relationship between language and culture. However, many teachers still lack enough resources and guidance to teach intercultural competence (IC) despite extensive research and attempts for a framework of reference. This volume will attempt to fill that gap.

The term "culture" could be described as follows: (a) traditional ideas and its attached values (Kroeber & Kluckhohln, 1952); (b) networks of meaning (Geertz, 1973); (c) ideas, experiences, feelings, and meanings that members of a society create (Hannerz, 1992); (d) offshoots of experience, learned or created by individuals of a group (Schwartz, 1992); (e) a combination of shared attitudes, values, beliefs, and behaviors (Matsumoto, 1996); (f) a system of the structural positioning of people (Thomas, 1996); or (g) a general ensemble of basic assumptions and values, beliefs, norms, procedures, and conventions which are shared by a group of people (Spencer-Oatey, 2008). Different perspectives, from anthropology (human beings), sociology (social relations), psychology (mind and behavior), linguistics (human language), and communication (interactions and sharing of information), have contributed to our understanding of "culture." Spencer-Oatey and Franklin (2009) find some common patterns on the characteristics of "culture": (a) it reveals itself through different types of regularities; (b) it is connected to social groups,

M. D. López-Jiménez (✉)
Universidad Pablo de Olavide, Sevilla, Spain
e-mail: mdlopezji@upo.es

J. Sánchez-Torres
Centro Internacional de Estudios Culturales, Sevilla, Spain
e-mail: jorge.sancheztorres@gmail.com

© Springer Nature Singapore Pte Ltd. 2021
M. D. López-Jiménez, J. Sánchez-Torres (eds.), *Intercultural Competence Past, Present and Future*, Intercultural Communication and Language Education,
https://doi.org/10.1007/978-981-15-8245-5_1

although two individuals from the same social group do not share exactly the same cultural characteristics; (c) it has an effect on the group's behavior and the interpretations of that behavior; and (d) it is acquired and/or constructed through interaction with others.

Similarly, the notion of "interculturality" is believed to have been central in L2 teaching and learning over the past 30 years. Although there is no general agreement on the meanings of interculturality, some principles may be shared across national borders. The word intercultural can be traced back to Hall's (1959) work on intercultural relationship in the 1950s. It literally means between cultures, and it could be defined as every interaction/communication among members of two social/cultural groups (Spencer-Oatey & Franklin, 2009). "Intercultural" as a term in language teaching emerged in the 1980s as a development of the concept of "communicative competence," which was by then widely agreed to be the aim of foreign language teaching and learning (Byram, 1997, p. 3). In addition, Zegarat (2007, p. 41) distinguishes "intracultural" from "intercultural." "Intercultural communication," from a cognitive point of view, is a situation in which the cultural distance of the participants is meaningful enough as to have a negative effect on successful communication, while in "intracultural communication" the cultural distance is not meaningful enough for having that negative effect. It is mostly through the concept of "intercultural competence" (IC) that interculturality has been developed for teachers and students.

The concept of IC was reintroduced by Byram (1997) through the notion of "intercultural communicative competence" (ICC) in his book *Teaching and Assessing Intercultural Communicative Competence*. His 1997 book arouse from a commission from the Council of Europe to define levels of sociocultural competence. However, the commission was not fulfilled due to the impossibility to define such levels. Instead, the notion of "intercultural speaker" (Byram, 1997) to refer to the learner and user of foreign language was conceptualized. For many years, the communicative competence had the native speaker as a model, but this was challenged due to the fact that the native speaker as a model not only sets an almost impossible objective for most of the students but also because it may be psychologically undesirable. Desirable learners have the ability to see and manage the relations between those who belong to their own culture, their own cultural beliefs, behaviors and meanings, as if they were expressed in a foreign language, and the cultural relations and beliefs of their interlocutors, expressed in the same language—or even in a combination of languages—that could, or not, be the main language repertoire of the interlocutors. Later, Kramsch (1998, p. 27) uses the term "competent user of the language," whose main characteristics are the adaptability skills to select the right forms of accuracy and the appropriate forms that are needed and demanded in a specific social use context. Besides, in most of the intercultural interaction cases, both interlocutors have different social identities and, with it, a way of interacting which is different from the one they have when interacting in the same language with individuals from their respective countries (Byram, 1997).

Byram's (1997) framework of reference, based on Van Ek's (1986), modifies some concepts in order to give more importance to the discovery, the interpretation, and the establishment of a relationship which he considers to be crucial for intercultural speakers (Byram, 1997). This way, he establishes the following components of ICC (Byram, 1997):

- Attitudes: curiosity and open-mindedness toward other cultures.
- Knowledge: knowledge of social groups and their products and practices in one's own country and in that of the interlocutor together with the general processes of social and individual interaction.
- Skills of interpreting and relating: skills to interpret a document or event from another cultural perspective in order to explain it and relate it to documents or events of one's own culture.
- Skills of discovery and interaction: skills for acquiring new knowledge of a culture and cultural practices and the skills to manage the knowledge, the attitudes, and the skills according to the limitations of real-time communication and interaction.
- Critical cultural awareness: skills to critically evaluate practices and products of one's own culture and those of other cultures.

According to Byram (1997), IC refers to peoples' "ability to interact in their own language with people from another country and culture" whereas ICC places its emphasis on language teaching and on "the ability to interact with people from another country and culture in a foreign language" (p. 71). However, Fantini (2009, p. 458) equates IC and ICC. He asserts that a monolingual speaker cannot acquire IC as the acquisition of IC in one or more foreign language (FL) results in ICC. Byram's (1997) assertion that "teaching for linguistic competence cannot be separated from teaching for intercultural competence" (p. 22) reflects the fundamental relationship between language and culture in second/foreign language teaching.

Byram's, 1997, model has not been exempt from criticism and, therefore, it has undergone developments since then for further refinements, as outlined in the following paragraphs. Firstly, most criticisms have centered on the concept of culture, that is, the fourth dimension identified by Rathje (2007, p. 255) as "foundation," which informs Byram's model. The 1997 model has been accused of being nationalist and essentialist (Belz, 2007; Holliday, 2011; Kramsch, 1998; Risager, 2007). Byram (1997, pp. 113–115), initially recommended focusing on British or American studies for teaching cultural content due to their dominance. Given the plurilingual and multicultural nature of societies, the model seems to be rather limited. It assumes that cultures are static, rigid, homogeneous, and nationally and geographically bounded notions (Kramsch, 1999). This association between a culture and a nation/country appears in one of the five components of ICC, that is, critical cultural awareness, since it is defined as the "ability to evaluate critically and on the basis of explicit criteria, perspectives, practices and products in one's own and other cultures and countries" (Byram, 1997, p. 53). However, Byram (2009, p. 330) stated that this is not "banal nationalism" but it is actually a necessity due to its use by FL teachers, apart from reflecting a reality in which people interact. Additionally, Byram (2008) stated that his model is not in conflict with a transnational paradigm expressed through the notion of "intercultural citizenship" (Alred, Byram, & Fleming, 2006), also developed by Risager (2007, p. 194) as "world citizen."

"Citizenship" is identified as a group of behaviors that belong to a single sociopolitical and cultural identity (singularity), whereas "interculturality" is usually associated with more than one identity (plurality). In their book, Byram and the rest of the editors and contributors emphasized the need for an intercultural dimension in citizenship education in which awareness of one's own identity is fundamental in order to deal with others' identity. Porto (2018) believes that the theory of intercultural citizenship in language education proposed by Byram (Byram, 2008; Byram, 2014; Byram, Golubeva, Han, & Wagner, 2017) can inform content and language integrated learning (CLIL) in theoretical terms as it bridges Coyle's 4Cs framework (Coyle, 2006, 2007a, 2007b) with Meyer, Coyle, Halbach, Shuck, and Ting's (2015) pluriliteracies approach to CLIL. Porto (2018) points out that nowadays CLIL faces certain difficulties in terms of conceptualization, research, pedagogy, and orientation. According to Nussbaum (2006), individuals' development and the values of democratic societies are not present in CLIL. Instead, CLIL has an exclusive instrumental orientation with a focus on content and/or language issues. In addition, many CLIL studies center on language outcomes (Aguilar & Muñoz, 2014; Heras & Lasagabaster, 2015), whereas no attention is paid to the learning process itself. Also, in CLIL pedagogy teacher talk dominates with almost no room for autonomous learning (Kääntä, Kasper, & Piirainen-Mash, 2018). Furthermore, CLIL has also been criticized for its Eurocentric orientation, a shortage of longitudinal studies, and little focus on primary and tertiary levels. Intercultural citizenship theory can inform CLIL in different ways. First, intercultural citizenship theory engages students in critical thinking not only at the cognition level, as it is the case of CLIL, but also at the level of action through social and civic action in the local/regional/national/global community. Education for citizenship deals with social themes (content learning) in a nonnative language (learning of an L2) that are relevant to the community (citizenship learning). CLIL, instead, lacks a citizenship orientation. Second, in relation to the concept of pluriliterate citizenship in CLIL, introduced by Meyer et al. (2015), the intercultural citizenship moves beyond the linguistic and intercultural aims which the theory shares with the pluriliteracies model, placing an emphasis on civic action.

Secondly, another criticism regarding the 1997 model is based on Kramsch's (2009) belief in Zarate and Byram still belonging to a structuralist perspective since that perspective facilitates assessment. According to Byram (personal communication), the concept of critical cultural awareness invites reflection and criticality. Therefore, as Byram points out, it emphasizes the symbolic power of language, which is associated with a poststructuralist perspective.

Thirdly, regarding assessment of IC, the achievement of an assessable threshold level of ICC (Byram, 1997, pp. 43, 76–78) is not compatible with cultural diversity (Belz, 2007). Any threshold level entails a standard that is unquestionably culture specific and value laden. Byram and Zarate (1994) proved from the original commission of the Council of Europe that defining levels of IC is an unattainable task because it is an interactional distributed ability. Instead, Byram, Gribkova, and Starkey (2002) proposed to test critical cultural awareness since it is an individual ability. Nowadays, there are assessing tools, for example the so-called Certificate of

Intercultural Competence in English (ICE) (Mader & Camerer, 2010). The ICE uses descriptors such as interaction, content, and language from the Common European Framework of Reference for Languages (CEFR) for assessment criteria. Another project that provides descriptors for the assessment of IC is the INCA project (www. incaproject.eu). This project has developed descriptors for three levels of competence, that is, basic, intermediate, and full competence.

Lastly, other criticisms related to the 1997 model revolve around its overt simplification and the passive role of the second language teacher together with a lack of guidance when observing the different processes found in practice. As for the first one, Byram (2009) asserts that his focusing on one identity of a learner and, thus, restricting the notion of multiple identities is a simplification needed for using the model in the context of foreign language learning. Concerning the second criticism, Houghton (2010) states that Byram endowed the teacher with a passive role since his task was to help students develop their own evaluative skills without any change in students' attitudes or fostering specific values. However, his shifting to a type of education for international citizenship has provided the teacher with a more active role when fostering students' values toward democratic principles and human rights (Houghton, 2010, p. 198).

In an attempt to define IC, Spencer-Oatey and Franklin (2009) explore different forms of differentiating among cultural groups and clarify that aspects such as values, beliefs, and conventions, among others, give human beings a system of reference and orientation to guide their behavior. With that exploration and clarification, they refer to "intercultural interaction competence" (IIC), which they define as "competence not only to communicate (verbally or not verbally) and behave effectively and appropriately with people from other cultural groups, but also to handle the psychological demands and dynamic outcomes that result from such interchanges" (Spencer-Oatey & Franklin, 2009, p. 51). These authors reviewed a number of empirical studies to identify the nature of IIC and developed a list of the components that play an important role in the creation of adequacy and effectiveness in intercultural interaction: (a) open-mindedness, (b) nonjudgementalness (sometimes referred to as interaction posture), (c) empathy, (d) tolerance for ambiguity, (e) flexibility in thinking and behavior, (f) self-awareness, (g) knowledge of one's own and other cultures, (h) resilience to stress, and (i) communication or message skills (including foreign language proficiency). These components are also present in the definitions of IC offered by other authors (see Wintergerst and McVeigh (2011) below), which is a form of validation of Spencer-Oatey and Franklin's (2009) revision of previous studies and list of components. Wintergerst and McVeigh (2011), for instance, explain that "understanding our own culture and that of others will help us achieve intercultural competence," which they define as "the skills, knowledge, attitudes, and cultural awareness we need to interact successfully with someone from another culture" (p. 9). In this introductory chapter, the expression "intercultural competence (IC)" will be used as an umbrella term not only for "intercultural communicative competence (ICC)," "intercultural interaction competence (IIC)," and "intercultural communication" but also for any issue dealing with aspects that involve more than one specific culture.

Recently, there has been an urgent need for theoretical frameworks and pedagogical suggestions for developing IC. When fostering IC, the Western/northern perspective has been questioned since a whole plethora of differing views of language and intercultural communication originate from different linguistic, cultural, territorial geographies, and communities (Parmenter, 2003; Santos, 2010). Also, and due to the peculiarities involved in every intercultural situation, not every methodology or pedagogy suits the concept of IC and vice versa. In addition, as previously stated, different meanings have been proposed for the word interculturality.

In spite of there not being a stage where the learner becomes fully interculturally proficient (Deardorff, 2009), Tobin and Abello-Contesse (2013), considering Bennett's (1993) work, refer to a series of stages, that is, denial, defense, minimization, acceptance, adaptation, and integration, which the intercultural learner goes through toward achieving IC. The first three stages indicate an ethnocentric view of the target culture where the other three help the learner move toward an ethnorelative position, being the L2 teacher the one who plays a fundamental role in guiding the learner through all those stages.

Although the foreign language classroom seems to be an especially appropriate environment for it, the development of this competence does not usually have a specific place in the educational curriculum, and it is integrated within the teaching of different subjects. However, a study commissioned by the General Board of Education and Culture of the European Commission entitled Languages and Cultures in Europe (LACE): The Intercultural Competencies Developed in Compulsory Foreign Language Education in the European Union (European Commission, 2007) reveals that, although there are many differences from one country to another within the 12 researched countries, the national curriculum pays more attention to the development of linguistic and communicative competences than to the development of (inter)cultural competences. This study also researched what didactic and methodological approaches were recommended in the national curriculum of these countries for the development of this competence and found out that this information was limited to the use of authentic materials in the target language (TV programs, newspapers, magazines, books), content and language integrated learning (CLIL), information on the target culture, oral production from the teacher, and online information.

In the abovementioned study, LACE, teachers were asked what methods, techniques, and procedures they use in their foreign language classroom for the development of IC. Although they were given Fowler and Blohm's (2004) classification of methods, the results were striking as there was an emphasized use of traditional "chalk-and-talk methods" (see examples in italics below). There was a (i) highly frequent use of "oral teacher input," "written information," "online information," "role plays," "task-based activities," and "literature and the arts"; (ii) medium use of the "Content and Language Integrated Learning," "information using other than online or written media," "Internet-based collaborative learning," "simulations and games," *"cross-cultural dialogues,"* and *"immersion, schools visits abroad and exchanges"*; and (iii) low frequent use of "tandem learning," "self-assessment," "case studies," *"critical incidents," "contrast culture training," "culture assimilator or intercultural sensitizer,*" and *"area studies"* (Spencer-Oatey & Franklin, 2009, p. 232).

Bandura and Sercu's (2005) study, corroborated by LACE (European Commission, 2007), discovered that little priority was given to values and beliefs. This is quite relevant if we consider that knowledge of values and beliefs of one's own and the target culture is essential for understanding cultural differences. It also revealed that the issues that target language teachers were facing were the lack of time, suitable resources, and specific guidance concerning intercultural competence development in their classrooms.

As stated above, many teachers still lack enough resources and guidance to teach IC in spite of extensive research and attempts for a framework of reference, and IC has been overtly simplified in language teaching. Although that degree of simplification is still a necessity in teaching, this creates an unavoidable tension with the complex nature of IC. Further refinements regarding the existing frameworks of reference and new teaching tools for IC are needed in order to understand the relationship between language, culture, and identity. In the next section, an overview of the book will be provided to show how this volume aims to meet that need.

1.2 Overview

This volume presents a collection of 12 chapters, some of which are revised, adapted, and extended versions of papers presented on July 2015 at the 12th University of Seville Conference on Applied Linguistics (ELIA)—organized by the research group The English Language in University Settings/La lengua inglesa en el ámbito universitario (HUM-397) based at the University of Seville—while the majority were commissioned for inclusion in this volume. To conclude, an epilogue is offered to foreground the strengths the volume holds in providing an understanding of the past, present, and future of intercultural competence and to "problematize ramifications and opportunities for further development across sociopolitical and geographical contexts."

The different chapters include (i) intercultural aspects such as "intercultural awareness" (Stracke), "teachers' awareness of interculturality and intercultural approach, teacher's reflection upon own culture, integration of language and culture" (Oranje), "intercultural communication, meaningful intercultural relationships, online intercultural communication" (Jackson), "critical intercultural awareness and intercultural communication, intercultural metalanguage and metaunderstandings" (Lubbers), "intercultural barriers to feedback" (Boyd & Donnarumma), "intercultural involvement, impediments in the target culture (C2) development, notion of 'third culture'/'third place', cultural hybridity" (Abello-Contesse), "promotion of critical cultural awareness, critical awareness and politeness, intercultural competence" (Guilherme & Sawyer), "critical cultural awareness, intercultural and visual competences promotion, exploration of otherness" (Mendez & Lindner), "PARSNIP as an essentialist and reductionist concept"

(Dinh & Siregar), "ELF in intercultural communication" (Chacón-Beltrán), "relationship between teacher confirmation and student motivation from a cross-cultural perspective" (Croucher, Galy-Badenas, Rahmani, Zeng, Albuquerque, Attarieh, & Nshom) and (ii) problematic/open to debate aspects such as "the roles of community (after-school) language schools," "language learning motivation (L2 Motivational Self System)," "heritage language learning," "stereotyping," "Otherization," "the effectiveness of feedback," "the role of reflection in teaching," "the immersion myth," "the individual differences," "external factors to learning," "'immersion' vs. moderate intensification," "online learning," "the role of culture in the L2 classroom," "the promotion of visual/media competence in the foreign language classroom," "PARSNIP and taboo in ELT," "ELF knowledge, awareness, attitudes, and beliefs from a teacher perspective," and "the relationship between teacher confirmation and student motivation," among others.

These debatable intercultural aspects are approached from different settings (study abroad education, local regular/mainstream education, after-school education, CLIL education, and online education) within different educational (community schools, primary, secondary, tertiary) and language (foreign, second, heritage) contexts under learning and/or teaching perspectives. In all, the chapters encompass qualitative and/or quantitative research from different countries around the globe, among them Australia, New Zealand, Great Britain, Spain, Finland, the United States, Portugal, Japan, Hong Kong, and Germany, and the concluding epilogue presents a general vision and one from South American countries such as Colombia and Argentina, among others, which incorporate further views from the Global South.

Regarding the types of research presented in this volume, it has to be mentioned that the goal of the IATEFL (International Association of Teachers of English as a Foreign Language) Research Special Interest Group, through the group's conferences, as stated by Dikilitaş, Wyatt, Burns, and Barkhuizen (2019) in *Energizing Teacher Research*, is to promote teacher research, "research by English language teachers into their own practice, for their own purposes and those of their students" (Burns, Dikilitaş, Smith, & Wyatt, 2017, p. 1). Dikilitaş et al. (2019, p. xv) explain that teacher research—contextualized relevant research, as they label it—in different parts of the world "is searching for new ways to introduce teachers to its possibilities, and to engage them in processes of professional investigation, analysis and reflection." This type of research in ELT, which has grown over the last two decades, is still growing, but, more importantly, "it has the capacity to provide deeply empowering and energizing personal and professional growth through which one's identity as a 'teacher-researcher' begins to expand" (p. xvi). In the same line, the chapters in this volume make consistent use of teacher research and contribute to legitimizing this professional activity in different contexts in order to provide other teachers and researchers with, in many cases, clear classroom implications, applications, and insights about their use regarding intercultural communicative competence. These implications, applications, and insights can be observed in chapters such as Lubber's (pedagogical problems of internationalizing and tools to embed intercultural metalanguage), Croucher et al.'s (effective pedagogical practices of teacher confirmation), Boyd and Donnarumma's (feedback as a pedagogical tool), Guilherme and Sawyer's (insights concerning the search for theoretical frameworks and pedagogical suggestions for understanding and promoting IC in different intercultural situations), Jackson's (online community for pedagogical interventions), and Méndez and Lindner's (visual media as a pedagogical resource), among others.

All these debatable intercultural aspects, issues, situations and/or contexts, implications, applications, and insights are organized in the 12 chapters of this edited volume and discussed in two interconnected parts: Part I: Respecting the Past and Problems in the Present and Part II: Forging the Future.

1.2.1   Part I: Respecting the Past and Problems in the Present

The first part consists of six chapters that deal with aspects of the past and issues in the present. The first two chapters address issues concerning heritage language learners and their desire "to learn and/or maintain the language and culture of their community and heritage" to maintain a link with their past. The past is also observed in other chapters when exploring the concept of intercultural competence, its meaning and growth, or through chapters that let us see the evolution of practices regarding intercultural competence and different approaches.

In addition, Chap. 2 considers community language schools in Australia, where heritage languages are taught, and awareness of differences between cultures, and Chap. 3 investigates the involvement and engagement of a year-long study abroad student in the host community and how that involvement and engagement may have an effect on the improvement of target language (heritage language in this case) proficiency level and (inter)cultural awareness. These two chapters—both approaching respect for the past by learning/maintaining heritage languages—are followed by four chapters that deal with problems in the present. Chapter 4 focuses on the problems of marginalization and alienation of international students. It explores the impact of the integration of critical intercultural awareness and the development of communicative competence in students enrolled in an Australian tertiary institution. Chapter 5 deals with teacher confirmation and how it is positively linked to student motivation but negatively related to the state receiver apprehension. It also takes into account the problematic and demotivating effect of school exclusion and low-self-concept. Chapter 6 explores how feedback provided by teachers in L2 study abroad classrooms can encounter barriers when the mother culture (C1) norms of these students differ from that of the teachers. Chapter 7 studies teachers' awareness of interculturality and practice of intercultural language teaching and highlights the problematic fact that teachers' practices are currently insufficient in terms of modeling, teaching, and supporting reflection on one's own cultural viewpoint.

Chapter 2, "Language Learning Motivation and Interculturality of Australian Community/Heritage Language Learners" by Elke Stracke, focuses on the role that

Australia's community language schools, after-hours institutions, play in overcoming or at least reducing the disconnection between the multilingual and multicultural profile of the Australian society and the current monolingual status of many Australians. It presents the findings of a qualitative interview study conducted for understanding (i) the reasons why these community/heritage language (CHL) learners learn their home language, (ii) their broader personal vision of who they are, and (iii) their developing awareness of differences between their community/ heritage culture and the Australian culture. The literature review of the chapter explores (a) the growing heritage language (HL) learning area, now one of the three main language learning contexts (foreign, second and heritage) studied by SLA researchers, and (b) the two theoretical frameworks on which this study rests: interculturality and its relevance for this type of learners and L2 Motivational Self System theory. The results indicate that the two main reasons why these students decided to learn a CHL were their desire to communicate and interact with their family members and the rest of the community and also their perceived value of the language for their future professional and personal life. In addition, it is the personal choice of these CHL learners as to where they position themselves on the bilingual/ cultural continuum between English and the HL. Finally, the learners show a strong cultural awareness of the differences between both cultures.

Christian Abello-Contesse's work, "Intermittent Second-Language Intensification in the Host Culture: An Ethnographic Case Study of a Heritage Speaker in a Study-Abroad Program" (Chap. 3), researches what year-long sojourners might do in their host community so that their proficiency levels in their target language and culture would grow significantly. It reviews some individual differences in SLA research such as anxiety, identity, and ambivalence, different aspects of heritage speakers, the notion of "third culture"/ "third place," and cultural hybridity. An ethnographic approach and longitudinal case study methodology was used to explore an American student's patterns, themes, issues, and emotions of L2 communicative situations while involved and engaged in the host community. The results show that (i) language and culture involvement was not successful and the experience cannot be described as "immersion," but rather as moderate intensification, because of a lack of direct contact with native classmates and of interpersonal use of the L2 in sustained interaction with local peers; (ii) over-presence of national and international tourism and everyday use of the L1 caused a discontinuity and was an impediment in the L2 and target culture (C2) development; (iii) the presence of sensitive issues that created anxiety-inducing situations made it difficult to achieve pursued objectives; and (iv) anxiety, identity issues, and resultant ambivalence—the coexistence of conflicting feelings, plans, and behaviors—made the participant create a "third culture" and "spectator behavior" and be unwilling to integrate into the host culture.

In light of the divide between the Australian tertiary sector's self-promotion as "internationalised" and the sense of marginalization and alienation reported by international students, Sue Lubbers' "Problems for Teachers of Culturally Diverse Classes: Investigating Strategies and Activities to Embed Intercultural Metalanguage in an Australian 'Internationalized' University Context" (Chap. 4) analyzes the impact of integrating critical intercultural awareness and communicative competence development on participation and interaction levels of international students enrolled in an Australian tertiary institution. This chapter also intends to demythify the reported image of international students, especially Asian students, and the misleading nature of the stereotype of "student as problem." At the same time, it also fosters and supports a more democratized approach to tertiary education. For that purpose, the author advocates for the construction of an intercultural metalanguage which consists of a negotiated language to talk about culture and interculturality in order to develop deep intercultural metaunderstandings. Qualitative data from a 13-week unit on media and popular culture was gathered through educator/researcher field notes, recorded and transcribed segments of group discussions, semi-structured group interviews, and one pair interview. The thematic data analysis of this pedagogically and politically motivated project suggests that embedding cultural awareness and intercultural communication in second language teaching brings many positive changes, such as (a) an increased participation in class discussions, (b) the development of intercultural awareness and empathy with cultural others, (c) the linking of experiences to theoretical perspectives, and (d) respectful group discussions, among others. The final implications of this study may be of high interest for tertiary educational contexts enrolling students from diverse cultural, language, and educational backgrounds.

Stephen Croucher and his colleagues in "Exploring the Relationship Between Teacher Confirmation and Student Motivation: The United States and Finland" (Chap. 5) state that perceived teacher confirmation, that is, teacher's communicating to their students that they are endorsed, recognized, and acknowledged, is positively linked to higher levels of motivation, emotional interests, and instructor credibility, among others. However, it is negatively related to the state receiver apprehension. Furthermore, perceived teacher confirmation also affects cognitive and affective learning. The authors researched (a) to what extent the relationship among teacher confirmation, emotional interest, perceived emotional support, emotional valence, emotional work, and student motivation differ between US and Finnish college students and (b) whether nation moderates the relationship among teacher confirmation, emotional interest, emotional support, emotional valence, emotional work, and student motivation. For that purpose, a group of 350 students from the United States and 128 students from Finland with ages ranging from 18 to 64 years and with diverse educational backgrounds participated in the study. The results showed a higher amount of perceived teacher confirmation and student motivation for the American students. The possible positive effect of the financial assistance from the Finnish government was neutralized by the demotivating effect of school exclusion and low-self-concept. Results for student emotions subscale could not be obtained due to a lack of structural factor confirmation. With respect to the role of nation, it was found that in spite of having a high motivation, Finnish students perceived (a) teacher's responses to class questions, (b) teacher's involvement and demonstration of interest in classroom activities, and (c) teacher's interactive method to be the opposite of what they expected according to their schooling culture.

Chapter 6, "Intercultural Barriers to Feedback in Study Abroad Settings," by Elaine Boyd and David Donnarumma investigates the perceptions and management of feedback by L2 learners according to their C1 norms and also teachers' consideration of the students' C1 when providing feedback. Current studies exploring the effectiveness of feedback to learners in study abroad settings focus on how a preagreed framework of feedback is delivered instead of researching on the nature of feedback and whether the model is right for the learners. In addition, previous research focus on feedback reception, feedback on written work, and feedback tips for teachers rather than on feedback perception and feedback on oral production. Using a mixed methods sequential transformative design and piloting different approaches (teacher led, student led, and negotiated) to managing feedback, this research explores (i) how international students perceive feedback, (ii) how English language teachers at university support students' understanding of feedback, and (iii) how far these teachers understand or make accommodations for students' C1 when delivering feedback. The results indicate that teachers and students agree on feedback being highly valued if delivered by the teacher itself and especially in a one-to-one situation. Also, teachers offer little or no support to students' understanding of the feedback process or its role in learning. However, teachers' ad hoc accommodations to intercultural sensitivities may take place when providing feedback, but they are much the product of their perceptions rather than a result of intercultural negotiation.

"Intercultural Language Teaching: On Reflection" (Chap. 7) by Jo Oranje examines language teachers' awareness of interculturality and reported practice of intercultural language teaching. It also provides modeling practice and reflection upon their own culture. This reflection is considered to be a crucial element of an intercultural language teaching (ILT) approach and fundamental for ICC. The chapter also relies on sociocultural theory as an appropriate paradigm for working with ILT. The research is composed of two phases. The first one consists of a questionnaire on New Zealand school language teachers' cognitions and practices related to teaching culture. The second one is an intervention through an activity called cultural portfolio projects (CPPs). Gathering quantitative and qualitative data, this study researches the extent to which participants value reflection in the language classroom and how the practice of an intercultural activity mediates teachers' understanding of the value of reflection in language education. The results shed light on teachers' practices being currently insufficient in terms of modeling, teaching, and supporting reflection on one's own cultural viewpoint. Nevertheless, teachers value reflection as a helpful tool for learning about one's own culture, but not so much about the target culture. However, reflection is not usually put into practice since it is not recognized as useful for target language learning. Besides, participating in the CPPs informed teachers on the practicalities of their implementation, the possible integrations of language and culture, and the ease with which they could be accommodated within the limited timeframes of a school program.

1.2.2 Part II: Forging the Future

The second part of this volume is concerned with aspects that will be forging the near future. More specifically, as a starting point, this part opens with two chapters that focus on L2 teachers' views on IC and critical cultural awareness, particularly their knowledge, attitudes, beliefs, and awareness about the relationship between the L2 and C2. In Chap. 8, the author researches prospective Spanish teachers of English as a lingua franca (ELF), whereas Chap. 9 takes into consideration a set of Portuguese and Japanese teachers of English as a foreign language for introducing new discussions on critical cultural awareness in intercultural education. With those new exchanges of views and debates in mind, the reader is presented tools that could shape future actions in the field. Chapter 10 examines how online intercultural communication courses could help study abroad students by promoting interculturality, meaningful intercultural relationships in the host community, and at the same time by avoiding stereotyping and Otherization. Lastly, Chaps. 11 and 12 discuss the effects of two instructional tools for teaching/learning a C2, that is, the Council of Europe's Images of Others: An Autobiography of Intercultural Encounters through visual media and PARSNIP (pork, alcohol, religion, sex, narcotics, ism, and politics) decoding. The first tool was used by teachers to encourage students' reflections on otherness, whereas the second one becomes a two-fold instrument as it was employed to research teachers' reactions to cultural taboos in an L2 classroom and to raise students' awareness of cultural diversity.

In Chap. 8, Rubén Chacón-Beltrán's "Attitudes Towards English as a Lingua Franca Amongst prospective EFL Teachers in Spain" examines, within the context of Spanish primary and secondary education, prospective English teachers' (i) knowledge and awareness of English as a Lingua Franca (ELF), (ii) the underlying reasons for their attitudes toward English as a Foreign Language (EFL), and (iii) their beliefs, both as language learners and also as future teachers. These explored perceptions, beliefs, and attitudes toward ELF among prospective teachers who are at different stages in their training are also compared to those of qualified serving teachers. As part of the literature review, the researcher explores the concepts of, and previous research on, lingua franca and ELF together with its connections with the areas of L2 (foreign/second language) Teaching and Second Language Acquisition. By means of an online questionnaire, both quantitative and qualitative data was gathered and contrasted within and across 4 groups of informants (a total of 175). The groups were progressive in terms of their linguistic competence (CEFR level B2 up to level C2) and their knowledge and understanding of the English-speaking culture. The results show that English teachers are generally aware of ELF and have a positive attitude toward it specially because they feel they are likely to use English to communicate mainly with nonnative speakers over the course of their lives. They recognize the value of teaching ELF for instrumental purposes without close association with culture. They perceive the advantages of learning English for intercultural communication, but with native speakers of other mother tongues that use ELF.

Manuela Guilherme and Mark Sawyer's "How Critical Has Intercultural Learning and Teaching Become? A Diachronic and Synchronic View of 'Critical Cultural Awareness' in Language Education" (Chap. 9) introduces new debates on critical cultural awareness in intercultural education. These new debates are instigated by (i) reconsidering the concepts of IC and critical cultural awareness within the literature review and (ii) undertaking a diachronic comparative analysis of two qualitative studies in Portugal, across a gap of 14 years, and a synchronic and contrastive analysis between the data from those studies and a new one in Japan. The focus of these studies, and of this chapter in general, is the teachers' promotion of critical cultural awareness among students, which is approached by assessing the teachers' general view of the role of culture in the L2 classroom, their understandings of a critical approach to culture, and various facets of their implementation of this approach, such as student responses to critical culture in the classroom together with experience and action in developing critical cultural awareness. The findings of the diachronic and synchronic analyses reveal that Portuguese teachers had similar beliefs and practices, but there was a diachronic move from the teachers' reference to the national syllabus—more innovative, challenging and inspiring to teachers in 2000—toward a more recent focus on the textbook, supplemented with authentic and updated materials selected by the individual teacher, although many teachers maintained their interest for cultural content. Synchronically, in general, the Japanese teachers had much lower consciousness than the Portuguese teachers regarding both culture and criticality, because of national identity issues and face-threatening matters, respectively.

Jane Jackson in Chap. 10 entitled "Building an Online Community to Contest Stereotyping and Otherization During Study Abroad" points out the need for research-driven approach interventions to foster intercultural learning, thus challenging the "immersion" myth. Within this context of study abroad, the author designs an eLearning platform to offer an online intercultural communication course to promote interculturality, meaningful intercultural relationships in the host environment, and avoid stereotyping and Otherization. The concepts of stereotyping, Otherization, guided critical reflection—as an interculturality-promoting way—and social constructivist orientation to online courses are reviewed. Specifically, the author investigates (a) how a group of 22 Asian international exchange students, who sojourn in different host countries and whose L2 is English, perceive stereotyping and Otherization before, during, and after the course and (b) to what extent the asynchronous forum fosters collaborative learning, critical reflection, and intercultural learning in relation to stereotyping and Otherization. The results indicate that participants at the end of the online course have become more cognizant of the ways in which stereotyping and Otherization can affect their perceptions and interactions with people with a different linguistic and cultural background. The students also began to move beyond the "us vs them" polarized orientations. Instead, they made an effort to get to know people as individuals rather than dealing with them as representatives of a particular culture or national group. Furthermore, the participants became more aware of strategies to develop meaningful intercultural relationships.

María del Carmen Méndez-García and Rachel Lindner, in "Promoting Intercultural and Visual Media Competence in the Foreign Language Classroom with the Autobiography of Intercultural Encounters Through Visual Media" (Chap. 11), emphasize the role played by visual media literacy, which involves developing students' cognitive skills to engage critically with print and digital images from all over the world, together with intercultural competence in learning a foreign language. The authors argued that intercultural and visual media competence are rarely promoted in foreign language education. The chapter reports on insights gained from using the Council of Europe's Images of Others: An Autobiography of Intercultural Encounters through Visual Media (AIEVM) in an online intercultural exchange (OIE) between preservice teachers of English at Dormund University (Germany) and preservice teachers at Jaén University (Spain). In this project, the AIEVM was the main tool around which activities were designed to help students reflect on cultural "otherness" through images. Specifically, the authors researched whether an OIE could enhance the potential of the AIEVM for developing intercultural and visual media competence. Results shed light on (a) students' image of the other; (b) critical thinking and knowledge discovery; (c) considerations of identity, self-awareness, and perspective-taking; and (d) students' views of the impact of the OIE context on working with the AIEVM. The findings of the study suggest that the AIEVM has a positive impact on OIE. In the same way, OIE presents itself as a useful framework for multiperspectival reflection and verbalization of encounters with otherness through images, thus promoting critical cultural awareness of visual media.

Chapter 12, "Intercultural Competence and PARSNIP: Voices from Teachers of English in Australia," by Thuy Ngoc Dinh and Fenty Lidya Siregar investigates how teachers decode PARSNIP (pork, alcohol, religion, sex, narcotics, ism, and politics) and how it is used in class. After reviewing the literature concerning English language teaching (ELT), IC in Australia, and PARSNIP in ELT, the chapter employs narrative action reflection and in-depth individual interviews as a methodology to generate data from five English teachers from different cultural backgrounds in Australia to explore two main issues: (i) teachers' response to PARSNIP (To what extent do they believe PARSNIP should be addressed in ELT to facilitate IC? What does PARSNIP mean to teachers of different cultural backgrounds? What issues, if any, have impacted teachers' decisions to avoid or address PARSNIP?) and (ii) teachers' integration of PARSNIP in practice (To what extent do they address PARSNIP in class?). The findings show that PARSNIP is a reductionist and essentialist concept as there are variations in the interpretations of cultural taboos across different cultures in multicultural classrooms. It also indicates that PARSNIP should be addressed appropriately to lift students' awareness of cultural diversity and to prepare them to ethically and pragmatically discuss global issues and controversial topics in English. Besides, the study points out that the teachers were cognizant of their own roles in today's era of English as an international language and IC. Furthermore, teachers' reflections on the study's workshop and materials helped them devise their own activities, considering the implications for both language and intercultural communication practice.

Darío Luis Banegas, in the epilogue, apart from foregrounding the strengths of the volume in providing a better understanding of the past, present, and future regarding intercultural competence within a broad applied linguistics perspective, explains the shifting in language understanding—from language as a system to language as discourse—the growth of IC in association with a complex array of analytical frameworks (applied linguistics, psychology, sociology, etc.) and highlights, among other things, the emerging of interesting concepts such as translanguaging, intercultural citizenship, and global citizenship education. It also clarifies that the volume opens the door for researchers to explore IC with younger learners in different settings, as the volume deals mainly with adult participants, or adopting different strategies and innovative research methods. In all, it sets new directions concerning language learning, global citizenship, and their impact on curriculum and teacher development.

The different debatable intercultural aspects, issues, situations, contexts, implications, applications, and insights covered in this edited volume are proof of how interculturality has been growing in importance in the last decades. The volume looks back to the past by presenting heritage language learners in different settings and educational contexts. It deals with different problems in the present, such as marginalization, alienation, exclusion, low-self-concept, barriers, or lack of reflection on one's own cultural viewpoint, among others. It faces the future by showing L2 teachers' views on IC and critical cultural awareness and presenting tools that could not only model further actions in education but also forge part of the uncertain future. It concludes, in the Epilogue, that the new doors opened by the volume will affect the curriculum and teacher development. This is just a new starting point toward new debates and changes that will make a difference since nowadays many teachers still lack enough resources and guidance to teach IC despite extensive research and attempts for a framework of reference. This volume will contribute to lead the way to transform society for common understanding and respect by providing teachers with a wider range of resources and guidance to teach IC with reference to the existing research and frameworks of reference, while respecting the complex nature and role of IC in language teaching.

References

Aguilar, M., & Muñoz, C. (2014). The effect of proficiency on CLIL benefits in engineering students in Spain. *International Journal of Applied Linguistics, 24*, 1–18.

Alred, G., Byram, M., & Fleming, M. (2006). *Education for intercultural citizenship: Concepts and comparisons*. Clevedon, UK: Multilingual Matters.

Bandura, E., & Sercu, L. (2005). Culture teaching practices. In L. Sercu, E. Bandura, P. Castro, L. Davcheva, C. Lascaridou, U. Lundgren, M. del Carmen, M. García, & P. Ryan (Eds.), *Foreign language teachers and intercultural communication: An international investigation* (pp. 75–89). Clevedon, UK: Multilingual Matters.

Belz, J. A. (2007). The development of intercultural communicative competence in telecollaborative partnerships. In R. O'Dowd (Ed.), *Online intercultural exchange* (pp. 127–166). Clevedon, UK: Multilingual Matters.

Bennett, M. J. (1993). Towards ethnorelativism: A developmental model of intercultural sensitivity. In R. M. Paige (Ed.), *Education for the intercultural experience* (pp. 21–71). Yarmouth, ME: Intercultural Press.

Burns, A., Dikilitaş, K., Smith, R., & Wyatt, M. (Eds.). (2017). *Developing insights into teacher research*. Faversham, UK: IATEFL.

Byram, M. (1997). *Teaching and assessing intercultural communicative competence*. Clevedon, UK: Multilingual Matters.

Byram, M. (2008). *From foreign language education to education for intercultural citizenship*. Clevedon, UK: Multilingual Matters.

Byram, M. (2009). Intercultural competence in foreign languages. The intercultural speaker and the pedagogy of foreign language education. In D. Deardorff (Ed.), *The SAGE handbook of intercultural competence* (pp. 321–332). Thousand Oaks, CA: Sage Publications.

Byram, M. (2014). Twenty-five years on—From cultural studies to intercultural citizenship. *Language, Culture, and Curriculum, 27*, 209–225.

Byram, M., Golubeva, I., Han, H., & Wagner, M. (2017). *From principles to practice in education for intercultural citizenship*. Bristol, UK: Multilingual Matters.

Byram, M., Gribkova, B., & Starkey, H. (2002). *Developing the intercultural dimension in language teaching: A practical introduction for teachers*. Strasbourg, France: Council of Europe.

Byram, M., & Zarate, G. (1994). *Definitions, objectives and assessment of socio-cultural competence*. Strasbourg, France: Council of Europe.

Coyle, D. (2006). Motivating teachers motivating learners through content and language integrated learning. *Scottish Modern Languages Review, 13*, 1–18.

Coyle, D. (2007a). Content and language integrated learning: Towards a connected research agenda for CLIL pedagogies. *International Journal of Bilingual Education and Bilingualism, 10*, 543–562.

Coyle, D. (2007b). The CLIL quality challenge. In D. Marsch & D. Wolff (Eds.), *Diverse contexts-converging goals. CLIL in Europe* (pp. 47–58). Frankfurt, Germany: Peter Lang.

Deardorff, D. K. (2009). Synthesizing conceptualizations of intercultural competence. In D. K. Deardorff (Ed.), *The SAGE handbook of intercultural competence* (pp. 264–269). Thousand Oaks, CA: Sage Publications.

Dikilitaş, K., Wyatt, M., Burns, A., & Barkhuizen, G. (Eds.). (2019). *Energizing teacher research*. Faversham, UK: IATEFL.

European Commission. (2007). *Languages and cultures in Europe (LACE): The intercultural competencies developed in compulsory foreign language education in the European Union*. Brussels, Belgium: European Commission. Retrieved from http://ec.europa.eu/education/languages/archive/doc/lace_en.pdf.

Fantini, A. (2009). Assessing intercultural competence: Issues and tools. In D. Deardorff (Ed.), *The SAGE handbook of intercultural competence* (pp. 456–476). Thousand Oaks, CA: Sage Publications.

Fowler, S. M., & Blohm, J. M. (2004). An analysis of methods for intercultural training. In D. Landis, J. M. Bennett, & M. J. Bennett (Eds.), *Handbook of intercultural training* (pp. 37–84). Thousand Oaks, CA: Sage.

Geertz, C. (1973). *The interpretation of cultures*. London: Hutchinson.

Hall, E. T. (1959). *The silent language*. New York: Doubleday.

Hannerz, U. (1992). *Cultural complexity: Studies in the social organization of meaning*. New York: Columbia University Press.

Heras, A., & Lasagabaster, D. (2015). The impact of CLIL on affective factors and vocabulary learning. *Language Teaching Research, 19*, 70–88.

Holliday, A. (2011). *Intercultural communication & ideology*. London: Routledge.

Houghton, S. (2010). Savoir se transformer: Knowing how to become. In Y. Tsai & S. Houghton (Eds.), *Becoming intercultural: Inside and outside the classroom*. Cambridge, UK: Cambridge Scholars Publishing.

Kääntä, L., Kasper, G., & Piirainen-Mash, A. (2018). Explaining Hooke's Laws: Definitional practices in a CLIL physics classroom. *Applied Linguistics, 39*, 694–717.

Kramsch, C. (1998). *Language and culture*. Oxford, UK: Oxford University Press.

Kramsch, C. (1999). Thirdness: The intercultural stance. In T. Vestergaard (Ed.), *Language, culture, and identity* (pp. 53–89). Aalborg, Denmark: Aalborg University Press.

Kramsch, C. (2009). Discourse, the symbolic dimension of intercultural competence. In A. Hu & M. Byram (Eds.), *Intercultural competence and foreign language learning* (pp. 107–122). Tubingen, Germany: Gunter Narr Verlag.

Kroeber, A. L., & Kluckhohln, C. (1952). *Culture: A critical review of concepts and definitions*. New York: Vintage Books.

Mader, J., & Camerer, R. (2010). International English and the training of intercultural communicative competence. *Intercultural Journal, 9*(12), 97–116.

Matsumoto, D. (1996). *Culture and psychology*. Pacific Grove, CA: Brooks/Cole.

Meyer, O., Coyle, D., Halbach, A., Shuck, K., & Ting, T. (2015). A pluriliteracies approach to content and language integrated learning—Mapping learner progressions in knowledge construction and meaning-making. *Language, Culture, and Curriculum, 28*, 41–57.

Nussbaum, M. C. (2006). Education and democratic citizenship: Capabilities and quality education. *Journal of Human Development, 7*, 385–395.

Parmenter, L. (2003). Describing and defining intercultural communicative competence–international perspectives. In G. Neuner, M. Byram, & Council of Europe. Directorate General IV--Education Culture Youth and Sport Environment (Eds.), *Intercultural competence* (pp. 119–147). Strasbourg, France: Council of Europe Publishing.

Porto, M. (2018). Intercultural citizenship in foreign language education: An opportunity to broaden CLIL's theoretical outlook and pedagogy. *International Journal of Bilingual Education and Bilingualism*.https://doi.org/10.1080/13670050.2018.1526886.

Rathje, S. (2007). Intercultural competence: The status and future of a controversial concept. *Language and Intercultural Communication, 7*. https://doi.org/10.2167/laic285.0.

Risager, K. (2007). *Language and culture pedagogy. From a national to a transnational paradigm*. Clevedon, UK: Mutilingual Matters.

Santos, B. S. (2010). *Refundación del Estado en América Latina. Perspectivas desde una epistemología del Sur. [A reconceptualization of the state in Latin America: Perspectives from an epistemology of the South]*. Lima, Peru: Instituto Internacional de Derecho y Sociedad.

Schwartz, T. (1992). Anthropology and psychology: An unrequited relationship. In T. Schwartz, G. M. White, & C. A. Lutz (Eds.), *New directions in psychological anthropology* (pp. 324–349). Cambridge, UK: Cambridge University Press.

Spencer-Oatey, H. (2008). Introduction. In H. Spencer-Oatey (Ed.), *Culturally speaking: Culture, communication, and politeness theory* (pp. 1–8). London: Continuum.

Spencer-Oatey, H., & Franklin, P. (2009). *Intercultural interaction: A multidisciplinary approach to intercultural communication*. New York: Palgrave Macmillan.

Thomas, A. (1996). Analyse der Handlungswirksamkeit von Kulturstandards. (analysis of the effectiveness of culture standards). In A. Thomas (Ed.), *Psychologie interkulturellen handelns* (pp. 107–135). Göttingen, Germany: Hofgrefe-Verlag.

Tobin, N., & Abello-Contesse, C. (2013). The use of native assistants as language and cultural resources in Andalusia's bilingual schools. In C. Abello-Contesse, P. M. Chandler, M. D. López-Jiménez, & R. Chacón-Beltrán (Eds.), *Bilingual and multilingual education in the 21st century: Building on experience* (pp. 203–230). Bristol, UK: Multilingual Matters.

Van Ek, J. A. (1986). *Objectives of foreign language learning. Volume I: Scope; volume II: Levels*. Strasbourg, France: Council of Europe.

Wintergerst, A. C., & McVeigh, J. (2011). *Tips for teaching culture: Practical approaches to intercultural communication*. New York: Pearson Education, Longman.

Zegarat, V. (2007). A cognitive pragmatic perspective on communication and culture. In H. Spencer-Oatey (Ed.), *Culturally speaking: Culture, communication, and politeness theory* (pp. 48–70). London: Continuum.

Part I
Respecting the Past and Problems in the Present

Chapter 2
Language Learning Motivation and Interculturality of Australian Community/Heritage Language Learners

Elke Stracke

2.1 Introduction

Australia is a multicultural society in which many languages are spoken in the community. The mainstream school system offers foreign language learning to all students, but the uptake is relatively low. Various reasons account for this low level of foreign language learning in Australia. These include that learning a second language as a subject in mainstream schools is usually not compulsory and young people are often not motivated to learn another language. Often the perception that English speakers do not need any foreign language proficiency prevails. Further, the number of foreign languages taught is limited. For instance, in the Australian Capital Territory (ACT), where the current study was conducted, the eight priority languages taught are four European languages (French, German, Italian, and Spanish) and four Asian languages (Indonesian, Japanese, Chinese/Mandarin, and Korean) (ACT Government, 2017).

Australia's community language schools[1] play a major role in overcoming or at least reducing the disjunction between the multilingual and multicultural profile of the Australian society and the prevailing monolingual habitus of its policymakers and many Australians. Community/heritage language (CHL) schools (also referred to as "ethnic schools" or, sometimes, as "Saturday schools") in Australia are

---

[1]In Australia, the term "community language" is the most commonly used term for such language. However, in literature from the United States, the term "heritage language" (HL) prevails, while literature from the United Kingdom refers to "complementary schools." For the purpose of this research, the terms "community/heritage language" (CHL) and "community/heritage culture" (CHC) are used for learners and learning in the Australian context.

E. Stracke (✉)
University of Canberra, Canberra, Australia
e-mail: Elke.Stracke@canberra.edu.au

© Springer Nature Singapore Pte Ltd. 2021
M. D. López-Jiménez, J. Sánchez-Torres (eds.), *Intercultural Competence Past, Present and Future*, Intercultural Communication and Language Education,
https://doi.org/10.1007/978-981-15-8245-5_2

nonprofit, after-hours institutions and open to students regardless of their linguistic backgrounds. CHL schools operate independently from within and outside mainstream schools and school hours. They are important, complementary providers of language education to mainstream schools in Australia. Approximately 700 CHL school authorities conduct classes in more than 1400 venues schools in Australia. In 2014, 69 languages were offered through CHL schools from Preparatory to Year 10 and 42 languages at Years 11 and 12 (the last year of high school). More than 100,000 CHL students attend CHL schools to learn and/or maintain the language and culture of their community and heritage in Australia (Community Languages Australia/Australian Federation of Ethnic Schools Associations Inc., 2016).

CHL learning and education in Australia take place in a situation in which English is the dominant and preferred medium. CHL learners live in deeply bilingual and bicultural spaces that shape their identity. This chapter aims to understand the reasons why these learners learn a CHL, their broader personal vision of who they are, and their (developing) awareness of differences between their community/heritage culture (CHC) and the Australian culture. Little is known about the reasons why Australian students of CHL attend their CHL school, often on a Saturday morning when many of their peers would typically play sports. Anecdotal evidence suggests that these learners only go to their CHL school because their parents want them to attend the school so they will maintain their language and culture. However, is it really just because of their parents or guardians that these young learners attend a CHL school? What is *their* motivation? And what is the impact of this CHL and CHC learning on the interculturality of these young learners?

This chapter reports on a qualitative interview study conducted to gain a deep understanding of the motivation and interculturality of young and adolescent Australian CHL learners. A learner's motivation correlates significantly with their success, and capacity for intercultural awareness is an essential capacity in a world where dialogue across nations and ethnic groups is crucial.

To start the chapter, the following section briefly sketches the growing area of heritage language learning and associated terminology, before it focuses on the two theoretical frameworks that underpin this study. Given the general focus of this volume on interculturality, this chapter discusses the relevance of interculturality for CHL learners before introducing the *L2 Motivational Self System*—the specific motivational theory that underpins this study. The chapter also evaluates the small number of studies that investigated the interculturality and motivation of CHL learners to clearly situate the current study.

2.2   Literature Review

2.2.1   *Heritage Language Learning and Learners*

Heritage language (HL) education and acquisition/learning—a form of second-language acquisition (SLA) and/or of bilingualism—is a relatively recent term and field of investigation, and research into HL learning and learners is growing. A clear sign of the growing awareness of this particular kind of language learning and learners is that recent textbooks of SLA research have included it as an area of investigation in its own right. Ortega, for instance, emphasizes that depending on the research questions, "distinguishing among specific contexts for L2 learning is in fact important. In such cases, SLA researchers make three (rather than only two) key contextual distinctions: *foreign, second* and *heritage* language learning contexts" (Ortega, 2009, p. 6). In their textbook, Gass and Selinker (2008) also note HLs as one type of language acquisition. HL learners differ with regard to such factors as exposure, use of language, and linguistic knowledge. Researchers have also observed linguistic differences between HL and non-HL learners (see, for instance, the 2011 special issue 'The linguistic competence of Heritage Speakers' (2011) of *Studies in Second Language Acquisition*). HL education is "now its own field" (Brinton, Kagan, & Bauckus, 2008, p. ix). Yet, "[d]espite the fact that much attention has been given to research on HL issues over the past 15 to 20 years, the field is still relatively new and continues to develop its theoretical focus" (Van Deusen-Scholl, 2014, p. 77).

The growing interest in HL learners has also seen a discussion develop around the definition of "HL learner." One definition that emerged was broad; the other was narrow. The broad definition focuses on the HL person's affiliation with the HL and culture; however, this person might not have the ability to speak or understand the language. The narrow definition defines an HL learner as someone "raised in a home where a non-English language is spoken, who speaks or at least understands the language, and who is to some degree bilingual in that language and in English" (Valdés, 2001). The vast majority of students who attend Australian CHL schools are HL learners as defined in the narrow definition. This definition is focused on the learner being raised in a home where their HL is spoken and they have some competence in that language. All research participants in this study fell under this narrow definition of "CHL learner."

2.2.2 Interculturality as a Platform to Investigate Bilingual and Bicultural Spaces

CHL learners live in intensely bilingual and bicultural spaces. They are raised in a home where HL is spoken, while their schooling is in another medium. In Australia, this is the medium of English. They may experience CHL and CHC at home, in the community, at their CHL school, and perhaps in religious practices. But Australian culture and Australian English are dominant in mainstream schools and in many other domains. These domains can also overlap as learners move between them and interact with peers and others from various linguistic and cultural backgrounds, including their own CHL and the dominant English language.

The concept of interculturality provides an adequate platform to investigate CHL learners' bilingual and bicultural spaces. "Intercultural competence entails an awareness and a respect of difference, as well as the socioaffective capacity to see oneself through the eyes of others" (Kramsch, 2005, p. 553). While the interculturality of language learners has been investigated in various contexts (this volume being one example), so far previous research has paid little attention to CHL learners. This is surprising given that HL researchers acknowledge that the "heritage culture is by definition a complex, developing, transnational, intercultural, cross-linguistic, and hybrid one" (He, 2010, p. 73). Kagan's (2012) work is one notable exception. Kagan reports on the results of the survey conducted by the National Heritage Language Resource Centre between 2007 and 2009 (N = 1800), which shows that "heritage language learners articulate a specifically intercultural understanding of their identities" (Kagan, 2012, p. 73). They are "well aware that they occupy an intercultural space" (p. 74). While Kagan (2012) investigated the intercultural knowledge and competence of HL speakers in the United States, the current study focuses on if, and how, young CHL learners in Australia show an awareness of cultural difference. Most importantly, interculturality "involves attitudes of curiosity and openness, skills in interpretation and mediation, and a critical awareness of conflicting value systems" (Menard-Warwick, 2008, p. 619; see also Byram, 1997). It is important to investigate whether and how Australian CHL learners show such attitudes.

2.2.3 The Important Role of Motivation in Learning Another Language

Motivation to learn another language is "simply conceived, the degree and type of 'wanting to learn'" (Van Patten & Benati, 2010, p. 111). Motivation correlates significantly with a learner's success. In the CHL context, motivation is likewise important: "Like L2 learners, heritage language learners need strong motivation to maintain and learn the heritage language, and issues of identity are very important" (Montrul, 2010, p. 7).

2.2.4 Components of the L2 Motivational Self System

This study draws on Dörnyei's *L2 Motivational Self System*, which integrates a number of L2 motivational constructs with findings of self-research in psychology (Dörnyei, Csizér, & Németh, 2006). Dörnyei introduced the concept of "possible selves"—originally developed in psychology—into SLA research:

> Possible selves are the ideal selves that we would very much like to become. They are also the selves we could become, and the selves we are afraid of becoming. The possible selves that are hoped for might include the successful self, the creative self, the rich self, the thin self, or the loved and admired self, whereas the dreaded possible selves could be the alone

self, the depressed self, the incompetent self, the alcoholic self, the unemployed self, or the bag lady self. (Markus & Nurius, 1986, p. 954)

For the context of language learning, the hoped-for *L2 Self* might be the fluent and confident self, while language learners might dread the idea of the incompetent *L2 Self* when, for instance, they find they are unable to use the target language in an important situation.

Dörnyei's *L2 Motivational Self System* consists of three main components: the *Ideal L2 Self*, the *Ought-to L2 Self*, and the *L2 Learning Experience*. While the psychologist Edward Tory Higgins originally described the *Ideal Self* as one's "representation of the attributes that someone (yourself or another) would like you, ideally, to possess (i.e., a representation of someone's hopes, aspirations, or wishes for you)" (1987, pp. 320–321), Dörnyei (2009) developed the concept of the *Ideal L2 Self* for language learning as the "L2-specific facet of one's ideal self" (p. 29). The *Ideal L2 Self* is "one's ideal self-image expressing the wish to become a competent L2 speaker" (Kormos & Csizér, 2008, p. 331). Traditional integrative and internalized instrumental motives belong to this component (Dörnyei, 2009). In *the L2 Motivational Self System*, the *Ideal L2 Self* has been replaced and now subsumes integrativeness. While integrativeness involved a sense of emotional identification with a language, an L2 community, their values, the emotional identification that the *Ideal L2 Self* conceptualizes refers to the broader personal vision of a language learner (Ryan, 2008). The *Ideal L2 Self* lies "at the heart of motivated L2 language learning behavior" (Csizér & Dörnyei, 2005, p. 30).

The *Ought-to L2 Self* contains "attributes that one believes we ought to possess to avoid negative outcomes—this motivational dimension may therefore bear little resemblance to our own wishes and desires" (Dörnyei et al., 2006, p. 145). The more extrinsic types of motivation belong to this component (Dörnyei, 2009). Finally, the *L2 Learning Experience* covers "situation specific motives related to the immediate learning environment and experience" (Dörnyei, 2005, p. 106). To conclude this short sketch of Dörnyei's *L2 Motivational Self System*, it is pertinent to understand that highly motivated L2 learners conceive their *Ideal L2 Self* as an L2-speaking self. Motivation is defined "as the desire to achieve one's ideal language self by reducing the discrepancy between one's actual and ideal selves" (Csizér & Dörnyei, 2005, p. 30).

Given how the language learning literature has considered motivation of central importance, it is not surprising that research into motivation in language learning that has employed Dörnyei's *L2 Motivational Self System* has flourished over the last decade, with "[o]ver 70% of studies focused on motivation for learning English" (Ushioda, 2016). While some research has also been conducted to understand the motivation of learners of other languages (including CHL learners) to learn a language, we still know very little about why CHL learners learn the CHL. Further, even fewer researchers have studied the motivation of CHL learners within the framework of the *L2 Motivational Self System*.

2.2.5   Motivation Research in CHL Education

Most motivation research on CHL learners has focused on the traditional dichotomy of instrumental and integrative motivation, as suggested by Gardner and associates (Gardner, 2001), or the complementary approach of intrinsic and extrinsic motivation (Noels, 2005). Results are not conclusive. Wilson and Martinez (2011) have shown one instrumental reason for learning the HL: its importance for the education and professional development of university Spanish HL learners in the United States. However, for Korean HL learners at university level in Lee and Kim's (2008) study (also conducted at two universities in the United States), "integrative orientation seems to play a more significant role in shaping their desire to learn the language consistently across different proficiency levels" (p. 168). Douglas (2008), also using Gardner's dichotomy of integrative and instrumental motivation, in his survey to profile the motivation of Japanese heritage learners at a university in the United States, showed that their reasons for studying the language were evenly spread between these two constructs. Beaudrie and Ducar (2005) investigated the linguistic and cultural attitudes of HL learners of first-year, university-level Spanish students. They found that these learners expressed both intrinsic and extrinsic motivation to learn Spanish.

In a comparative study, Noels (2005) found that university-level HL learners and non-HL learners endorsed the integrative/instrumental and intrinsic/extrinsic orientations in their learning of German to the same extent. The only exception was that HL learners found German important for their self-concept. To find out why younger learners learn their HL, Yi (2009) investigated the personal reasons of HL learners of Korean at junior high school and high school in an HL-learning program in the United States. Yi (2009) identified five major reasons that positively affected the motivation of language learners: "good school atmosphere," "living with heritage language speakers," "using heritage mass media," "parents' strong encouragement," and "preparation for further study."

In a comparative study of Chinese university language learners in the United States, Weger-Guntharp (2006) highlights the importance of the sense of social identity that university CHL learners experience in a language classroom setting. Weger-Guntharp used an earlier version of Dörnyei's *L2 Motivational Self System* to contrast their comments with those of non-CHL learners. Also, from a comparative perspective, Xie's (2011) study of the motivation of HL and non-HL Chinese college level learners in the United States supported previous studies on the theoretical legitimacy of the *L2 Motivational Self System.* Xie (2011) suggested that its application could be extended to a language other than English and to second-language settings. More recently, Kurata's (2015) research into the motivation of university Japanese learners at an Australian university also moved away from the traditional dichotomy and drew on Dörnyei's *L2 Motivational Self System* as one of the theoretical frameworks in her study. Kurata's study showed that the motivational selves of the Japanese HL learners in this study ($N = 7$) "are more properly described as a process" (p. 110) and so provide a different explanation from the previous understanding of motivation as an individual static characteristic. This process emerges through the CHL learners' interaction with their social activities, relationships, and experiences and in multiple contexts. Kurata's findings also point to the important link between "learners' motivational selves and issues related to their identities as HL speakers" (p. 126), such as language inheritance and affiliation.

To conclude, the field of CHL learning lacks research in many areas. Motivation and interculturality are two such areas. Recently, researchers (Kurata, 2015; Weger-Guntharp, 2006; Xie, 2011) have started using the *L2 Motivational Self System* to investigate the motivation of university students. In so doing, their research has helped to expand our understanding of CHL learners' motivation beyond the traditional instrumental vs integrative dichotomy. Kagan's (2012) analysis of survey data from HL learners in the United States is an important starting point to reflect on what Kagan calls "the intercultural theme in relation to heritage language learners" (p. 72). The current interview study adds to this small, yet growing, body of research that seeks to understand the motivation of young CHL learners through both the lenses of the *L2 Motivational Self System* and these learners' sense of interculturality.

The learners in this study are children and adolescents (aged 11 to 16) who study at a CHL school in Australia. The study aims to understand why these learners choose to learn their CHL and CHC. It focuses on three key questions:

1. Why are the CHL learners learning the language?
2. How does their *CHL Self* contribute to their vision of a future user of that language?
3. How does their interculturality contribute to their language learning?

2.3 Methodology

2.3.1 Context and Participants

At the time of the interview all interviewees were attending one of the ACT CHL schools. The ACT is the capital territory of the Commonwealth of Australia and its smallest self-governing internal territory. The ACT Community Language Schools Association Incorporated is the umbrella body for community-based language schools in the ACT. The association offers approximately 30 languages in more than 40 member schools with over 1700 registered students (ACT Community Language Schools Association, n.d.). Even though schools vary in size, and each school has their own vision, their common main objectives are:

- To promote understanding and mutual respect among Ethnic Communities
- To promote the teaching of languages, history, and culture of ethnic communities
- To coordinate and promote interethnic school social and cultural activities
- To promote the concept of multicultural education

Table 2.1 Details of school-age participants from the ACT

Name	CHL	Gender	Age
David	Chinese	Male	14
Ying	Chinese	Female	12
Lena	German	Female	12
Mona	German	Female	16
Yoko	Japanese	Female	11
Naoko	Japanese	Female	16
Ken	Japanese	Male	12
Aroha	Māori	Female	13
Henare	Māori	Male	15
Mya	Mon	Female	14
Abinaash	Punjabi	Female	15
Jasleen	Punjabi	Female	12

Note: All names are pseudonyms

- To provide language programs for all students within the ACT (ACT Community Language Schools Association, n.d.)

Twelve students from six schools participated in this study. The languages taught were Chinese, German, Japanese, Māori, Mon, and Punjabi. Table 2.1 provides an overview of the 12 participants. They studied Chinese (Mandarin) ($N = 2$), German ($N = 2$), Japanese ($N = 3$), Māori ($N = 2$), Mon ($N = 1$), or Punjabi ($N = 2$). Nine participants were female and three male. Table 2.1 lists the participants in language groups (in alphabetical order).

Because this research was conducted with research participants under the age of 18, particular care was taken to ensure an ethical procedure. All participants in this study and their parents gave informed consent before being interviewed.

2.3.2 Data Collection

This study draws on qualitative interview data to gain a deep understanding of each CHL learner's motivation to learn a language and their intercultural awareness. The interviews were semistructured to allow for both a focus on the phenomena under investigation and for flexibility during the interview process. The interviews were conducted in English and in various locations, taking the preferences of both the interviewees and their parents into account. Most interviews took place in the interviewee's home (usually in the lounge), on the school grounds, or, in one case, in a neighborhood café.

Usually, one or both of the interviewee's parents attended the interview; it was rare that the parent greeted the interviewer and then moved away from the interviewer and their child. Often, the interview became, to some extent, a family event. However, the interviews were conducted with each child individually, even in the case of Abinaash and Jasleen, who are sisters. The parents' presence might have influenced what their child told us; however, due to the ethical procedures agreed upon, it was not appropriate to ask the parents to leave. The parents' presence might have hindered some children from discussing topics fully; others less so. Even so, all interviews were conducted in a pleasant and friendly atmosphere. Most interviews lasted 25–30 min.

2.3.3 Data Management and Analysis

All interviews were, with the consent of the participants, recorded and then transcribed *verbatim* after the interview. After the repeated reading of all transcripts, to ensure a good overall sense of the complete dataset, each interview was first analyzed individually. As the research interest was designed to understand the participants' views, no work was undertaken with any a priori categories when analyzing the data. First the process identified salient and repeated themes; these were then grouped, for each interview, into categories (Flick, 2014; Strauss & Corbin, 1990). The second step in the process determined major categories in the data from the students by examining all the cases together.

For the purpose of this chapter, the data analysis focuses on the cross-case analysis of those sections in the interviews where the interviewees talked about their reasons for learning the CHL and their *Ideal CHL Self* and showed awareness, attitudes, and skills that can be attributed to interculturality. The results are presented and discussed in the next section.

2.4 Results and Discussion

Despite the small sample size of the study, the interviews offer deep insights into the lived reality of these learners as CHL learners and speakers of languages (including English). Their reasons to learn the CHL vary, and their *Ideal CHL Selves* differ, depending on the importance given to the (imagined) use of the language with the family and in the community, and in the working world.

2.4.1 Research Question 1: Why Are the CHL Learners Learning the Language?

The learners' (a) desire for communication and interaction with family members (in Australia or in the "heritage" country) and the broader community and (b) the perceived value of the language for their future professional and personal life are important factors in the formation of these learners' motivation. Often, the learners' motivation to learn their CHL spans these factors.

(a) *Desire for communication and interaction with family members and the broader community*

The learners' desire to communicate and interact with their family is the strongest driver across this group of young learners. They wish to be a member of that community. The emotional attachment to their CHC and the love for their family lie at the heart of their motivation. For Abinaash, for instance, the Punjabi language, music, and dance play an important part in her life:

> I love being I love speaking and I love singing in Punjabi especially the songs because they usually have a really upbeat and fast tone to them so and it's fun to dance to the songs (Abinaash)

Instrumental reasons do not seem to matter much to her; what matters is the Punjabi heritage, its culture, and her family. Learning the language allows Abinaash to be part of that heritage:

> I won't I can't really get a job with it in the future whereas science I can make a career out of that but um I enjoy learning Punjabi and especially the culture or part of it I enjoy more but it's sort of links in together (Abinaash)

> I would consider it my language um (pause) and probably part of um like my heritage, culture because all my cousins um and in our family like we all speak Punjabi so it's kind of like our communication (Abinaash)

The ability to connect with family and friends through the language is a main motivator for these learners, as the following three quotations show for Japanese, German, and Māori, respectively:

> um because I have friends there [. . .] um yes because most of my family is Japanese [. . .] it's sort of my family like extended families they're setting standards for me and I try to aspire to be like them and to be successful (Yoko)

> um and it's good that like to me liking German is also liking my mum (Lena)

> I really enjoy the dancing and singing [. . .] when I was younger they used to send me to the group so I could learn more about myself like my culture and um I really I really enjoyed it as I grew up [. . .] I just I just got more mature I learnt that I really enjoy and I really want to be a part of it yeah [. . .] um (pause) I just feel that it's important to me (Aroha)

Aroha's reflection points at how his motivation has changed over time. While his parents initially sent him to the school, he started to enjoy going to the Māori school and wanted to become a part of it.

David also admits frankly that his parents expect him to go to the Chinese school, but he also points to the importance of him being able to communicate in Chinese to people outside his immediate family and in the broader community:

> [I]t is my language cos I'm a Chinese person and I love to embrace my culture and while I have to say probably the main reason why I learn it is cos of my parents another reason I considered learning Chinese language is cos I consider communication as a really important thing I've learnt the language so I can use it to talk to more people so I'd say language is

important to me cos it allows me to communicate but why I'm learning it actually because my parents are pushing me to do it (David)

(b) *Perceived value of the language for their future professional and personal life*

David's statement shows that he sees some value in being able to communicate in Chinese, while Abinaash's earlier statement that she "can't really get a job with it [Punjabi] in the future" shows her negative assessment of the value of Punjabi in the job market.

Both Chinese learners in this study, David and Ying, believe in the value of the Chinese language for their school learning and, at the same time, for their communications skills beyond the school context. The following statements clearly show David's parents' influence on his developing instrumental motivation. At the same time, they also show the importance of David's peers, of "people", who make his learning enjoyable and allow for "happy moments in Chinese":

> I think it will be useful like I mainly learn because my parents say it going to be useful in the future and there's a sense and I personally learn to aim to be fluent in two languages to seek more opportunities in the future I also like cos my brother told me about how you could do the there's a there's a International Baccalaureate how you could you have to know second language so I'm sort of using Chinese as my second language so maybe for school (David)

> I meet a lot more people like right there one of my friends was there so I definitely find coming to this school I do meet a lot more people and I'm able to use my language and be exposed to a lot of other backgrounds and same with cos they always at our school there's this emphasis on some call the 'Asians' so I think having my background gives me have an advantage over others but just the happy moments in Chinese definitely I think it's just the people that I'm able to meet and learn with I find (David)

Ying strongly believes in the value of the Chinese language for her future life, which she relates to China's overall influence in the global market. Ken and Mya point out the benefit of meeting people and travelling overseas:

> China is a growing country [...] it's leading in trade and other stuff [...] so it's very important in the world [...] China has always been big (Ying)

> [I]t's just I guess useful and useful to know two languages um [...] I like being cultural as well like multicultural so [...] I get to see a lot more people (Ken)

> I also have the ability to speak another language which is an advantage for me when I um go overseas or something [...] yeah and you get mobility (Mya)

For Ying, working hard for being proficient in Chinese is "value: it's valuable" so that "in the future [she] can work internationally overseas and relations between other countries." In contrast, Henare's desire for a future apprenticeship as a carver is closely connected to his motivation to learn the Māori language so that he can be a full member of the Māori community:

> [O]h yeah when I finish school I want to go to a carving school in (words unclear) so we learn the traditional carvings and I'll stay there for two or three years and I'll get my diploma and while we're there we're learning the Māori language of our ancestors yeah (Henare)

The quotations show the wide variety of reasons why these young learners choose to learn CHL. Looking at their motivation from the integrative/instrumental dichotomy only partly describes their motivation. For some, like Ying, the motivation is primarily instrumental; for others, like Abinaash, the motivation is mainly integrative. Henare's desire to become a wood carver goes hand in hand with his strong wish to learn the Māori language and culture, and can best be described as an integrated, holistic motivation. Compared with Yi's (2009) study, which investigated the motivation of Korean HL learners at junior high school and high school, this study confirms "living with heritage language speakers," "parents' strong encouragement," and "preparation for further study" as the reasons that positively influenced the motivation of the students to learn a language. Yi's (2009) study shows that "good school atmosphere" only had a marginal effect on student motivation, and while the students in this study do not refer to school atmosphere, the school as a conducive place to meet their friends plays an important role. The learners in this study did not mention "heritage mass media," another positive factor in Yi's (2009) study; however, more traditional media like songs and dances played an important role for some learners. To sum up, the learners in this study emphasize the ability to communicate, in the family and beyond, and the value of the language for their future working life.

Lo Bianco (2014) predicts a battle between two conflicting views on language education, namely:

> the contest of value between those wishing to wrest language education from its construction as a tool of narrowly conceived economic interests, to defend a rival vision of humanistic, cultural, and intellectual goals, and those wishing to consolidate the utilitarian reasoning of much contemporary language education, with its bias toward a world auxiliary English and a small number of other international languages. (Lo Bianco, 2014, p. 322)

Similarly, Scarino (2014) highlights the tension between the economic value of language learning as opposed to more general educational benefits in Australian education. Even so, for the particular learners in this study, practical proficiency in their CHL for study and/or future work can go hand in hand with their desire for linguistic and cultural enrichment. Ushioda (2016) recently described that motivation research has started to move from an instrumentalist to a more holistic constitutive view. Coffey (2016), in a qualitative study with English language learners of modern foreign languages, emphasizes: "Most significantly, the value of language study as an asset is articulated as a form of cultural capital in an educational discourse of liberal, humanistic tradition of education rather than purely as an instrumental goal" (p. 1). The Australian CHL learners in this study echo these modern foreign language learners in England.

The next section focuses on a description of these learners' *HL Selves*. The analysis shows that often learners have a vision of themselves as multilinguals in which the use of the CHL and the use of English are described holistically. Essentially, this means that these learners do not hold language-specific visions of themselves.

2.4.2 Research Question 2: How Does Their CHL Self Contribute to Their Vision of a Future User of that Language?

When asked about their future self, these young learners expressed overall positive visions of themselves as competent language users of their CHL. Some had short-term visions; others had visions linked to long-term goals:

> I'm kind of imagining myself up on the stage doing a speech um at multicultural festival um like like at a festival (Abinaash)

> I'm thinking around a career choice around travel and foreign affairs and speaking another language interacting with my clients would be quite helpful for that (Jasleen)

> [T]hey're like musicians and um they all can speak Māori right and Māori fluent and Māori and it's just like yeah something that I want to do I really want to kind of be like them one day (Henare)

Henare's vision illustrates the strong link between the Māori language and culture and his own identity. His *CHL Self* is best described when he says:

> Māori's me and yeah that's yeah it's me [...] yeah it's me (pause) it's never gonna leave me it's always gonna be with me and (pause) for other people it could be there but it's always gonna be with me personally (Henare)

Naoko also describes very clearly that the HL is an integral part of her and will stay with her for good: "I guess since like I obviously love my parents it's their language it's already with me and I can't really take it away so it's something that will be with me forever."

Henare refers to both English and Māori as "my language": the only difference for him is that as for Māori, he is "still learning [...] bits and pieces of it it's not fully there yeah." Meanwhile, Naoko gives clear weighting to English and Japanese:

> [M]y goal is to Kyoto University for a year or maybe two um just just to be able to live in Japan again and you know learn Japanese but I don't really want to get married there and get a job so the university is really where it stops.

Naoko and also Ying typically identify themselves more strongly with their Australian culture and identity:

> I don't really want to become like a fully Japanese person (Naoko)

> Chinese is sort of my second culture and learning Chinese here helps think of even though I haven't been growing up in China and I've learned English and everything about me is more Australian (Ying)

In contrast, Mona's bilingual/cultural identity has allowed her to develop a *Language(s) (L) Self* that is best described as integrated or holistic. She does not distinguish between the two languages (English and German) that are part of her life: "[I]t's me that's pretty much to sum it up I cannot imagine not knowing being bilingual." Later she says, "I don't have a first language."

Analyzing these statements from an *Ideal CHL Self* perspective, it is clear that the quotations show that the *CHL Selves* of these learners vary. Perhaps one would be tempted to say that Henare's *Ideal CHL Self* is stronger than that of Ying or Naoko. However, such an implicitly judgmental categorization would divert our attention from, for instance, Naoko' full awareness of the bilingual space she lives in and, most importantly, her ability to clearly position herself. Where these CHL learners position themselves on the bilingual/cultural continuum between English and HL is a personal choice. To avoid the somewhat negative descriptor of a low *Ideal CHL Self*, moving beyond the learner's individual languages and the corresponding *Ideal CHL Self* might be more adequate when describing these learners' reality and self-perception. Instead, looking at these learners' *L Self*, which includes all the languages (and varieties) that the learner uses, might allow for a better foundation to understand their motivation to learn a language. Some learners (such as Mona) see themselves as having no first language. As Mona emphasizes, she has a holistic vision of herself as a bilingual person. The construct of the *L Self* allows to adequately describe these learners' choices by viewing and understanding the learner's languages and cultural repertoire as a single factor. Previous research has suggested the term *Multilingual Self* (Henry & Thorsen, 2017; Lvovich, 1997) or *Linguistic Self* (Lemmer, 2014).

The following section describes how living in a bilingual/cultural space and the intercultural experiences that are an integral part of it help these learners develop interculturality.

2.4.3 Research Question 3: How Does Their Interculturality Contribute to Their Language Learning?

2.4.3.1 Awareness of Linguistic and Cultural Difference

The learners in this study show a strong awareness of the cultural differences that they have learnt about. David, for instance, reflects on what he has learnt about Chinese politics in his history lesson at school:

> I also see China on a global perspective I see China as a rising or one of the greatest economies in the world right now I see China as (words unclear) when we study China at school especially in history we often discuss how the totalitarian so there are many side of Chinese language and culture that I see when I think about language (David)

The desire to understand differences in the cultures involved and of the people who are part of these cultures is very strong, as Aroha, Ken, and Mona point out for Māori, Japanese, and German, respectively:

> um well I have a lot of cousins over in New Zealand [. . .] and learning a bit more about it it sort of helps you understand how they feel as well (Aroha)

I like Japanese [. . .] um the culture, like the language, the way you write, the style, the food um all the people you get to see like the way people are different according to the country (Ken)

[I]t's more than just the language it's to understand the way to communicate it has got to do with culture how you say things word phrases they all come from the history of that country and yeah if I want to travel I really have to understand the people so I wanna do it (Mona)

Naoko also sees the benefits of her bilingual identity in a broader understanding of the world when she says, "it shows me a whole new spectrum of things that I can't experience if I just spoke English." At the same time, her awareness of linguistic and cultural differences is manifested in her specific language choice and behavior:

because one thing we do bond over is that we're from different racial cultures but we're all Australian and we speak English so it would distance my me from them and when I am with my friends I don't speak about Japanese or I'd never speak Japanese in front of them just stuff like that it would distance me (Naoko)

2.4.3.2 Using Their Skills as Mediators to Help Others

The students in the study show not only awareness of difference but also attitudes and skills—or desire to acquire skills—in mediating in their interactions with speakers of English and other languages. They see themselves as a person who now and in the future can assist and support peers at school, migrants, foreigners, and people without the same level of language proficiency, either in the CHL or in English. It is worth noting that learners often use the verb "help" in this context, as the following quotations show:

and teaching Japanese to my friends helping them with the Japanese tests (Yoko)

[T]hat was the first image that came to me but after that like also working in the office talking to someone who has migrated and like helping them understand English as well (Jasleen)

Mon people who would come to Australia and don't know any English I would help them around and also when I go overseas when I go to Burma I can also talk and it's easy for me to get my way round (Mya)

[I]f there were people having trouble for example they came from Germany or even France or anywhere um if they if I knew the language they could speak then I could help them out . . .a lot (Lena)

For Ying, the willingness to help others extends to a political level. She believes that people like her can help Australia connect better with other countries. Speaking both English and Chinese "helps make Australia sort of connected to the rest of the world in a way that we can speak to them we can communicate with them." Such comments show the CHL learners' deep sense of interculturality that adds to their language learning.

2.5   Conclusion

By applying Dörnyei's *L2 Motivational Self System* and the concept of interculturality to the Australian CHL learning context, this study has extended the applicability of these theoretical frameworks. The study provides evidence that "heritage language learners articulate a specifically intercultural understanding of their identities" (Kagan, 2012, p. 73), use their skills in mediation, and demonstrate critical awareness of value systems.

Regarding research question 1 (*Why are the CHL learners learning the language?*), the two main reasons why learners chose to learn the CHL are their desire for communication and interaction with family members and the broader community and their perceived value of the language for their future professional and personal life. These reasons need to be understood from a holistic angle; in other words, motivation research must move beyond language-specific orientations. In response to the second research question (*How does their CHL Self contribute to their vision of a future user of that language?*), the study shows that the construct of the *L Self* allows for an adequate description of these learners' choices and of the vision of future users of the language(s), as the construct seeks to understand the learners' languages and cultural repertoire as a single factor. Finally, regarding research question 3 (*How does their interculturality contribute to their language learning?*), the intercultural competence of these learners is often highly developed and closely connected to their language learning. Their lives in a bilingual/cultural space and their intercultural experiences help them develop a capacity to look at cultural issues from more than one perspective.

Despite the small number of participants, the study provides significant insight into these young learners' *L Selves*. These *L Selves* vary, depending on the learner's motivation for learning the language and on interculturality. At the same time, the learners embrace the bilingual/cultural space in which they live and shape it according to their needs and desires. So, the study adds to our understanding of both the motivation of Australian CHL learners and interculturality. Such knowledge is useful for CHL teachers, parents, and other stakeholders. Practical implications for CHL classrooms emerge from the findings of this current study. The link between the *L Selves*, the learners' motivation and sense of interculturality invites teachers, teacher trainers, and curriculum developers alike to help support CHL learners in their multilingual development through their teaching and developing materials that reflect the learners' bilingual/cultural lived experience.

Finally, this research falls into a growing body of research into CHL learners that recognize CHL learners as a "resource rather than a problem" (Hornberger & Wang, 2008, p. 23). It shows that the value of learning a CHL is not necessarily an economic utility: one of its main assets is the capacity of these young Australians to show intercultural awareness—an essential capacity in a world where dialogue across nations and ethnic groups is crucial.

References

ACT Community Language Schools Association. (n.d.). Retrieved from https://actclsa.wordpress.com/home/, 14 May 2019.

ACT Government. (2017). *2017 languages pathway plan in Canberra public schools.* Retrieved from https://www.education.act.gov.au/__data/assets/pdf_file/0006/123396/2017-Language-Pathways-PEA.pdf, 14 May 2019.

Beaudrie, S., & Ducar, C. (2005). Beginning level university heritage programs: Creating a space for all heritage language learners. *Heritage Language Journal, 3*(1), 1–18.

Brinton, D. M., Kagan, S., & Bauckus, S. (2008). Preface. In D. M. Brinton, O. Kagan, & S. Bauckus (Eds.), *Heritage language education: A new field emerging* (pp. ix–xiii). New York: Routledge.

Byram, M. (1997). The intercultural dimension in "language learning for European citizenship". In M. Byram & G. Zarate (Eds.), *The sociocultural and intercultural dimension of language learning and teaching* (pp. 17–20). Strasbourg, France: Council of Europe.

Coffey, S. (2016). Choosing to study modern foreign languages: Discourses of value as forms of cultural capital. *Applied Linguistics,* 1–20. https://doi.org/10.1093/applin/amw019.

Community Languages Australia/Australian Federation of Ethnic Schools Associations Inc. (2016). Retrieved from http://www.communitylanguagesaustralia.org.au, 24 April 2017.

Csizér, K., & Dörnyei, Z. (2005). The internal structure of language learning motivation and its relationship with language choice and learning effort. *Modern Language Journal, 89*, 20–36.

Dörnyei, Z. (2005). *The psychology of the language learner: Individual differences in second language acquisition.* Mahwah, NJ: L. Erlbaum.

Dörnyei, Z. (2009). The L2 motivational self system. In Z. Dörnyei & E. Ushioda (Eds.), *Motivation, language identity and the L2 self* (pp. 9–42). Bristol, UK: Multilingual Matters.

Dörnyei, Z., Csizér, K., & Németh, N. (2006). *Motivational dynamics, language attitudes and language globalization: A Hungarian perspective.* Clevedon, UK: Multilingual Matters.

Douglas, M. O. (2008). Profile of Japanese heritage learners and individualized curriculum. In D. M. Brinton, O. Kagan, & S. Bauckus (Eds.), *Heritage language education: A new field emerging* (pp. 215–226). New York: Routledge.

Flick, U. (2014). *An introduction to qualitative research* (5th ed.). Los Angeles: Sage.

Gardner, R. C. (2001). Integrative motivation and second language acquisition. In Z. Dörnyei & R. Schmidt (Eds.), *Motivation and second language acquisition* (pp. 1–19). Honolulu, HI: University of Hawai'i Second Language Teaching & Curriculum Center.

Gass, S., & Selinker, S. (2008). *Second language acquisition: An introductory course* (3rd ed.). New York: Routledge.

He, W. H. (2010). The heart of heritage: Sociocultural dimensions of heritage language learning. *Annual Review of Applied Linguistics, 30*, 66–82. https://doi.org/10.1017/S0267190510000073.

Henry, A., & Thorsen, C. (2017). The ideal multilingual self: Validity, influences on motivation, and role in a multilingual education. *International Journal of Multilingualism.* https://doi.org/10.1080/14790718.2017.1411916.

Higgins, E. T. (1987). Self-discrepancy: A theory relating self and affect. *Psychological Review, 94* (3), 319–340.

Hornberger, N. H., & Wang, S. C. (2008). Who are our heritage language learners? Identity and biliteracy in heritage language education in the United States. In D. M. Brinton, O. Kagan, & S. Bauckus (Eds.), *Heritage language education: A new field emerging* (pp. 3–35). New York: Routledge.

Kagan, O. (2012). Intercultural competence of heritage language learners: Motivation, identity, language attitudes, and the curriculum. *Proceedings of Intercultural Competence Conference,* September 2012, Vol. 2, 72–84. Retrieved from http://citeseerx.ist.psu.edu/viewdoc/download?doi=10.1.1.466.2881&rep=rep1&type=pdf, 14 May 2019.

Kormos, J., & Csizér, K. (2008). Age-related differences in the motivation of learning English as a foreign language: Attitudes, selves, and motivated learning behavior. *Language Learning, 58*, 327–355.

Kramsch, C. (2005). Post 9/11: Foreign languages between knowledge and power. *Applied Linguistics, 26*(4), 545–567. https://doi.org/10.1093/applin/ami026.

Kurata, N. (2015). Motivational selves of Japanese heritage speakers in Australia. *Heritage Language Journal, 12*(2), 110–131.

Lee, J. S., & Kim, H. (2008). Heritage language learners' attitudes, motivations and instructional needs: The case of postsecondary Korean language learners. In K. Kondo-Brown & J. D. Brown (Eds.), *Teaching Chinese, Japanese, and Korean heritage language students: Curriculum needs, materials, and assessment* (pp. 159–186). New York: Lawrence Erlbaum Associates.

Lemmer, K. (2014). Examining the linguistic self in a multilingual context: Reflecting on a South African adaptation of Shaw's Pygmalion. *South African Theatre Journal, 27*(3), 183–196. https://doi.org/10.1080/10137548.2014.910963.

Lo Bianco, J. (2014). Domesticating the foreign: Globalization's effects on the place/s of languages. *The Modern Language Journal, 98*(1), 312–325. https://doi.org/10.1111/j.1540-4781.2014.12063.x.

Lvovich, N. (1997). *The multilingual self: An inquiry into language learning.* Hillsdale, NJ: Erlbaum.

Markus, H., & Nurius, P. (1986). Possible selves. *American Psychologist, 41*(9), 954–969.

Menard-Warwick, J. (2008). The cultural and intercultural identities of transnational English teachers: Two case studies from the Americas. *TESOL Quarterly, 42*(4), 617–640.

Montrul, S. (2010). Current issues in heritage language acquisition. *Annual Review of Applied Linguistics, 30*, 3–23. https://doi.org/10.1017/S0267190510000103.

Noels, K. A. (2005). Orientations to learning German: Heritage language learning and motivational substrates. *Canadian Modern Language Review/La Revue Canadienne des Langues Vivantes, 62*(2), 285–312.

Ortega, L. (2009). *Understanding second language acquisition.* London: Hodder.

Ryan, S. (2008). *The ideal selves of Japanese learners of English.* Unpublished doctoral thesis. University of Nottingham, Nottingham, UK, United Kingdom.

Scarino, A. (2014). Situating the challenges in current languages education policy in Australia— Unlearning monolingualism. *International Journal of Multilingualism, 11*(3), 289–306. https://doi.org/10.1080/14790718.2014.921176.

Strauss, A., & Corbin, J. (1990). *Basics of qualitative research: Grounded theory procedures and techniques.* Newbury Park, CA, London: Sage.

The linguistic competence of heritage speakers. (2011). Guest editor S. Montrul. Special issue of *Studies in Second Language Acquisition*, 33(2).

Ushioda, E. (2016, December 5). *Motivation and making connections across the multilingual mind.* Plenary paper presented at the Applied Linguistics Association of Australia (ALAA) Annual Conference 2016, Monash University, Australia.

Valdés, G. (2001). Heritage language students: Profiles and possibilities. In J. K. Peyton, D. A. Ranard, & S. McGinnis (Eds.), *Heritage languages in America: Preserving a national resource* (pp. 37–77). Washington, DC/McHenry, IL: Center for Applied Linguistics & Delta Systems.

Van Deusen-Scholl, N. (2014). Research on heritage language issues. In T. G. Wiley, J. K. Peyton, D. Christian, S. C. K. Moore, & M. Liu (Eds.), *Handbook of heritage, community, and native American languages in the United States* (pp. 76–84). New York: Routledge.

Van Patten, B., & Benati, A. G. (2010). *Key terms in second language acquisition.* New York: Continuum.

Weger-Guntharp, H. (2006). Voices from the margin: Developing a profile of Chinese heritage language learners in the FL classroom. *Heritage Language Journal, 4*(1), 29–46.

Wilson, D. V., & Martinez, R. (2011). Diversity in definition: Integrating history and student attributes in understanding heritage learners of Spanish in New Mexico. *Heritage Language Journal, 8*(2), 115–133.

Xie, Y. (2011). *Representations of L2 motivational self system with beginning Chinese language learners at college level in the United States: Heritage and nonheritage language learners.* Unpublished doctoral thesis. Liberty University, VA, United States.

Yi, C. (2009). *Motivational factors in heritage language learning in the context of Korean community.* Unpublished doctoral thesis. University of Biola, CA, United States.

Chapter 3
Intermittent Second-Language Intensification in the Host Culture: An Ethnographic Case Study of a Heritage Speaker in a Study-Abroad Program

Christian Abello-Contesse

This chapter is dedicated in loving memory to my dear sister, Eliana Abello Contesse (Santiago de Chile, 1955–2015).

3.1 Introduction

It may be claimed that study-abroad research has recently achieved more balanced perspectives and a reasonably mature stage where there is ample recognition of the coexistence of complex, interconnected processes and dimensions that have challenged early intuitive assumptions or sheer idealization. It is currently accepted, for example, that direct availability of opportunities for out-of-class second language learning does not mean that sojourners will automatically want to experience the target language or culture (L2 or C2) firsthand. Similarly, it is recognized that members of the host community may not be willing to engage in sustained, supportive interaction with L2 learners whose overall proficiency level in the L2 may be more than adequate for formal lectures, but not necessarily for sustained, colloquial interaction in the local variety of the target language. Regarding the target culture (C2), in addition to the widely expected host-culture integration (as implied, for example, in explicit references to "immersion experiences" and "immersed learners" in the study-abroad literature), both "third culture/place" formation and passive "spectator," rather than (pro)active "participant," behavior have also been observed and reported. As a result, it has become patent that students decide to go abroad for a wide variety of reasons, have different strengths and weaknesses regarding their individual learner differences, and set various goals that are not necessarily as immediate or clear-cut as is often assumed.

C. Abello-Contesse (✉)
University of Seville, Seville, Spain
e-mail: chac@us.es

© Springer Nature Singapore Pte Ltd. 2021
M. D. López-Jiménez, J. Sánchez-Torres (eds.), *Intercultural Competence Past, Present and Future*, Intercultural Communication and Language Education,
https://doi.org/10.1007/978-981-15-8245-5_3

3.2　Literature Review

3.2.1　Individual Differences in Second Language Acquisition Research

This section briefly reviews some individual differences (IDs) that became salient over the course of the longitudinal study reported in this chapter. Two IDs gradually became more prominent in this case; these were *anxiety* and *identity*; both of them generated high levels of *ambivalence*. Within identity as a multidimensional factor, aspects related to family, ethnic, language, and national identity became noticeable, mainly as a result of the participant's dual role as a heritage Spanish speaker and a Spanish-as-a-second-language learner/user in Spain. As it turned out, the specific effects of these IDs did not seem to favor much host culture integration in practice.

Loewen and Reinders (2011) claim that the term ID "refers to a broad area of SLA research that investigates characteristics that L2 learners bring to the task of L2 learning and how those characteristics may differ from learner to learner" (p. 88). According to Richards and Schmidt (2010), these are:

> Factors specific to individual learners which may account for differences in the rate at which learners learn and their level of attainment. While much research in second language learning has the goal of discovering processes and stages of development that are common to all learners, this has always been accompanied by a complementary concern for differences among learners. Given the same learning environment, it is often observed that some learners are highly successful and others are not. (p. 278)

3.2.2　Anxiety

Research on anxiety in second language acquisition (SLA) has often been described as a dimension of personality rather than as an autonomous ID among L2 learners. Lightbown and Spada (2013, p. 85) deal with anxiety under personality and define *learner anxiety* as "feelings of worry, nervousness, and stress that many students experience when learning a second language." Saville-Troike (2012) asserts that:

> Anxiety has received the most attention in SLA research along with lack of anxiety as an important component of self-confidence. Anxiety correlates negatively with measures of L2 proficiency [. . .], meaning that higher anxiety tends to go with lower levels of success in L2 learning. In addition to self-confidence, lower anxiety may be manifested by more risk-taking or more adventuresome behaviors. (p. 96)

Colman (2001) makes a basic distinction between *state* anxiety (defined as "a temporary form of anxiety related to a particular situation or condition that a person is currently in") and *trait* anxiety (defined as a "person's general or characteristic level of anxiety" (pp. 703, 750). Winstanley (2006, p. 26) defines anxiety as "a psychological feeling of fear and apprehension that an individual experiences, which is usually associated with physical symptoms such as increased heart and pulse rates, sweating, blushing and nausea." She makes the following distinctions:

> Anxiety can be seen as normal, short-lasting *response* to particular internal or external *stimuli*, or can be long lasting in which case it may be viewed as abnormal. [...] State anxiety is defined as a transitory emotional state or condition of an individual that is characterized by *subjective*, consciously perceived feelings of tension and apprehension and by heightened physical activity. In contrast, *trait* anxiety, is defined as a relatively stable individual proneness to anxiety, and refers to a tendency to respond with anxiety to perceived threats in the environment. (p. 26)

Much of the applied research has centered on specific anxiety reactions among *L2* learners in *classroom* situations. Horwitz and Young (1991) state that:

> Many people claim to have a mental block against learning a foreign language, although these same people may be good learners in other situations [...]. In many cases, they may have an anxiety reaction which impedes their ability to perform successfully in a foreign language class. Anxiety is the subjective feeling of tension, apprehension, nervousness, and worry associated with an arousal of the autonomic nervous system [...]. (p. 27)

3.2.3 Identity in SLA

Identity is a comparatively recent and fast-growing ID within SLA research. According to Swann, Deumert, Lillis, and Mesthrie (2004), identity is "a term used to refer to an individual's or group's sense of who they are, as defined by them and/or others" (p. 140). Field (2011) defines identity as "How one views oneself; a person's concepts of [their] own individuality or group reference/affiliation" (p. 86). Block (2007a) relates the concept of identity to negotiation of status changes (social, professional, etc.) in challenging middle-of-the-road or intermediate positions and situations:

> Identities are about negotiating new subject positions at the crossroads of past, present, and future [...]. The entire process is conflictive as opposed to harmonious, and individuals often feel ambivalent [...]. Identities are related to different, traditionally demographic categories, such as ethnicity, race, nationality, migration, gender, social class and language. (p. 27)

Overall, it may be claimed that the current SLA literature characterizes identity as a process that is (i) socially constructed and negotiated in interaction (co-constructed in both equitable and inequitable relations of power); (ii) multiple and complex; (iii) a site of instability or even struggle; (iv) involving both compatible and contradictory identities that may coexist within a single individual; (v) age related as adults normally have more (quantity) and stronger (quality) identities as compared with teenagers or children; (vi) not uniform, but rather in constant flux; (vii) subject to modification and change across time and place; and (viii) closely related to the concepts of individual bi/multilingualism and bi/multiculturalism (i.e., individuals having two or more different cultural identities).

3.2.3.1 Ambivalence

In this study, ambivalence is examined as an essential component within the broader concept of individual and collective identity. Block (2007a) explicitly emphasizes the relationship between the concepts of identity and *ambivalence*:

> Ambivalence is the uncertainty of feeling a part and feeling apart. It is the mutually conflicting feelings of love and hate. Moreover, it is the simultaneous affirmation and negation of such feeling [...]. Ambivalence, it would seem, is the natural state of human beings who are forced by their individual life trajectories to make choices where choices are not easy to make. However, a natural state is not necessarily a desirable state and in studies of individuals' life stories, there are attempts to resolve the conflicts that underlie ambivalence. (pp. 864-865)

Reber (1995) defines "ambivalence" as "1. Having simultaneous contrasting or mixed feelings about some person, object or idea. 2. A tendency to 'flip-flop' one's feelings or attitudes about a person, object or idea" (p. 28).

3.2.3.2 Heritage Spanish Speakers in the United States

Language identity involves three different types of relationships (Block, 2007b), "language expertise," "language affiliation," and "language inheritance." Block defines *inheritance* as "being born into a family or community setting that is associated with a particular language or dialect" (p. 40). Kinginger (2013) relates the notion of "inheritance" to research done on *heritage language learners/speakers* abroad.

The terms *heritage speaker* and *heritage language learner* tend to be used synonymously in much of the SLA literature. Montrul (2016), however, provides a relevant distinction between them as used in the United States:

> [...] *heritage speaker* refers to individuals from language minority groups who grow up exposed to a minority language in the home and the majority societal language. In essence, this is a bilingual situation, and heritage speakers are bilingual individuals. (p. 19)

Montrul (2016) claims that heritage language *learners* are "speakers who seek to (re)learn their heritage language in the classroom and are taking formal classes" (p. 19); she asserts that *heritage language learners* are not a subset of *heritage speakers* since "having some proficiency in the heritage language is crucial for the linguistic definition of a heritage speaker" and adds:

> Not all the students who sign up for heritage language classes are heritage language speakers. In fact, some *heritage language learners* do not have any proficiency in the heritage language but may come to the classroom because they want to learn the language from zero. These *heritage language learners*, who do not speak or understand the language, [...] are in fact no different from the second language learners. (p. 19)

3.2.4 The Notion of "Third Place"/"Third Culture" and Sociocultural Hybridity

Block (2007b) also relates identity to the notion of a *third place*:

> In particular, when individuals move across geographical and psychological borders, immersing themselves in new sociocultural environments, they find that their sense of identity is destabilised and that they enter a period of struggle to reach a balance. [...] In such cases, the ensuing and ongoing struggle is not, however, a question of adding the new to the old. Nor is it a half-and-half proposition whereby the individual becomes half of what he or she was and half of what he or she has been exposed to. Rather, the result is what has come to be known as a *third place* [...], where there is what Papastergiadis (2000) called a *negotiation of difference* during which the past and the present "encounter and transform each other" in the presence of fissures, gaps and contradictions [...]. (p. 864)

According to Swann et al. (2004), the concept of third space "is used by researchers to refer to a relatively abstract notion of space which is defined in terms of culture and identity rather than primarily in terms of geographical or physical location" (p. 314). Thus, the "third place"—or "third space"—is closely related to the concept of hybridity (sociocultural heterogeneity). Mikula (2008) claims that:

> Recent scholarship has interpreted hybridity as a potential challenge to existing hierarchies and essentialist worldviews. According to [Homi] Bhabha, hybridity occupies a "third space" in between the subject positions of the colonizer and the colonized. This space in between does not recuperate the essence of its constitutive elements, but rather enables new positions to emerge. (p. 90)

3.3 Methodology

3.3.1 Qualitative Research Design: Ethnographic and Case Study Approaches

One of the methodological approaches used in this study was ethnography. In line with the exploratory and emergent nature of ethnographic research, there were no *explicit foci* of attention at the beginning of the project (Richards & Schmidt, 2010) in favor of patterns and themes/categories that would come up from and during the study. As Swann et al. (2004, p. 101) suggest, "categories used to interpret activities tend to emerge during the study rather than being fixed at the outset [...]." Broadly speaking, however, the study aimed to explore aspects of L2 involvement and sociocultural engagement in the host community, that is, what year-long sojourners would do so that their proficiency levels in their target language (L2) and culture (C2) might grow significantly. Thus, initial attention was given to communicative situations where input was typically received and output was produced as well as those where the dimensions of their C2 were experienced firsthand—in terms of products, practices, and perspectives (Moran, 2001).

The ethnographic approach was used in conjunction with case study methodology. Thus, in order to investigate sojourners' individual strategies for additional language and culture learning within a second language context, a case study research project was conducted during one academic year. It was felt that, by doing a longitudinal study (October to May), the patterns, themes, issues, and emotions that the participants faced while fulfilling their new roles in the host community could be investigated more thoroughly. While it is sometimes claimed that the findings of case studies are unlikely to be generalized, generalizability was not a major purpose in this study in view of its *constructivist* orientation. Case-study methodology has been used extensively and productively in the field of SLA research; van Lier (2005) claims that: "We can thus conclude that, far from being marginal studies of merely anecdotal value, case studies have played a key role in shaping the knowledge base of SLA" (p. 198).

Consequently, while the study was broadly intended to explore the ways in which the L2 and C2 were used by the participants in their host community, its theoretical framework was based on specific IDs. On the one hand, learner involvement is likely to be closely related to the personal factors that sojourners bring with them; on the other, such IDs are likely to become more obvious among year-long participants in study-abroad programs. The roles of anxiety, identity, and ambivalence within this second language context of learning became increasingly salient during the study and, thus, became the overarching focus of the study (Beaven & Spencer-Oatey, 2016; Block, 2007a, 2007b; Brown, 2009; DuFon & Churchill, 2006; Gallucci, 2013; Jackson, 2008; Kinginger, 2009, 2013; Yang & Kim, 2011).

3.3.2 Participant

The criteria for the selection of the participants in the case were (i) length of stay, (ii) an overall intermediate or higher level of L2 proficiency, and (iii) personal commitment, that is, the participant was expected to be a year-long, intermediate/ high intermediate sojourner who was willing to take part in a longitudinal study which required some time for oral and written output in the L2; the student, in turn, would benefit from additional use of the language with a native interlocutor in an informal environment. Two students volunteered for participation; the present paper focuses on one of these year-long participants in the study.

In her initial background questionnaire for this study, Marta (a pseudonym, henceforth referred to as M) noted that she was 20 years old, a third-year university student double-majoring in International Studies and Spanish at a US public university. Unlike the vast majority of the other study-abroad students in her program, M wrote that she had been learning Spanish formally since first grade in elementary school (see Participant's Personal Data Sheet) (Table 3.1).

Table 3.1 Participant's personal data sheet

Name: Marta/M (pseudonym)
Age: 20. Sex: Female
Place of origin: US Midwest
Nationality: US American
Ethnic/family background: Latino/Mexican-American and Anglo-American
Parents' names: Pedro and Martha
Brothers and sisters: Two sisters (Patricia and Sharon)
Family's socioeconomic status (SES) in the US: Upper-middle class
Religion (if any): Catholic (currently, a nonpracticing Catholic)
Current occupation: A junior at a large public university
Academic major(s): International Relations and Spanish
Prospective employment: Undecided. Would like to work at an international organization, such as the UNO.
Total time learning Spanish in a school setting: 15 years (since first grade)
Time spent in a Spanish-speaking community before this sojourn: Costa Rica (1 week), Ecuador (2 weeks), Peru (2 weeks), and Spain (2 weeks)
Present housing option in Spain: Home stay
People she reported speaking Spanish with frequently outside class in Spain: Her host family (parents, 16-year-old brother, 14-year-old sister) and some friends
Learning disabilities: None were reported

3.3.3   Data Collection and Analysis

The data-gathering procedures consisted of the following complementary sources: (i) six in-depth interviews with the participant, (ii) five journal entries; (iii) one interview with the resident coordinator of M's program; (iv) several short oral and written tasks (sometimes done in order to assess new lexical items along with their semantic transparency and/or cultural implications); and (v) naturally occurring e-mail messages between the informant and the researcher during the study. Both the interviews and journal entries constituted the primary data for the study. Relatively unstructured interviews of approximately 1 h (55–75 min) were conducted six times during the 8-month period; all interview sessions were based on face-to-face, one-to-one interaction performed exclusively *in Spanish* and were held at reasonably quiet places, such as a cafeteria on a university campus or a coffee shop opposite the campus. Each interview was audio-recorded and transcribed with the participant's previous written consent. The transcriptions were subjected to the phases of thematic analysis suggested by Braun and Clarke (2006); the analysis was conducted in Spanish, and extracts were translated into English by the researcher later on. A total of five journal entries (400–500 words each) were collected over the research period. Because the aim was to have access to the participant's practices, perspectives, and changes in different registers and styles in her target language, interviews were conversational—intended to provide informal spoken samples—and the participant was typically encouraged to focus on the topics/subtopics that she found most relevant. Conversely, all five journal entries were intended to provide relatively formal, reflective samples of the target language in writing.

3.4 Results

3.4.1 Emerging Themes, Issues, and Emotions

A total of seven interconnected themes that gradually emerged from the data sources identified above are described, exemplified, and interpreted below.

3.4.1.1 Is this Actually Immersion or Rather Intermittent L2 Intensification?

Although M's second language learning context is usually described—although with surprisingly little sociolinguistic rigor—as *immersion*, it is clearly not the case that the various situations that occur in it constitute immersion. The study-abroad program model in M's destination may be described as "combined" in that it offers an "integrated" enrollment program option (where US students are placed in local university classrooms with local students) and an "island" program option (designed specifically for American study-abroad students). Almost all of the classes that M took during her study-abroad experience were within the "island" program, which largely replicates in Spain practices found in American college classrooms.

Due to this and other decisions M made in Spain, her linguistic and sociocultural situation may be described more objectively as *intensification*. Thus, the expression *L2 intensification with potential access to C2* is used as a more accurate alternative in this chapter. This is defined as comparatively intensive periods of receptive contact and productive use of L2 Spanish where direct access to naturally occurring cultural situations (C2) is *available* at varying degrees of involvement. This *intensification* tends to be *intermittent* as it is present in short periods which often cover 4 days a week since students in this program type do not normally have classes or other mandatory academic activities from Friday to Sunday. Because M's host city was a major urban center, students—who are part of a *temporary micro-culture* within the dominant host culture from the initial orientation sessions in September—may have access to the local culture *if they wish* to do so and *to the extent* they desire (i.e., potential rather than automatic or unavoidable access to the C2).

According to the answers to the written statement *Using my Spanish orally has been more frequent and more sustained on weekdays than on weekends* posed to a subgroup of 25 students—all of them participating in M's program—towards the end of the first semester, higher percentages were assigned to their use of Spanish *during* the week—in some cases, twice as high or even higher—while considerably lower percentages were assigned to weekend use. Specifically, 68% of these students "agreed" with the statement, whereas 24% evaluated it as "it depends/varies," and only 8% "disagreed" with it. The students also commented that the higher percentage awarded to this 4-day week was mainly due to their *classes* and other class-related activities. Those students who lived with local families also benefited from interacting with members of their families at varying levels.

These comments on the relative weight that instructional activities have also showed that much of the time the students spend "in Spanish" actually continues to take place in a formal, academic variety of Spanish, in what is typically a *protected* L2 environment. This is defined here as settings where there is a widespread presence of *simplified* and *modified* input, *negotiated* interaction (i.e., mutual clarification of unfamiliar language content), and occasional *L1 use* by (bilingual) professors or administrative staff. Therefore, the language available on weekdays often provides reduced levels of sociolinguistic and discursive variation (e.g., styles, registers, types of interlocutors, topics covered). A typical example might include minimal or no use made of *intergenerational* language resources as found naturally in the local community. In an interview conducted in February, it became clear that M had no contact with Spanish-speaking peers the previous week. In addition, although she had already been in Spain for 5 months, until then she had never used Spanish with Spanish-speaking senior citizens, and although she had recently had an opportunity to talk with Spanish-speaking children, the conversation had simply been a brief exchange with children who were visiting her host family (still, M commented that it had been "difficult" for her to talk to them in Spanish).

M soon realized that she was faced with an ongoing dichotomy between the relative easiness of the *protected* Spanish environment found in the classroom at the American Center for Study Abroad (ACSA) and the added difficulty of Spanish "out in the street." This was evidenced in a journal entry in November, where she stated: "There are some local practices that are still challenges for me, like the local accent. I have no problem with communication with my professors here or with my Spanish family, but sometimes the accent is quite difficult to understand. The other day a cousin of my Spanish family was at home and asked my host mother, 'Trini. Why are you talking like that?'" I then realized she did not talk like that in her everyday life. She speaks more slowly so I understand everything. And now I'm used to the way she talks, but in the street with other people, the local accent is very difficult for me."

Given that the only class that M took at the local university during her first semester was part of the *Courses-for-Foreigners Unit*, M actually had no contact with *Spanish* peers in *any* of her classes between late September and mid-December. Her only on-campus class was different in that it was larger and made up of international students with various *non-Spanish* nationalities and mother tongues. Therefore, the most noticeable feature of the Spanish with which M had contact during a typical week was the minimal presence of *unmodified* language and *sustained*, *informal* conversation with *local peers*—as opposed to brief transactional exchanges (service encounters) in stores, cafes, or restaurants.

Before M finished her first semester, she already had an opinion on the only class she was taking on campus: that class was "strange." When asked what she meant by that, M identified several features related to teaching styles or classroom culture.

However, M did not seem to be aware that such features, as not having some predetermined material to prepare (as announced on the syllabus) for every class session or being given limited oral participation time for class discussion, usually occur in the Spanish system of university education. M felt it was the opposite of the equivalent situation back home, and she concluded that she liked her (US-style) classes at ACSA "much more." This situation was reinforced later, given that out of the six classes that M took during the second semester, all were taught at ACSA for American students. In an interview with the resident coordinator of the ACSA Liberal Arts program in May, a person who knew M well during her stay, she confirmed there were relevant personality differences among her students: "Some of the other year-long students (in M's program) enrolled in classes at the university with Spanish students, although that is actually a *challenge* because they must be more proactive and independent, and they also have to be away from their family for another month (i.e., from early May to early June) in order to observe the official academic calendar at the local university."

3.4.1.2 Elusive Local Spanish-Speaking Peers Even in a Spanish-Speaking Community

M's "social/communicative" use of Spanish during a given time period (typically the previous week or month) was present as a topic in all of the interviews; the focus was on her interaction in establishing and/or maintaining human relations. *In the mid-December interview, immediately after the end of the first semester, M mentioned that she felt satisfied that she had not come for just one semester: "It's not long enough to get to know people well."* She also commented on the relative ease and difficulty she had in meeting people who would give her opportunities to socialize and *concluded, "It's easy to meet people here, but it's difficult to maintain the relationship." The first 4 months had shown her* the difficulty of having to *seek out* Spanish-speaking local peers as interlocutors. Although M originally liked the idea that local Spanish-speaking peers could provide her with communicative practice and sociocultural support, the notion soon became ambivalent and she seemed unwilling or unable to put it into practice.

A month later, in January, she told the interviewer that she had attended the reception for the ACSA students who had arrived for the second semester. She commented that the orientation for incoming students had taken place the previous week and emphasized that she had been "the only year-long student (out of 16 year-long students in her program) who had participated in it to *meet people*." This was probably the occasion where M's ambivalence regarding her interactions with Spanish-speaking peers was most evident as she reverted to the simpler route of meeting new American peers to socialize with. According to the information provided by the resident coordinator of M's program at ACSA, M showed great interest in getting involved in these welcome activities to make friends, although many full-year students do not normally participate in them any longer: "What interests them is their relationship with *Spanish* students, because they have already passed that initial stage—back in September—and see themselves as being 'different' in January. Others still prefer to be more sheltered, to feel more secure and protected."

In January, M also recognized that she had not had many opportunities to use her Spanish over the Christmas break and that during recent weeks she had used Spanish mainly at home, with her host mother. Continuing to address the subject of the *regular* presence of Spanish-speaking *peers* in her daily activities, M stated, "I have a friend named Tere who is 19, and a university student here." The interviewer commented that she had previously mentioned that Tere was "related" to her local family since Tere's parents were very close friends of her host parents and asked her if there were people her age—*unrelated* to her family—with whom she had some social relationship in Spanish. She replied, "Well, with my professors. . ., but that's all there is." Later in the same interview when asked to identify "something you would *not* do this semester that you did do in the previous one," she replied that she was trying to (i) go out with Tere more often instead of going out with her American acquaintances, as had happened earlier, and also (ii) speak more Spanish outside the home, since that semester there was another US student living with her Spanish family. In theory, at least, her explicit intentions were to meet more local people and use more Spanish beyond her host parents.

However, a month later, in February, when the interviewer asked her if she had used Spanish with peers in the past week, for the first time her answer was straightforward: "No." In the fifth interview in April, M was asked the same question, albeit on a shorter time scale: "Who did you speak with in Spanish this past weekend?" Her response— "With my Spanish parents and with. . . waiters"— revealed both (i) the absence of peers and (ii) situations of unsustained talk, most often limited to service encounters. Her use of strategies apparently intended to minimize the lack of interpersonal interaction of a certain length and depth was also shown in that interview. M commented that her recent visits to the doctor (due to the heart problem she had experienced), and her new yoga classes, had increased her contact with spoken Spanish. A little later, however, it became clear that the yoga instructor was an American woman residing in Spain and that the visits to the doctor had been made with a bilingual assistant from ACSA, in case it had been necessary to act as an interpreter in addressing specific medical aspects.

Tere appears on M's list of "Spanish conversation partners" that she wrote in mid-December, identifying people she had used Spanish *regularly* with during the first semester. At the top of that list were her local parents (Pablo, 50, and Trinidad, 45) and then her local brother (16) and sister (14). It is revealing to note that while there were several explicit references to interactions with Pablo and, especially, Trinidad (Trini) in the recordings, there was absolutely no mention of her local brother or sister. Actually, Tere features in this study as the *only peer* with whom M socialized in Spanish in a relatively stable manner during her year in Spain. Their relationship was probably facilitated by the fact that Tere was a second-year student in English Studies and planned to take a trip to the US the following academic year.

3.4.1.3 Does a College Student Need to Be Familiarized with the University System in the Host Culture?

In December, M answered some questions about her experience during the first semester, which had just concluded. One of the key questions was: "Do you think you now have a *good idea* how the Spanish university system works?" She replied, "I don't know yet. I think my 'Courses-for-Foreigners' class was weird in the way it was taught. So I don't think so."

During the study, it became increasingly clear that M was aware that the American and Spanish university systems did not work the same way. An explicit example of this was recorded in the January interview. M mentioned that something that was difficult for Spaniards to understand was that in the US someone may study at a university in a place that is far away from their hometown. In an interview a month later, M was aware that there were *other* differences, although she could not identify what those differences were specifically. She mentioned that sometimes people asked her about American university life, since in Spain there was no distinction between undergraduate and graduate studies. "They don't have undergrad and then graduate school here." "They ask me: 'What are you majoring in?'" "So I answer International Relations and Spanish, but that is not a specific degree program here…" "So then they ask me: 'And what are you going to do after graduating?'"

These statements—ironically addressed to a person M knew was working in the local educational system—may have been the result of topics that emerged spontaneously (probably in conversations with other US students who also had limited experience with the Spanish system) and, thus, gave rise to misinterpretations on the part of M that never seemed to be clarified. It is worth pointing out that in these interviews M *rarely requested* clarifications or practical examples of sociocultural information that might have been unclear to her. The virtual absence of local university students in M's academic environment did not help clarify these confusions. Near the end of her sojourn, there was no evidence that M had come to understand any of the following educational/cultural aspects: in Spain (i) there is indeed a clear distinction between undergraduate and graduate degrees; (ii) a student's undergraduate major usually indicates their future professional career; thus, it is highly relevant to consider what specific job opportunities are available with a given major; (iii) just as there are traditional undergraduate majors in both systems (e.g., a modern language such as French), there are also other majors that are much less common (e.g., international relations in Spain or translation and interpreting in the United States); (iv) the presence of two different yet *related* academic majors (double majors) is rather uncommon in Spain; and (v) the presence of double majors in fields that are *unrelated* to each other is practically nonexistent at Spanish universities.

In early May, just 5 days before her return to the United States, M seemed to be ready to wrap up her academic experience in Spain; it should be mentioned that those of M's fellow year-long ACSA students who had chosen to take one or more classes at the local university would have to stay in Spain for another full month. M was "satisfied" with the grades she would get on the classes she had just completed. In fact, of the total of 6 classes that M took in the second semester, she got a final grade of A in 5 of them and a B+ in one. In indirectly responding to the question, "How would you define yourself as a *student*: Excellent, good, fair, or bad?" M said, "Well, in the US, if you get As in everything, if you're on the Dean's List—I don't know if that exists here [it does *not*]—and if you participate in many activities in your school..." The interviewer preferred to confirm her indirect reference by saying, "So, is that *your* situation, then?" To which M answered, "Yes." When asked if it had been difficult to maintain that high academic standard here in Spain, M agreed, and recalling the only class that she took at the university, she commented, "That was the worst grade I've ever gotten in my life... a *B* -."

Given that all the interviews were conducted fully in Spanish, it should be noted that, when commenting on her grades, M used the American option of *letter* grades—rather than the Spanish system of *number* grades. Apparently, there had been no need for her to learn what the equivalent terms were during her school year in Spain. Later in the same interview, when asked about what she would not do again if she had the chance to do it all over again, she replied, "I would take more classes at the university because I think the experience I had scared me." This comment also shows M's ambivalence considering that she had previously done the opposite by choice.

3.4.1.4 Her Destination as a Home Base for Frequent National and International Trips

In early November, when M let the researcher know the times she had available to schedule the project interviews, she wrote, "Fridays: All (day) free, if I'm not *traveling*." By the end of the first semester, M had traveled to five destinations, each of them at least 1000 kilometers/620 miles from her destination (two inside Spain and three abroad). When this subject arose in an interview in December, M responded quite naturally, "This is almost everyone's expectation (among ACSA students)." In an activity done in December concerning her experience during the first semester regarding her oral interaction in Spanish outside her classes, M responded that she had used it about 50% of the time during the week, but only 20% of the time on the weekends.

One of the most recurrent aspects of the data obtained in the study is the presence of brief periods of self-planned tourism, a characteristic that is facilitated by the fact that ACSA's academic program—as opposed to the regular academic practice in Spain—does not schedule classes on Fridays. Although this tourism varied, trips often lasted for 2–4 days and took place every 3 or 4 weeks, including both domestic and foreign travel of short and long distance. Weekends, local holidays, and vacation periods throughout the sojourn were typical options. However, from the perspective of further developing an L2 and a C2, this form of tourism without academic guidance is most likely to be *counterproductive*, since students usually make little or no use of Spanish during most trips. From the point of view of social relationships and cultural adaptation with their local families, this tourism does not seem to help strengthen family ties as the trips are not experiences shared with the other members of the family core.

Another relevant aspect worth considering is that international travel within Europe these days usually puts the student in direct contact with the use of English as a lingua franca (ELF). Specifically, within the scope of these trips (e.g., international airports and flights, downtown hotels, sightseeing tours, fast-food chains), English usually serves as an international language of wider communication or lingua franca.

A valid example of how this added tourism can clearly "compete" for time and attention with the target language and culture can be seen in an interview conducted in the spring. In April, M answered some simple questions that were related directly to aspects of one of the "major fiestas" held annually in her destination. It caught the researcher's attention that she could recognize the meaning of several of the typical expressions used, yet not of other equally common ones. Later on, it became clear that M relied heavily on what she had learned in two of her classes in previous weeks, since she had only had a chance to observe a small part of the on-site celebration. Specifically, M had planned an international trip for the same week the city celebrates this major festival; she had received information on the characteristics of the celebration in two of her classes by way of preparation but had only been physically present at the celebration on the last day and a half, which is ironically the portion that is typically considered the least representative.

According to data from this study, in early May M had undertaken a total of *15 trips* to 13 destinations (seven destinations within Spain and six foreign destinations; two of the overseas destinations were visited two times each). Only two of these 15 trips had been educational ones organized by ACSA. From a quantitative perspective, this situation in no way represents the norm for the average university student in Spain either at the undergraduate or the graduate level.

3.4.1.5   An Active Role for English in Everyday Life: L2 *Intensification* in a *Bilingual* Setting

Obviously, "full immersion" or "full contact" with the L2 in a new community cannot be expected to be a homogeneous feature that is applicable a priori to an individual student—let alone a large group of students—while living and studying abroad. As stated earlier, the study-abroad context does offer second language *intensification*. However, the nature of such intensification is highly personal, subjective, and volitional and, thus, an extremely *variable* feature. A relevant question that came up along the study was the extent to which sociolinguistic immersion may actually be claimed to exist these days, even among highly promising sojourners.

This case study revealed that although there *was* L2 intensification, there was *no* such thing as sociolinguistic *immersion*; it further revealed that there was a Spanish/

English *bilingual* setting (Abello Contesse & Ehlers, 2010) all along the study. Moreover, it raises the additional question of whether today, through the frequent use—or abuse—of ICT among college students, it is accurate, rather than misleading, to continue to speak of "immersion" as a typical feature within this context.

The presence of the students' L1 during stays abroad has been extensively documented (e.g., Citron, 2002; Isabelli-García, 2006; Kinginger, 2009; Wilkinson, 1998). However, in this research project *everyday* use of English became the *norm*: both in oral and written media, through face-to-face interaction and through electronic devices, with interlocutors from different language backgrounds. M's use of English was documented in the following activities: (i) various trips both inside and outside Spain, (ii) visits by American family and friends from her home university, (iii) academic activities conducted with American classmates, (iv) breaks between class and during free time at the local ACSA center, (v) social and recreational activities (e.g., going to the movies or the beach) with American acquaintances from ACSA, (vi) the presence of a second American student (with a lower level of proficiency in Spanish) living with the same local family, (vii) voluntary activities, such as participation in English-language support classes, and (viii) Skype, phone calls, text messages, emails, etc. through the daily use of her computer and cellular phone. M used English daily during the 2-week visit from her mother and sisters over the holidays and during her father's stay in the spring. At the beginning of the second semester (January to May), M's local family decided to host another American student from the same institution who, in M's opinion, had a much lower level of proficiency in Spanish than her own. At least for the first 2 months, this situation required M to use English *at home*—a domain hitherto reserved for the more consistent use of Spanish—in order to act as interpreter for the new sojourner in family activities.

The April interview included a question about how many days M had gone *without* having oral or written contact in *English* with people in the United States. M replied that since September she did not remember having spent "*a single day*" without getting news in English, and then added, "It is almost impossible not to hear from the US on a *daily* basis." Kinginger (2009) points out that the impediments to development of close local ties are significant [. . .] as students "may remain attached to their communities of origin through the electronic umbilical cord of computer-mediated communication" (p. 149). When the researcher asked M if she thought that the daily news reported in English had a favorable, neutral, or unfavorable effect on her experience here, she replied (after thinking about it for a few seconds) that "It was *not* a positive thing." When asked *why*, M replied, "I think it's not a good thing because it's harder to be here in the moment and easier to miss people and things back home." M's response highlights two of the most tangible limitations of information and communication technology abuse within this context and among year-long students. First, without even realizing it, M was *permanently* connected to two different languages and cultures, each competing for further attention. Second, such "competition" prevented her from achieving the longed-for, but increasingly elusive, *sustained* intensification in the target language and culture.

3.4.1.6   An Ever-Present American Mother and Family

In December, M undertook a written activity where she had to identify eight items (people, places, activities, dates, feelings, etc.) related to her *personal identity*, making a distinction between those that were felt to be direct and indirect for her. Interestingly, none of such identities alluded to any person/group, practice or product related to M's L2 or C2. Among her direct identities, M identified her American family (parents, sisters, and grandmothers) and, in particular, emphasized her role as "daughter." She also included her hometown and the city where she studied. Among her indirect identities, M identified "the importance my family gives to traveling" and "the importance of school and learning new things."

Through the interviews it became increasingly clear that her family of origin was particularly meaningful for her. Actually, her family became a recurring theme. In the last 2 interviews, it also became clear that a local cultural practice that she liked in Spain was the value given to the family and family unity in general.

At the end of the first semester, when M seemed quite satisfied to stay an additional semester in Spain, she was asked why she had decided to come for a full academic year. She replied that it had been her *mother*'s idea. This was one of the first signs of M's influence from, and sometimes dependence on, her family in the United States. This influence/dependence (concerning ideas, practices, behaviors, and personal decisions) seemed considerably more noticeable regarding her *mother* than any other family member. Comments where a strong mother figure emerged— although it was not the subject of the conversation—became common; for example, in describing her impressions from a recent trip to Morocco, she added—without prompting—that her mother planned to travel to Morocco that summer.

It is relevant to note that the influence of her American mother tended to be repeated at times when M made comments about her *local* family. M chose to live with a local family as her housing option; when asked if her homestay option had been what she expected towards the end of the first half of her stay, M replied, "Yes, I love my Spanish family. I think I have had more exposure to Spanish daily life and Spanish culture." For this reason, she had chosen to *continue* living with the same family during the second semester. However, this was not a common decision among continuing full-year students, as explained by the resident coordinator of M's program at ACSA.

In late January, M recognized that the most significant situation for her during the last 5 weeks had been the visit from her mother and sisters for Christmas and New Year's (M always referred to this situation as "my family's visit"). She was also aware that while being in Spain, she missed her mother and her sister Patricia most: "They are the most significant people for me." In comparison, the anticipated subsequent visit from her father, who was coming on his own in the spring, seemed to create both tension and emotion. On that occasion, she commented that her parents' separation a few years earlier remained a complicated matter for her; she found it difficult to accept since her idea of "the family" included *both* parents, although she clarified, by way of justification, that it had been her *mother* who had asked for separation. It was also during the spring when M's maternal influence became most evident. Shortly before her father's visit, M planned a 6-day trip to Turkey with an American friend. However, during the first day at her destination there was an attack, and M received a call from her mother in the United States, who—in tears—asked her to return to Madrid to avoid any unnecessary danger. M decided to return immediately, even though her friend did not think it necessary to return and continued the trip as originally planned. Curiously, in describing this particular situation, M did not seem overly regretful that the 6-day stay had been cut short.

3.4.1.7 Keeping Calm Under Stress: Identity Challenges in Need of Accommodation in the New Community

In November, M spoke briefly with her only on-campus professor after class on the subject of "cultural stereotypes" as part of an assignment in one of her ACSA classes. The informant that M chose for the task was a professor of modern history with experience in teaching American and other international students at the local university. M summarized the professor's view as follows: "For him, compared to Spaniards, Americans were very competitive, politically correct, puritanical, patriotic, and arrogant individuals. He said that *we* think *we* are the center of the world, but we have to realize that the world has many centers." And then she added her own viewpoint: "All the stereotypes my Spanish professor holds relate to the idea that Americans believe they are part of the 'best' country in the world. It is important for us not to judge other cultures. That's where the most ethnocentric stereotypes come from."

In the final interview in May, this issue was still present when the researcher asked her whether her national identity as a US citizen had changed during this period (if it was stronger, roughly the same, or weaker). She replied, "I think it's a little stronger, and I don't know exactly why" (nervousness, sobbing). "I recognize that the U.S. is a power; it's stronger worldwide than I thought it was. That may be a very good thing, but sometimes it doesn't seem very good, but I think it's a good thing." She then commented that her impression was based on the observations made by one of her professors (in November), and that before that she was unaware there were people in the world who felt antipathy toward Americans.

One of the most revealing aspects of the December interview was discovering M's high levels of anxiety, although she was able to function with apparent normality. There was virtually nothing regarding the topics covered or the informal atmosphere that might have caused M to feel uneasy, but the fact was that she showed signs of emotional instability, expressed through crying, to the extent that the interviewer told her that they did not need to continue with the interview. However, M assured him that she was "fine" and added that she did *not really know why* she was crying. The day after that interview, M sent the researcher an email where she wrote, "I'm sorry about what happened yesterday. I'm under a lot of *stress*, but I *didn't know* why I was crying so much. I'm very happy here. Thanks for everything and see you in January. Happy holidays."

As it seems contradictory for a sojourner to cry in an environment where she claims to be happy, her reaction was probably due to nonacademic reasons related to the recent departure of her American friends who had recently completed their semester abroad or to the visit of her mother and sisters who were arriving the following week—or a combination of both.

Furthermore, in the January interview, it became clear that the identity issue surrounding her family led to strong emotions and mixed feelings; this included her parents, her two sisters, and her dear grandmothers, her traditional Spanish-speaking paternal *"abuela"* and her unconventional English-speaking maternal *"grandma."*

In the interviews conducted in February and April, the issue related to her parents' separation—which had taken place about 3 years earlier—came up, as well as the changing relationship that M had at that time with her father ("He has changed; he's more distant and has a new partner now"). Although these family matters were not a core part of the interviews, they emerged spontaneously. She looked emotional and sobbed, although at no time did she try to avoid or change the topic. During this period, she even decided to take yoga classes in order to overcome these tensions. The ACSA program resident coordinator later commented that the anxiety that M had experienced during the second semester was unusual among full-year students: "they typically experience some anxiety in the *first* semester." She also suggested that in April M was probably looking forward to her coming reentry into the US in May rather than focused on her host community.

Actually, there were episodes of discomfort that M began to experience during the first few weeks in Spain that she claimed she was unfamiliar with up to then. These situations were related to her ethnic identity, specifically her first name as a US American of Mexican descent on her father's side. Through simple questions regarding her social identity (e.g., *What's your name?*) from her Spanish interlocutors, M claimed she discovered an unexpected situation, which caused her to feel deeply sensitive. In a journal entry that M wrote in October, she made it clear that her first name had been a problematic matter since September: "One of the most confusing things for people I've met in Spain is to understand why I have a 'Spanish'—rather than an English—name." She added: "My name has roots as a Spanish name, but it is now an American name." And she concluded, "I like my name, because it's an example of the two cultures in my life. I have a name with Spanish roots, but I'm also M because my mother's name is Martha."

In an interview conducted in late January, the researcher returned to this subject to check whether it had been successfully accommodated over time. The way she addressed the topic revealed that it was not simply an initial, but a continuing discomfort. Between sobs, M pointed out that Spanish people's first reaction was typically related to the origin of her name ("How come you have a name in Spanish?"). M said that her response usually was, "My father was born in Mexico." She considered her father was an American not only because of his current nationality but also because he had lived, gone to college, and worked most of his life there. This was one of the occasions where M showed evident signs of anxiety through sobbing and tears. When the researcher asked her why she was crying, she replied, "I think it's a sensitive issue that I wasn't aware of, because in the past I've never had problems talking about this." This statement relates to the fact that although M's given name is Spanish, in her opinion, the name is no longer Spanish in that it is not necessarily associated with a Spanish-speaking person in a multicultural society like the US. Nevertheless, it is the case that her *last name* is also a common Spanish-speaking surname. This seems to show that her statement—that this situation was *new* to her—may have been an ambivalent effort to explain that although she was aware her full name is of Spanish origin, she did not *anticipate* that particular circumstance might turn into an issue while in Spain.

3.4.2 Relating These Recurrent Themes to M's Personal Goals for Her Sojourn

As a major part of the final interview in early May, a few days before M returned to the US, the researcher asked her to identify the original goals of her sojourn and evaluate her relative level of accomplishing them. The conclusions to be drawn in this section relate the seven recurrent themes described above as part of the ethnographic study to the four personal, long-term goals that M set regarding her stay. The researcher's etic perspective is added to M's emic perspective in cases where there are discrepancies.

In M's view, two of her four objectives were fully achieved: (i) "improve her Spanish" and (ii) "mature." On the other hand, she said that an additional objective had only been partially fulfilled: (iii) "meet Spanish college-age people." One goal she did not achieve was (iv) "learn to live a more relaxed life."

In explaining the one goal that was not fully achieved (iii) and the one that was not achieved at all (iv), M stated that the first might be due to her not being an outgoing person at first, and also due to the fact that by having taken classes at ACSA, she did not have that contact with Spanish students in her classes. As for the objective of achieving a more relaxed life, M explained that she was a very active, although also anxious, person and that she "was usually either busy with something or worried about something."

The first two themes—discussed in Sects. 3.4.1.1 and 3.4.1.2 above—focus on the sociolinguistic characteristics of the Spanish that M was exposed to and the very limited availability of native peers with whom she interacted on a sustained basis. The theme discussed in Sect. 3.4.1.3 on the Spanish university system combines features of both her L2 and C2 and is interpreted here as a cultural and intercultural component that is inherent to the experience of university students in their new academic environment. One characteristic shared by these three themes is the presence of the aphorism "so close and yet so far." There were two findings showing that M's language and culture involvement in her host community was not exactly successful; these findings also show that M's experience cannot be described as "immersion" but rather as *moderate intensification*: (i) she did not have direct contact with Spanish classmates in any of the 12 classes she took in Spain between late September and early May, and (ii) in terms of interpersonal use of Spanish, her "typical week" during the *second* semester was characterized by a minimal presence—or simply absence—of sustained interaction with local peers.

If M's perception of her sojourn is accepted, it is not possible to objectively explain that her limited communicative interaction with Spanish-speaking peers would not have an adverse effect on the improvement of her Spanish *accuracy*—as her fluency level was comparatively high from the start. Consequently, there is no shared conclusion in this regard. From M's emic perspective, the overall goal of "improving her Spanish" had been "completely fulfilled." From the researcher's etic perspective, however, this would indicate that M's expectations of accuracy improvement concerning her Spanish phonology and morphology were low. Regardless of her expectations for improvement, it is also likely that M's perceptions while in Spain were largely based on maintaining her self-esteem high as a learned strategy that would allow her to avoid the debilitating effects of anxiety.

From an etic perspective, M's original choice not to integrate into the local university system, despite having a more advanced proficiency level in Spanish—particularly spoken and written fluency—than many of her peers at the outset, may be interpreted as a *play-it-safe* strategy: (i) the safety of functioning within the familiar American system limited her anxiety and allowed (ii) the subsequent achievement of higher academic performance. Although this decision might be considered academically legitimate, an emphasis on *studying* for top grades rather than *experiencing life abroad* seems to contradict one of the fundamental tenets of an international, educational experience. However, more challenging views favoring sustained sociocultural integration might have clashed in practice with M's proneness to trait anxiety.

At the end of her stay, M felt the goal of meeting college-age Spaniards had been partially fulfilled. The etic interpretation is that this appears to be an example of overly high self-esteem on her part, probably an attempt to save face vis-à-vis the researcher at a significant moment, such as the final interview. By way of conclusion, however, the oral and written data from the study consistently show that this particular objective was not met.

Regarding the over-presence of national and international tourism as well as the everyday use of English in this case—discussed in Sects. 3.4.1.4 and 3.4.1.5 respectively— the *discontinuity* in progress that such trips probably caused to M's ongoing process of L2 and C2 development might only have contributed to strengthening her process of maturation. As to the daily presence and use of English, the conclusion is that this practice was of no use in achieving any of the four objectives. Rather, it may well have been an impediment to her aim of improving her Spanish, preventing her from improving her—phonological and morphological—accuracy in Spanish.

Considering the frequent presence of her American family—addressed in Sect. 3.4.1.6—as well as her dependence on her omnipresent mother while she was in Spain (and the fact that both behaviors were sometimes replicated with her local family), it came as a surprise to the researcher that in the final interview M identified her *having matured* as one of the original objectives that she had met through her sojourn. Having matured, in this case, may well refer to her *emotional* maturity. Although defining this type of maturity is a relative matter, since it depends in part on the sociocultural norms of particular communities, it generally reflects an *adult-type* balance in emotional behavior, a feature that does not characterize M's behavior Therefore, an etic interpretation by way of conclusion is that M probably felt that her having been able to go through with her mother's recommendation to live in Spain for 8 months—away from her family and friends—and experiencing some problems but no major complications was more than enough proof *to her* that she had achieved greater personal maturity.

As for the tensions related to M's identities—discussed in Sect. 3.4.1.7 above— and the presence of higher levels of anxiety during the second half of her stay, it is concluded that these factors did not have a positive effect on any of the four objectives identified above. To the contrary, the presence of these sensitive issues that created anxiety-inducing situations may have made it difficult for M to achieve the objectives she pursued. This is probably why M evaluated her goal of "learning to live a more relaxed life" as not fulfilled by the end of her sojourn; this conclusion does fit the data obtained throughout the study.

3.5 Concluding Remarks and Implications

The present ethnographic case study was intended to examine what a full-year American sojourner—whose incoming situation seemed highly promising—would do in the host community in order to boost her proficiency levels in the L2 and C2. Several themes and issues that gradually came up from the longitudinal study were identified and described. The primary theoretical framework of the study was based on two IDs—anxiety and identity—while the role played by ambivalence (as a major component of identity) was highlighted. In addition, due to the nature of the single participant under study, the roles played by the notions of heritage Spanish speakers in the United States and the initial building of a third place in new sociocultural settings became salient and were also addressed as secondary foci.

M's overall L2 involvement and C2 engagement may be described as noticeably *inferior* to what she could have achieved over an 8-month period. However, from an academic perspective M was a student with an outstanding record, accustomed to receiving high grades in her two academic majors. Her family background was both Latino and Anglo, and she was looking forward to working at an international organization in the future. She also claimed to have positive attitudes toward both the target language and culture from the beginning of her sojourn. Consequently, what attenuated the solid progress that she could have made?

One factor that appears to be at the heart of M's lack of progress is her *chronic, trait anxiety* due to its greater weight and hindering nature. As Winstanley (2006, p. 26) asserts, this is the "general tendency to respond with anxiety to perceived threats in the environment." Regrettably, this particular anxiety type continues to be underresearched in the SLA literature. Thus, M prioritized the security of *familiar* practices (e.g., American fellow students, US-style classes, brief transactional exchanges, tourism) and people (e.g., middle-aged host parents) over the—real or imaginary—risks that prompted anxiety when she faced unexpected situations. Risk-taking and adventuresome options were consistently bypassed.

Another major factor includes the identity aspects that arose and gradually increased during her sojourn; these new subject positions created sensitivities that she perceived as "unexpected" or "unfavorable," but because she systematically *avoided* confronting them, such aspects only wound up *increasing* her existing levels of tension. The hybrid nature of some of her identities—as interpreted in a different sociocultural environment (Spain)—especially her national, ethnic, social, and familial identities—as both Mexican-American (father) and Anglo-American (mother)—produced high levels of ambivalence characterized by the coexistence of conflicting attitudes, feelings, and behaviors. This ambivalence, which played a prominent role during the second half of her sojourn, was characterized by the frequent dichotomy between what was, in her own view, "desirable for her to do" and what she "actually did" in the end.

As a result of the combined effects of her chronic, trait anxiety, her identity issues, and her resultant ambivalence in behavior, she appeared to be largely unwilling to integrate into the host culture. It may well be claimed that while M was a member of a temporary micro-culture in Spain, she essentially favored passive "spectator"—rather than (pro)active "participant"—behavior. This is one of the characteristics that Ogden (2007) identifies with contemporary US students in study-abroad programs: "Rather than immerse themselves into the host community to the extent possible, they embrace the privileges afforded to them as short-term guests" (p. 5). She also showed some initial "third culture" formation (Citron, 2002; Kramsch, 2009), a sociocultural adaptation where she gradually started repositioning herself in a place roughly between her C1 and her C2. M's positive outlook in October did translate into academically successful results but did not translate into an immersive socio-linguistic/sociocultural experience.

These findings seem to have significant implications for study-abroad and SLA specialists who continue to assume that *sociolinguistic* (L2 and C2) *immersion* in the host community is a given simply because students are *motivated* and *physically located* in their new setting. The sociolinguistic situation observed in this study was consistently limited to *L2 intensification*, a context where comprehension and production of the L2 increased considerably when compared with the previous at-home context. However, such quantitative increase often occurred in *protected* language environments and at irregular intervals; it was *intermittent* rather than reasonably steady. Moreover, due to the fact that the sojourner's L1 was never absent from communicative use, this overall situation has been described here as *intermittent L2 intensification in a bilingual setting with potential access to the C2* (in M's case, this access was mainly limited to her host mother and family). This is felt to be a more accurate description that challenges the still widespread notion of *immersion* as an automatic feature within this context. This study suggests that *full sociolinguistic immersion* may well be the exception rather than the rule, at least in urban centers in Western European destinations, such as the one explored in this chapter, and that further empirical studies should address this relevant phenomenon in different destinations and through various research designs.

This study reinforces the strikingly individual, complex, multidimensional, and time-consuming nature of the process of adapting to the language and cultural dynamics of life abroad, which combines factors in the student's personal background—particularly emotional ones—with unique aspects of the experience in the location abroad.

References

Abello Contesse, C., & Ehlers, C. (2010). Escenarios bilingües: una visión global. In C. A. Contesse, C. Ehlers, & L. Q. Hernández (Eds.), *Escenarios bilingües. El contacto de lenguas en el individuo y la sociedad* (pp. 7–39). Bern, Switzerland: Peter Lang.

Beaven, A., & Spencer-Oatey, H. (2016). Cultural adaptation in different facets of life and the impact of language: A case study of personal adjustment patterns during study abroad. *Language and intercultural communication, 16*(3), 349–367.

Block, D. (2007a). The rise of identity in SLA research: Post Firth and Wagner (1997). *Modern Language Journal, 91*, 863–876.

Block, D. (2007b). *Second language identities*. London: Continuum.

Braun, V., & Clarke, V. (2006). Using thematic analysis in psychology. *Qualitative Research in Psychology, 3*(2), 77–101.

Brown, L. (2009). An ethnographic study of the friendship patterns of international students in England: An attempt to recreate home through conational interaction. *International Journal of Educational Research, 48*(3), 184–193.

Citron, J. L. (2002). U.S. students abroad: Host culture integration or third culture formation? In W. Grünzweig & N. Rinehart (Eds.), *Rockin' in Red Square: Critical approaches to international education in the age of cyberculture* (pp. 41–56). Piscataway, NJ: Transaction.

Colman, A. M. (2001). *A dictionary of psychology*. Oxford, UK: Oxford University Press.

DuFon, M. A., & Churchill, E. (Eds.). (2006). *Language learners in study abroad contexts*. Clevedon, UK: Multilingual Matters Ltd..

Field, F. W. (2011). *Key concepts in bilingualism*. London: Palgrave Macmillan.

Gallucci, S. (2013). Emotional investments during the year abroad: A case study of a British ERASMUS student in Italy. *Journal of Applied Language Studies, 7*(2), 17–37.

Horwitz, E. K., & Young, D. J. (1991). *Language anxiety. From theory and research to classroom implications*. Englewood Cliffs, NJ: Prentice Hall.

Isabelli-García, C. (2006). Study abroad social networks, motivation and attitudes: Implications for second language acquisition. In M. A. DuFon & E. Churchill (Eds.), *Language learners in study abroad contexts* (pp. 231–258). Clevedon, UK: Multilingual Matters Ltd..

Jackson, J. (2008). *Language, identity, and study abroad. Sociocultural perspectives*. London: Equinox.

Kinginger, C. (2009). *Language learning and study abroad. A critical reading of research*. New York: Palgrave Macmillan.

Kinginger, C. (2013). Identity and language learning in study abroad. *Foreign Language Annals, 46*(3), 339–358.

Kramsch, C. (2009). Third culture and language education. In V. Cook & L. Wei (Eds.), *Contemporary applied linguistics* (Vol. 1, pp. 233–254). London: Continuum.

Lightbown, P. M., & Spada, N. (2013). *How languages are learned*. Oxford, UK: Oxford University Press.

Loewen, S., & Reinders, H. (2011). *Key concepts in second language acquisition*. London: Palgrave Macmillan.

Mikula, M. (2008). *Key concepts in cultural studies*. London: Palgrave Macmillan.

Montrul, S. (2016). *The acquisition of heritage languages*. Cambridge, UK: Cambridge University Press.

Moran, P. (2001). *Teaching culture. Perspectives in practice*. Boston: Heinle.

Ogden, A. (2007). The view from the veranda: Understanding today's colonial students. *Frontiers: The Interdisciplinary Journal of Study Abroad, 15*, 2–20.

Papastergiadis, N. (2000). *The turbulence of migration: Globalization, deterritorialization and hybridity*. Cambridge, UK: Polity Press.

Reber, A. S. (1995). *The penguin dictionary of psychology*. London: Penguin Books.

Richards, J. C., & Schmidt, R. (2010). *Longman dictionary of language teaching and applied linguistics*. Harlow, UK: Longman Pearson.

Saville-Troike, M. (2012). *Introducing second language acquisition*. Cambridge, UK: Cambridge University Press.

Swann, J., Deumert, A., Lillis, T., & Mesthrie, R. (2004). *A dictionary of sociolinguistics*. Edinburgh, Scotland: Edinburgh University Press, Ltd..

van Lier, L. (2005). Case study. In E. Hinkel (Ed.), *Handbook of research in second language teaching and learning* (pp. 195–208). Mahwah, NJ: Lawrence Earlbaum Associates, Publishers.

Wilkinson, S. (1998). On the nature of immersion during study abroad: Some participant perspectives. *Frontiers: The Interdisciplinary Journal of Study Abroad, 4*(2), 121–138.

Winstanley, J. (2006). *Key concepts in psychology*. London: Palgrave Macmillan.

Yang, J.-S., & Kim, T.-Y. (2011). Sociocultural analysis of second language learner beliefs: A qualitative case study of two study-abroad ESL learners. *System, 39*, 325–334.

Chapter 4
Problems for Teachers of Culturally Diverse Classes: Investigating Strategies and Activities to Embed Intercultural Metalanguage in an Australian 'Internationalized' University Context

Sue Lubbers

4.1 Introduction

4.1.1 The Problem

The research problem reported in this chapter relates to the educator-researcher's (the author's) experience of pedagogical problems in several Australian university contexts over a period of two decades. The problems emerged with the rapid increase, from the late 1990s, in enrolments of international students, the majority of whom have come from countries in Asia. This has resulted in campus populations with high levels of 'Western-Eastern' diversity.

A persistent problem of 'internationalizing' the Australian university sector has been the deficit perception and stereotyping of 'Asian students'. Anglo-Euro-Western educators have tended to '[position them] within a discourse of deficient learning styles, such as rote learning or non-critical learning and as deficient personally—passive and quiet, non-contributing' (Koehne, 2004, p. 5). Chalmers and Volet (1997), Dale and Lubbers (2005), Mayuzumi, Motobayashi, Nagayama, and Takeuchi (2007), Wang (2010) and Lubbers (2016) have documented continuing deficit stereotypes of students from Asian backgrounds.

This has left many who begin their studies in Australia with high hopes, not only of successfully achieving a degree but also of developing enduring friendships and professional relationships with Australian and other international students, experiencing the opposite. A continuing sense of marginalization, alienation and loneliness has been reported by many international students of Asian background

S. Lubbers (✉)
Western Sydney University, Sydney, Australia

© Springer Nature Singapore Pte Ltd. 2021   67
M. D. López-Jiménez, J. Sánchez-Torres (eds.), *Intercultural Competence Past, Present and Future*, Intercultural Communication and Language Education, https://doi.org/10.1007/978-981-15-8245-5_4

(Baik, 2013; Hellsten, 2002; Lubbers, 2008, 2013, 2016; Sawir, Marginson, Deumert, Nyland, & Ramia, 2008; Summers & Volet, 2008).

The persistence of deficit stereotyping and *essentializing* (Abdallah-Pretceille, 2006; Risager & Dervin, 2015) of Asian students suggests a lack of *critical intercultural self and other awareness* (Byram, 1997) and other *intercultural communicative competences* (Byram, 1997; Byram & Zarate, 1994) in educational institutions.

The problems are not easy for classroom teachers to manage (see Sects. 4.4 and 4.5). Teachers across a range of educational levels and contexts are unsure about how to meet the complex, context-related and continually changing challenges of culturally and linguistically diverse classes. The intercultural and related fields are awash with contesting theoretical perspectives, yet there are few evidence-based intercultural communicative competence (ICC) pedagogical models which can readily be adapted to manage the kinds of context-specific problems teachers experience. Moreover, educational disciplines have tended to draw on pedagogical traditions and understandings which can be hard to change. In the field of foreign language pedagogy and teacher education, for example, there is a 'natural', historic tendency, as evident, for example, in German schools and universities, of *Landeskunde*, with cultural-intercultural aspects taught through comparison of characteristics of the countries of the target language and of the learners. This tends to result in an essentialized understanding of intercultural communicative competence in both teachers and learners (Risager, 2007).

Thus, despite an abundance of theories and models, and extensive research in the area, many teachers still do not know how to develop the intercultural communication competences which the literature in the area suggests are critical to participation of students with cultural, linguistic and educational backgrounds different to those of the dominant group. As a consequence, meaningful interactions among students and between teacher and students are impeded.

This problem is not unique to Australia, as the literature on internationalization in the tertiary sector in Canada, the United States and Britain reveals. Zhang and Zhou (2010) report on the sense of loneliness and isolation of Chinese international students in Canada, linked to the difficulty of developing close relationships with Canadian students. Glass and Westmont's (2014) study of eight American universities on the psychological concept of belongingness, similarly, details feelings of isolation, depression and marginalization, also of experiences of racism, of non-Western students. Holliday (2011) describes a similar problem in British universities, of "East Asian" students [who] ... were constructed [by their lecturers] as those "problem students" who didn't speak and therefore were "passive" and didn't think' (Holliday, 2011, p. 170).

Attempts in Australia to address this problem have been intermittent and pursued mainly by individual researcher-practitioners (for example, Arkoudis, Baik, Marginson, & Cassidy, 2012; Briguglio, 2006; Briguglio & Smith, 2012; Collett, 2015; Lubbers, 2016), rather than as a whole-of-institution approach.

Stereotyping and marginalization of students are serious problems which teachers working with culturally diverse cohorts should be capable of ameliorating. The lack of ICC praxis should not, however, be blamed on individual teachers, since the problem needs, but rarely appears to be understood as an issue for the education system as a whole, as Svarstad (2016) recognizes. In Svarstad's context of school language education and language teacher education, the 2013 Danish Teacher Education Reform mandated intercultural communicative competence modules for future primary and secondary teachers. Even so, as Svarstad's (2016) research demonstrates, 'conceptualization of new understandings of culture and the teaching of interculturality [are] highly demanding' (Svarstad, 2016, p. 227). Teachers with full teaching loads are left with little time for lesson preparation, let alone for the time required to 'conceptualize and transform [interculturality]' (Svarstad, 2016, p. 228) into teaching. This study applies to the concept of interculturality a similar understanding of Svarstad (2016), as 'discourses of the world that foreground diversity and encounters' (Svarstad, 2016, p. 36).

4.1.2   The Project

The pedagogical-research project reported in this chapter discusses first theoretical-pedagogical frameworks. It then outlines, problem by problem, a series of interlinked cultural-intercultural problems experienced by the educator-researcher in teaching a culturally diverse class of undergraduate international students enrolled in a film, media and popular culture course in a university in Sydney. Next, it describes the intercultural strategies and activities employed in attempts to ameliorate problems. It then reports findings. Finally, it considers the findings' implications, including consideration of the challenges the problems presented may pose to teachers faced with similar challenges in other pedagogical contexts.

The class consisted of 18 international students from non-Western/Asian and Western cultural, language and educational backgrounds. The unit was a full credit-bearing course of 13 weeks' duration, included in a suite of such units offered to international students from language backgrounds (L1) other than English. Lecturers were specialists in both course content areas and applied linguistics and/or Teaching English to Speakers of Other Languages (TESOL). As such, they were expected to provide language support as needed. The course was not classified as CLIL (Content and Language Integrated Learning), but resembled CLIL in the expectation to address language-related issues in a content-based program. This class comprised students from China (4), Japan (5), Korea (1), Spain/Madrid (2), Spain/Catalonia (2), Italy (1), Argentina (1), Turkey/Germany (1) and Germany (1). Lecturers were encouraged to adapt course content and resources as appropriate to the interests and needs of each cohort.

Classes were held once a week. Each class lasted two hours. A course schedule is provided in Sect. 4.4 (Key Strategies, Activities and Findings). The first class of the semester-long course employed the first intercultural pedagogical strategy of this project, an 'intercultural orientation'. This comprised six *experiential and theoretical* (Guilherme, 2002) activities designed to support the development of critical intercultural awareness and other intercultural communicative competences (ICC). These activities are described in Sect. 4.4. Educator input and student responses from the orientation session were subsequently used throughout the course as reference points for further class discussion on culture and intercultural interaction and/or to support the second intercultural pedagogical strategy, intercultural intervention by the lecturer. The final class, Week 13, was dedicated to group interviews and one pair interview. These also aimed to further develop intercultural *reflection* and *critical self-reflection* (Guilherme, 2010; Jack, 2009). Data and data collection methods are described in Sect. 4.3.

4.1.3   *Project Aims*

First, the project aimed to mitigate seven of the most serious problems repeatedly experienced by the educator-researcher in teaching and observing culturally/linguistically diverse university cohorts. The educator-researcher employed a range of strategies and activities in an attempt to develop intercultural communicative competence in the students. The main competences focused on were (a) *critical intercultural awareness* and (b) *intercultural* communicative competences relating to *knowledge, affect, skills and attitudes* (Byram, 1997; Byram, Golubeva, Hui, & Wagner, 2016; Byram & Zarate, 1994). These are explained in Sect. 4.2 (Theoretical-Pedagogical Framework).

Second, the pedagogical strategies and activities aimed to support the active participation of all students in all aspects of learning and teaching, with focus on encouraging participation in group and class discussions.

Third, the project aimed to investigate the impact of *embedding intercultural metalanguage*. This concept is explained in Sect. 4.5 (Implications).

Fourth, the study aimed to investigate the potential of the strategies and activities to develop *deep intercultural meta-understanding(s)* in individuals as well as among the participants. This concept is also explained in Sect. 4.5.

Fifth, the project aimed to support a more *democratized* (Rancière, 1991; Singh & Meng, 2013) approach to Australian internationalized tertiary education. It links to other pedagogical efforts by the educator-researcher (see, for example Lubbers, 2016) to challenge hegemonic Anglo-Euro-Western dominance of learning and teaching approaches in Australian universities, through implementation of pedagogical strategies and activities which aim to enable all students, including those of marginalized or silenced students, to voice their ideas, knowledges and perspectives.

4.2 Theoretical-Pedagogical Framework of the Research

The variety and number of theoretical-pedagogical perspectives and concepts utilized in this study may be understood as reflecting the educator-researcher's search over time for theoretical perspectives and pedagogical support to address numerous problems as they arose. No one theoretical framework or theoretical-pedagogical model, unadapted and/or unsupplemented, offered enough deep understandings and/or comprehensive pedagogical approaches for the nature and range of problems experienced. Guilherme (2014), among others, has concluded that 'intercultural communication and interaction is more intricate than it has been perceived' (Guilherme, 2014, p. 362). This study is informed by a similar realization forged through personal and professional intercultural experience. It is evident that it is extremely challenging for teachers to locate in the literature, context-appropriate, theoretically informed approaches.

Perhaps the most daunting experience for the educator-researcher has been navigating the literature and, often mutually unsettling, if not mutually excluding, theoretical perspectives on the complex and contested (Gallie, 1955) concepts of culture, interculturality and intercultural communicative competence. It was frustrating, for example, to read, and to hear at international conferences, theoretical points of view which appeared to reject any reference, even in initial class discussions and activities, to national culture as *essentialist* (Holliday, 1999), when intercultural activities which appeared to enable students to discuss their own cultural, linguistic and educational experiences and perspectives, and to reflect critically on these, very often resulted in the students themselves linking these to their country of birth, societal and family norms and expectations and language (L1).

In the interests of researcher-practitioner openness and as a self-reflexive admission (Byrd Clark & Dervin, 2014), the author would describe her personal and professional experiences and perspectives on the concepts of culture and interculturality as generally aligning comfortably with post-structuralist theoretical perspectives. At the same time, her deep and lifelong engagement at a professional and personal level with many cultural and linguistic others has brought her to an understanding similar to that of Jullien (2014): 'For my part, I have been able to characterize a little more closely what constitutes "Europe" only by going to China' (p. 162). Brief visits by Westerners to non-Western destinations are hardly sufficient to develop understanding(s) of any depth. Time, openness, open-mindedness, curiosity (Byram, 1997) and *deep engagement* are called for: one needs to leave, physically and metaphorically, one's own Western world-view, to be able to develop deep understandings of non-Western ways of being, seeing and doing.

In such a contested area, the question therefore arises: what and how many theoretical perspectives and pedagogical approaches can provide a useful, balanced and sufficiently encompassing starting point, and which might also promote longer-term intercultural development? This is indeed a daunting prospect for teachers already time-challenged by lesson preparation, assessment, reporting and administrative responsibilities.

To help answer this hugely challenging but essential question, the educator-researcher has turned to Rancière's (1991) belief in the *equal intelligence* of all students. The educator-researcher draws on extensive pedagogical experience (over 30 years spent in universities and several years in schools) in relying upon her understanding that students from all cultural, linguistic, socioeconomic and educational backgrounds are equally capable of reflecting, and engaging in dialogue, on culture and interculturality. Moreover, she does not believe it is the role of a teacher to 'tell students what to think' about these concepts. A more open-minded approach is to encourage students to explore their multiple meanings and relevance for themselves, and with cultural others, in a *personal experiential* approach through exposing them, over time, to diverse scholarly points of view through a maximum of interpersonal, intercultural interactions and discussions.

The main intercultural theoretical-pedagogical intercultural communicative competence model and concepts employed for this study are those developed by Byram (1997), which added a further competence to the four previously developed by Byram and Zarate (1994). Nonetheless, the educator-researcher's personal and professional cultural-intercultural understandings, as well as pedagogical praxis, have been illuminated, inspired and motivated by seminal theorists from a range of disciplines. Their perspectives, ideas and concepts have both deeply informed this pedagogical research project theoretically and also provided content for Activity 6.

The three potential alternative frameworks considered and decided against as inappropriate for this project are *cultural competence, cultural intelligence* and *cultural understanding*:

– *Cultural competence* has been defined by the Office of Minority Health in the United States as 'a set of congruent behaviours, attitudes, and policies that come together in a system, agency, or among professionals that enables effective work in cross-cultural situations' (as cited by the Canadian Paediatric Society, 2018, n. p.). In Australia, a cultural competence framework underpins significant work of educational, human service departments and organizations which focus on addressing historic and current disadvantage among First Nations Peoples. In this context, importance has understandably been placed on developing knowledge and understanding of First Nations Peoples' history, culture, traditions and beliefs in staff of non-First Nations Peoples background to support more effective engagement and culture-appropriate service delivery to First Nations individuals and groups (Centre for Cultural Competence, 2018). Despite sharing some key understandings of Byram's ICC model, such as development in teachers of 'critical reflection' (Jones, Bustamante, & Nelson, 2016, p. 4), cultural competence has tended to be used in contexts which emphasize cross-cultural differences of racial, ethnic and socioeconomic background, as in the highly segregated school system in the United States, making it less appropriate to the aims of this study.
– *Cultural intelligence* (CQ) is defined as 'an individual's ability to function effectively in situations characterized by cultural diversity' (Ang & Van Dyne, 2015, p. xv). Cross-disciplinary collaboration of researchers in social psychology,

cross-cultural psychology, cross-cultural management, international management and applied linguistics have led to a conceptual framework which proponents claim to be theoretically sound and empirically proven (Goh, 2012). This claim, together with fixed rather than more fluid (Baumann, 2007) notions of culture, would appear to render cultural intelligence a less appropriate theoretical framework for a study aiming to address stereotyping through a self-reflective rather than an externally assessed lens.

– *Cultural understanding* research recognizes, as does this study, the vital importance of developing in students the knowledge, skills and attitudes to interrogate and to resist, or in other words, to work actively against, cultural stereotypes and stigmatizing identities (Porto, 2010). It would appear, however, that cultural understanding could be viewed as one, albeit significant, part of a broader theoretical framework, rather than as providing a theoretical and pedagogical model for a study such as this one, which aims to develop a broad repertoire of intercultural competences through a range of theoretical perspectives.

There are three main reasons why the educator-researcher believes that Byram's (1997) ICC approach provides the soundest, if adapted, model for both the theoretical and the pedagogical purposes of this study.

First, Byram's key concepts and understandings have stood the relevance test of time. Byram remains one of the most widely and frequently referenced scholar-educators in the fields of language education and intercultural education, the fields most closely associated with this study. Byram's conceptualization of the *attitudes and feelings, behaviour, knowledge* and *skills* (Byram, 1997; Byram & Zarate, 1994) as key to developing *interculturally effective global citizens* (Byram, 2010) has significance beyond one educational discipline. For example, in relation to the kinds of knowledge Byram, with Zarate (Byram & Zarate, 1994), has suggested to develop ICC in individuals, 'knowledge of self and other and of individual and societal processes' (Byram, 1997, p. 34), are convincing at a point in time, yet sufficiently fluid, or open, to allow for individual, cultural and societal change. They also imply a meta-level of understanding which should accompany individuals on their intercultural journey, potentially deepening and complexifying understanding over time. Intercultural skills such as the ability *to de-centre*, *to interpret* and *to relate* should similarly stand the test of time, regardless of changing theoretical conceptualizations of culture and interculturality. This is so because they simultaneously promote ongoing development, reflection and critical self and other awareness.

Second, Byram's intercultural research and practice have remained firmly situated in pedagogy, as have the educator-researcher's attempts to mitigate the cultural stereotyping and sense of marginalization of Asian students in Australian tertiary contexts.

The third reason this study aligns with Byram's ICC model is his inclusion in the 1997 model (Byram, 1997) of the fifth *savoir* or competence, *savoir s'engager*. Associated with the German tradition of *Bildung—education—* this concept refers to developing 'critical cultural-intercultural awareness [linked to] political education' (Byram, 1997, p. 34). A similarly politically-motivated goal of developing ICC as a way of enabling the voices of students marginalized in a hegemonic Anglo-Euro-Western dominated tertiary education system underpins this study.

Byram's (1997) ICC model comprises five key *savoirs*, all of which are drawn on in this project. These are *intercultural: knowledge, attitudes, skills to interpret and to relate, skills to discover and/or interact and education*. Byram explains intercultural knowledge as *knowledge of self and others*. Intercultural skills are of two kinds: *to interpret and to relate;* [and] *to discover and/or interact*. Attitude refers to the ability to *relativize self* or to *de-centre* and to *value others*; it includes such attributes as *openness* and *curiosity affect/feelings* (see Byram et al., 2016) appear to be foregrounded more than was clear in the 1997 model.

The most significant starting point, arguably, for any effective intercultural communication to take place is critical cultural-intercultural awareness, added by Byram (1997) to the four dimensions of sociocultural competence developed earlier by Byram and Zarate (1994). It is viewed as the ability to apply *evaluative* (Byram, 1997, emphasis added) skills to critique both positive and negative aspects of cultures and of intercultural interactions, including of one's own behaviours, attitudes and values. Byram (2010) associates this concept with conceptualizations of *politische Bildung*, developing in Germany around the same time. Potential misunderstandings of this concept led Byram to link it to Himmelmann's (2006) conceptualization of *Demokratielernen*, 'where the emphasis [is] on learning to be and act in a democracy' (Byram et al., 2016, p. xxi). This concept better captures the notion of the *transformative* power of education in 'that interplay between the individual and the world' (Byram, 2010, p. 318).

Critical intercultural awareness has underpinned the study in two ways: first, in its focus on employing pedagogical strategies to support the development of this understanding and ability in students (and educators); and second, in relation to the project's underlying goal to support democratization of 'internationalized' tertiary education by enabling all students, whatever their cultural, language and educational backgrounds, to engage fully in pedagogical processes. The second goal and the ways in which this is aimed for in this project are discussed in Sect. 4.5 (Implications).

In addition to Byram's model, the project draws on several theoretical-pedagogical perspectives and concepts from related fields. Rancière's (1991) critical sociology of education provides powerful motivation through his development of Jacotot's (see Rancière, 1991) notion/*discovery* of *equal intelligence* in his students. This concept underpins and motivates the educator-researcher's attempts to democratize approaches to education by addressing problems which appear to impede equal expression of ideas, knowledge and perspectives in classrooms. Pedagogical praxis is also deeply informed by Freire's (1985) understandings of critical pedagogy. Freire's conviction that no human beings are so ignorant or submerged in the *culture of silence* that they lack capability *to educate each other through* critical reflection *in dialogical encounters with others* provides, as well, theoretical input for Activity 6. *Critical self-reflection* (Guilherme et al., 2010; Jack, 2009) and *reflexivity* are integral to the project. For the purposes of this study, reflexivity is understood as

Bhabha (1994) conceptualizes it, as involving a capacity to question hegemonic assumptions of dominant groups. The anthropologist Hall's (1989) notion of the necessity for *a shock of contrast and difference* and Phipps' (2007) elucidation of the important role played by *perception of risk* in the development of intercultural competence are also employed as theoretical content for dialogical discussion.

The post-modern, post-colonial literary and cultural theorist Bhabha (1994) provides a more richly informed, while also subtle, response to those intercultural theorists who denote much of current intercultural practice in universities as 'soft essentialist recidivism' (Holliday & MacDonald, 2016, Abstract). As Deardorff and Jones (2012) point out, there needs to be a starting point in the process of intercultural understanding and competence development. Deeper knowledge and more complex cultural-intercultural understandings can be developed over time. Bhabha recognizes the phenomenon of culture, as expressed through the notion of *cultural difference*, as deeply contestable, while differing from Dervin's (2015) argument that, in discussions of the concept of culture, 'we see difference where there is none'. Bhabha (1994) pleads, rather, for recognition of 'knowledges or a distribution of practices that exist beside each other, *abseits* designating a form of social contradiction or antagonism that has to be negotiated rather than sublated' (p. 232). The undermining of fixed conceptualizations of culture occur as *transcultural contestations*:

> Cultural difference introduces into the process of cultural judgement and interpretation that sudden shock... [whereby] the very possibility of cultural contestation, the ability to shift this ground of knowledges, or to engage in the 'war of position' marks the establishment of new forms of meaning, and strategies of identification. (p. 233)

This perspective is employed in Activity 6 in an attempt to engage students from self-designated 'different cultures' to engage with the complexities, perplexities and rich potentialities of intercultural dialogue. Bhabha thus serves to inform theoretical-pedagogical understanding of the educator and of the project, as well as to 'entice' students to begin to explore demonstrations of complexities such as *the hybridity of cultures* (Bhabha, 2006).

Theoretical understandings and pedagogical strategies and activities draw as well on post-structuralist theories of language inspired by Bakhtin's (1981) *dialogic* principle. Bakhtin's conception of *heteroglossia* is employed. Kim (2004, p. 54) explains this notion whereby 'the entire world can be viewed as *polyglossic* [author's italics] or multi-voiced since every individual possesses their own unique world view which must be taken into consideration through dialogical interaction'. The educator-researcher believes that the concept of heteroglossia can be related, in intercultural dialogical contexts, to Rancière's notion of equal intelligence.

The sociolinguist Halliday (1978) conceptualizes linguistic structure as '*the realization of* social structure, actively symbolizing it in a process of mutual creativity' (Halliday, 1978, p. 186). He explicates the property of language not only 'to transmit social order but also to ... potentially modify it' (Halliday, 1978, p. 186). These theoretical understandings are also applied in the pedagogical praxis of the study. Sociolinguists Scollon, Wong-Scollon, and Jones (2012) offer understandings of *face* and differing expectations of interpersonal politeness forms, which likewise inform the project's theoretical-pedagogical frame.

The French philosopher and sinologist Jullien (2014) provides illuminating insights in relation to the educator-researcher's experienced personal and professional conception of the complex and contested concepts (Gallie, 1955) of culture and interculturality. Jullien (2014) refers to the *fluidity* and *forever self-transformative* nature of culture. Moreover, Jullien's deep, long-term engagement with China and Chinese philosophies, together with his mastery of Chinese (Mandarin), provides a convincing *theoretical experiential* (Guilherme, 2014) understanding through which to approach the development of deeper intercultural understandings in students and in educators. The depth and duration of Jullien's engagement with Chinese language and philosophy has led him to a position of critical self-reflection whereby he recognizes that 'in spite of its goodwill [for example on human rights] European thought has still not left home' (Jullien, 2014, p. 162). Jullien's (2014) view, which resonates with the educator-researcher's personal and professional intercultural experience(s), is that the key to establishing effective intercultural interactions lies in developing *mutual intelligibility*. The process of developing deep understanding of, and with, people from diverse cultures therefore points to the need for an integrated, or *embedded*, learning and teaching approach. There is a need for teachers to develop, as Guilherme (2014) suggests, 'a critical language and intercultural communication pedagogy ... to overcome avoidance, suspicion, prejudice and misunderstanding [which] ... requires time for reflection, experiential learning, dialogue' (p. 368).

Finally, the researcher-educator's cultural-intercultural knowledge and praxis have been informed by other investigations of classroom behaviours of students of Asian educational and language backgrounds enrolled in Anglo-Euro-Western universities. These include Nakane's (2002, 2006) study on ways in which Japanese students are silenced by more confident and rapid responses of Australian students. Liu's (2000) research on the silence of Chinese students in American universities is also referenced:

> Silence as a way of implicit communication may fit more with Chinese communication norms ... Silence in class sometimes meant showing respect for teachers and classmates, especially when there were lots of students in class, and it sometimes meant agreement and harmony with others' opinions. (Liu, 2000, p. 47)

4.3   Description of Data and the Methods of Data Collection

A mixed method of research was used in the project. Data is qualitative, consisting of researcher-participant field notes and annotated class logs; recorded and transcribed segments of group discussions; semi-structured group interviews; and one pair interview. All interviews were audio recorded and transcribed. A written log was kept for each of the 13 classes. Individual contributions to whole-class discussions were noted in number by annotating a class list and for key ideas and content as far

Table 4.1 Course schedule: Media and popular culture

Class schedule	Class content, structure + activities
Week 1	Intercultural orientation: 1. Introductions + creation of divergent groups 2. Group discussion: Behaviours, attitudes, values 3. Group discussion: A good student? 4. Video: Hana's response to Western academic argument style 5. Dialogical language script 6. Theory input + group + class discussion
Week 2	Student input and questions: Expectations of course Lecturer input + student questions: Course + assessment overview Lecturer-supported group + whole-class discussion: Favorite films Lecturer input: 6 elements of film + film viewing: Gallipoli (first half)
Week 3	Film viewing: Gallipoli (second half) Lecturer-supported group + whole-class activity: Analyzing film elements of Gallipoli Group discussion comparing cultural stereotyping in Gallipoli (e.g. Australian larrikin as hero) with films depicting students' national cultures/national hero types Lecturer-supported group + whole-class discussion + reference to dialogical language script: Film and media as reflection or shaper of society and culture? * [lecturer intervention in whole-class discussion: Kazuaki on Japanese speakers' pause time]
Week 4	Lecturer input: Language of films: Semiotics Film-viewing: Australian outback gothic genre, Priscilla, queen of the desert Lecturer-supported group and whole-class discussion + reference to language script: Semiotics of Priscilla
Week 5	Lecturer input: Analysis of film review text type model + lecturer-supported group analysis of second film review model Lecturer-supported group discussion of plot, character, setting, values, ideology of Priscilla as preparation for assignment 1 Film viewing: Australian idyll genre, Baz Luhrmann's Australia (first third)
Week 6	Film-viewing: Australia (to end of film) Lecturer-supported group analysis of film elements of Australia
Week 7	Lecturer-supported group + whole-class discussion: Semiotics of Australia + comparison of Australian stereotypes in Gallipoli and Australia Film-viewing: Japanese story (first half)
Week 8	Film-viewing: Japanese story (second half) Lecturer-supported group + whole-class discussion of Japanese story: Cultural-intercultural representation in cross-cultural/intercultural relationships in Japanese story and other films students have viewed
Week 9	Lecturer input: Overview of current media in Australia Student input: Comparison with students' national and international media experiences Public broadcasters vs. commercial media Media via the internet Lecturer input + lecturer-supported group analysis of academic discussion essay text type as preparation for assignment 2
Week 10	Lecturer input + group + whole-class discussion: Analysis and discussion of news and current affairs programs in Australia and internationally: Choices made, cultural meanings, political and ideological pressures, role of media in democracy, as further preparation for assignment 2 Lecturer-supported group discussion with reference to discussion essay model

(continued)

Table 4.1 (continued)

Class schedule	Class content, structure + activities
Week 11	Lecturer input + film clips from Jedda and Rabbit Proof Fence: Representations in film of First Nations Peoples+ the Stolen Generation: from Jedda to Rabbit Proof Fence
	Group and whole-class discussion: Film and media representation of indigenous peoples across the globe
	Lecturer input + student questions: Analysis of oral presentation text type
	Lecturer-supported group discussion on students' choices of topic for assessment task 3
Week 12	Assessment task 3: Individual oral presentations + initial written feedback for each student from lecturer
Week 13	Group and pair interviews for research study + encouraging further critical intercultural reflection, reflexivity

and as accurately as was possible, given the researcher-participant nature of the research.

The course structure, content and activities are summarized in Table 4.1. Intercultural interventions occurred throughout the course, as perceived necessary or constructive by the lecturer. Reference is made in the schedule to the Week 3 intervention *, described in Sect. 4.4 (Key strategies, Activities and Findings).

Thematic analysis and coding (Braun & Clarke, 2006) were applied to the content of discussion contributions (audio recorded and/or from field notes) and of interview data. Use of multiple sources of evidence enabled development of *contiguity relations* (Maxwell & Miller, 2008), for example between class input, lecturer interventions and student interview responses. Focus in analyzing thematic patterns and developing codes was on theoretical-pedagogical aspects relating to developing: (a) critical intercultural awareness, (b) respect for the 'other', (c) sensitivity, (d) openness, (e) curiosity, (f) discovery, (g) intercultural knowledge, (h) empathy and (i) relationship building through dialogical interactions. Rates of individual student contributions to whole class discussion, as observed and logged, were compared with student interview data.

4.4   Key Strategies, Activities and Findings

The participation of all students in discussions in culturally diverse classrooms is a recurring problem. The question arises, does *embedding of intercultural metalanguage* and development of *deep intercultural meta-understanding(s)* in any way address these issues? These concepts are defined and explained in Sect. 4.5 (Implications).

This section addresses two critical problems. First, there is lack of a classroom language for discussing cultural, language and educational backgrounds; and second, teachers lack strategies to support the participation of all students in peda-gogical processes.

There are two important elements, representing contributions to knowledge, in this evidentiary section:

(a) The individual activities for teachers
(b) The overarching process of moving from one problem to the next, and devel-opment over time, through educator-researcher critical reflection

Two key intercultural strategies were employed in an attempt to mitigate a problem perceived as an underlying one, that is, differences in experiences and understandings of behaviours, attitudes, and values: first, intercultural orientations, incorporating six experiential theoretical activities; and second, 'educator intercultural interventions'.

First, each problem is outlined; next, the key strategy and/or activity used to address the problem is/are described. Finally, key findings are given. Findings are informed by the most thematically representative data.

The pedagogical practice and research presented in this chapter began primarily as a search over time for solutions to problems incurred in the educator-researcher's professional contexts. The frequency and nature of the problems suggested issues related to different understandings and expectations among students, and in teachers, in relation to behaviours, attitudes and values: the underlying problem of differing behaviours, attitudes and values. These appeared to relate to differences in cultural, language and educational backgrounds and expectations among students.

4.4.1 Strategy 1: Intercultural Orientations

This prompted the educator-researcher to develop intercultural orientations. These constituted the first one or two sessions of each course. Two to three hours was the usual duration of class time given over to the orientations. In addition, orientation input and student responses served as reference points for educator-researcher interventions, as perceived appropriate and/or needed throughout courses. The intercultural orientations developed over time, as further problems were experienced and/or an intercultural activity threw light on a related problem.

Fictive names are used for student participants. None of the students' responses have been modified or corrected.

4.4.1.1 Problem 1: Discussion Groups

The educator-researcher's pedagogical experience and research (Lubbers, 2008, 2016) has been that students commonly opted initially to sit in starkly demarcated 'cultural/language blocs'. These reflected Western-Eastern backgrounds, rather than a spread of the cultural, language and educational backgrounds of the class. This pattern tended to continue throughout the course.

The tendency of culturally-linguistically diverse cohorts to separate into blocs raised the concern that students who do not sit together do not share knowledge and ideas. Moreover, they do not get to know each other either as cultural beings or as fellow human beings. As a consequence, they do not learn about other cultural-linguistic-educational perspectives and experiences. This separation within class spaces they share with diverse others also means that opportunities to develop close and long-term friendships across different cultures and languages are limited. Activity 1 was designed as an initial step in alleviating this problem.

4.4.1.1.1   Activity 1: Creation of Culturally Divergent Discussion Groups

Students introduced themselves to the class by name and language/s, self-identified cultural and educational background. They were then asked to form groups reflecting this diversity and to avoid grouping along 'Western/Eastern' lines. They were informed that all discussion and activity groups throughout the semester were to be similarly diverse.

4.4.1.1.2   Findings

In this project, students were provided with multiple opportunities over 13 weeks to interact, and to reflect on, their own culturally-linguistically-educationally influenced individual behaviours, attitudes and values through discussions embedded in the course, with cultural-linguistic-educational background others. Course-end group interviews revealed an overwhelming preference (100 percent) for culturally diverse over 'homogenous' groups. Adelberto (Spain) elucidates her preference:

> Before I came to Australia, I thought all Asians were the same. I mean, I did not know anything much about them or their cultures and I did not realise they are all as different in their personalities as Europeans … I thought they were all quiet and shy but now I have spent so much time talking with them in class I have learned they all have their individual opinions and personalities, just like us Spanish and Europeans.

Annike (Germany) also articulates a radical change in cultural-intercultural understanding through her interactions with Baris. Annike's response is reproduced in full as an example of the depth of personal cultural-intercultural change that can occur as an outcome of sustained intercultural interaction. This is explicated in Sect. 4.5 (Implications).

> In Germany we don't think very much of the Turkish people. We think they do not want to mix with the Germans and we think they are not very well educated and do not want to learn German so we ask, 'Why do they come to Germany if they want to live only with other Turkish people?' But Baris speaks such great German and he studies now in Germany and now he also studies in English in Australia and he's such a great guy – so nice and

[considerate] ... such a nice person. So now I have completely changed my idea about Turkish people and when I go back to Germany, I will try to find some Turkish friends.

4.4.1.2   Problem: Behaviours, Attitudes, and Values

The problem, which negative stereotypes such as those articulated by Adelberto and Annike suggested to the educator-researcher, was a mutual lack of knowledge or understanding of behaviours, attitudes and values different from the students' own. The next activity was developed to address this issue.

4.4.1.2.1   Activity 2: Discussion of Behaviours, Attitudes and Values

This activity consisted of five questions for group and class discussion. The questions were designed to elicit viewpoints, exchange of similarities and differences, as well as discussion of changes in cultural-socialization norms over time. Responses or issues raised in these discussions are related to the later theoretical input and discussions, as relevant. Selected responses taken from recorded group discussions, observational field notes and post-course interviews are given here to illustrate the variety and nature of responses. For the purposes of this chapter, just two questions are reported on.

The question '*What do you call your lecturer at university in your tertiary context?*' (Question 1) is intended to lead into a discussion of cultural-institutional customs and expectations as well as to provide explicit and context-appropriate information to international as well as to domestic students.

4.4.1.2.2   Findings

Claudio (Italy) and Jin Kyong (South Korea) express discomfort with the more informal Australian approach. Claudio explains his discomfort as stemming from a confusion of hierarchical roles and expectations and relates this to a similar experience recounted by Emiko (Japan) about her embarrassment when she is asked by American lecturers to address them by their given name:

> In Japan we never call our Japanese professors with their first name, only some American or Australian professors ask this. And some students can do it but for me ... uh ... uh ... it embarrasses me.

Korean-born and educated Jin Kyong responds to Claudio:

> This is very interesting for me to hear, what you are saying, because I think when I come to university here to Australia, I was thinking maybe it is just in Asia we must show respect to our teachers. I mean ... I was thinking it is maybe the same in all of the Western countries like here.

The purpose of Question 2 (*'What questions can you ask someone you have just met? That is, what topics are polite and not polite? Is this the same for your grandparents and parents? For example, do they ask new acquaintances questions that you might not ask?'*) is to promote discussion of cultural/social/personal behaviours, values and attitudes relating to politeness. It aims to develop students' critical self and other awareness and reflexivity, as well as to share educational experiences and language-specific knowledge. Jin Kyong stresses the importance of questions about another's age:

> If we meet other students in a new class, we must first ask them how old they are because if another student is older than us, we must use a different ... uh ... maybe a more polite language with them. In Korea we just expect this. It is very bad manners to use the wrong language to talk to someone older than you.

Jin Kyong then suggests to Emiko that this may be similar to her experience (in Japan), which Emiko confirms by stating that relative age does play an important role in determining who might speak first or last and/or for longer than others in a group. Claudio suggests that age does not play a role in determining discussion participation in his Italian context. He alludes rather to individual personality differences, describing a friend who likes 'to argue a lot in class' whereas he is 'quite quiet'. Jin Kyong then comments to Claudio, laughing in a friendly way, 'Maybe you are a bit Japanese, Claudio!'.

The following problem suggested itself as a result of previous cohorts' responses to Activity 2.

4.4.1.3   Problem: 'What Is a Good Student?'

The problem raised by students in the preceding activity suggested differing expectations and educational experiences of 'a good student'. Activity 3 was developed to promote mutual sharing of cultural-educational experience, curiosity, discovery, open discussion, critical self-awareness and reflexivity.

4.4.1.3.1   Activity 3: Group Discussion 'What Is a Good Student?'

This activity asked the groups to discuss and describe behaviours, experience(s) and their own expectations of 'a good student'. The most thematically representative responses have been selected.

4.4.1.3.2   Findings

Annike describes her undergraduate experience in Germany as depending to some extent on individual lecturers; however, a consistent expectation is that 'we should be ready to discuss about the main ideas and to give our opinions about the questions or topics'. Baris, educated to the end of undergraduate level in Turkey, and at the time undertaking postgraduate studies in Berlin, relates similar expectations to Annike's in both contexts.

Duyi (from China) describes traditional expectations of classroom behaviours in China of his mother and her peers, high school teachers who had recently undertaken teacher professional development in Australia:

> [They practised] many different ways to teach. For example, she told us how they had to talk about all the ideas and do many activities in small groups, not in the whole class. Not just be a good student who listen to the teacher and take many notes. The [Australian] teachers ask them to argue against other Chinese teachers. And my mother says this is very hard for her and also for her friends because she does not want to make the other teachers sad or angry or insult them with a different opinion or idea.

Duyi emphasizes the level of difficulty the different pedagogical approach represents for his mother and other teachers of her generation. While she accepts the authority of her school principal, who was responding to recent demands from the Chinese Ministry of Education that teachers support the development of students' 'critical thinking', public contradiction of a peer's opinion is 'rude for her'. Duyi expresses awareness of generational changes in educational experience: 'I am younger, so I can change my way maybe more quicker than my mother'. Baris responds:

> That is very interesting for me. For your mother it is some other way to be a good student, I think. I mean, to listen to the teacher and to take many notes. When the teacher is good you can learn many things on this way.

Kazuaki's (Japan) response concerning his perception-experience of his need to pause before speaking is reproduced in full, as it is a characteristic which Japanese students have repeatedly conveyed to the educator-researcher as being integral to their understanding of polite dialogue:

> We should not interrupt other people when they speak. So . . . uh . . . one example for me is . . . uh . . . one day my teacher from America asked me to say my opinion about the topic and . . . uh . . . uh . . . I always need some time to think about my ideas . . . but then I tried to say my opinion because he kept asking me to say something . . . uh . . . uh . . . then I start to say my idea and then . . . uh . . . he started to speak again so . . . I was quiet again . . . uh . . . uh . . . and I knew he wanted me to say some more . . . uh . . . but it was too hard for me because I did not know what . . . uh . . . if he would speak again. And I think he was . . . uh . . . quite angry with me. But I should not interrupt him. In Japan, we do not speak . . . uh . . . we wait . . . before we speak.

Similar responses from other students from Asian backgrounds to this activity highlighted the need to address the issue of the Anglo-Euro-Western academic approach to argument. This led to Activity 4.

4.4.1.4 Problem: Anglo-Euro-Western Academic Argument

At another tertiary institution in Sydney, the educator-researcher had engaged in a dialogue with a postgraduate student from Japan. Hana, a veterinary surgeon with six years of professional experience in Japan, was undertaking a postgraduate degree in accounting. Hana expressed a high level of anxiety in response to an in-class explanation of the conventions of the style of Anglo-Euro-Western argument. She then requested a one-on-one meeting after class to explain her problem. She agreed to a video recording of this dialogue and to the video being used to illustrate this issue to other students, educators and researchers. Hana's perspective and student responses to Activity 3 led to the inclusion of this videoed discussion as the focus of Activity 4.

4.4.1.4.1 Activity 4: Hana's Perspective

Following on from the discussion of a good student, the class was shown the video of Hana's dialogue with the educator-researcher. The purpose of this activity was to develop empathy and deeper understanding in Western students of the extent of the challenges which students from Asian/Eastern cultural-educational-language backgrounds can face during their studies in Anglo-Euro-Western institutions. It was also to extend the preceding discussions on differing expectations of a good student. A further purpose was for the educator to model openness to educational experiences, behaviours and values of the Asian background students, which may differ from those of their Western peers. Hana explains her perspective:

> It's totally different. I've never been taught by arguing against someone's idea, especially in the classroom or in front of everyone. If I ... argue with someone's idea I feel ... like I'm fighting with someone in the class [Hana balls her fists and hits knuckles against knuckles]. I feel as if I'm criticising them in front of everyone and I feel ... I am embarrassing them in front of everyone. That also applies to me.

4.4.1.4.2 Findings

For the students of Asian backgrounds in this class, Hana's response appeared to align with their own educational experiences. Annike's comment is representative of the Western background students in this cohort:

> It is so different for me ... us in Germany. In our group I told the others how the professors expect German students to discuss about all the topics in every class. Hana helps me to see how hard this might be for her and other students like her.

Addressing the problem of differing context-dependent expectations of styles of discussion and dialogue raised awareness of the need to respond to the issue of differing levels of language confidence, which is evident in linguistically diverse classes. Activities 3 and 4 led to the development of the following activity.

4.4.1.5 Problem: A Need for Language Support

In Australia, international students with L1 other than English are admitted into universities with an IELTS (International English Language Testing System), or equivalent levels, which range from as low as overall IELTS 6, with individual band scores (speaking, listening, reading or writing) of 5.5, through 6.5, the most common level, to IELTS 8 in some faculties such as medicine and law. The educator-researcher has taught international students across this range. Students with a lower English level are extremely challenged by the language demands of academic English. Even international students entering university with IELTS 8 and L1 English students initially find the specific spoken and written text type demands of their academic discipline unfamiliar and difficult (Birrell, 2006; Dale & Lubbers, 2005; Evans, Tindale, Cable, & Hamil-Mead, 2009). For many international students, lack of confidence and hesitance in relation to fluency (Nakane, 2002, 2006) add to their challenge.

Students from Asian backgrounds raise the additional concern elucidated by Hana of the expectations placed on them by Western educators and class peers to participate in discussions they perceive as confrontational and potentially humiliating to others (Chen & An, 2009; Liu, 2002). These concerns around language led the educator-researcher to develop context-appropriate language support, starting with the following orientation activity focused on a model *dialogical* (Bakhtin, 1981) language script.

4.4.1.5.1 Activity 5: Dialogical Language Support Script

The purpose of providing a dialogical language script which focuses on intercultural theoretical perspectives, is to develop confidence in oral language as well as to model dialogic intercultural engagement and critical intercultural awareness and other intercultural attitudes, skills and knowledge exchange. A cline or gradation is provided, ranging from mild or non-confrontational modes of disagreement (and agreement) to stronger, more direct modes. The script is initially practiced with the class to support comprehension, pronunciation, intonation and fluency. The educator-researcher subsequently provides additional support throughout the course, as appropriate for individuals, through active monitoring of group discussions.

4.4.1.5.2 Findings

Interview responses and research field notes detailing individual as well as group utilization of language models (for example, of sentence syntax, lexis, discourse markers, collocations, phrases) from the script, demonstrate the provision of language and dialogical models in such oral text types to be a significant factor in the developing confidence of several students in this project cohort to participate in group as well as in whole class discussions. Students' drawing on the script and asking questions about adapting it provide evidence of its perceived usefulness. The class was also encouraged to adapt models of language provided in 'a process of mutual creativity' (Halliday, 1978, p. 187). In the context of this pedagogical research, Halliday played out in the following way. Active monitoring by the educator-researcher of group discussions throughout the semester encouraged the process of mutual creativity by providing responses and suggestions to questions on grammatical usage, syntax, lexis and context-appropriate pragmatics as students adapted, with and for each other, elements of the scripted dialogue. Evidence for this mutual support and adaptation is given in the findings of Activity 6.

4.4.1.6 Problem: Theory

The issues around cultural-linguistic-educational differences raised by the preceding pedagogical problems and activities suggested a need to develop theory-related reflexivity, critical intercultural self and other awareness, knowledge and communication skills. As discussed in Sect. 4.2, literature searches across the intercultural language, education and related fields yielded a wide range of contesting theoretical perspectives, together with a dearth of evidence-related classroom approaches appropriate to the educator's context. These issues led to the development of Activity 6.

4.4.1.6.1 Activity 6: Presentation and Discussion of Theory

Students were introduced, through a presentation on power point and handouts, to an overview of historical and current theoretical perspectives on culture, intercultural (communicative) competence and intercultural interaction. These perspectives and quotes range from structuralist to post-structuralist conceptions and approaches. Groups were then instructed to discuss a range of contesting quotes and to relate these to their own cultural-intercultural experience and perspectives. They were also asked to consider theoretical perspectives in relation to the current discussion and interactions with their group peers. Key ideas out of each group were then shared and discussed with the whole class.

4.4.1.6.2 Findings

An earlier group discussion on context-appropriate levels of eye contact in conversations involving new acquaintances had elicited from Emiko an admission of the extreme discomfort Claudio's overly (for Emiko) sustained direct eye contact caused for her during their first exchange: 'All the time he was looking at my eyes'. Claudio subsequently relates the shock Emiko's response had induced in himself to Hall's (1989) notion that *a shock of contrast and difference* is necessary for the development of cultural understanding and successful intercultural communication. Jin Hyong empathizes with Claudio, describing her conflicted feelings about her 'messy, noisy [Australian/Western] flatmates'. On the one hand, she understands and expects people to behave differently in different cultural places, while on the other hand, there is a big difference for me between the theory and my experiences now'. Emiko supports both Claudio and Jin Hyong by referring to her own lack of confidence in politeness norms of different contexts. She links the experience of the shock such uncertainty causes to theoretical input on Phipps' (2007) notion of the important role played by perception of risk in the development of intercultural competence. Emiko shares with her group her strategy of observation of the behaviours of others, for example of 'the Australian students', in her search for context-appropriate responses. Jin Hyong compliments Emiko on her intercultural strategy: 'You think about how other people do things and say things, so you are already one very good intercultural person in our group'. Claudio relates his and Emiko's intercultural shock regarding eye contact to theoretical input on Bhabha (1994), which he reads out to his peers:

> Cultural difference introduces into the process of cultural judgement and interpretation that sudden shock . . . The very possibility of cultural contestation, the ability to shift the ground of knowledges, or to engage in the "war of position", marks the establishment of new forms of meaning, and strategies of identification. (Bhabha, 1994, p. 233)

Claudio tentatively expresses his sense of developing 'a new identity' as a result of the shock of his intercultural encounter with Emiko through his realization that his 'normal' is 'not always normal for other people'. Jin Hyong also relates theoretical input to her group's discussion. She expresses appreciation of Bakhtin's (1981) concept of heteroglossia: 'that the whole world is full of many voices'. She suggests that in intercultural encounters like theirs, no viewpoint is more or less 'stupid or clever'. She refers to Freire's (1996, p. 71) notion: 'At the point of encounter there are neither utter ignoramuses nor perfect sages; there are only people who are attempting, together, to learn more than they know now' (p. 71). Jin Hyong reflects further on the current intercultural encounter: 'Like we do now, I think . . . because in our group we all learn today something new, but no person knew all of it until we told to each other about it—our ideas, our feelings'.

Perspectives from Scollon et al. (2012) were subsequently used by the educator-researcher to provoke further in-depth discussion and critical reflection (Guilherme, 2010; Jack, 2009):

> One of the most important ways in which we reduce the ambiguity of communication is by making assumptions about the people we are talking to. In a monolingual speech community that is rarely a problem, but in the increasingly multilingual business community it is becoming a major issue, to be solved right at the outset of communications. (Scollon et al., 2012, p. 46)

The class was then asked to consider this quote in relation to their earlier group discussions and their individual experiences in the linguistically diverse context of this class. Claudio responded for his group, suggesting that in Italy the question of age in relation to who speaks first in a conversation tends to be a matter of an individual's confidence or personality rather than of relative status by age. For Claudio, the importance placed by Emiko and Jin Kyong on age as a significant factor in conversation turns 'is something that is quite different'. Claudio compares the Italian language's use of formal and informal address but finds it a less strict system of politeness, whereby formal address is restricted to use with older or higher status individuals, or with strangers. This difference in politeness expectations is both interesting and confusing, even unsettling, for Claudio:

> Now I can understand more what the quote is meaning. In one way I think a know a little more from Emiko and Jin Kyong about these different ways of speaking politely in their countries but in another way, it is now for me more confusing. Now I am not certain how I should behave to be polite all the time with all the students in this class.

Jin Kyong responds to Claudio's uncertainty with a question-suggestion: 'So maybe . . . uh . . . can we just ask the other person how we should be polite to them?'

4.4.1.7   Recurrent Problems

These intercultural orientation activities, held in the first class of each course, understandably, did not address recurrent problems which the educator-researcher perceived as arising out of cultural-linguistic-educational differences in behaviours, values and beliefs. These issues led to the employing of educator interventions, as described in Strategy 2.

4.4.2   Strategy 2. Educator Intervention

Notwithstanding the introduction of the topic of culture and intercultural communication at the start of the course, the problem of including all students in class discussions recurred throughout the semester. Western background students continued to dominate responses to questions, and Asian background students (Korean, Chinese and Japanese) were relatively silent. The intercultural orientation served as a reference point for intercultural interventions throughout the course as the educator-researcher observed a need to draw attention to classroom behaviours which appeared to be impeding the contributions of some students.

4.4.2.1   Findings

In this example, Kazuaki was asked for his viewpoint on the discussion topic. After approximately five seconds of silence, Adelberto offered a further contribution to her previous response. The educator acknowledged her response but suggested that Kazuaki might have some interesting thoughts on the topic.

Kazuaki: [pause] Sorry ... I cannot speak too quickly after you ask a ... after anyone asks a question.

Educator: You talked about this in our first intercultural session, didn't you, Kazuaki? Could you please remind us?

Kazuaki then repeated the gist of his orientation session contribution on his experience of Japanese speakers' need for pause time to respond to a question. Adelberto remained quiet while Kazuaki gave a thoughtful, insightful and original response to the question.

In the end-of-program interview, Hisayo responded to a question concerning her increasing participation in class discussion over the semester:

We [the Japanese students] want to give our opinions in class but it is very difficult for us to speak. The Spanish students speak too fast for us. In Japan it is ... uh ... very rude to interrupt other people. But the Spanish students understood. We cannot give our opinion if the Spanish students always speak, but then they let us speak ... uh ... after you helped Kazuaki in the class ... uh ... they realised this fact. Now it is much more easy for me to speak in class—even to the whole class.

In the weeks following this lecturer intervention in Week 3, Hisayo's contributions to class discussion from Week 4 to end of semester increased from none to an average of two and a half, approximately the class average for this period.

4.5   Implications

Based on the evidence, the following key ideas or concepts are suggested as worthy of consideration for moving the field forward: 1. *embedding intercultural metalanguage;* 2. *developing deep intercultural meta-understanding(s);* 3. *intercultural epiphany* and 4. *development through educator-researcher critical reflection of a problem-responsive, context-appropriate model of intercultural communicative competence development.* These ideas are explained below and discussed in relation to the literature and findings of the study. Consideration is also given to their potential for use in other areas, such as foreign language teaching, TESOL, teacher education and CLIL.

Embedding Intercultural Metalanguage
Embedding intercultural metalanguage refers to integrating into pedagogical processes a mutually understood language to talk openly, critically and self-reflexively about aspects of behaviour, values, attitudes and feelings relating to the cultural, language and educational backgrounds and experiences of students and teachers. Findings of this study suggest that utilization over the duration of a course, by students and educator, of a mutually intelligible (Jullien, 2014) language to talk about culturally, linguistically and/or educationally influenced differences and similarities appears to ameliorate some of the problems which teachers can face working with diverse cohorts. In addition, provision of context-appropriate oral text types designed to develop fluency and confidence (Nakane, 2002), together with ongoing

language support, intercultural activities and educator interventions as needed, appear to encourage participation of students who lack confidence to speak up in class. The educator-researcher's experience has been that the problems described here do not occur in isolation from each other. This suggests the potential efficacy of a combination of theoretical-pedagogical forms of support, as the findings of this project seem to illustrate.

In the context of the educator-researcher, embedding intercultural metalanguage also offers potential to address the persistent problem of classrooms separated into cultural-linguistic-educational background blocs (see also Briguglio, 2006; Collett, 2015). Activity 1, for example, aims to alleviate two problems in the following ways: first, sharing from the beginning of a course of cultural-language-educational background self-identification, together with insistence by the educator on a classroom structured into diverse groups, can signal to all students, if only implicitly, that students from commonly marginalized backgrounds (Baik, 2013; Lubbers, 2016; Sawir et al., 2008) will be integrated into group and class activities and discussions; and second, initiating a course with reference to students' self-identifications may indicate to students the educator's awareness of, and openness to, aspects of backgrounds and experiences which can impact on classroom behaviours and expectations. It offers a response to a common student complaint, 'We want to talk about culture, but none of our lecturers ever mention it' (Student Cultural Ambassadors, University of Sydney, 2015).

Findings suggest that embedding intercultural metalanguage, through the kinds of context-responsive strategies and activities attempted in this project, which focus explicitly on aspects of culturally-linguistically-educationally influenced behaviours, attitudes and values, appears to support mutual sharing of those experiences and perspectives. It also appears to provide a vehicle for experiential and theoretical development (Guilherme, 2002, 2014) of critical intercultural awareness of self and others, intercultural skills, feelings and attitudes (Byram, 1997; Byram et al., 2016; Byram & Zarate, 1994) conducive to effective intercultural engagement. It seems to encourage these students to interact and to relate (Byram, 1997; Byram & Zarate, 1994). Thematic analysis of Emiko, Claudio and Jin Kyong's interactions during Activity 2, for example, illustrates sensitive, empathic, open and mutually respectful and informative dialogue (Byram, 1997; Byram et al., 2016; Byram & Zarate, 1994). There is evidence, also, that these students' curiosity leads them to cultural-intercultural discovery and knowledge (Byram, 1997; Byram & Zarate, 1994). These represent first tentative yet significant steps, it could be argued, in the 'endless [intercultural] journey where each day brings more knowledge and more questions' (Guilherme, 2014, p. 358).

Moreover, it is through dialogical discussion (Bakhtin, 1981) of theoretical perspectives, read aloud to their peers and then interpreted (Byram, 1997) in relation to their interaction, by Emiko and Claudio, that significant intercultural understandings, including reflexivity and critical self- and other awareness, appear to have been realized by both. They relate a comparable sense of intercultural disruption to their 'normal' experience and expectations of polite behaviours. Emiko links her personal experience of uncertainty about politeness norms (Scollon et al., 2012) to Phipps'

(2007) notion of the need to perceive risk. Claudio responds by linking Hall's (1989) notion of the need for a shock involving contrast and difference with Bhabha's 'sudden shock' (Bhabha, 1994, p. 233), through his discovery that his normal level of eye contact was upsetting to another. By reading the quote from Bhabha (1994, p. 233) to his peers, Claudio signals apparent recognition of a personal 'experience of cultural contestation, the ability to shift this ground of knowledges'. He also appears to realize, for himself, an ensuing 'establishment of new forms of meaning, and strategies of identification' (p. 233). His articulation of this may also, potentially, have triggered understanding of this intercultural experience in his peers. Claudio's sense of 'new identity' may even, for himself, at least, if not also for the other actors in the dialogue, signal foregrounding of *cultural hybridity* (Bhabha, 1994).

In addition, embedding intercultural metalanguage through initial intercultural activities and repeated educator intercultural interventions may partially, at least, serve to ameliorate the problem of the persistent stereotyping of students of Asian backgrounds studying in Anglo-Australian tertiary contexts. Adelberto, for example, articulates an undoing of essentializing (Abdallah-Pretceille, 2006), or *unstereotyping*, of 'Asian people' she has experienced through sustained interaction and discussion with her class peers. Annike's sustained engagement with Baris through intercultural discussion, through the vehicle of intercultural metalanguage, seems to have led to a similar unstereotyping of 'Turkish people in Germany'.

Importantly, an intercultural metalanguage provides a vehicle for discussion for teachers who recognize conflicting patterns of behavioural and attitudinal differences in students which appear to relate to cultural, language and educational backgrounds (Deardorff & Jones, 2012). A common language is needed to address these differences in an explicit, but at the same time open and unjudgemental, way. As well, suggestions, for example, to take the word/concept *culture* out of *interculturality* (see, for example, Dervin, 2014), do not, it may be argued, provide a constructive response, for example, to this Chinese-background international student's anguished expression of alienation and loneliness, 'I studied three years in Australia and no-one asked me even one time about my culture' (Lubbers, 2008).

Moreover, as Spivak (1988, p. 205), in her discussion of subaltern studies, alerts us, Western post-structuralist intellectuals such as Foucault have a voice that can easily be, and is, heard, while hegemonies which are 'economic, but also (post)-colonial, male, ethnic, spatial and so forth' continue to silence the voices of those on the periphery. Her question 'Can the subalterns speak?' (Spivak, 1988) has relevance to the position of students of Asian backgrounds enrolled in Australian and other Anglo-Euro-Western universities. The educator-researcher would argue that their position, as they continue to be stereotyped and marginalized in and by the dominant, for the most part un-self-critiquing Western pedagogical contexts, is not unlike that of the subaltern peripheries Spivak discusses. These, Spivak asserts, are in need of some form of temporary *positive strategic essentialism*. Additionally, despite critiquing all forms of essentialism, Spivak argues that, without any identification as a collective or group, the domination of any group cannot be represented and subsequently addressed.

Deep Intercultural Meta-understanding(s)

This concept refers to understanding(s) of a cognitive and theoretical nature. Importantly, it also incorporates understanding at a *felt*, human to human, or *inter-human* level. Deep intercultural meta-understanding(s) crystallizes the end-goal of the educator-researcher's attempts to mitigate the problem of cultural-linguistic blocs. The stereotyping and marginalization of Asian background international students are ways of *de-humanising* the Other.

Evidence from students' in-class interactions and interview responses in this project suggests that activities which support development of intercultural communicative competences (Byram, 1997) have potential to develop deep intercultural meta-understanding(s). The warmth of liking and personal admiration Annike expresses towards Baris—'such a nice *person*'—(emphasis added), it is suggested, constitutes not only developing intercultural openness, discovery, knowledge and critical intercultural awareness of self and other at a cognitive level but also a person-to-person warmth, which may represent the seeds of deeper human understanding of previously stereotyped Others. The developing ease, accompanied by moments of humour, with which the group of Emiko, Jin Hyong and Claudio relate personal encounters, which include experiences of shock, discomfort, unsettling, uncertainty and confusion, is also worth considering in relation to this concept. Their developing relationship involving mutual understanding, increasing knowledge of each 'other' and empathy could be regarded as *deepening intercultural meta-understanding.*

Intercultural Epiphany

This concept could be understood as an *intercultural lightbulb moment* or *experience*. It refers to a sudden dawning in an individual, through deep intercultural engagement with another individual or group, of critical intercultural awareness, often involving understanding of difference and of similarity. Instead of leading to further stereotyping and tendency to marginalize, an intercultural epiphany represents the first seed of understanding of the common humanity of another individual and, potentially, through reflection, extension of this to the group of Others the individual has appeared to represent. Out-groups begin to become in-(humankind)groups; *they*, supported by carefully constructed and sensitively supportive intercultural activities, begin to become *we*. Annike's revelation of a complete reversal in her perception of Turkish people in Germany is potentially evidence of her unstereotyping, through intercultural engagement over time with an individual cultural other, of a whole group ('Turkish people in Germany').

Adelberto's previous view of Asians as quiet and shy is, as already discussed, a well-documented perception of Asian students among Australian academics and students. Both Adelberto's and Annike's heterostereotypes exemplify "'collective meta-attitudinal" discourses that lay boundaries between groups' (Dervin, 2014, p. 186, citing Moore, 2003). They also have, as Scollon and Wong-Scollon (2001) suggest, an ideological basis, deriving from a sense of superiority created out of sociopolitical and historical factors. The educator-researcher believes that the significance of the radical attitudinal shift articulated by these young people, from a strongly negative national-cultural stereotype to a strongly positive perspective on one individual 'representative' of a group should not be underestimated. It could even be argued that the radical shift in understanding of one Other, or a group of Others, such as those articulated by Annike and Adelberto, represents a significant, if not critical, first step in a lifelong intercultural journey. Moreover, that both students declared this shift to be the most important aspect of their sustained interactions in culturally diverse groups argues for the responsibility of the educator to structure learning and teaching in ways which promote sustained intercultural engagement of students.

A final implication to be drawn from this study is the clear evidence of the equal intelligence (Rancière, 1991) of the students, regardless of background and previous experience-s, to reflect critically on, and to discuss, complex and contesting (Gallie, 1955) theoretical concepts and perspectives on culture and interculturality. They are also equally capable of relating this to their own past and current developing intercultural interactions.

Development Through Educator-Researcher Critical Reflection of a Problem-Responsive, Context-Appropriate Model of Critical Intercultural Awareness and Intercultural Competence Development

This theoretically informed pedagogical process is illustrated in each section of this chapter. Below is an outline of the process.

(a) The introduction sets out the overarching problem of stereotyping and margin-alization of Asian international students experienced and observed over time by the educator-researcher's pedagogical context.

(b) Literature searches resulted in a lack of theoretical-pedagogical models which offered comprehensive responses to the specific problems of this context. The educator-researcher then decided to apply the theoretical-pedagogical model which offered the most comprehensive and relevant approach. Notwithstanding this 'decision', a range of other concepts and understandings from areas engaging with culture, language and/or education was considered. Those which appeared most appropriate were selected and adapted to context and a specific problem.

(c) Each problem was critically reflected on, and an intercultural strategy and/or activity was/were developed and implemented.

(d) The pedagogical-research nature of this project enabled gathering of data, analysis and deep understanding of the problem. It also deepened the educator-researcher's own intercultural knowledge and understanding.

(e) Increasing knowledge and understanding helped the educator recognize a related or another problem and to develop a strategy/activity to ameliorate that problem.

(f) This repeated 'loop process', in which student responses and input and critical reflection were critical throughout to deepening intercultural awareness, under-standing and knowledge in the educator-researcher, has led to the pedagogical research project presented in this chapter.

4.5.1   Relevance to Other Educational Areas

CLIL, foreign language teaching/FL, TESOL and teacher education suggest themselves as most accessible to integration of ICC using a context-appropriate, problem-response approach. Regrettably, the amount of content and activity flexibility available to the educator-researcher in this project, such as freedom to select films promoting discussion on national cultural stereotyping, is not available to too many teachers. This is mainly because most curricula, and therefore too often even class programming as well, are set at an institutional, state, provincial or even national level.

CLIL should be open to flexibility. Underlying principles of CLIL, such as the belief that all teachers should be able to teach language through their discipline (Bullock, 1975), should in theory also mean that ICC could be integrated with language development. In practice, however, most teachers of disciplines other than those with a clear focus on language, such as foreign language teaching and TESOL, are not provided with enough pre-service or professional development to develop the depth of linguistic knowledge and skills needed to teach the language aspect effectively, let alone to integrate informed ICC praxis into their lessons.

As already discussed, foreign language teaching has traditionally tended to 'teach culture' through comparison of lists of concrete differences between the target language country/countries and those of learners, producing national generalizations and cultural stereotypes (see, for example, Svarstad, 2016). Svarstad's (2016) study suggests a way forward for integration of ICC into English language teaching in lower secondary schools in Denmark through collaboration of researchers, teachers, students and teacher educators. This should be a rewarding approach, but it might also be time-challenging for all involved.

In relation to the educator-researcher's professional area, TESOL, stereotyping by national group is surprisingly common (see Kumaravadivelu, 2003). In response to this problem, compulsory ICC professional development was developed and facilitated in the early 2000s by the educator-researcher (Director of the centre) for teachers, administrative and student support staff of the English language and academic preparation centre at NCELTR (National Centre for English Language and Research) at Macquarie University, Sydney. As far as she is aware, no other such centres, even in universities in Australia, offered ICC professional development for all teachers. This is regrettable, since university pathway centres potentially offer ideal 'crucibles' to develop intercultural competence in teachers and students. Extension of this to post-entry university academic and professional communication support programs, as developed in the above context, through close collaboration between the English centre and academic disciplines, such as that developed at that time with the university's Master of Accounting, moreover, can promote cultural-intercultural awareness and greater openness in academic staff. Such collaborations can lead to reduced stereotyping, as documented by Evans et al. (2009).

Teacher education is the area in which intercultural communicative competence development needs to be mandatory. In a country whose population is as diverse as

Australia's, with longstanding migration from all parts of the globe, diversity of cultural and language background is the norm. Here, however, as indicated in the introduction, integration of ICC is patchy. In the educator-researcher's experience, few university educators across subject (discipline) areas are currently equipped to develop ICC in their students, since few, particularly those of the dominant (Anglo-Western) background (see Lubbers, 2018), appear themselves to evince critical intercultural awareness or ability to de-centre. Australian educational institutions, teachers and students could potentially benefit enormously from compulsory intercultural competence development in teacher education, as mandated in 2013 by the Danish Teacher Education Reform (Svarstad, 2016).

4.6 Conclusion

This study involved a problem-oriented approach aimed at enabling the ideas, perspectives and knowledge of all students, including those of commonly marginalized and silenced international students of Asian backgrounds, to contribute to the learning and teaching pool.

The educator-researcher believes there are three contributions to knowledge arising out of the approach:

(i) The individual *activities* for teachers.
(ii) The overarching *process of moving from one problem to the next* (development over time, through educator-researcher critical reflection).
(iii) *Three innovative concepts* are offered as a way forward for addressing the present problems in the field:

    (a) *Embedding intercultural metalanguage*
    (b) *Deep intercultural meta-understanding(s)*
    (c) *Intercultural epiphany*

The chapter has outlined the cultural-intercultural problems experienced by the educator-researcher in teaching diverse cohorts in Australian university contexts. It has described the strategies and activities implemented to address these and presented the findings of this theoretically informed pedagogical investigation. Finally, implications of the research study have been discussed.

The literature makes clear the persistence of such problems, both in Australia and in other countries, where diversity in classrooms is already considerable, and in many countries, including in Australia, it continues to increase. Growing nationalism, stereotyping and scapegoating by ethnic, religious and cultural background, of asylum seekers and migrants driven from their homes by conflict and poverty, are among other factors driving the rise of racist populist governments across the world. This makes development of intercultural awareness and competences an even more urgent challenge for universities, schools and educators.

Goh (2012, Abstract) alerts us to the problematic reality that 'while the literature … in Asia and the Pacific often mentions intercultural understanding and global-mindedness as desirable outcomes, few models exist that translate effortlessly into … classroom pedagogy'.

The approach presented in this chapter represents a process developed over time through theory-informed pedagogical practice and continuous critical reflection by the educator-researcher. Effortless translation of this, or any other models, into classroom practice is not realistic. Rather, it is hoped that a problem-responsive, context-appropriate intercultural model, strategies and activities, as presented in this study, together with the innovative concepts suggested as potentially helpful across a number of pedagogical contexts, might offer teachers some fresh ideas and an adaptable approach to ameliorating the kinds of intercultural problems confronted by other teachers.

References

Abdallah-Pretceille, M. (2006). Interculturalism as a paradigm for thinking about diversity. *Intercultural Education, 17*(5), 475–683.

Ang, S., & Van Dyne, L. (2015). Preface and acknowledgements. In S. Ang & L. Van Dyne (Eds.), *Handbook of cultural intelligence: Theory, measurement and applications* (pp. xv–xviii). London: Routledge.

Arkoudis, S., Baik, C., Marginson, S., & Cassidy, E. (2012). *Internationalizing the student experience in tertiary education: Developing criteria and indicators*. Melbourne, Australia: University of Melbourne. Retrieved from https://melbourne-cshe.unimelb.edu.au/__data/assets/pdf_file/0010/1490851/Janu_2012AEI_indicators.pdf.

Baik, C. (2013). Internationalising the student experience. In S. Marginson (Ed.), *Tertiary education policy in Australia* (pp. 131–138). Melbourne, Australia: Centre for the Study of Higher Education. Retrieved efrom https://melbourne-cshe.unimelb.edu.au/.../1489174/Tert_Edu_Policy_Aus.pdf.

Bakhtin, M. ([1935]1981). Discourse in the novel. In M. Holquist (Trans.), C. Emerson, & M. Holquist (Eds.), *The dialogic imagination: Four essays by M.M. Bakhtin* (pp. 269–422). Austin, TX: University of Texas Press.

Baumann, Z. (2007). *Consuming life*. Cambridge, MA: Polity Press.

Bhabha, H. K. (1994). *The location of culture*. London: Routledge.

Bhabha, H. K. (2006). Cultural diversity and cultural differences. In B. Ashcroft, G. Griffiths, & H. Tiffin (Eds.), *The post-colonial studies reader* (pp. 155–157). New York: Routledge.

Birrell, B. (2006). *The changing face of the accounting profession in Australia*. Melbourne, Australia: CPA Australia.

Braun, V., & Clarke, V. (2006). Using thematic analysis in psychology. *Qualitative Research in Psychology, 3*, 77–101.

Briguglio, C. (2006). Intercultural communication competencies in higher education and management. In *Proceedings of the international conference on intercultural communication competencies: Can structured intervention improve intercultural communication in multinational student teams?* (pp. 143–164). Singapore, Singapore: Marshall Cavendish Academic.

Briguglio, C., & Smith, R. (2012). Perceptions of Chinese students in an Australian university: Are we meeting their needs? *Asia Pacific Journal of Education, 32*(1), 17–33.

Bullock, A. (1975). The Bullock report: A language for life, 1975. Great Britain Department of Education and Science.

Byram, M. (1997). *Teaching and assessing intercultural communicative competence.* Clevedon, UK: Multilingual Matters.

Byram, M. (2010). Linguistic and cultural education for Bildung and citizenship. *The Modern Language Journal, 94*(ii), 317–321. Retrieved from https://www.jstor.org/stable/40856134.

Byram, M., Golubeva, I., Hui, H., & Wagner, M. (Eds.). (2016). *From principles to practice in education for intercultural citizenship.* Clevedon, UK: Multilingual Matters. Retrieved from http://ebookcentral.proquest.com/lib/uws/detail.action?doc=4722509.

Byram, M., & Zarate, G. (1994). *Definitions, objectives and assessment of socio-cultural objectives.* Strasbourg, France: Council of Europe.

Byrd Clark, J., & Dervin, F. (Eds.). (2014). *Reflexivity in language and intercultural education.* Milton Park, UK: Taylor & Francis.

Canadian Paediatric Society. (2018). Cultural competence for child and youth professionals. In V. Dzung & M. Mayhew (Eds.), *A guide for health professionals working with immigrant and refugee children and youth.* Retrieved from https://www.kidsnewtocanada.ca/culture/competence.

Centre for Cultural Competence Australia. (2018).. Retrieved from https://ccca.com.au/

Chalmers, D., & Volet, S. (1997). Common misconceptions about students from South-East Asia studying in Australia. *Higher Education Research and Development, 16*(1), 87–99.

Chen, G. M., & An, R. (2009). A Chinese model of intercultural leadership competence. In D. K. Deardorff (Ed.), *The sage handbook of intercultural competence* (pp. 196–208). Thousand Oaks, CA: Sage.

Collett, D. (2015). *'Everyone at every rank matters': Inclusive intercultural communication in higher education.* Doctoral dissertation. Retrieved from http://researchdirect.westernsydney.edu.au/islandora/object/uws%3A33426

Dale, M., & Lubbers, S. (2005, October). *Internationalising universities: Adopting an ethical position while continuing to attract international students.* Refereed paper presented at the Australian International Education Conference (AEIC), Gold Coast, Queensland. Copy in possession of author.

Deardorff, D., & Jones, E. (2012). Intercultural competence: An emerging focus in internationalized higher education. In D. K. Deardorff, H. de Wit, J. D. Heyl, & T. Adams (Eds.), *The sage handbook of international higher education.* Retrieved from http://ebookcentralproquest.com/lib/uwsau/detail.action?doc=1995626.

Dervin, F. (2014). Cultural representation, identity and othering. In J. Jackson (Ed.), *The Routledge handbook of language and intercultural communication* (pp. 181–194). London: Routledge.

Dervin, F. (2015, November). *Intercultural competences in teacher education: An example from Finland.* Combined Symposium of the School of Education and IEC, Linguistics, Macquarie University, Sydney.

Evans, E., Tindale, J., Cable, D., & Hamil-Mead, S. (2009). Collaborative teaching in a linguistically and culturally diverse higher education setting: A case study of a postgraduate accounting program. *Higher Education Research & Development, 28*(6), 597–613. Retrieved from https://doi.org/10.1080/07294360903226403.

Freire, P. (1985). *The politics of education: Culture, power and liberation.* South Hadley,, MA: Bergin & Garvey.

Freire, P. (1996). *Pedagogy of the oppressed.* London: Penguin Books Ltd..

Gallie, B. (1955). Essentially contested concepts. *Proceedings of the Aristotelian Society, New Series, 56*, 167–198. Retrieved from http://www.jstor.org/stable/4544562.

Glass, C., & Westmont, C. (2014). Comparative effects of belongingness on the academic success and cross-cultural interactions of domestic and international students. *International Journal of Intercultural Relations, 38*, 106–119.

Goh, M. (2012). Teaching with cultural intelligence: Developing multiculturally educated and globally engaged citizens. *Asia Pacific Journal of Education, 32*(4), 395–415.

Guilherme, M. (2002). *Critical citizens for an intercultural world.* Clevedon, UK: Multilingual Matters.

Guilherme, M. (2010). Introduction. In M. Guilherme, E. Glaser, & M. C. Méndez-García (Eds.), *The intercultural dynamics of multicultural working* (pp. 1–20). Clevedon, UK: Multilingual Matters.

Guilherme, M. (2014). Critical language and intercultural communication pedagogy. In J. Jackson (Ed.), *The Routledge handbook of language and intercultural communication* (pp. 357–371). London: Routledge.

Hall, E. T. (1989). *Beyond culture*. New York: Anchor Books.

Halliday, M. A. K. (1978). *Language as social semiotic: The social interpretation of language and meaning*. London: Edward Arnold.

Hellsten, M. (2002, October). Students in transition: Needs and experiences of international students in Australia. New times, new approaches. *Paper presented at the 16th IDP Australian International Education Conference, Hobart, Tasmania*. Retrieved from www.aiec.idp.com/uploads/pdf/Hellsten_p.pdf

Himmelmann, G. (2006). Concepts and issues in citizenship education: A comparative study of Germany, Britain and the USA. In G. Alred, M. Byram, & M. Fleming (Eds.), *Education for intercultural citizenship. Concepts and comparisons*. Clevedon, UK: Multilingual Matters. Retrieved from http://trove.nla.gov.au/version/19879497.

Holliday, A. (1999). Small cultures. *Applied Linguistics, 20*(2), 237–264.

Holliday, A. (2011). *Intercultural communication and ideology*. Los Angeles: Sage.

Holliday, A., & MacDonald, M. (2016, November). *On paradigms, recidivism and 'soft' essentialism: Resisting neoliberalism in intercultural research*. Paper presented at the International Association for Languages and Intercultural Communication (IALIC) Conference, Barcelona, Spain. Abstract copy in possession of author.

Jack, G. (2009). A critical perspective on teaching intercultural competence in a management department. In A. Feng, M. Byram, & M. Fleming (Eds.), *Becoming interculturally competent through education and training* (pp. 95–114). Clevedon, UK: Multilingual Matters.

Jones, B., Bustamante, R., & Nelson, J. (2016). Cultural competence preparation: Pre-service teachers' perceptions of their needs. In K. Lowell (Ed.), *Cultural competence: Elements, developments and emerging trends*. New York: Nova Science Publishers. Retrieved from https://ebookcentral.proquest.com/lib/uwsau/reader.action?docID=4586661&ppg=1.

Jullien, F. (2014). *On the universal, the common and dialogue between cultures* (M. Richardson & K. Fijalkowski, trans). Cambridge: Polity Press.

Kim, G. (2004). Mikhail Bakhtin: The philosopher of human communication. *The University of Western Ontario Journal of Anthropology, 12*(1), 53–62.

Koehne, N. (2004, November–December). *Positioning international education and international students: Multiple discourses and discursibe practices*. Paper presented at the AARE conference, Melbourne. Retrived from https://www.aare.edu.au/data/publications/2004/koe04870.pdf

Kumaravadivelu, B. (2003). Problematizing cultural stereotypes in TESOL. *TESOL Quarterly, 37*(4), 709–719. https://doi.org/10.2307/358219.

Liu, J. (2000). Understanding Asian students' oral participation modes in American classrooms. *Journal of Asian Pacific Communication, 10*(1), 155–189. Retrieved from https://benjamins.com/catalog/japc.10.1.09liu.

Liu, J. (2002). Negotiating silence in American classrooms. *Language and Intercultural Communication, 2*(1), 37–54. Retrieved from https://www.tandfonline.com/doi/abs/10.1080/14708470208668074.

Lubbers, S. (2008, October). *What quality of global impact? Intercultural awareness and communication skills: A missing link in international education*. Paper presented at the Australia Education International Conference (AEIC), Sydney. Copy in possession of author.

Lubbers, S. (2013, July). *Enhancing learning and teaching in multicultural educational contexts: Developing intercultural awareness and a shared intercultural metalanguage*. Paper presented at the European Conference on Education (ECE), Brighton, Britain. Copy in possession of author.

Lubbers, S. (2016). Democratising the multicultural learning and teaching environment through the development of a shared intercultural metalanguage. In F. Klippel (Ed.), *Teaching languages - Sprachen lehren* (pp. 317–329). Münster, Germany: Waxmann.

Lubbers, S. (2018, July). Helping all our students to thrive: Challenging western educators' stereotyping of "Asian students". In *Paper presented at the European conference on education (ECE)*. Brighton, UK: Copy in possession of author.

Maxwell, J. A., & Miller, B. A. (2008). Categorizing and connecting strategies in qualitative data analysis. In P. Leavy & S. Hesse-Biber (Eds.), *Handbook of emergent methods* (pp. 461–477). New York: Guilford Press.

Mayuzumi, K., Motobayashi, K., Nagayama, C., & Takeuchi, M. (2007). Transforming diversity in Canadian higher education. *Teaching in Higher Education, 12*(5), 581–592. https://doi.org/10.1080/13562510701595200.

Moore, D. (2003). *Les représentations de langues et de leur apprentissage*. Paris: Didier.

Nakane, I. (2002). Silence in the multicultural classroom: Perceptions and performance in Australian university classrooms. *Inter-Cultural Studies, 2*(1), 17–28.

Nakane, I. (2006). Silence and politeness in intercultural communication in university seminars. *Journal of Pragmatics, 38*, 1811–1835.

Phipps, A. (2007). The sound of higher education: Sensuous epistemologies and the mess of knowing. *London Review of Education, 5*(1), 1–13.

Porto, M. (2010). *Cultural understanding in EFL reading in Argentina*. New York: Nova Science Publishers. Retrieved from https://www.worldcat.org/title/cultural-understanding-in-efl-reading-in-argentina/oclc/751990878.

Rancière, J. (1991). *The ignorant schoolmaster: Five lessons in intellectual emancipation*. Stanford, CA: Stanford University Press.

Risager, K. (2007). *Language and culture pedagogy: From a national to transnational paradigm*. Clevedon, UK: Multilingual Matters.

Risager, K., & Dervin, F. (2015). Introduction. In F. Dervin & K. Risager (Eds.), *Researching identity and interculturality* (pp. 1–25). Abingdon, UK: Routledge.

Sawir, E., Marginson, S., Deumert, A., Nyland, C., & Ramia, G. (2008). Loneliness and international students: An Australian study. *Journal of Studies in International Education, 12*, 148–180. https://doi.org/10.1177/1028315307299699.

Scollon, R., & Wong-Scollon, S. (2001). *Intercultural communication: A discourse approach*. Oxford: Blackwell.

Scollon, R., Wong-Scollon, S., & Jones, R. (2012). *Intercultural communication: A discourse approach*. Chichester, UK: Wiley.

Singh, M., & Meng, H. (2013). Democratising western research using non-western theories: Rancière and mute Chinese theoretical tools. *Studies in Higher Education, 38*(6), 907–920. https://doi.org/10.1080/03075079.2011.607493.

Spivak, G. C. (1988). Can the subaltern speak? In C. Nelson (Ed.), *Marxism and the interpretation of culture* (pp. 271–313). Chicago: University of Illinois. Retrieved from https://postcolonialismuon.wordpress.com/category/can-the-subaltern-speak.

Student Cultural Ambassadors. (2015, December). *Live performance given at the cultural competence colloquium conducted at the University of Sydney*. Sydney, Australia.

Summers, M., & Volet, S. (2008). Students' attitudes towards culturally mixed groups on international campuses: Impact of participation in diverse and non-diverse groups. *Studies in Higher Education, 33*(4), 357–370. https://doi.org/10.1080/03075070802211430.

Svarstad, L.K. (2016). *Teaching interculturality: Developing and engaging in pluralistic discourses in English language teaching*. PhD Thesis. Copenhagen, Denmark: Department of Educational Theory and Curriculum Studies, Aarhus University.

Wang, P. (2010). A case study of an in-class silent postgraduate Chinese students in London Metropolitan University. *TESOL Journal, 2*, 207–214.

Zhang, Z., & Zhou, G. (2010). Understanding Chinese international students at a Canadian university: Perspectives, expectations, and experiences. *Canadian and International Education/Education Canadienne et Internationale, 39*(3), 43–58. Retrieved from https://www.researchgate.net/publication/266969601.

Chapter 5
Exploring the Relationship Between Teacher Confirmation and Student Motivation: The United States and Finland

S. M. Croucher, D. Rahmani, F. Galy-Badenas, C. Zeng, A. Albuquerque, M. Attarieh, and E. N. Nshom

5.1 Introduction

Teacher communication behaviors have enormous impacts on students' learning processes and thus have attracted extensive scholarly attention (Mazer, 2013). Teacher confirmation is the process through which teachers communicate to students that they are endorsed, recognized, and acknowledged as valuable individuals (Ellis, 2000). In primarily US-based research, teacher confirmation has been linked to a variety of effective pedagogical practices, student motivation, and emotional outcomes (Ellis, 2004). As McCroskey and McCroskey (2006) stated, it is not likely that instructional practices in other instructional cultures are always as effective as they are in the United States. To understand the classroom dynamics in a global setting, instructional communication researchers increasingly have examined the

S. M. Croucher (✉) · D. Rahmani · F. Galy-Badenas
School of Communication, Journalism, and Marketing, Massey University, Wellington, New Zealand
e-mail: s.croucher@massey.ac.nz

C. Zeng
Department of Communication, North Dakota State University, Fargo, ND, USA

A. Albuquerque
Department of Language and Communication Studies, University of Jyväskylä, Jyväskylän, Finland

Business Department, Yamanashi Gakuin University, Yamanashi, Japan

M. Attarieh
Department of Language and Communication Studies, University of Jyväskylä, Jyväskylän, Finland

E. N. Nshom
California State University San Marcos, San Marcos, CA, USA

© Springer Nature Singapore Pte Ltd. 2021
M. D. López-Jiménez, J. Sánchez-Torres (eds.), *Intercultural Competence Past, Present and Future*, Intercultural Communication and Language Education, https://doi.org/10.1007/978-981-15-8245-5_5

extent to which teaching practices enacted in the United States can be applied to other countries. Goldman, Bolkan, and Goodboy (2014) observed that teacher confirmation has a greater effect on students learning in the United States than in China or Turkey. Goodboy, Bolkan, Beebe, and Schultz (2010), investigating the cross-cultural behavioral alteration techniques and affinity-seeking strategies with instructors, reported that while Chinese students use more behavioral alteration techniques, American students use more diverse varieties of affinity-seeking. These classroom differences were mainly attributed to the national cultural differences such as individualism vs. collectivism and power distance.

Individualism–collectivism is a cultural spectrum with a collective extreme end that puts emphasis on the goals of some collective, such as a stable in-group, rather than individuals' personal goals, whereas an individualist extreme puts emphasis on personal goals and the goals of various smaller in-groups rather than a bigger collective group (Triandis, Bontempo, Villareal, Asai, & Lucca, 1988). Power distance refers to how much inequality among the individuals in different parts of a society is perceived to be normal (Smith & Hume, 2005).

In addition to the national cultural dimensions, a few cross-cultural studies on teaching behaviors claimed other contextual factors such as differences in education values, parents' involvement, and locus of control may also contribute to the differences manifested in classrooms across cultures (Zhang, 2007; Zhang & Huang, 2008; Zhang & Oetzel, 2006). However, the need for and reactions to confirmation are related to the social and psychological characteristics of culture such as self-perception and self-esteem (Pajares & Schunk, 2002), which are contextual notions or, in other words, they are different from culture to culture (Heine, 2001; Heine, Lehman, Markus, & Kitayama, 1999). Previous cross-cultural studies have compared North American and European cultures with East Asian cultures and paid little attention to these contextual factors. To emphasize the contextual influences, the researchers of this study aim to explore the constructs of teacher confirmation and student motivation in two cultures which are both Western but have vastly different educational values and social systems: Finland and the United States.

5.2 Literature Review and Theoretical Discussion

Teacher confirmation is a significant factor in developing a positive instructional condition and results in a stronger sense of community and stronger relationships in the classroom (Ellis, 2000; Schrodt, Turman, & Soliz, 2006). Perceived teacher confirmation, which strongly predicts students' positive educational outcomes, is positively correlated with higher levels of student motivation and emotional interests, instructor credibility, and perceived use of reward, expert, and referent power. On one hand, it is negatively associated with state receiver apprehension and indirectly affects students' cognitive and affective learning and their motivation to learn (Edwards, Edwards, Torrens, & Beck, 2011; Ellis, 2004; Schrodt et al., 2006; Turman & Schrodt, 2006). Three ways in which teacher confirmation may be demonstrated behaviorally are (a) communicating interest in the comments and concerns of the students, (b) general interest in students' education and learning, and (c) application of a variety of instructional techniques to help students with their learning process (Ellis, 2000, 2004).

Previous research has shown the effect of teacher confirmation on positive student motivation and affective learning is mediated by the sense of classroom community. As confirmation makes students feel more comfortable in classroom environments, their feelings of community belonging and membership increase, which in turn increases student motivation (Edwards et al., 2011). Teacher credibility also partially mediates this relationship, and confirmation from a less credible teacher is more likely not to encourage students or heighten their self-regard (Schrodt et al., 2009).

The effect of confirmation on student success has different manifestations such as higher student motivation and more positive classroom emotions. Student motivation –in the form of disposition either toward learning in general, namely, trait motivation (Pogue & Ahyun, 2006), or toward a specific subject, namely, state motivation (Christophel, 1990) – is related "to approach and avoidance of goal-directed effort expenditures" (Heggestad & Kanfer, 2000, p. 753). Student motivation is affected by various educational factors such as the educational environment and the instructor (Brophy, 1998; Chesebro & McCroskey, 2001; Frymier, 1994). It is positively linked to teacher immediacy (Christophel & Gorham, 1995; Pogue & Ahyun, 2006), perceived teacher credibility (Martin, Chesebro, & Mottet, 1997), out-of-class communication (Jaasma & Koper, 1999), and confirming teacher/instructor behaviors (Ellis, 2000, 2002; Goodboy & Myers, 2008). Also, classroom emotions such as emotional interest, perceived emotional support, emotional valence, and emotional work are organized according to their relationship to a motivational system and a wide range of unconditioned stimuli (Lang, Bradley, & Cuthbert, 1998) such as teacher confirmation, which raises more emotionally positive feelings among students (Andersen & Guerrero, 1998; Ellis, 2000, 2002; Goldman & Goodboy, 2014).

Emotional interest is the psychological excitement or happiness people get from actions or behaviors, and it is positively related to effective teaching practices and student motivation (Mazer, 2012, 2013). Another construct of classroom emotion is perceived emotional support, which is "the extent to which students perceive that their instructor is available and able to provide emotional support about topics that are directly and indirectly related to school" (Titsworth, Quinlan, & Mazer, 2010, p. 438). Essentially, students have emotional support in the classroom when they perceive their teacher as giving them supporting messages, such as confirming messages. Perceived emotional support is positively correlated with student motivation (Titsworth et al., 2010). Another construct of classroom emotion is emotional valence, which is related to the extent to which students rate aspects of their classroom from positive to negative. In a class setting, when students view the situation as more positive (more valence), they are more likely to have higher motivation (Titsworth et al., 2010). Finally, emotional work is the amount of emotional energy individuals must exert in a particular setting (classroom, organization, etc.). For students, emotional work includes things like studying and/or thinking about course materials. Emotional work is negatively related to student motivation (Titsworth et al., 2010).

Student motivation and consequently classroom emotions are related to student self-esteem and self-perception. Human beings are more motivated and confident and function more cohesively while feeling they are cared about and supported by significant others (Behrends & Blatt, 1985). Actually, motivation, self-reliance, and confidence are directly related to individuals' experiential sets (Ryan, Stiller, & Lynch, 1994).

The role of self-perception and self-reliance in individuals' social and psychological life is emphasized by different theories such as terror management theory (Greenberg & Arndt, 2012). Terror management theory aims to explain how people's awareness of their mortality affects their psychological functioning. It posits that individuals develop faith in worldviews that help them feel significant and enhance their self-esteem. As with faith, self-esteem and motivation are also related to one's positive feeling about oneself, especially in instructional contexts such as classrooms.

Student motivation is also influenced by inside and outside cultural factors. Explaining the influence of culture on student motivation, personal investment (PI) (Maehr & Braskamp, 1986) asserts that in a cross-/intercultural context, differences in the sense of self, perceived goals, and facilitating conditions explain the student motivational variation (King & McInerney, 2013). Students with higher self-esteem or with more-established perceived goals are more motivated in educational context.

The influence of self-efficacy on student motivation is evident in how students' self-perception and the confirmation they receive from their teachers influence their performance in educational settings. Previous research on self-efficacy has shown the role of self-related constructs such as academic self-concept (the confidence one has in oneself in academic performance), sense of purpose (the sense of identifying oneself with education and perceiving the importance of education in one's life), and self-reliance (the identification of oneself as a competent and independent individual within the academic context) in improving achievement-related behavior (Bandura, 1997; King & McInerney, 2013). Also, previous studies revealed higher amount of teacher confirmation enhances students' self-esteem and motivation to participate in class activities (Goodboy & Myers, 2008). Therefore, a relationship between teacher confirmation with student motivation and classroom emotions is likely to occur. Thus, the following hypotheses are presented:

H1: Teacher confirmation is positively related to student motivation, emotional interest, perceived emotional support, and emotional valence in US and Finnish college students.

H2: Teacher confirmation is negatively related to emotional work in US and Finnish college students.

From a sociopsychological point of view, people's self-concepts are formed as part of their search for meaning in the context of the culture they live in and so are affected by cross-cultural differences (Heine, 2001). While the common understanding of self-perception is rooted in an independent reading of personality, due to the necessities the social context sets, in many Asian cultures, personality is constructed interdependently (Markus & Kitayama, 1998). Because of this influence of culture on self-concept, a contextual investigation of self-regard is a proper opportunity to perceive (cross)cultural variations in sociopsychological structures such as confirmation, motivation, and emotional reactions which develop in relation to the individual's perception of self (Heine, 2001).

Although the cultural differences in self-perception have been studied in a number of cultural contexts, more research is needed to determine the different cultural aspects of self-perception. For example, Heine et al. (1999) represented this cultural difference in self-perception among North American and East Asian cultures. This anthropological, sociological, and psychological study of self-regard in Japan refuted the universality of the idea that people seek positive self-regard and empirically showed insufficient evidence of a need for positive self-regard among the Japanese as the construction of self and regard is different in this culture than in the more widely investigated North American cultures (Heine et al., 1999). However, less research has been conducted outside North America (Heine et al., 1999), and there is not enough information available regarding the possible differences between North America and other cultures, such as in Nordic countries. It is important to make such a comparison as there are cultural and educational differences between Nordic countries such as Finland and US American culture.

With a student-centered approach, US classrooms are known for having small power distance and high intimacy between students and instructors (Neuliep, 1997). Anderson and Powell (1991) stated that US classrooms predominantly adopt the Socratic ideal, where teacher and student pursue knowledge together through interactions. Thus, students have higher autonomy, and openly disagreeing with teachers is common in US classrooms (Smithee, Greeblatt, & Eland, 2004). In addition, teachers using authoritative power are generally rejected by US students (Goldman et al., 2014). Students in the United States expect their instructors to exhibit confirming behaviors and to meet their needs individually (Ellis, 2000; Kopp, Zinn, Finney, & Jurich, 2011). In a study exploring cultural differences between students in the United States and Taiwan, Niehoff, Turnley, Yen, and Sheu (2001) reported US students expect greater teacher availability, have lower preference for mandatory class attendance, and are more prone to question their grades.

From the instructors' perspective, intimacy between students and instructors is manifested through affinity-seeking and immediacy behaviors. Affinity-seeking is the desire of an individual to be perceived positively by others. Immediacy has been defined as "the extent of the use of communication behaviors that enhance closeness and reduce physical and/or psychological distance between communicators" (Zhang, 2005, p. 112). US instructors tend to use various strategies to establish close relationships with students to facilitate the learning process. However, such closeness between instructors and students in the United States can also be considered "superficial," and it hardly lasts beyond the end of the course (Roach & Byrne, 2001).

The educational system in Finland is famous for being egalitarian and efficient. Finland has gained international recognition for its consistently outstanding performance in the Program for International Student Assessment (PISA). Like the United States, the Finnish classroom also belongs to a low-context culture and is defined by its small power distance. However, one way in which the Finnish school system differs significantly from the US system is in instructor intimacy. Unlike in other countries, students' academic performance is negatively associated with teacher–student relations in Finland (Linnakylä & Malin, 2008). Finnish students also showed relatively low school satisfaction, and the student–teacher relationship in Finland was the most negative among all researched countries in a study exploring quality of life of students in 1991 (Linnakylä, 1996; Linnakylä & Malin, 2008). The poor teacher–student relationship might be due to the fact that both students and instructors in Finland tend to be verbally and nonverbally low expressive (McCroskey, Richmond, Sallinen, Fayer, & Barraclough, 1995). Students rarely receive encouragement from teachers. In addition, teachers in Finland tend to minimize interactions with students and their families after school to keep a "professional distance." Thus, the differences in instructor intimacy and teacher–student relationship between the United States and Finland are likely to impact on students' classroom learning.

The similarities and differences in teacher confirmation and learning outcomes between the United States and Finland might help explain cross-cultural differences in teachers' communication styles. As there are no comparisons of teacher confirmation and learning outcomes (student motivation and classroom emotions) between these two different educational cultures, it is difficult to cross-culturally understand these relationships. Therefore, to further our understanding of the relationship between teacher confirmation and learning outcomes in the United States and Finland, particularly the instructional differences, the following research questions are proposed:

RQ1: To what extent do the relationships between teacher confirmation and each of emotional interest, perceived emotional support, emotional valence, emotional work, and student motivation differ between US and Finnish college students?

RQ2: To what extent does nation moderate the relationships between teacher confirmation and emotional interest, emotional support, emotional valence, emotional work, and student motivation?

5.3 Method

5.3.1 Participants and Procedures

A total of 478 participants in the United States (n = 350) and Finland (n = 128) participated in this study. The US participants ranged in age from 18 to 32 (M = 21.65, SD = 3.24), while Finnish participants ranged in age from 18 to

64 (M $=$ 28.22, SD $=$ 8.44). In the United States, men (n $=$ 175) and women (n $=$ 175) were equal in number. In Finland, women (n $=$ 76, 59.4%) were more prevalent than men (n $=$ 52, 40.6%). The participants from both nations had relatively diverse educational backgrounds. In the United States, 30.3% had completed high school (n $=$ 106), 36.6% had a 2-year degree (n $=$ 128), 21.4% had a bachelor's or equivalent degree (n $=$ 75), 10% had some graduate education (n $=$ 35), and 1.7% (n $=$ 6) had the equivalent of an MA. In Finland, 8.6% completed high school (n $=$ 11), 58.6% had a 2-year degree (n $=$ 75), 12.5% had a bachelor's or equivalent degree (n $=$ 16), and 1.6% (n $=$ 2) had the equivalent of an MA. Regarding areas of study (major), in the United States, 20.3% reported sciences (n $=$ 71), 10.9% education (n $=$ 38), 4.3% communication (n $=$ 15), 3.4% history (n $=$ 12), 8.9% music (n $=$ 31), 20.9% languages (n $=$ 73), 8.6% IT (n $=$ 30), 4.3% mathematics (n $=$ 15), 4.3% sociology (n $=$ 15), 4.3% psychology (n $=$ 15), 8% business (n $=$ 28), and 2% sports (n $=$ 7). In Finland, 10.2% reported sciences (n $=$ 13), 7% education (n $=$ 9), 7% communication (n $=$ 9), 5.5% history (n $=$ 7), 4.7% music (n $=$ 6), 14.8% languages (n $=$ 19), 3.9% IT (n $=$ 5), 3.1% mathematics (n $=$ 4), 3.9% sociology (n $=$ 5), 4.7% psychology (n $=$ 6), 3.9% business (n $=$ 5), 7.8% sports (n $=$ 10), and 23.4% were undeclared (n $=$ 30).

Before data collection took place, the English version of the survey was translated into Finnish through a process of back translation. Two independent bilingual Finnish English speakers translated the English version of the survey into Finnish. The translated version of the survey was significantly (89%) similar to the English version as the kappa reliability statistic ($\kappa =$ 0.89) is well above the 0.70 threshold for reliability. Data were collected in 2014 and 2015 through self-administered online and paper surveys in Finland and the United States. Both online and paper versions of the questionnaires were identical, and students were given paper or online versions based on their accessibility. Participants in both nations were contacted via classroom announcements after appropriate institutional review board approval. Participants were awarded extra credit for completion of the survey. The confidential survey took approximately 20–30 minutes to complete. Students were notified that they were permitted to end their participation at any time.

5.3.2 Instruments

5.3.2.1 Teacher Confirmation

Perception of teacher confirmation was assessed using Ellis's (2000) Teacher Confirmation Scale (TCS). There are three dimensions to the teacher confirmation scale: teachers' responses to questions (e.g., "My instructor takes time to answer students' questions fully"), demonstrated interest in students and their learning (e.g., "My instructor makes an effort to get to know students"), and style of teaching (e.g., "My instructor uses an interactive teaching style"). A total of 16 items were measured using a 5-point Likert-type scale ranging from 0 (strongly disagree) to 4 (strongly

Table 5.1 Teacher confirmation scale change in model fit

	χ^2	df	CFI	RMSEA
All items (16 items)	6365.94	303	0.80	0.15
Reduced model (10 items)	1308.59	90	0.95	0.08
Δteacher confirmation	5098.74	213	0.15	0.07

agree). Previous Cronbach's alpha[1] reliabilities have ranged from 0.83 to 0.95. Larwin and Harvey's (2012) jackknifing procedure was followed to assess the factorial structure of the teacher confirmation scale in Finland. As revealed in Table 5.1, a final model of 10 items demonstrated appropriate fit (1, 2, 3, 6, 7, 8, 10, 13, 14, and 15). Thus, these items were retained for the final analysis for both nations (see Table 5.1 for the change in model fit). Moreover, pursuant with Muethel and Bond (2013), the researchers tested the scalar equivalence between the United States and Finland. A scalar invariance test (($\chi2(72) = 1297.20$, CFI $= 0.95$, and RMSEA $= 0.04$), Δ $\chi2(18) = 11.39$, $p < ns$) revealed that scalar equivalence does exist. Essentially, the same modified factor structure fits in both nations. Basically, it shows that US American and Finnish students have the same perception of the questions of the examined scales.

5.3.2.2 Student Motivation

Respondent perceptions of motivation toward specific classes were assessed. To that end, a scale developed by Beatty, Forst, and Stewart (1986) and refined by Richmond (1990) and Christophel (1990) was used. This 16-item semantic differential scale is composed of bipolar adjectives including motivated–unmotivated, interested–uninterested, involved–uninvolved, stimulated–not stimulated, want to study–don't want to study, inspired–uninspired, challenged–unchallenged, invigorated–uninvigorated, enthused–unenthused, excited–unexcited, aroused–not aroused, fascinated–not fascinated, not dreading it–dreading it, important–unimportant, useful–useless, and helpful–harmful. The reliability of this measure has been established in previous studies with alpha coefficients ranging from 0.93 to 0.96^2 (Christophel, 1990). Larwin and Harvey's (2012) jackknifing procedure was again followed to assess the factorial structure of the student motivation scale. As revealed in Table 5.2, a final model of 6 items demonstrated appropriate fit (4, 5, 7, 8, 9, and 12). Thus, these items were retained for the final analysis for both nations (see Table 5.2 for the change in model fit). Moreover, in accordance with Muethel and Bond (2013), the researchers tested the scalar equivalence between the United States and Finland. A scalar invariance test (($\chi2(9) = 149.42$, CFI $= 0.99$, and

---

[1]This shows the measure (scale) functions similarly in different contexts. If a scale does not perform similarly in different contexts or groups, it is not a reliable measure of a construct.

[2]This means previous studies have used the same scale, and they also found and report it to be extremely reliable.

Table 5.2 Student motivation scale change in model fit

	χ^2	df	CFI	RMSEA
All items (16 items)	2387.66	104	0.83	0.22
Reduced model (six items)	202.73	24	0.95	0.11
Δstudent confirmation	2184.93	80	0.12	0.11

RMSEA $= 0.18$), $\Delta \chi^2(15) = 53.31$, $p < 0.001$) revealed that scalar equivalence does not hold. Nonequivalence can occur for a variety of reasons, such as response bias, answering in extreme cases, and/or linguistic misunderstandings (Byrne & Campbell, 1999; Muethel & Bond, 2013). All scores in this study have been standardized to help adjust for nonequivalence. As the samples of the US American and Finnish students are different in terms of size, cultural backgrounds, etc., standard statistical calculations were done to modify the results based on these differences.

5.3.2.3 Classroom Emotions

Classroom emotions were assessed using Titsworth et al.'s (2010) Classroom Emotions Scale (CES). There are three dimensions to this scale: emotional valence (e.g., "I would generally describe the emotions I feel toward this class as positive"), emotional work (e.g., "Interacting with this instructor requires a lot of emotional energy"), and emotional support (e.g., "My instructor is willing to discuss my feelings and emotions about school"). Participants used a 5-point Likert scale with response options ranging from 1 (strongly disagree) to 5 (strongly agree). Confirmatory factor analysis (CFA) revealed the three-dimensional scale was an acceptable[3] fit in Finland ($\chi^2 (28) = 170.58$, p < 0.001, CFI $=0.00$, RMSEA $=0.20$). Even following the jackknifing procedure (multiple reiterations), an acceptable model fit could not be found for the scale. Thus, the Classroom Emotions Scale was not considered in the final analysis.

5.3.2.4 Emotional Interest

Emotional Interest was assessed with a 9-item measure from Mazer (2012). The scale assesses students' emotional interest in a specific course using a 5-point Likert scale ranging from 1 (strongly disagree) to 5 (strongly agree). Previous Cronbach's alpha reliability ranged from 0.95 to 0.97. CFA revealed the emotional interest scale did not function appropriately in Finland ($\chi^2 (27) = 995.13, p < 0.001$, CFI $=0.83$, RMSEA $=0.27$).

---

[3]This means the result is significantly strong enough to not have occurred by accident.

Table 5.3 Means, standard deviation, reliability coefficients, and correlations

Both nations

Variables	M	SD	α	(1)	(2)	(3)	(4)
(1) Responding to questions	1.89	1.27	0.96	–			
(2) Demonstrating interest	1.99	1.29	0.96	0.91**	–		
(3) Interactive teaching style	1.89	1.19	0.95	0.90**	0.95**	–	
(4) Student motivation	3.24	1.38	0.98	0.57**	0.64**	0.63**	–

Finland

Variables	M	SD	α	(1)	(2)	(3)	(4)
(1) Responding to questions	2.88	1.22	0.80	–			
(2) Demonstrating interest	2.89	0.82	0.91	0.70**	–		
(3) Interactive teaching style	2.55	1.15	0.83	0.70**	0.88**	–	
(4) Student motivation	3.59	1.15	0.92	−0.12	0.01	−0.04	–

United States

Variables	M	SD	α	(1)	(2)	(3)	(4)
(1) Responding to questions	1.54	1.09	0.97	–			
(2) Demonstrating interest	1.66	1.17	0.98	0.97**	–		
(3) Interactive teaching style	1.65	1.12	0.98	0.98**	0.98**	–	
(4) Student motivation	3.11	1.44	0.92	0.80**	0.83**	0.82**	–

Note: $* p < 0.05$, $** p < 0.001$

5.4 Results

To address *H1* and *H2*, Pearson correlations were conducted (see Table 5.1 for correlations). H1 predicted there would be a positive correlation between teacher confirmation (responding to questions, demonstrating interest, and interactive teaching style) and student motivation, emotional interest, emotional support, and emotional valence. For the combined sample (United States and Finland), after removing classroom emotion and emotional interest, H1 was partially supported as the three factors of teacher confirmation were positively correlated with student motivation. However, when analyzing the nations separately, there are differences to note. In the United States, student motivation was positively correlated with responding to questions ($r = 0.24$, $p < 0.001$), demonstrating interest ($r = 0.83$, $p < 0.001$), and an interactive teaching style ($r = 0.82$, $p < 0.001$). In Finland, there were no significant correlations between student motivation and the three dimensions of teacher confirmation. Thus, H1 was partly supported (Table 5.3).

H2 predicted a negative correlation between teacher confirmation and emotional work for both the American and Finnish samples. However, because the three-dimensional scale of classroom emotions was unacceptable in Finland, H2 was not considered for further investigation.

RQ1 asked the extent to which the correlations between teacher confirmation and each of emotional interest, perceived emotional support, emotional valence, emotional work, and student motivation differed between the United States and Finland. A Fisher's z comparison of correlations was computed. Significant differences

Table 5.4 Correlations coefficients and their corresponding Fisher z

Variables	(1)	(2)	(3)	(4)	(5)
(1) Responding to questions	–				
(2) Demonstrating interest	14.88[a]	–			
(3) Interactive teaching style	5.77[a]	14.52[a]	–		
(4) Student motivation	4.33[a]	1.48	3.55[a]	–	

[a]Statistical difference in the correlations using Fisher's r-to-z statistic ($p < 0.05$).

Table 5.5 Hierarchical regression results for responding to questions (teacher confirmation)

Variables	Model 1	Model 2
Intercept	1.54	−0.34
Finland	0.47***	1.28***
Student motivation		0.66***
Student motivation*Finland		−0.97***
F	132.21***	203.19***
ΔF		186.93***
R^2	0.22	0.56
R^2_{adj}	0.22	0.56

Note: * $p < 0.05$, **$p < 0.001$, ***$p < 0.0001$

between the United States and Finland were observed. The results showed significant differences between correlations of teacher confirmation with student motivation[4]. These results are displayed in Table 5.4.

RQ2 asked the extent to which nation moderated the relationships between teacher confirmation and emotional interest, emotional support, emotional valence, emotional work, and student motivation. Three multiple regressions were constructed with two models for each regression. In each regression, a dimension of teacher confirmation (responding to questions, demonstrating interest, and interactive teaching style) served as the outcome variables. The criterion variables were student motivation, nation (United States $= 0$; Finland $= 1$), and the cross product of nation*student motivation. The Classroom Emotions Scale and Emotional Interest Scales were not included in the final analysis as the CFAs suggested these scales' factor structures were not an acceptable fit. Student motivation was mean centered before the cross product was generated (for full regression results, see Tables 5.5, 5.6 and 5.7).

In model 1, for responding to questions, nation was entered into the regression ($R^2 = 0.22$). In model 2, student motivation and the cross product testing if nation moderated the relationship between nation and confirmation were entered into the regression ($R^2 = 0.56$, $\Delta F = 186.93$, $p < 0.0001$). Model 2 was a significant improvement over model 1. Based on model 2, student motivation has a significant positive effect on the perception/belief that teachers respond to questions ($b = 0.66$,

---

[4]This means the correlations between teacher confirmation and student motivation in the United States are different from the same correlations in Finland.

Table 5.6 Hierarchical regression results for demonstrating interest (teacher confirmation)

Variables	Model 1	Model 2
Intercept	1.67	−0.42
Finland	0.42***	1.12***
Student motivation		0.72***
Student motivation*Finland		−0.86***
F	101.45***	223.73***
ΔF		234.91***
R^2	0.18	0.59
R^2_{adj}	0.17	0.58

Note: * $p < 0.05$, ** $p < 0.001$, *** $p < 0.0001$

Table 5.7 Hierarchical regression results for interactive teaching style (teacher confirmation)

Variables	Model 1	Model 2
Intercept	1.65	−0.32
Finland	0.33***	1.11***
Student motivation		0.74***
Student motivation*Finland		−0.95***
F	59.69***	186.21***
ΔF		221.73***
R^2	0.11	0.54
R^2_{adj}	0.11	0.54

[1]* $p < 0.05$, ** $p < 0.001$, *** $p < 0.0001$

$p < 0.0001$). Nation did in fact moderate the relationship between student motivation and perception/belief that teachers respond to questions. In this case, compared to Americans, the more motivated Finnish students are, the less they perceive/believe teachers respond to their questions and/or confirm them ($b = -0.97$, $p < 0.0001$).

In model 1, for demonstrating interest, nation was entered into the regression ($R^2 = 0.18$). In model 2, student motivation and the cross product testing if nation moderated the relationship between nation and confirmation were entered into the regression ($R^2 = 0.59$, $\Delta F = 234.91$, $p < 0.0001$). Model 2 was a significant improvement over model 1. Based on model 2, student motivation has a significant positive effect on the perception/belief that teachers demonstrate interest in students ($b = 0.72, p < 0.0001$). Nation did in fact moderate the relationship between student motivation and perception/belief that teachers demonstrate interest in students. In this case, compared to Americans, the more motivated Finnish students are, the less they perceive/believe teachers demonstrate an interest in them and/or confirm them ($b = -0.86$, $p < 0.0001$).

In model 1, for interactive teaching style, nation was entered into the regression ($R2 = 0.11$). In model 2, student motivation and the cross product testing if nation moderated the relationship between nation and confirmation were entered into the regression ($R2 = 0.54$, $\Delta F = 221.73$, $p < 0.0001$). Model 2 was a significant improvement over model 1. Based on model 2, student motivation has a significant positive effect on the perception/belief that teachers use an interactive teaching style ($b = 0.74, p < 0.0001$). Nation did in fact moderate the relationship between student motivation and perception/belief that teachers demonstrate an interactive teaching style. In this case, compared to Americans, the more motivated Finnish students are, the less they perceive/believe teachers have an interactive teaching style and/or confirm them (b $= -0.95$, $p < 0.0001$).

5.5 Discussion

The objective of this study was to evaluate the utility of teacher confirmation as a culturally universal pedagogical behavior. To do this, the relationships between teacher confirmation and student motivation in US and Finnish classrooms were first analyzed. Second, the way teacher confirmation influences student motivation across Finnish and US classrooms was evaluated. For the entire sample, H1 was partially supported, which suggests that when US and Finnish students are combined, teacher confirmation is positively correlated with student motivation, which confirms previous research asserting increased teacher confirmation is related to heightened student motivation and more positive emotional outcomes (Goldman & Goodboy, 2014). However, when the data were split between the two nations, the correlations were not as clear. The Finnish students' motivation is not correlated with their perception of teacher confirmation. This is in line with the result of the previous investigation of student motivation and teacher–student relationship in Finland, which showed the Finnish teacher–student relationship as being the weakest (in 1991) and the second weakest (in 2003) among the Nordic countries, despite Finnish students' positive view of the role of education in their future (Linnakylä & Malin, 2008). Linnakylä and Malin (2008) explained that Finnish students' high performance does not guarantee teacher and peer acceptance and that Finnish students, more than those in other Nordic countries, believe that the teachers do not listen to what the younger generation say. It is most likely that this approach to the teacher–student relationship at universities is in the continuation of the students' perception of the teacher–student relationship in the previous educational stages. *H2* tested whether teacher confirmation was negatively related to emotional work. As the factorial structure of the student emotion scale could not be confirmed for the present study, this hypothesis cannot be examined.

RQ1 investigated the possible difference in the relationship between teacher confirmation, emotional interest, perceived emotional support, emotional valence, emotional work, and student motivation between US and Finnish college students. The results showed a higher amount of perceived teacher confirmation and student motivation for the US students, while the results for the student emotions subscale could not be investigated due to the lack of structural factor confirmation. The finding is consistent with PI theory (Maehr & Braskamp, 1986), which explains that cultural influences from inside or outside of society affect student motivation in academic settings. According to PI theory, due to cultural variations, students from different cultures have different sense of self, perceived goals, and facilitating conditions, which results in motivational variation (King & McInerney, 2013).

The analysis showed Finnish students have less motivation and perceived teacher confirmation than US students. This is in line with the previous research that modestly reports Finnish students have lower student engagement in school life compared to other Nordic countries (Linnakylä & Välijärvi, 2005). However, it is more likely that the Finnish students' lack of motivation is not related to their senses of self-reliance and purpose. As already mentioned, both US and Finnish classrooms share the characteristics of low power distance, low context, higher autonomy, and general higher self-reliance (Linnakylä & Malin, 2008; Neuliep, 1997). In the same way, a previous study reported Finnish students had a more positive view of the benefits of education for the future of students (higher sense of purpose) compared to the other Nordic countries (Linnakylä & Malin, 2008). Higher self-reliance and sense of purpose are related to higher student motivation (King & McInerney, 2013).

However, Finnish students' lack of motivation could be related to other factors such as students' feeling toward school. Linnakylä and Malin (2008) reported exclusion due to the weak peer support, low teacher intimacy, and relatively low school satisfaction as a major element in the disengagement of students in Finnish schools. They showed that students with a lower (academic) self-concept and self-efficacy are more disengaged and less satisfied with school. As mentioned before, cross-cultural instructional self-concept studies are mostly focused on the American-Asian context.

Another major effect in student motivation is facilitating conditions. Theoretically, the financial assistance Finnish students receive from the government and the free access they have to colleges and universities should make pursuing higher education easier for the Finns and increase their educational motivation. However, practically, Finnish students recorded less motivation than Americans. Finnish students do not feel the financial urge to compete as much as their US counterparts. Finland has a relatively small population, there are fewer international students migrating to Finland for education, and Finnish students also receive a monthly study allowance from the government (Students, 2014). However, despite this monthly study allowance, many students need to work. Furthermore, Finnish students enjoy flexibility in the completion of their studies. It is not uncommon to take 7 or more years to obtain a bachelor's and a master's degree instead of the official 5 years. Thus, Finnish students feel less pressure in educational contexts to work on their emotional relationships and enjoy higher levels of emotional interest. Meanwhile, US classrooms are more competitive. There is national and global competition for better educational positions and places. At the same time, students and researchers from around the world migrate to US universities where there is a higher research capacity (Marginson, 2006). Financial reasons can intensify competition among US students seeking to pursue a postsecondary education (Davies & Hammack, 2005). Students in the United States, unlike in Finland, pay tuition fees, and there are different subsidies to help students financially (Marginson, 2006). This intense competition to enter the undergraduate education system will also result in more intensive competition to enter postgraduate programs. It is likely that competition in US classrooms makes students put more effort or motivation into presenting themselves to their teachers and instructors and into making emotional connections in educational contexts. In 2014, 103,900 Finnish students attended high school, while there were 89,900 students attending undergraduate programs in the nation (Number of university students, 2015). In 2015, while 50.1 million US students attended high school, 20.1 million students are expected to attend US universities and colleges (Fast facts, n.d.). Two explanations are possible for the lower motivation of the Finnish students despite the higher financial facilitation they received. First, financial assistance may not affect student educational motivation; second, the possible positive effect of the financial assistance on Finnish students may be neutralized by the demotivating effect of other elements such as school exclusion (state of emotional and/or physical detachment from and losing connection with school or peer groups) and low self-concept.

RQ2 investigated the moderating role of nation on the relationship between teacher confirmation, student motivation, and emotions. The results showed, when nation is not taken into consideration, student motivation has a positive effect on teacher confirmation subscales. But when considering the role of nation, the data showed the more Finnish students are motivated, the less they perceive teachers responding their questions, demonstrate an interest in them, or follow an interactive teaching style. Previous research has shown that despite good academic achievement, weak student–teacher relationship needs to be improved to enhance school engagement and satisfaction (Haapasalo, Välimaa, & Kannas, 2010). Compared to the US and other Nordic countries, Finnish students have more negative feelings toward school, which was found to be related to the teacher–student relationship and school culture (Malin & Linnakyllä, 2001). The Finnish education system heavily emphasizes the autonomy of students including the idea that the definition of the needs for guidance and searching for support services is done by the students (Jääskelä, Nykänen, & Tynjälä, 2016; Sahlberg, 2007). Along with student autonomy, as mentioned before, Finnish students, more than other Nordic country students, perceive that their teachers do not listen to them (Linnakylä & Malin, 2008). It is likely such practices and perceptions result in a school culture that pushed the students to be independent of the teachers, regardless of their approach to the role of education in their future. Therefore, despite the higher motivation of the students, they could perceive frequent teacher's response to class questions, teacher's involvement and demonstration of interest in classroom activities, and teacher's interactive method to be opposing to their schooling culture. However, student autonomy is a value pursued by various nations' educational systems such as in the United States, despite the variations at the level of autonomy (Levesque, Zuehlke, Stanek, & Ryan, 2004). Levesque et al. (2004) found out American students are less autonomous but more competent than German students. Future research comparing Finnish and US students could provide a better understanding of the dynamics of student motivation and teacher confirmation.

5.6 Implications

These results could have practical implications for educational decision makers in Finland. The present study proposes more innovative approaches and methods for integrating and relating teacher confirmation techniques to student motivation and emotional interest. Theoretically, the study implied that inconsistency between students' cultural background and classroom cultural values could affect students' perceptions of teacher confirmation techniques, which in turn could affect the utility of teacher confirmation as a culturally universal teaching behavior (McCroskey & McCroskey, 2006). The results suggest teacher confirmation behaviors, as followed in the United States, may not be as effective in the Finnish educational context.

5.7 Limitations

As with all studies, there were some limitations. First, although the focus of the study was on college/university students, the current sample is limited in the fact that it is a convenience sample. Future studies could be more representative if they were random samples of college/university student populations. Second, the method of data collection for this study was self-reports. While self-reports provide information about participants' perceptions, other methods of data collection, such as classroom observations, interviews, teacher self-reports, and other reports, would provide different perspectives on these crucial issues. Also, due to differences between seminars and lectures, future studies could focus on only one of these class formats.

5.8 Conclusions

Overall, the current study contributes to our understanding of the relationships between teacher confirmation and student motivation in university/college classrooms in Finland and the United States. Students' perceptions of confirming techniques, emotional interest, and motivation in Finland differed significantly from those in the United States. Ultimately, researchers, as well as instructors, would be well served by recognizing that instructional practices in the United States might not always be suitable for non-US-based educational systems. At the same time, more confirmation from a teacher could facilitate the process of learning as it establishes higher amounts of positive emotion among the students and heightens their motivation. Future cross-/intercultural research is asked for to study the academic self-concept across other cultures such as the Nordic countries, which, although they share more cultural characteristics with the US than Asian cultures, nonetheless represent major differences, as is the case in the present study.

References

Andersen, P. A., & Guerrero, L. K. (1998). *Handbook of communication and emotion: Research, theory, and constructs*. San Diego, CA: Academic Press.

Anderson, J. F., & Powell, R. (1991). Intercultural communication and the classroom. In L. A. Samovar & R. W. Porter (Eds.), *Intercultural communication: A reader* (6th ed., pp. 208–214). Belmont, CA: Wadsworth.

Bandura, A. (1997). *Self-efficacy: The exercise of control*. New York: Freeman.

Beatty, M. J., Forst, E. C., & Stewart, R. A. (1986). Communication apprehension and motivation as predictors of public speaking duration. *Communication Education, 35*, 143–146.

Behrends, R. S., & Blatt, S. J. (1985). Internalization and psychological development throughout the life cycle. *The Psychoanalytic Study of the Child, 40*, 11–39.

Brophy, J. (1998). *Motivating students to learn*. Boston: McGraw Hill.

Byrne, B. M., & Campbell, T. L. (1999). Cross-cultural comparisons and the presumption of equivalent measurement and theoretical structure: A look beneath the surface. *Journal of Cross-Cultural Psychology, 30*, 555–574.

Chesebro, J. L., & McCroskey, J. C. (2001). The relationship of teacher clarity and immediacy with student state receiver apprehension, affect, and cognitive learning. *Communication Education, 50*, 59–68. https://doi.org/10.1080/03634520109379232.

Christophel, D. (1990). The relationships among teacher immediacy behaviors, student motivation, and learning. *Communication Education, 39*, 323–340. https://doi.org/10.1080/03634529009378813.

Christophel, D. M., & Gorham, J. (1995). A test-retest analysis of student motivation, teacher immediacy, and perceived sources of motivation and demotivation in college classes. *Communication Education, 44*, 292–316. https://doi.org/10.1080/03634529509379020.

Davies, S., & Hammack, F. M. (2005). The channeling of student competition in higher education: Comparing Canada and the U.S. *Journal of Higher Education, 76*, 89–106.

Edwards, C., Edwards, A., Torrens, A., & Beck, A. (2011). Confirmation and community: The relationships among teacher confirmation, classroom community, student motivation and learning. *Online Journal of Communication and Media Technologies, 1*, 17–43.

Ellis, K. (2000). Perceived teacher confirmation: The development and validation of an instrument and two studies of the relationship to cognitive and affective learning. *Human Communication Research, 26*, 264–291. https://doi.org/10.1111/j.1468-2958.2000.tb00758.x.

Ellis, K. (2002). Perceived parental confirmation: Development and validation of an instrument. *Southern Communication Journal, 67*, 319–334. https://doi.org/10.1080/10417940209373242.

Ellis, K. (2004). The impact of perceived teacher confirmation on receiver apprehension, motivation, and learning. *Communication Education, 53*, 1–20. https://doi.org/10.1080/0363452032000135742.

Fast facts. (n.d.). Retrieved from http://nces.ed.gov/fastfacts/display.asp?id=372

Frymier, A. B. (1994). A model of immediacy in the classroom. *Communication Quarterly, 42*, 133–144. https://doi.org/10.1080/01463379409369922.

Goldman, Z. W., Bolkan, S., & Goodboy, A. K. (2014). Revisiting the relationship between teacher confirmation and learning outcomes: Examining cultural differences in Turkish, Chinese, and American classrooms. *Journal of Intercultural Communication Research, 43*, 45–63. https://doi.org/10.1080/17475759.2013.870087.

Goldman, Z. W., & Goodboy, A. K. (2014). Making students feel better: Examining the relationships between teacher confirmation and college students' emotional outcomes. *Communication Education, 63*, 259–277. https://doi.org/10.1080/03634523.2014.920091.

Goodboy, A. K., Bolkan, S., Beebe, S. A., & Schultz, K. (2010). Cultural differences between United States and Chinese students' use of behavioral alteration techniques and affinity-seeking strategies with instructors. *Journal of Intercultural Communication Research, 39*, 1–12. https://doi.org/10.1080/17475759.2010.520834.

Goodboy, A. K., & Myers, S. A. (2008). The effect of teacher confirmation on student communication and learning outcomes. *Communication Education, 57*, 153–179. https://doi.org/10.1080/03634520701787777.

Greenberg, J., & Arndt, J. (2012). Terror management theory. In P. A. M. Van Lange, A. W. Kruglanski, & E. T. Higgins (Eds.), *Handbook of theories of social psychology* (pp. 398–415). Thousand Oaks, CA: Sage.

Haapasalo, I., Välimaa, R., & Kannas, L. (2010). How comprehensive school students perceive their psychosocial school environment. *Scandinavian Journal of Educational Research, 54*, 133–150. Retrieved from https://doi.org/10.1080/00313831003637915

Heggestad, R., & Kanfer, R. (2000). Individual differences in trait motivation: Development of the motivational trait questionnaire. *Educational Research, 33*, 751–776. https://doi.org/10.1016/S0883-0355(00)00049-5.

Heine, S. J. (2001). Self as cultural product: An examination of East Asian and North American selves. *Journal of Personality, 69*, 881–906. https://doi.org/10.1111/1467-6494.696168.

Heine, S. J., Lehman, D. R., Markus, H. R., & Kitayama, S. (1999). Is there a universal need for positive self-regard? *Psychological Review, 106*, 766–794. https://doi.org/10.1037/0033-295X.106.4.766.

Jääskelä, P., Nykänen, S., & Tynjälä, P. (2016). Models for the development of generic skills in Finnish higher education. *Journal of Further and Higher Education, 40*, 1–13. Retrieved from https://doi.org/10.1080/0309877X.2016.1206858.

Jaasma, M. A., & Koper, R. J. (1999). The relationship of student-faculty out-of-class communication to instructor immediacy and trust and to student motivation. *Communication Education, 48*, 41–47. https://doi.org/10.1080/03634529909379151.

King R. B., & McInerney, D. M. (2013). Culture's consequences on student motivation: Capturing cross-cultural universality and variability through personal investment theory. *Educational Psychologist, 49*, 175–198. Retrieved from https://doi.org/10.1080/00461520.2014.926813.

Kopp, J. P., Zinn, T. E., Finney, S. J., & Jurich, D. P. (2011). The development and evaluation of the academic entitlement questionnaire. *Measurement and Evaluation in Counseling and Development, 44*, 105–129.

Lang, P. J., Bradley, M. M., & Cuthbert, B. N. (1998). Emotion, motivation, and anxiety: Brain mechanisms and psychophysiology. *Biological Psychiatry, 44*, 1248–1263. Retrieved from https://doi.org/10.1016/S0006-3223(98)00275-3

Larwin, K., & Harvey, M. (2012). A demonstration of a systematic item-reduction approach using structural equation-modeling. *Practical Assessment, Research & Evaluation, 17*(2), 1–19.

Levesque, C., Zuehlke, A. N., Stanek, L. R., & Ryan, R. M. (2004). Autonomy and competence in German and American university students: A comparative study based on self-determination theory. *Journal of Educational Psychology, 96*, 68–84. https://doi.org/10.1037/0022-0663.96.1.68.

Linnakylä, P. (1996). Quality of school life in Finnish comprehensive school: A comparative view. *Scandinavian Journal of Educational Research, 40*, 69–85. https://doi.org/10.1080/0031383960400105.

Linnakylä, P., & Malin, A. (2008). Finnish students' school engagement profiles in the light of PISA 2003. *Scandinavian Journal of Educational Research, 52*, 583–602. https://doi.org/10.1080/00313830802497174.

Linnakylä, P., & Välijärvi, J. (2005). *Arvon mekin ansaitsemme. Kansainvälinen arviointi suomalaisen koulun kehittämiseksi* (Worthy of recognition? International assessment and the development of the Finnish school; in Finnish). Jyväskylä, Finland: PS-kustannus.

Maehr, M. L., & Braskamp, L. A. (1986). *The motivation factor: A theory of personal investment*. Lexington, MA: Lexington.

Malin, A., & Linnakyllä, P. (2001). Multilevel modelling in repeated measures of the quality of Finnish school life. *Scandinavian Journal of Educational Research, 45*, 145–166. Retrieved from https://doi.org/10.1080/00313830120052732

Marginson, S. (2006). Dynamics of national and global competition in higher education. *Higher Education, 52*, 1–39. https://doi.org/10.1001/s10734-004-7649-x.

Markus, H. R., & Kitayama, S. (1998). The cultural psychology of personality. *Journal of Cross-Cultural Psychology, 29*, 63–87. https://doi.org/10.1177/0022022198291004.

Martin, M. M., Chesebro, J. L., & Mottet, T. P. (1997). Students' perceptions of instructors' socio-communicative style and the influence on instructor credibility and situational motivation. *Communication Research Reports, 17*, 431–440. https://doi.org/10.1080/08824099709388686.

Mazer, J. P. (2012). Development and validation of the student interest and engagement scales. *Communication Methods and Measures, 6*, 99–125. https://doi.org/10.1080/19312458.2012.679244.

Mazer, J. P. (2013). Associations among teacher communication behaviors, student interest, and engagement: A validity test. *Communication Education, 62*, 86–96. Retrieved from https://doi.org/10.1080/03634523.2012.731513

McCroskey, J. C., & McCroskey, L. L. (2006). Instructional communication: The historical perspective. In T. P. Mottet, V. P. Richmond, & J. C. McCroskey (Eds.), *Handbook of instructional communication: Rhetorical and relational perspectives* (pp. 33–47). Boston: Allyn & Bacon.

McCroskey, J. C., Richmond, V. P., Sallinen, A., Fayer, J. M., & Barraclough, R. A. (1995). A cross-cultural and multi-behavioral analysis of the relationship between nonverbal immediacy and teacher evaluation. *Communication Education, 44*, 281–291. https://doi.org/10.1080/03634529509379019.

Muethel, M., & Bond, M. H. (2013). National context and individual employees' trust of the out-group: The role of societal trust. *Journal of International Business Studies, 44*, 312–333.

Neuliep, J. W. (1997). A cross-cultural comparison of teacher immediacy in American and Japanese college classrooms. *Communication Research, 24*, 431–451. https://doi.org/10.1177/009365097024004006.

Niehoff, B. P., Turnley, W. H., Yen, H. R., & Sheu, C. (2001). Exploring cultural differences in classroom expectations of students from the United States and Taiwan. *Journal of Education for Business, 76*, 289.

Number of university students decreased and that of degrees increased in 2014. (2015, May 6). Retrieved from http://www.stat.fi/til/yop/2014/yop_2014_2015-05-06_tie_001_en.html

Pajares, F., & Schunk, D. H. (2002). Self and self-belief in psychology and education: A historical perspective. In J. Aronson (Ed.), *Improving academic achievements: Impact of psychological factors on education* (pp. 3–21). Orlando, FL: Elsevier.

Pogue, L. L., & Ahyun, K. (2006). The effect of teacher nonverbal immediacy and credibility on student motivation and affective learning. *Communication Education, 55*, 331–344. https://doi.org/10.1080/03634520600748623.

Richmond, V. P. (1990). Communication in the classroom: Power and motivation. *Communication Education, 39*, 181–195. Retrieved from https://doi.org/10.1080/03634529009378801

Roach, K. D., & Byrne, P. R. (2001). A cross-cultural comparison of instructor communication in American and German classrooms. *Communication Education, 50*, 1–14. https://doi.org/10.1080/03634520109379228.

Ryan, R. M., Stiller, J. D., & Lynch, J. H. (1994). Representations of relationships to teachers, parents, and friends as predictors of academic motivation and self-esteem. *The Journal of Early Adolescence, 14*, 226–249. https://doi.org/10.1177/027243169401400207.

Sahlberg, P. (2007). Education policies for raising student learning: The Finnish approach. *Journal of Education Policy, 22*, 147–171. Retrieved from https://doi.org/10.1080/02680930601158919

Schrodt, P., Turman, P. D., & Soliz, J. (2006). Perceived understanding as a mediator of perceived teacher confirmation and students' ratings of instruction. *Communication Education, 55*, 370–388. https://doi.org/10.1080/03634520600879196.

Schrodt, P., Witt, P. L., Turman, P. D., Myers, S. A., Barton, M. H., & Jernberg, K. A. (2009). Instructor credibility as a mediator of instructors' prosocial communication behaviors and students' learning outcomes. *Communication Education, 58*, 350–371. https://doi.org/10.1080/03634520902926851.

Smith, A., & Hume, E. C. (2005). Linking culture and ethics: A comparison of accountants' ethical belief systems in the individualism/collectivism and power distance contexts. *Journal of Business Ethics, 62*, 209–220. https://doi.org/10.1007/s10551-005-4773-1.

Smithee, M., Greeblatt, S. L., & Eland, A. (2004). *U.S. culture series: U.S. classroom culture.* NAFSA: Association of International Education Publications. Retrieved from http:// http:// www.nafsa.org/uploaded-Files/NAFSA_Home/Resource_Library_Assets/Publications_ Library/u.s.pdf

Students (2014, September 22). Retrieved from http://www.kela.fi/web/en/students.

Titsworth, S., Quinlan, M. M., & Mazer, J. P. (2010). Emotion in teaching and learning: Development and validation of the classroom emotions scale. *Communication Education, 59*, 431–452. https://doi.org/10.1080/03634521003746156.

Triandis, H. C., Bontempo, R., Villareal, M. J., Asai, M., & Lucca, N. (1988). Individualism and collectivism: Cross-cultural perspectives. *Journal of Personality and Social Psychology, 54*, 323–338.

Turman, P. D., & Schrodt, P. (2006). Student perceptions of teacher power as a function of perceived teacher confirmation. *Communication Education, 55*, 265–279. https://doi.org/10. 1080/03634520600702570.

Zhang, Q. (2005). Immediacy, humor, power distance, and classroom communication apprehension in Chinese college classrooms. *Communication Quarterly, 53*, 109–124. https://doi.org/10. 1080/01463370500056150.

Zhang, Q. (2007). Teacher misbehaviors as learning demotivators in college classrooms: A cross-cultural investigation in China, Germany, Japan, and the United States. *Communication Education, 56*, 209–227. https://doi.org/10.1080/03634520601110104.

Zhang, Q., & Huang, B. (2008). How does teacher clarity affect student learning? A multi-cultural test for the mediated effect. *Texas Speech Communication Journal, 33*, 10–19.

Zhang, Q., & Oetzel, J. G. (2006). Constructing and validating a teacher immediacy scale: A Chinese perspective. *Communication Education, 55*, 218–241. https://doi.org/10.1080/ 03634520600566231.

Chapter 6
Intercultural Barriers to Feedback in Study Abroad Settings

Elaine Boyd and David Donnarumma

6.1 Introduction

An increasing number of young people are studying abroad, typically in language settings "grounded in national English norms" (Jenkins, 2011, p.926). This can present multiple cultural challenges to students, not just in terms of lifestyle but specifically in how they master the two new language cultures they are operating in – that of generic academic English (L2Ac) as well as the expected discourse of their chosen specialist field (L2Sp). The progression and quality of their learning within these new cultures can depend on two factors: (a) their own cultural background (C1) and the consequent expectations they bring with them and (b) the way in which the university where they choose to study manages their learning in L2Ac and L2Sp. Naturally, there are multiple threads to their learning, but this chapter focuses on one key aspect – that of feedback.

Feedback is seen as an essential pedagogical tool (Race, 2001) in national English language academic settings. However, students' own cultural background (C1) and the influences this brings into the L2/culture abroad (C2) setting can affect how students perceive and value feedback as well as how they utilize it and thus, ultimately, how effective that feedback is at progressing their learning in L2Ac and L2Sp. Arguably, students today live in a world where various forms of feedback not only prevail but are actively sought in social media contexts (via likes and shares, etc.). Yet, in the high-stakes context of academic study in English language settings,

E. Boyd (✉)
University College, London, UK
e-mail: elaine.boyd@ucl.ac.uk

D. Donnarumma (✉)
BPP University, London, UK
e-mail: daviddonnarumma@bpp.com

© Springer Nature Singapore Pte Ltd. 2021
M. D. López-Jiménez, J. Sánchez-Torres (eds.), *Intercultural Competence Past, Present and Future*, Intercultural Communication and Language Education,
https://doi.org/10.1007/978-981-15-8245-5_6

the significance of feedback and the expectations around its force as a learning tool in those settings are not always recognized or understood by international students. This has the potentially damaging effect of slowing their progress in L2 and/or C2. Thus, investigating the potential barriers to understanding, together with proposing ways to improve the perceptions of and practices around feedback, seems critical.

Current literature on feedback in academic contexts generally investigates how feedback is received and suggests a variety of solutions to improve this (e.g., Hedgecock & Lefkowitz, 1994; Hyland & Hyland, 2006), but these studies do not fully consider how feedback is perceived by students. From the teachers' perspective, feedback is seen as critical to the effective acquisition of all competences in L2Ac and L2Sp, so it is nonnegotiable and is a much-used tool intended to progress learning quickly. Despite this belief, something is not working. Universities regularly report low satisfaction levels with how feedback is implemented and managed, and this is captured in their overall satisfaction statistics, despite a positive spin by the central universities organization, Universities UK, which reports:

> Universities frequently assess student satisfaction with feedback and assessment. In 2015, 77% of Non-Native Speaker respondents in Higher Education Institutions (HEIs) in England reported that assessment and marking criteria are fair and 67% reported that feedback has helped them clarify things they didn't understand. (Hammond, 2016)

The cited 67% is well below other statistics relating to course content and, if feedback is a key learning tool, shows a lost opportunity for these international students. It suggests there is a significant miscommunication in the channel between teachers and international students regarding the purpose, utility, and delivery of feedback.

In order to explore this apparent gap in understanding about feedback, this study investigates the perceptions of feedback and how it is managed in the light of students' own C1 norms and teachers' own beliefs about and understanding of feedback. The study focuses on whether the effectiveness of feedback is challenged by cultural differences and thus how far feedback supports international students' learning in an academic study setting. The study also pilots three new approaches to feedback, and the outcomes suggest that it is the teachers in the C2 who may need to adjust their management of feedback in all settings in order to reach a negotiated understanding with students from diverse C1 backgrounds.

6.2   Literature Review

This study cuts across several fields of previous research. Principally, there are studies into the impact of feedback in academic settings, but the intercultural nature of this investigation means it is necessary to also explore what studies of intercultural challenges in academia have reported, as well as considering the role and training of the teacher in the university setting under investigation.

As outlined above, current studies generally focus on how students receive feedback and look at ways in which this could be improved (e.g., Hedgecock & Lefkowitz, 1994; Hyland & Hyland, 2006). The focus is very much on helping students understand and utilize feedback rather than investigating how feedback is perceived by those receiving it. The studies tend to ignore the facet of an alternative worldview (C1) which may be the root cause of either a resistance to feedback or make it a challenge for students to apply in the most useful way for learning. Studies tend to focus on, for example, what kind of feedback to give and when or the management of feedback looking within the socio-culture of the university setting but without consideration of how C1 might affect students' perceptions or understanding of this feedback.

Additionally, the research has been heavily weighted toward feedback given on written English (the assumption perhaps being that this is where the challenge to progressing in L2Ac and L2Sp lies) even though students nowadays have to regularly give spoken presentations of their work to demonstrate understanding and fluency. This spoken mastery is important because it is where a face threat occurs, not just in their delivery but also in the consequent feedback. So we need to consider a more holistic view of feedback and how far that view travels outside both the linguistic and the academic culture in which it is rooted.

The work on feedback in English language (EL) academic contexts (summarized in, e.g., Johnson, 2013; Entwhistle, Karagiannopoulou, Olafsdotti, & Walker, 2015) means there is now a wealth of advice for teachers on how to manage feedback. Stenger (2014) offers research-based tips which sound very robust. However, while confirming that research data supports feedback as critical for student learning, these tips pay no attention to how the feedback is being received and managed. These suggestions appear to support the idea that learners need to be involved in the process but as recipients – not as partners or even drivers. None of this work suggests that any initial research into student expectations or previous experiences with feedback has been conducted. The conclusion is that feedback is seen by the teaching profession as a key tool for learning, but this does not take account of the fact that other learning styles or experiences may challenge this assumption.

Other studies do indicate that a problem is brewing. Di Loreto and McDonough (2013) highlight the results of a poor communicative relationship between teachers and students on feedback. This is to the extent that certain types or methods of delivery of feedback can actually increase student anxiety and therefore surely stall learning. The warning signs are also there in Lee's (2008) paper which investigates how teachers can be unaware of the impact of their feedback practices. In other words, there is an issue with teachers not discussing the expectations around giving feedback nor checking how it is received. This is especially surprising given that "concept checking" is a cornerstone of EL teaching methodology. This lack of awareness on the part of teachers will surely exacerbate negative consequences in a setting with international students.

A later study by Lee (2009) showed how teachers tended to focus their feedback on scores, errors, and other quantitative details and continued with this practice even though they saw no difference or improvement in their students' competences. This is an alarm bell which is supported by the study reported in this chapter – an indication of an unwillingness to change on the part of the teacher and a corresponding and unfair expectation that it is the students who need to adapt. Duff and Anderson (2015) refer to the hurdles or actual barriers C1 students face in "adapting" to a C2 culture, and perhaps the least we can expect is that academic institutions and their teachers are sensitive to this and put in place steps or a framework that specifically supports these students.

Given the gap in understanding of how students from abroad perceive feedback in an EL setting, together with the indications of the challenges they face and signs that teachers are not managing feedback in the most effective way, this study is intended to explore these issues. In other words, the study seeks to explore whether C1 acts as a barrier or hurdle in processing feedback and how far teachers are able or willing to accommodate learners whose C1 experiences of learning may be considerably different from the C2 they are operating in.

6.3 Research Design

6.3.1 Methodology

This study aims to investigate three questions:

RQ1: How do international students operating in English language as an L2 perceive feedback?

RQ2: How, if at all, do English language teachers at university support students' understanding of the feedback approach and process?

RQ3: How far do English language teachers in the host organization understand or make accommodations for students' C1 when delivering feedback?

The study was designed using a mixed methods sequential transformative design (Creswell, 2008; Creswell & Plano Clark, 2011). This methodology is characterized by the collection and analysis of either qualitative or quantitative data, depending on which best serves the theoretical perspective.

> There is currently general agreement that concentrating on participant viewpoints and the meaning individuals attach to educational issues is not only valid, but even preferred in specific cases, over quantitative methodologies. (Creswell, 2008)
> The movement to focus on student satisfaction and needs eventually led to qualitative methods of evaluating student services and the impetus to justify the cost of co-curricular activities led to the current focus on learning outcomes. (Herdlein & Zurner, 2015, p.2)

This research was designed around three focus groups in a layered approach to gather data which then informed a trial of three different approaches to managing feedback. The object of the focus groups was to have an organized discussion with a group of individuals for them to comment on specific points that the researchers had selected (Powell, Single, & Lloyd, 1996). The results from each focus group are then analyzed and integrated into the next focus group. Such a methodology can help generalize qualitative data and validate a particular instrument, in this case feedback and how it is given and received.

The first focus group (A) involved a sample of experienced students from abroad, and their responses were analyzed and used to inform the next phase of the study, which was a focus group composed of teachers (B). Based on responses, a small set of teachers were then given guidelines on how to manage feedback with their classes. Following this, a third focus group with those teachers who had been involved in the trialing was organized (C).

6.3.2 Participants

All participants – teachers and students – were based in a UK university with the students either preparing for or studying degree courses. All students were from abroad and functioning in L2 and C2. A total of 48 students participated in the study either in the focus group or in the trial classes.

6.3.2.1 Focus Group A: Experienced Students

This consisted of six students from various countries who had been studying in the United Kingdom for a while (Table 6.1).

In order to inform the issues under investigation, an initial focus group with students who were at the end of their English course was undertaken. It was important that the group was at the end of their program of study as they would have had a complete program of feedback and would be in a better position to reflect on both their own previous experiences (if any) in their home country and those in

Table 6.1 Student focus group at the end of their course

Student reference	Gender	Home country	Length of time studying English in UK	Age	Native language	Program of study
100	Male	Saudi Arabia	3 years	20	Arabic	Academic English
101	Female	Ecuador	6 months	22	Spanish	Academic English
102	Female	Colombia	6 months	37	Spanish	MSc business and finance
103	Female	Vietnam	1 year	24	Vietnamese	MSc business and finance
104	Female	Cameroon	10 months	28	French	BSc nursing
105	Female	Russia	1 year	23	Russian	MSc business and finance

the L2 classroom. The students were from a wide range of countries covering different continents, L1 and C1s.

6.3.2.2   Focus Group B: Teachers (Prior to Trial)

A focus group was run with a group of 10 expert English-speaker teachers of academic English and English for specific academic purposes (i.e., L2Ac and L2Sp). Two teachers focused on teaching English for specific academic purposes on in-sessional programs of English, and eight teachers focused on teaching academic English on pre-sessional English courses. There were five female and five male teachers. All teachers had taught general and academic English for 6 to 10 years, and six had between 15- and 20-year experience. All teachers had a CELTA or DELTA qualification in TESOL.

6.3.2.3   Focus Group C: Teachers (Post Trial)

This was made up of four teachers, three males and one female. The teachers had all participated in focus group B. These were the teachers who had conducted the trialing of the various approaches to feedback in the classroom.

6.3.3   Process

As outlined in Sections 1 and 2 above, studies which explore the effectiveness of feedback to students in study abroad settings tend to focus on how a pre-agreed framework of feedback is delivered or made more understandable rather than investigating the nature of feedback itself and whether or not the model is right for the learners. In the light of this, the study followed a four-step sequential process.

Stage 1: Focus group A was an attempt to understand what problems experienced international students perceived with feedback and even how the students themselves would like to manage feedback. This initial collection of data was then analyzed for both themes and issues and used to guide the shape of the feedback approaches (teacher-led, explanatory, and student-led negotiated) used in the trial and to be conducted by selected teachers on new students.

Stage 2: Focus group B consisted of 10 teachers, and the purpose was to determine how feedback was currently taking place. This group was not informed of what group A had said but was asked for their own perceptions about and practices in giving or managing feedback.

Stage 3: Four teachers from stage 2 were then invited to trial different approaches for giving feedback over a period of 4 weeks with 42 new students from abroad (see Table 6.2). The approaches were informed by the issues raised in focus group A. The trial consisted of three different approaches:

Table 6.2 Overview of the students involved in stages 3 and 4

Teacher	Group	Number of students	Origins
1	Control group	9	Colombian (4), Vietnamese (1), Chinese (1), Turkish (1), Brazilian (1), Indian (1)
2	Explanatory group	10	Colombian (6), Vietnamese (2), Cameroonian (1), Ugandan (1)
3	Negotiated group A	11	Colombian (4), Vietnamese (3), Uzbekistan (2), Moroccan (1), Ecuador (1)
4	Negotiated group B	12	Colombian (4), Vietnamese (2), Chinese (2), Uzbekistan (1), Argentinian (1), Jordanian (1), Turkish (1)

- Trial (a): A control group (see Table 6.2) where the teacher simply conducted feedback as usual and in accordance with his own training and what was required in terms of meeting university demands.
- Trial (b): An "explanatory" group (see Table 6.2) where the teacher was asked to trial an approach to feedback where he spent some time explaining to and working with his group on how feedback would be conducted and how the students could best manage and benefit from the feedback they were given, that is, what the teacher or university expectations were.
- Trial (c): A "negotiated" group (see Table 6.2) where two teachers were each asked to work with their classes to jointly decide on the type of feedback the students wanted, how and when feedback was given, and how the students would manage that feedback. This was intended to take account of any of the students' expectations derived from their C1 understandings or experiences.

Stage 4: A third focus group (C) was organized with the four teachers who had trialed the different approaches in order to discuss how successful they felt it had been, what, if any, differences they had noticed from their previous practice, and what issues had arisen.

Details about the teachers and the instructions provided to teachers for stage 3 trialing can be found in Table 6.3.

6.4 Results

The intention of the study was to explore how different cultures (see Table 6.2) and thus potentially different perceptions of feedback influenced the effectiveness of the feedback process. Within this, it also explored the potentially different perceptions of students from abroad (C1) and their teachers (C2). For the students, the study explored the role of students' C1 and what impact their cultural perceptions and reception of feedback might have on their acquisition of L2. For the teachers whose first language was English (Teachers 1, 2, and 4), we intended to explore the assumptions they made in regard to feedback especially focusing on any

Table 6.3 Overview of teachers and instructions for stage 3 trialing

Teacher	Description of teacher	Overview of role	Instructions given
Teacher 1	First language: English. He has over 15 years of experience of teaching English at both school and university level. He has taught students in different countries and worked with both home and international students. He holds a CELTA and a degree in linguistics.	No change in how feedback should be given [control group]	I am wondering if you might be able to help us with a study my colleague and I are doing on feedback. You wouldn't need to do anything different in how you give feedback, apart from being available in the third week of June to be in a focus group and asked questions about how you give feedback.
Teacher 2	First language: English He has over 25 years of teaching English experience at both school and university level. He holds a CELTA, DELTA, and masters in TEFL.	Explanatory approach	Set aside some time for explaining feedback to the group of students. How you give feedback, for example, the focus, method, degree, purpose, etc. How feedback can work in UK, for example, teacher, peer, self, and the benefits of each. Expectations around how students should deal with feedback, that is, you expect to see them try to improve points in next assignment, find out more about something, that is, self-engage, and so on. Allow students to ask questions as you are explaining and get agreement from them about how they will participate and value feedback.
Teacher 3	First language: Language other than English She has over 15 years of teaching EFL, ESOL, and EAP at university level. She has a DELTA, masters in linguistics, and a PhD.	Negotiated approach to feedback [student-led]	Have a discussion with the students about the concept of feedback: a) Have students had experience of feedback? Was it helpful or not? Why? Why not?
Teacher 4	First language: English He has over 15-year experience of teaching EFL and ESP and has 2 years of experience in teaching at university level. He has a CELTA and a recently acquired DELTA.		b) How do the students want to receive the feedback? How will they manage it? c) What sort of feedback do students find helpful? Just the correct answers or prompts to help them get to the answers? From peers? Group vs one-to-one? Agree with them how to manage even if it goes against your normal practice, but it must be a group decision.

accommodations they made and on the universality of understanding feedback and its acceptance as a learning tool.

6.4.1   Focus Group a: Experienced Students

a)   Different Understandings About Feedback

All students, with the benefit of hindsight, identified feedback as being essential to learning, but they had very different perceptions of what feedback was. One student commented, "Feedback was only given on things you did wrong so that next time you would not make the same mistake," while others believed feedback was given on things you did correctly or wrongly, and both were helpful. However, one student commented that feedback is not always important, as sometimes "you don't want it." One student found that receiving feedback helped her feel more confident, and another found feedback given in the United Kingdom was quite different to that given in Asia (in their C1), and it was more useful in the United Kingdom. Finally, one student commented, "Feedback is not always what you want, you don't know. Very important is it helps you understand something you do well or that you don't do well. Feedback is very useful."

(b)   Different Perceptions of Who Should Give Feedback

Again, there were differences regarding what students were used to in their home countries (see Table 6.2). Some students (from Ecuador and Colombia) commented that all feedback should come from the teacher because the language level of their fellow students was not high enough. Some of this was expressed in comments that indicated peer feedback might be a face threat. Other students (Russian and Vietnamese) thought all feedback from teachers and students was helpful, especially when commenting on presentations. One student (Russian) believed peer feedback to be important because some teachers are "not great." As one student (Saudi Arabian) identified, "Feedback is more important from teacher than from students because of the level. Teacher is important."

(c)   Timing of Feedback

When asked when they wanted to receive feedback, all were keen to receive it immediately – "Yes, every time. Immediate feedback to delay will mean you might forget and not learn from it." For one student, receiving feedback was an entirely new experience, so she reported being happy to receive any and that the timing of it was not an issue.

(d)   The Focus of Feedback

All were in agreement that grammar mistakes need to be corrected, although one student thought it important to also correct her own mistakes. The group had a poor or nonexistent understanding of what other elements of their English they might need to improve in order to be successful at degree level.

In summary, the key points to emerge were that students recognized that positive feedback was key to feeling confident when operating in C2 environments and a strong belief that the teacher is the expert who should deliver feedback. This latter belief appears to be driven by their C1 teacher-centered learning experiences and consequent expectations, where they see feedback as being the responsibility of the teacher. The students felt their position in the feedback process was primarily that of a receiver. It was also clear that their expectations and understanding of feedback was that it had very prescribed limits around linguistic competence, and their experiences of learning in a C2 environment had not helped them understand how feedback might enhance their strategic, pragmatic, or discourse competences. This is reflected in the literature which highlighted the quantitative focus of much feedback for both teachers and students.

6.4.2 Focus Group B: The Teachers – Pretrial Reflections

Teachers stated that they provide students with a range of feedback which varies from one-to-one individual feedback to group and peer feedback. In contrast to the students, teachers commented that "peer feedback is less threatening, but students don't believe it." Another teacher also commented, "Students are harder on each other when giving feedback but are happy to do so." They also commented that their impression was that some nationalities (such as Colombians and Ecuadorians) do not like to receive feedback at all. It might be in part because "...certain nationalities find feedback hard to take, and so I need to build in the reason for feedback. Colombians don't like to be singled out on pronunciation." In terms of timing, they said that sometimes feedback is given immediately, sometimes a week later.

The teachers' comments acknowledged that the different ways they use to give feedback tends to be tied to the task or skill rather than student needs. Teachers commented that they "...give common feedback across all students. This is due to time and the nature of the courses." The teachers demonstrated a strong belief in peer feedback, but it was unclear where this comes from. It could be from prior training in the EL academic setting and/or it could be based on their own learning experiences. It was also clear that they had identified issues, but they did not explain if they were addressing them or how – there seemed to be a resigned acceptance.

Following the information about current practices elicited from the two focus groups A and B, the trialing was set up as described in 3.3 above. This was operationalized with 42 new students for a period of 4 weeks, and the results of the trialing in terms of perspectives and issues arising were captured in focus group C.

6.4.3 Focus Group C: Posttrial Reflections from the Teachers Who Conducted the Trials

Four of the teachers from focus group B agreed to participate in the next phase of the study and implement the different new approaches for giving feedback over a period of 4 weeks. The focus group was led by one of the researchers and recorded, while the other researcher took notes and made notes of any other comments. The focus group, which had a duration of 1 h, centered on two main areas: (a) reiterations of teacher's perceptions and approaches to feedback prior to the project and (b) their perceptions and approaches during and after the project. The following section notes the key points made during focus group C.

(a) Student Focus on Linguistic Competences in Feedback

Generally, all teachers agreed the focus for them was on giving feedback on writing (a key challenge for L2 speakers in L2Ac). Specifically, the teachers expressed frustrations with students who always want to receive feedback on grammar. The students' focus on grammar, as explained earlier, was often related to their previous learning experiences in their own culture.

> Always divide into two – macro and micro – hard to get the balance, students dive straight into grammar. (Teacher 1)
> Students need to learn how to prioritize as they automatically go straight for the grammar. (Teacher 2)

In the case of spoken tasks, all agreed that feedback is given on pronunciation. This mirrors the micro-focus on grammar and accuracy in writing.

> [I] try to give feedback on pronunciation. One of the reasons is they ask for it. . .Students [are] worried about [the] communicative elements. . . . (Teacher 1)

(b) One-to-One Feedback

All teachers agreed that the stronger students receive more one-to-one feedback.

> They [stronger students] get it during in the task. Others wait and get less one-to-one feedback, and it is group feedback, picking individuals for answers (all agreed). (Teacher 1)

All teachers agreed that if there were more time, then one-to-one feedback would be the best approach. Even when written feedback had been given, Teachers 1 and 2 emphasized the importance of following up on written comments with face-to-face feedback:

> Sometimes, I have been complacent about comments I have written, look back, and think what would a student do with the mechanical comments that appear on an essay, hoping something will get through. Success rate is probably very low. On the other hand, what does make a difference is how you follow that up – maybe follow up with a face-to-face meeting. (Teacher 2)
> Scribbling stuff on an essay generally gets me nowhere, and them nowhere, [it's] always conversation that works. (Teacher 1)

This point ties in with one of the issues under investigation, which is the need for feedback to be culturally and individually relevant and questions whether or not feedback can ever be "universally" relevant.

It is worth noting that all commented that feedback delivered as a conversation worked best:

> It has to be individualized, may start by being general, same feedback form will apply to everyone, but you do realize that certain individuals need a different approach. But time permitting, I've tried to take that approach. (Teacher 2)
> [. . .] Depends on class size. [If] 6–8 [students in a] class, [then you are] able to give feedback on a one-to-one basis in a class situation. (Teacher 2)
> The problem is me, [I have] an EFL background. . . . To be able to sit with someone one-to-one means everything [must be] planned. (Teacher 1)

(c) Universality of Feedback

All teachers agreed that feedback needed to be individualized and culturally sensitive:

> [. . .] with South Asian students, [I am] more assertive – you listen [to what I say] and you do. (Teacher 2)
> while [I am] more gentle with Chinese students, [I] listen more, [as they are] not used to receiving feedback from teacher. (Teacher 1)
> I think it depends on [the] cultural or educational background of the students. They don't understand [the] importance of structure and doing things on their own. (Teacher 3)

Despite these idealized wishes, the issue of time in giving feedback was an overriding concern. All teachers questioned the amount of time required to give individual and culturally sensitive feedback and stated that even though one-to-one feedback was the ideal, the demands of the syllabus in preparation for the end of term assessments required the majority of their time.

(d) Feedback on Wider Communicative Competences

Although the universality of how feedback is managed is questionable, teachers commented that, in their view, what students needed feedback on was as much in strategic, pragmatic, and discourse competences (such as addressing a question or task and structure of a piece of writing) as in linguistic competence. Both Teachers 2 and 4 agreed.

> Answering the question. . .seems to be an ongoing battle. For example, in argument essays, [the students] seem to fall back [to the] default position of advantages and disadvantages, which I know is evaluative, but it's not exactly an argument essay. (Teacher 2)

This often leaves teachers thinking:

> Well, we've talked about this, but still not getting it don't seem to get it, question myself, what is missing? What am I not doing right? (Teacher 2 and Teacher 1 agreed)

(e) Peer Feedback.

Teacher 3 was focused on making sure students engaged with peer feedback:

Those students who generally don't get involved are forced to when they give peer feedback, in a way I think it is a good practice to encourage students to get involved more with each other's work. (Teacher 3)

In the study, Teacher 3 had given the students the choice, and they chose teacher-led feedback: "I gave students the choice, [they] didn't want peer feedback, so we gave them teacher-led feedback" (Teacher 3). Teacher 3 expressed disappointment that students did not take on peer feedback and appeared to reluctantly allow students to have their choice of teacher feedback: "I tried, even [using their] written work, but. . .they were [still not] involved" (Teacher 3). Here, the teacher appears to be drawing on her own C1 and trying to enforce her C1 beliefs, that is, peer feedback is a helpful tool for giving feedback. However, both Teachers 1 and 2 commented that peer feedback meant students lost interest. This supports the comments of those students from Ecuador, Colombia, and Saudi Arabia that all feedback should come from the teacher.

[Students] rush through peer feedback, go off topic, [there] didn't seem to be much discussion between them. [They] weren't interested, didn't see the point in it, [I] reflected back how they saw their own feedback was interpreted. (Teacher 1)

(f) Feedback on Speaking

Teachers felt that giving feedback on spoken tasks is easier as you can monitor a group activity through listening and commenting:

When they are doing brainstorming or working in groups. You can actually stand with them for 5 minutes and what they have been discussing. Generally, with brainstorming sessions, it's a much freer and relaxed atmosphere, so critical thinking can take place. (Teacher 3)

Teachers found that, despite earlier comments on peer feedback (Colombians and Saudi Arabian students not wanting peer feedback) and self-reflection, peer feedback and self-reflection worked well for feedback on speaking activities:

Self-correction – students record their presentations, listen to themselves, and correct themselves. [They are] very keen on it and aware. (Teacher 3)

This agreement around how speaking feedback is managed possibly reflects an almost universal view on the primacy of communicative effectiveness and may be the only element where diverse cultures agree.

(g) Concerns Over Changes to Feedback

Teachers who were asked to trial the "negotiated" approach to feedback (group (c)) raised concerns about the timing of what they were doing as they were starting this study at the beginning of students' arrival in the United Kingdom. They felt that a process that required them to elicit or negotiate student needs would have been better placed later in the course:

Because we did right at the beginning of course, they didn't know me, 9 Chinese students + 3 others, and Chinese being Chinese was too far out for them. Better to ask at end of the course. (Teacher 4)

This comment indicates that attempts to explain and negotiate how feedback is managed with students are not straightforward. Students, such as the Chinese, coming from a C1 "teacher as expert" culture clearly need time to absorb the C2 "teacher as facilitator" approach in most UK academic settings.

(h) Operational Concerns

Teachers mentioned some concerns related to the situation or context in which they are teaching, such as the tension between general and academic English which confronts many universities when students come from abroad. This manifests itself in the fact that the teachers often feel they are correcting form when perhaps function and performance of competences might be more appropriate.

> When a spoken task, I try to give feedback on pronunciation. One of the reasons is they ask for it, nature of the classes. Uncomfortable nature of academic and general English. Students worried about communicative elements, nothing wrong with it [all agreed]. Listening, personally, I'm slightly controlled by the nature of their exams in the listening into how to give the feedback. I identify key points, how they have written bullet points. (Teacher 1)

They all seemed to feel that focusing feedback on the wider set of study skills that international students might need was impossible:

> At least in our level, general speaking skills we don't work on – focus on presentation not general skills; drill them; talk to the audience, speak very slowly, not their language we work on, but their delivery, and you see more pauses. (Teacher 4)

This appears to be exacerbated by the dominance of exams in the curriculum which can dictate the focus for the kind of feedback they give:

> You are right, note-taking is hard, and exams can hijack the whole process of giving feedback – but I always remind them that it is not just for the exam, but for their postgraduate study, longer term. Note-taking skills is something that they will need, so we might focus on this after listening. (Teacher 2)

In summary, the teachers seem to feel constrained by their situation in the type or focus of the feedback they give but are very aware of the cultural differences (mentioned in 4.1, such as unwillingness to receive criticism of work, a focus on grammar and accuracy, a demand for teacher rather than peer time) in how feedback is managed and received by the students. Nevertheless, the results show that there is no evidence that they are reflecting on this or changing their approach which supports Lee's (2009) findings.

6.5   Discussion

These results indicate that feedback is both perceived and received very differently from the teachers' expectations which prevail in the C2 study setting and that these differences may well emerge from the students' expectations of how learning and feedback happens in C1. Interestingly, the student from a country (Cameroon) which, reportedly, has no process of feedback in its education system seemed to absorb the C2 approach better and use feedback as a very effective learning tool. Others, especially Latin American Spanish speakers, seemed to perceive feedback as face threatening and have strongly held beliefs about how feedback should be conducted.

6.5.1 Students' Perceptions of Feedback

The initial focus group A indicated that the issue of feedback was a rich seam to explore. The participants felt strongly about it, and in the midst of their conclusions, it was clear that these experienced students were generally frustrated about how feedback was managed. What emerged was a desire for feedback to be much more controlled or driven by the student receiving the feedback through a one-to-one interaction. This suggested they had not understood the range and purpose of feedback they were given. It was also interesting to note that all students, judging from their demeanor and on the economic investment they have made in studying abroad, were very keen to progress quickly but seemed to consider feedback as an add-on or an irritant rather than core to learning and progression. Students generally, both in the focus group and in reporting by teachers, did not appear to understand how feedback could support them in developing wider academic skills and competences. They were very much focused on feedback in micro or quantitative terms of what is correct or not, for example, with their grammar or pronunciation. In fact, one of their comments on peer feedback, a thorny issue throughout the study, focused on the inability of their peers to correct their grammar. This in itself raises concerns about how peer feedback is managed in the classroom by the teacher; that is, the teacher should probably ensure that students understand that the focus should be on whether or not they have understood the key points in a presentation rather than the micro-focus on grammar.

The study also raised questions about what exactly constitutes feedback or where it sits in terms of importance for the progression of learning. The fact that bald quantitative elements, such as scores from tests, seem to sit under the blanket term of feedback equally with the more in-depth qualitative considerations of feedback, such as skills, is interesting. Broader feedback on "expected" performance, in, for example, speaking and writing in terms of cohesion, argument, and critical thinking, indicates that feedback in the classroom is starting to be lost in a general methodology, and this, in turn, makes it hard for teachers or students to pay attention to. The notion of paying attention is critical to learning across all cultures. This means that if C2 strategies or approaches, which are new to international students, are not highlighted, then they will struggle to absorb or manage their relevance (James, 1950).

6.5.2 Teachers' Communications about Feedback

A lack of skills or knowledge on the part of the teacher in managing intercultural issues that affect learning seems to militate against more positive perceptions of feedback on the part of the students. It suggests a lack of communication in the classroom about the beliefs in the benefits of feedback within the EL academic setting, where it should be the responsibility of the teachers to communicate C2 expectations or approaches to learning. In addition, the students' comments raise concerns about how feedback is being conducted. It appears to be forced on them without any discussion of what their C1 expectations might be around this. Although most students said they valued feedback – in whatever form – especially those who had had nonexistent or negative experiences at home (C1), only one student out of the group of six sample students seemed to have learned how to manage feedback according to C2 expectations. Perhaps this is a failure of teachers to manage their resistance and/or confusion. This can easily build up over time, so one could see where those negative reports in university surveys come from.

6.5.3 The Teacher/Peer Role in Feedback

In general, international students perceive the teacher as an "expert" and are willing to accept feedback on their language choices. However, teachers reported that feedback on L2Ac and L2Sp competences is less successful where students are required to amend features of academic discourse which conflict with their L1/C1 understanding. There is also a contrast with teacher-centered cultures, such as those in many SE Asian countries, which appear to affect how peer feedback, a common practice in EL study settings, is solicited and received. Generally, students do not like feedback from their peers (both students and teachers reported this) – they only want expert input. And this ties in with students' emphasis on language over content in that they don't trust their peers to correct their grammar, etc. Interestingly, however, teachers reported far fewer issues with peers giving feedback on spoken work, and students supported this view. Overall, this general resistance to peer feedback suggests a contrast to Jenkins' (2011, p. 934) observations that international students shift to peer modelling their multilingual contemporaries during their study abroad.

One of the key points to emerge from the study was, in fact, not so much a difference in how feedback was utilized but significant cultural differences in the understanding of the role of the teacher. Teachers reported that some students in their classes, especially those from teacher-centered cultures such as China, struggled to participate in contributing to the management of their feedback in a way that would be expected and encouraged in the culture of study settings with perceived "native English-speaker" teachers. Thus, it transpired that a flaw in the study was assuming that, by consulting students in order to tailor feedback to their cultural expectations, the feedback cycle would have the same meaningful impact as it has in English study settings within which English is the first language (even if not delivered in the same way). Arguably, this requirement for participation in learning could have been delayed until students had settled in to the C2 educational mores and approaches, but it does raise the question of how far that process in itself is a challenge for them and to what extent it is holding back their learning. This has certainly been explored in previous literature in terms of recognizing this challenge, but the premise has always been *how do we get students (C1) on board to our (C2) way of thinking* rather than *how do we (teachers) manage intercultural issues so that we can accommodate different ways of learning?*

6.5.4   Responsibility for Managing Intercultural Negotiations

In general, the trialing of three different approaches to feedback supported the initial views which emerged from the focus groups. However, the final focus group C indicated that a much greater challenge is being presented that cannot be resolved by a simple shift to intercultural negotiation. This is the teachers' inability to step outside their own cultural beliefs, despite their recognition that C1 learning experiences and/or beliefs about face threats impair the effectiveness of feedback.

The trialing of the three different approaches produced varied results. At best, it caused the teachers to reflect on their approaches and, despite time issues, to consider how they might manage feedback in new ways. But what shocked the researchers was the rigidity of the belief system of these experienced teachers. Despite the opportunity to reflect on their practices (e.g., in focus group (B)) coupled with the fact that they all have to manage the expectations of a very wide range of cultures in their daily working lives, they seemed immoveable from their training and the UK academic system into which they are locked. For example, they resolutely refused to give up on peer feedback, despite student resistance to this. Some even blamed the student for a lack of understanding or pressed on with the expectation that the student would eventually grasp the purpose over time.

Teachers did, however, express sensitivity to the different attitudes that other cultures may bring to the process and acknowledged that this variety existed within their classes. They further claimed to adjust or accommodate the way they delivered feedback based on their understanding of various C1s. However, they managed this in a way which was dominated by their own academic culture. This manifested itself in the way teachers delivered the same feedback by adjusting the way it was delivered rather than perhaps considering that the content may also need to be modified.

The fact that all teachers felt that individual conversations worked best (and the building of understanding through interaction that this involves) implies there does need to be a more negotiated approach to how feedback is delivered. This perception ties in with the experienced students' stated needs of wanting a two-way conversation. It may be that teachers understand that conversation works best as a feedback tool without actually having paid attention to the fact that this is because they are negotiating student needs and issues as they talk. The teachers clearly feel this is more successful in terms of perhaps being listened to and in improving student performance but have possibly not reflected on why or how they can give more consideration to students' voices. Nonetheless, the individual nature of these exchanges means that students have an opportunity to express their needs in terms of their C2 to which the teacher can then potentially adapt.

It has to be said that the two teacher focus groups, although small, represented some variety in teacher background although all had a CELTA or DELTA qualification. This sets up concerns about the perpetuation of a model or methodology of teaching that is very much based in native EL speaker C2 norms. The teachers feel stuck in one of Kuhn's (1996) paradigms, unable to see an alternative world. The teachers' general lack of reflection on how students were bringing diverse C1 models of learning to the classroom needs to be addressed rather than responded to with a prescriptive model. The research indicates a need for further teacher training in this area. To be fair to the teachers it seems, although the universities are sitting looking at survey results which show weak levels of satisfaction with feedback, these institutions are not endeavoring to pull together a coherent approach or training model for the teachers, nor are they exploring what the students might require to feed into that process.

6.5.5   Limitations

Clearly, there are significant limitations to such a small-scale study, yet it is only by the nature of such in-depth qualitative studies that one can get at the underlying issues here in the first phase. The sample did not include representation from all the different university disciplines, and the focus was on the academic English class. This was in order to catch students in their first contact with feedback in this context. The trial of approaches may need to be implemented on a wider scale across several universities. However, the consistency of responses does give good evidence of the problem. Herdlein and Zurner (2015) point out that with the growth in the tertiary education market, institutions of higher education do need to research and review how they manage learning. They state, "Although asking the very clients (students) how to approach the teaching/learning model may seem anathema to many higher educational professionals across the globe, educators have an imperative to find and implement best practices" (p. 9).

Overall, the focus groups indicated that the effectiveness of feedback in a C2 setting is shaped by C1 in diverse ways, indicating it is critical for teachers to take account of this diversity if their feedback practice is to enhance effective language acquisition. It is likely that an understanding of how to receive and utilize feedback would need to be negotiated between students and teachers and be built in a series of layers. Thus, for a true alignment between C1 and C2, the process would require a two-way effort from both students and teachers, as the students pointed out.

6.6 Conclusions

In terms of the research questions, the study provided a wealth of data on how international students operating in C2 perceive feedback, RQ1. This was especially evidenced in focus group A plus perceptions of teachers which indicate that feedback is only really valued if it is delivered by the teacher and preferably in a one-to-one situation. The study worryingly indicated that, in terms of RQ2, EL teachers at university offer little or no support to students' understanding of the feedback process or its role in learning. However, in addressing RQ3, there are responses which demonstrate that teachers do make some accommodations to intercultural sensitivities when delivering feedback, but this is rather ad hoc and based very much on teachers' perceptions rather than being a result of intercultural negotiation.

6.6.1 Implications and Applications

Overall, the results indicate that there are several possible ways forward in ensuring that feedback is working for all, that is, the institutions that accept students from abroad, the teachers who are introducing students to a learning tool that will apply well beyond the doors of the classroom, and, most importantly, the students who approach this tool from multiple perspectives and who do not always connect feedback with faster progression. We have to consider that teachers in study settings for whom English is their first language (e.g., the United Kingdom, United States, Australia, Canada) who are working with an English language model of academic competence would be severely challenged by a methodological shift that would see them "giving away" answers rather than the more inductive approach they expect students to absorb. Such a shift also flies in the face of the dominant current perceptions of higher education which prizes critical evaluation and self-reflection in how knowledge is filtered and presented.

At the least, this study has indicated that feedback needs to be given much more forethought by teachers in terms of understanding how different cultures accept and absorb feedback information. The role and purpose of feedback need to be managed early on in induction classes with students being allowed to relay their own C1 experiences and expectations and this information being used to negotiate how feedback will work for that particular class (it may vary from class to class depending on the makeup of the students). While the students, in choosing to study in an international setting, probably need to accept the learning style of the institution they have chosen, it is far more important that the teachers in that institution consider how feedback can be used as an effective tool with students from diverse C1s. Having clarified that, any approaches which might focus on negotiating feedback between C1 and C2 are inevitably hampered by the time and resources available. All the teachers raised concerns regarding this. The approach adopted for Trial Group C, where methods and purposes of feedback are negotiated at the onset of a course, might save time later on. In terms of ongoing feedback, one possible solution might be to give less but more focused feedback. So rather than provide feedback on every task, teachers could provide feedback on more critical tasks or cover all feedback in a weekly conversation session.

6.6.2 A New Approach to Managing Feedback

The early study indicates that the current literature on feedback, largely targeted at teachers, does not take enough account of student perceptions specifically in a C1/C2 cultural mix. Although some literature investigates student responses, it does not target student beliefs and expectations before feedback has taken place. In highlighting this issue, the approaches piloted in this study suggest that methods for managing feedback will be more effective if the students, not the feedback, are the starting point, and these approaches – and their impact – should be investigated further. Looking at the specific issues of students in international study abroad settings, we should also consider Torday-Gulden's strong and plausible claim about the dominance of the English academic language model in tertiary education and its impact. Speaking specifically about epistemic language, she says:

> Knowledge that has been construed in accordance with other cultural norms often has to be radically reformulated in translation to bring it into line with English discourse expectations. Such domestication procedures (which often go far beyond the word or sentence level to involve textual organization and the whole rhetorical approach) effectively repackage the text in terms of the dominant epistemology, thereby rendering invisible rival forms of knowledge. (Torday-Gulden, 2013: Karen Bennett, call for paperse, 2011)

This concern seems to suggest that, as there is a global English version in which each L1 is allowed its voice and identity, so the same must be true for culture. The disquiet that Torday-Gulden (2013) expresses could be extrapolated to conclude that, if we fail to negotiate the cultural center point, we exclude voices. Thus, it seems urgent that EL teachers in international study settings learn to recognize and value alternative approaches to feedback and that they are supported in this by their institutions. This is not, of course, to suggest that there is anything as simplistic as a universal culture but rather that the mores of sensitivity, awareness, and overall accommodation that prevail in a global language setting need to extend to international cultural settings, such as in higher education, so that each can learn within their own identity.

References

Creswell, J. (2008). *Educational research: Planning, conducting and evaluating quantitative and qualitative research.* Upper Saddle River, NJ: Pearson Education.
Creswell, J. W., & Plano Clark, V. L. (2011). *Designing and conducting mixed methods research.* Los Angeles, CS: Sage.

Di Loreto, S., & McDonough, K. (2013). The relationship between instructor feedback and ESL student anxiety. *TESL Canada Journal, 31*, 21–41. Retrieved from http://teslcanadajournal.ca/index.php/tesl/article/view/1165.

Duff, P., & Anderson, T. (2015). Academic language and literary socialization for second language students. In N. Markee (Ed.), *The handbook of classroom discourse and interaction* (pp. 337–352). New Jersey: Wiley.

Entwhistle, N., Karagiannopoulou, E., Olafsdottir, A., & Walker, P. (2015). Research into university learning and teaching. In J. Case & J. Hulsman (Eds.), *Researching higher education: International perspectives on theory, policy and practice* (pp. 190–208). Oxford, UK: Routledge.

Hammond, W. (2016). *Are students satisfied with their courses? Interpreting the statistics.* Universities UK. Retrieved from http://www.universitiesuk.ac.uk/blog/Pages/are-students-satisfied-with-their-courses-interpreting-the-statistics.aspx

Hedgcock, J., & Lefkowitz, N. (1994). Feedback on feedback: Assessing learning receptivity to teacher response in L2 composing. *Journal of Second Language Writing, 3*, 141–163.

Herdlein, R., & Zurner, E. (2015). Student satisfaction, needs, and learning outcomes. A case study approach at a European university. *SAGE Open April – June, 2015*, 1–10. Retrieved from http://sgo.sagepub.com/content/5/2/2158244015580373.

Hyland, K., & Hyland, F. (Eds.). (2006). *Feedback in second language writing: Contexts and issues*. Cambridge, UK: CUP.

James, W. (1950). *The principles of psychology. Volume 1*. New York: Dover Publications.

Jenkins, J. (2011). Accommodating (to) ELF in the international university. *Journal of Pragmatics, 43*, 926–936.

Johnson, A. (2013). Facilitating productive use of feedback in higher education. *Active Learning in Higher Education, 14*, 63–76.

Kuhn, T. (1996). *The structure of scientific revolutions*. Chicago: University of Chicago Press.

Lee, I. (2008). Student reactions to teacher feedback in two Hong Kong secondary classrooms. *Journal of Second Language Writing, 17*, 144–164.

Lee, I. (2009). Ten mismatches between teachers' beliefs and written feedback practice. *ELT Journal, 63*, 13–22.

Powell, R. A., Single, H. M., & Lloyd, K. R. (1996). Focus groups in mental health research: Enhancing the validity of user and provider questionnaires. *International Journal of Social Psychology, 42*, 193–206.

Race, P. (2001). *Using feedback to help students learn*. The Higher Education Academy. PDF retrieved from https://www.heacademy.ac.uk/resource/using-feedback-help-students-learn.

Stenger, M. (2014). *5 research-based tips for providing students with meaningful feedback*. Edutopia. Retrieved from http://www.edutopia.org/blog/tips-providing-students-meaningful-feedback-marianne-stenger

Torday-Gulden, A. (2013). *English as the academic 'lingua franca': Looking back in anger and looking forward*. Paper presented at BALEAP conference, 2013. Retrieved from: http://qmlanguagecentre.on-rev.com/baleap/archive/media/uploads/conferences/nottingham-2013/papers-slides/Ann-Torday-Gulden-baleap_13.pdf

Chapter 7
Intercultural Language Teaching: On Reflection

Jo Oranje

7.1 Introduction

Across the world, language education studies have reiterated a general finding that despite most teachers being "favorably disposed" (Sercu et al., 2005, p. 10) toward intercultural language teaching and learning, fewer report practicing an intercultural approach in the classroom (e.g., Larzén-Östermark, 2008; Sercu et al., 2005). This chapter draws from a large research project that not only measured language teachers' awareness and reported practice of intercultural language teaching but also sought to enhance teachers' understanding and application of the approach. The results, generated through both quantitative and qualitative research methods, showed that reflection upon one's own culture—a fundamental element of intercultural teaching—was not commonly modeled, practiced, or taught by teacher participants. It is argued that insufficient emphasis on reflection on one's own cultural viewpoint is a defining feature of teachers who do not practice intercultural teaching, even if they report cognitions that support the approach.

J. Oranje (✉)
University of Otago, Dunedin, New Zealand
e-mail: jo.oranje@otago.ac.nz

© Springer Nature Singapore Pte Ltd. 2021
M. D. López-Jiménez, J. Sánchez-Torres (eds.), *Intercultural Competence Past, Present and Future*, Intercultural Communication and Language Education, https://doi.org/10.1007/978-981-15-8245-5_7

7.2   Literature Review

7.2.1   *Intercultural Language Teaching in the Study Context of New Zealand*

Intercultural language teaching (ILT) integrates language and culture at all stages of language education. Through exploration of cultures, reflection on one's own culture/s, and comparison of languages and cultures—including the learner's (and the teacher's) own—learners develop intercultural communicative competence (ICC). An interculturally competent individual has the affective and cognitive attributes necessary to effectively mediate intercultural interactions and to predict and avoid, or recognize and resolve, misunderstandings.

The notion of ICC being the goal of language teaching originated in the 1990s (most influentially, in Byram, 1997). However, decades on, research has shown the practice of the associated teaching approach of ILT to still be limited, even by teachers with beliefs that accord with ILT (Byram, 2014). This has been described as a mismatch between beliefs and practices and has been attributed to teachers' reports of insufficiencies in terms of (a) time to teach culture (e.g., Sercu et al., 2005), (b) teacher education in the approach (e.g., Peiser & Jones, 2013), (c) awareness of the target culture (e.g., Byram & Risager, 1999), (d) supporting materials (e.g., Larzén-Östermark, 2008; Moeller & Osborn, 2014), and (e) references to ILT in education policy (e.g., Castro, Sercu, & Méndez-García, 2004; Scarino, 2014).

Like their peers abroad, New Zealand language teachers have demonstrated minimal knowledge and limited practice of ILT (East & Scott, 2011; Roskvist, Corder, Harvey, & Stacey, 2011). Language education in New Zealand, the context of the study reported here, is administered in accordance with a national school curriculum that *implicitly* refers to an intercultural approach with language knowledge "strands" supporting the "core communication strand" (Ministry of Education, 2007, p. 24). The online curriculum guide for learning languages (Ministry of Education, 2016) *explicitly* refers to Intercultural Communicative Language Teaching (iCLT), comprising six principles established by Newton, Yates, Shearn, and Nowitzki (2010) to support the development of intercultural teaching and learning programs. The curriculum guide recommends explicit comparison between cultures and languages, and the development of an "actively reflective disposition" (Ministry of Education, 2016, 'What's new or different', sect. 6, para. 6). Nevertheless, New Zealand language teachers are uncertain about how to integrate culture in the language class and are confused by the perception of a language focus in assessment (East & Scott, 2011).

7.2.2 Teacher Cognitions as a Means of Assessing Reflection in ILT

If teachers are to be assisted in changing their practices to become more aligned with ILT, research needs to take account of their cognitions, that is, what they "think, know, believe and do" (Borg, 2003, p. 81), and analyze how those cognitions influence the choices they make in the classroom. Teacher cognitions are generally accepted as strongly influencing a teacher's decision-making and practice in the classroom (Birello, 2012; Borg, 2003; Feryok & Oranje, 2015). However, an individual's beliefs may not necessarily be internally consistent, be attributed equal importance, or regulate their practice in a consistent way (Birello, 2012). Central, or core, beliefs are grounded in personal experience, long held, 'tried and true', and are often given priority over peripheral beliefs, being those that are unsupported by experience and/or newly acquired (Rokeach, 1968). A similar distinction can be made between abstract, or theoretical, beliefs and concrete, or practical, beliefs (Birello, 2012; Feryok & Oranje, 2015; Mangubhai, Marland, Dashwood, & Son, 2005). For example, a teacher might report a particular belief in relation to an abstract concept (e.g., the integration of language and culture is valuable) but report an alternative belief in relation to the operationalization of the concept in a particular context (e.g., linguistic focus is necessary for examinations). These conflicting "subsets of beliefs" could account for some practices appearing to be at odds with beliefs or where teachers' knowledge is not always translated directly into classroom behaviors (Birello, 2012, p. 91).

The focus of this chapter is teachers' cognitions associated with the role of reflection on their own culture in teaching and learning languages and cultures[1]. Objective and critical reflection on one's own culture is a crucial element of an ILT approach and a requisite of ICC. Reflection fosters a "meta-level understanding of oneself and one's own culture" (Moeller & Osborn, 2014, p. 681) and is necessary to enable comparisons with the target culture, another key element of ILT. Reflection is, therefore, both a learning goal of ILT and a strategy for developing ICC (Blasco, 2012). Through reflection, an individual can decenter and avoid an ethnocentric stance of treating one's own culture as the norm or right way against which others are judged as abnormal or wrong (Barrett, 2007). For reflection to be critical, one must ask not only "*What* does my culture do?" but "*Why?*" and "*How?*" and analyze the responses from the perspective of others to recognize the influence of one's cultural perspective on an intercultural interaction and on assumptions made about the interactants.

The absence or presence of critical reflection on one's culture is a significant indicator of whether a teacher's orientation is intercultural. Although a teacher might have cognitions that align with ILT, it is often the absence of critical reflection that

---

[1]It is important to note that in this chapter, "reflection" refers to reflection on one's own culture as a key element of ILT to be practiced by teachers *and* learners. It does not relate to the much greater field of reflective teaching in education research.

means the approach practiced in the classroom is not wholly intercultural (e.g., Han & Song, 2011; Sercu et al., 2005). Reflection is not a natural activity for everyone, so it is important for teachers to explain it, encourage it, and model it. Furthermore, relativization of one's culture is not always explicitly promoted in education policy, curricula, and programs (Castro et al., 2004; Scarino, 2014), so the importance of the role of reflection needs to be actively brought to the attention of teachers. This study sought to do that by seeking to answer the following research questions:

1. To what extent do participants value reflection in the language classroom?
2. How does the practice of an intercultural activity—cultural portfolio projects— mediate teachers' understanding of the value of reflection in language education?

7.2.3   Theoretical Framework: Sociocultural Theory

Sociocultural theory (SCT) served as the theoretical framework for this study. In SCT, learning is co-constructed by individuals as they participate in social interaction. Crucially, interaction both socializes and mutually transforms the participants. Transformation is a key difference between SCT and constructivism, the approach used in most of the extant literature on culture teaching. From a constructivist perspective, development occurs as a result of a learner's experiences as they manipulate the world, but the construction of knowledge does not manifestly change the individual him/herself (Packer & Goicoechea, 2000, p. 228).

Particularly relevant is SCT's notion of mediation. In an SCT perspective, all activities are mediated by others, by tools, or by both. Tools can be physical, such as computers or a national curriculum, or intangible, such as language or theoretical concepts. In order for a tool to empower, rather than hinder, an activity, the tool must be appropriate for the task, be accessible, and be used properly (Wertsch, Del Río, & Álvarez, 1995). According to Vygotsky (1978), development occurs when the mediated external social activity becomes internally controlled by the individual and able to be applied in other similar situations. This process is enhanced by the activity being relevant and of value to the learner and within their grasp—that is, within their zone of proximal development.

SCT is an appropriate theoretical paradigm for working with ILT. SCT emphasizes the crucial prefix of "co-"; learning is dialogical, co-constructed by individuals as they interact with one another (Swain, Kinnear, & Steinman, 2011). This aligns well with the implication of the prefix "inter-" of intercultural language teaching. Far from meaning merely an interaction between people of different cultures, the prefix carries richer and more dynamic connotations through the continuously dialectic, mutual, and jointly transformative process of an interaction between individuals, each of whom is a collection of histories and experiences, seeking to comprehend and to be comprehensible (Scarino, 2014).

Here, SCT is used both to highlight the value of reflection in the internalization process of language learning and to interpret the value of cultural portfolio projects in terms of developing teachers' understanding of the role of reflection.

7.3   Methodology

The greater study from which this chapter is drawn comprised two phases. Phase 1 was a questionnaire gathering New Zealand secondary school language teachers' cognitions related to teaching culture in their language classes. Phase 2 was an intervention involving three classes in an activity called cultural portfolio projects. The general methodological procedures of each phase are described below.

7.3.1   Questionnaire

In Phase 1, teacher cognitions about culture teaching were gathered through a questionnaire. Following piloting, the questionnaire was mailed to all language teachers (i.e., of foreign languages, New Zealand's indigenous language, *Te Reo Māori*, and English as an additional language) at all secondary schools in the South Island of New Zealand.

Learning languages is the only non-compulsory learning area in the New Zealand national curriculum (Ministry of Education, 2007). Consequently, many schools employ only two or three language teachers. It is common for teachers to teach more than one language, and in some cases, schools share language teachers. In all, 393 questionnaires were sent to 121 schools based on a minimum of three questionnaires to each school (more if a school's website suggested more than three teachers were employed). A total of 76 completed questionnaires were returned from across 39 schools, representing 32% of all schools approached.

Many of the questionnaire items were replications or adaptations from the surveys conducted in Sercu et al.'s (2005) multinational study and Byram and Risager's (1999) British-Danish comparative study. Other items were inspired by related literature (e.g., Jedynak, 2011; Larzén-Östermark, 2008). The questionnaire items were mostly Likert type, presenting a statement and asking participants to select the response that best matched their view. These included rating their level of agreement with cognition and practice statements on a scale of 1 (*do not agree at all*) to 4 (*strongly agree*) and rating the extent to which they practiced listed intercultural activities using a scale of 1 (*I never use this activity*) to 4 (*I frequently use this activity*). For example, one item presented the cognition statement, "It is important to deepen students' knowledge about their own cultures while learning about a new culture," another presented the practice statement, "I critically analyze my own culture in class activities," and another listed the intercultural activity, "I ask my students about their experiences in the culture." No neutral or "don't know" options were provided, so participants were forced to make a choice. In addition to Likert-type items, a small number of items produced short-answer responses that fell within a limited range (e.g., familiarity with ILT or teaching qualifications).

Using only one indicator to measure a concept risks skewed results arising from misunderstandings or different interpretations of question items (Dörnyei & Csizér,

2012). This was managed by key concepts being measured by multiple-indicator scales of items associated with the same concept. Scale scores were calculated by summing a participant's response scores (i.e., 1 to 4) for the items related to the key concepts of (i) ILT cognitions, (ii) reported ILT practices, and (iii) reported use of ILT activities. During the analysis of data from both phases, it became clear that reflection was also a key concept. The questionnaire data was reconsidered, and the 13 items pertaining to modeling or teaching the skill of reflection were grouped as the reflection scale.

Initial descriptive statistics revealed patterns of interest in the frequencies, central tendencies, and dispersion. Inferential statistics were then calculated, including Pearson's product-moment correlation coefficients to determine the probabilities of variables being related by anything other than chance and Cronbach's alpha to assess the reliability of the multi-item scales (all were deemed to have high consistency). The scales were also subjected to principal components analyses to define the factors by which the variables were related.

7.3.2   Cultural Portfolio Projects

In the second phase, an in-class intervention was carried out in three secondary school languages classes. The participants[2] were:

1. Greenview School's Year 12[3] German class. This class of six students, aged 16–17 years, was taught by Ada, of German nationality, resident in New Zealand for 10 years.
2. City School's combined Years 12 and 13 German class. The six students in this class were aged 16–18 years and were taught by Craig, of New Zealand nationality who had spent some years living in Germany as a university student 20 years ago.
3. Muirside School's Year 11 French class. These 11 students were aged 15–16 years and were taught by Helene, of German nationality, resident in New Zealand for 20 years but frequent visitor to France throughout her life.

The intervention involved engaging the teachers and their students in a language learning activity called cultural portfolio projects (CPPs), essentially individual research projects about an aspect of the target culture. CPPs have been used in other studies (e.g., Allen, 2004; Byon, 2007; Su, 2011) but never in association with ILT.

Four steps of the CPPs remained generally consistent across the three classes with minor adaptations made to suit the specific environment and preferences of the teachers. Those steps were:

---

[2]All school names and all participant names are pseudonyms.

[3]Year 12 is the penultimate year in New Zealand secondary schools.

1. The class generated a list of statements that represented their existing beliefs about the target culture. Examples raised by this study's participants included "German people are comfortable with nudity" and "French people are very formal."

2. Each student chose a statement to treat as a hypothesis about the target culture and tested its validity by searching a range of primary (e.g., users of the language) and secondary (e.g., books, Internet) sources. Students completed a reflection sheet after each search, consolidating the information, analyzing its impact on their hypothesis, and noting similarities or differences with respect to their own culture. These searches took place over a number of lessons.

3. Students reformulated their hypotheses to relate to their own culture, for example, "New Zealanders are comfortable with nudity," and tested its validity. This step, based on Allen's (2004) work, was included in response to studies that demonstrated a lack of reflection in language classes (e.g., Roskvist et al., 2011) and to counter Bagnall's (2005) assertion that the school and classroom environments can inhibit reflection.

4. Students presented their findings. Ideally, these presentations should be made to the whole class. In these cases, the teachers requested that the findings form the basis of speeches required for assessment.

Data were gathered from various sources: (a) audio-recorded planning sessions with the teachers, scheduling the lesson-by-lesson implementation of the CPPs, (b) classroom observations of the CPPs in progress, (c) students' reflection sheets, (d) audio-recorded class discussions at the conclusion of the project, (e) students' brief evaluative questionnaires, and (f) audio-recorded teachers' interviews post-CPPs. The data were analyzed using qualitative methods with the assistance of MaxQDA software (http://www.maxqda.com). All data were coded and iteratively analyzed to reveal repeating or conflicting ideas and patterns, which were gathered into themes, then organized into theoretical constructs.

7.4 Results and Findings

The results of the reflection-based elements of the questionnaire are presented first and provide a general overview of New Zealand language teachers' cognitions and practices with respect to reflection in the language class. Then, the findings of the classroom-based study are presented, demonstrating how the participant teachers' initial and developing impressions of the role of reflection were influenced by their engagement in the CPPs.

7.4.1 Results from Questionnaire

The 76 participants ranged in age from 20–29 to 60–69 years with teaching experience extending from less than 1 year to more than 30 years and teaching qualifications from certificate to doctorate level; five individuals (6.6%) had no
qualifications. The significant majority (90.8%, $n = 69$) were female, and nearly
one-third (31.6%, $n = 24$) were teaching their mother tongue.

One questionnaire item was central to this study. Inspired by Jedynak's (2011)
survey, it asked, "Have you heard of intercultural language teaching as a teaching
approach?" Four response options were provided. In total, nearly two-thirds of
participants reported being unfamiliar with ILT, either having heard of ILT but
being unfamiliar with its principles ($n = 15$, 20.3%) or not having heard of ILT at all
($n = 31$, 41.9%). Nearly one-third ($n = 23$, 31.1%) advised that they understood and
practiced ILT. The remaining five individuals (6.8%) reported understanding ILT
but not practicing it. These reports were not verified in any way.

As explained, scales were developed to provide robust measures of the extent to
which cognitions, practices, and activities aligned with ILT and, most relevant here,
the extent to which reflection was valued, taught, or modeled. Due to space restric-
tions, this chapter presents only summaries of results for all but the reflection scale,
which is presented in some detail.

The lowest possible score for the 18-item ILT cognitions scale was 18, and the
maximum was 72; the higher the score, the more the participant's reported cognitions aligned with ILT. The range of scores extended from 40 to the maximum
possible 72, with a mean of 59.17 ($SD = 7.12$). The ILT practices scale had a lowest
possible score of 14 and a maximum of 56; scores ranged from 22 to the maximum
56, and the mean was 42.07 ($SD = 7.31$). The ILT activities scale had a minimum
possible score of 17 and a maximum of 68. Scores extended from 28 to 67, and the
mean was 49.36 ($SD = 12.01$).

Of most relevance in this chapter on reflection is the extent to which participants
reported cognitions, practices, and activities that valued the teaching and modeling
of reflection on one's culture. The 13 reflection-related questionnaire items were
grouped to form the reflection scale detailed with responses in Table 7.1 below.

Participants agreed moderately to strongly that they were aware of their own
culture when teaching ($M = 3.49$, $SD = 0.74$) and that they regularly used activities
in which they shared their experiences of the culture with their students ($M = 3.49$,
$SD = 0.95$). There was also moderate to strong agreement that language education
includes development of reflective understanding of one's own culture ($M = 3.42$,
$SD = 0.72$). The aspect with the lowest score ($M = 2.71$, $SD = 0.92$) was the
teacher's practice of critical analysis of their own culture in class activities.
Rounding out the three lowest scores were the practice of providing opportunities
for students to reflect on their own cultures through the eyes of others ($M = 3.04$,
$SD = 0.89$) and the cognition that to learn a new culture, one needs to consider how
it is similar to, or different from, one's own ($M = 3.07$, $SD = 0.85$).

Table 7.1 Responses to items on reflection scale

Reflection-related item	M	SD
(C12) Language education includes development of reflective understanding of one's own culture.	3.42	0.72
(C23) Language teaching ought to contribute to students' understanding of their own identities.	3.38	0.71
(C24) It is important to deepen students' knowledge about their own cultures while learning about a new culture.	3.11	0.93
(C27) To learn a new culture, you need to consider how it is similar to, or different from, your own.	3.07	0.85
(C29) Comparing languages and cultures draws students' attention to the influence of invisible culture in their lives.	3.34	0.74
(P5) I am aware of my own culture when I am teaching.	3.49	0.74
(P8) I purposefully plan to talk about my own experiences of the culture that I teach.	3.11	0.84
(P10) I provide opportunities for students to make connections with their own cultural backgrounds and experiences.	3.28	0.84
(P11) I provide opportunities for students to reflect on their own culture(s) through the eyes of others.	3.04	0.89
(P13) I critically analyze my own culture in class activities.	2.71	0.92
(A7) I talk to my students about my own experiences in the culture.	3.49	0.95
(A8) I ask my students about their experiences in the culture.	3.21	1.00
(A10) I ask my students to describe an aspect of their own culture in the target language.	2.54	1.09

Notes: C = cognitions statements, P = practice statements, and A = activities. Means and standard deviations relate to response scales where 1 = *do not agree at all* and 4 = *strongly agree* for cognitions and practices and 1 = *never use* and 4 = *frequently use* for activities.

Pearson's product-moment correlation coefficients revealed a number of significant positive relationships between scores on the reflection scale and other variables of interest. More likely to score highly on the reflection scale were those who scored highly on the ILT cognitions ($r = 0.73$, $p < 0.01$, $r^2 = 0.53$), practices ($r = 0.79$, $p < 0.01$, $r^2 = 0.62$), and activities scales ($r = 0.53$, $p < 0.01$, $r^2 = 0.28$). In addition, reflection scale scores were also positively related, at a significant level, with awareness of ILT ($r = 0.43$, $p < 0.01$, $r^2 = 0.18$).

The relationship between the reflection scale and awareness of ILT was examined further by re-coding the scale as a dichotomous variable, grouping responses as "high reflection" or "low reflection" in relation to the median of 41. The scales were compared using chi-square, where X^2 (1, N = 74) = 6.65, $p < 0.01$. The results of the cross-tabulation showed that 63% of those not aware of ILT scored in the low half of the reflection scale. Put another way, of those scoring low on the reflection scale, 76% were not aware of ILT. The high reflection scores were reasonably equally distributed regardless of reported awareness of ILT. In other words, awareness of ILT was not a prerequisite for high reflection scores, but if a low level of reflection was reported, it was more likely that the participant was not aware of ILT.

7.4.2   Findings from Cultural Portfolio Projects (CPPs)

Turning to the findings from the qualitative analysis of the CPPs data, reflection arose in three key situations:

(i). Teachers' pre-CPPs cognitions about reflection, ascertained in the planning sessions
(ii). The practice and evaluation of the reflective steps of the CPPs
(iii). Teachers' post-CPPs cognitions on the value of reflection, ascertained in the interviews.

Each situation is discussed in turn.

7.4.2.1   Teachers' Cognitions on Reflection Pre-CPPs

In discussing and planning the CPPs, Helene and Ada made some early responses regarding students' reflection on their own cultures. Helene revealed awareness of the value of reflection, believing it desirable to get students to think about these questions: "Does that happen in my culture?" and "how it might be different, how it might be similar?" These responses demonstrated an understanding of ILT's accent on critical reflection and comparison. In contrast, Ada believed the reflective steps of the CPPs would hinder her students in learning the language needed for assessments by taking up lesson time that should be devoted to language. Ada's view on students' reflection was that "they're gonna do that automatically anyway, aren't they?" This is indicative of a cultural (rather than an intercultural) orientation, and although Ada expected comparisons to be made, she thought they would be done without critical self-awareness and without the learner being transformed or relativizing their own cultural perspective (Byram, 1997; Liddicoat, 2005, 2011; Newton et al., 2010; Scarino & Liddicoat, 2009).

7.4.2.2   The Reflective Elements of the CPPs

Reflection featured prominently in two aspects of the CPPs. Firstly, it was a component of the reflection sheets that students completed after every research session, with students being required to consider whether and how the information discovered was the same or different to their own cultural view. Secondly, reformulating the hypotheses to relate to the student's own culture forced them to analyze whether their topic was relevant to their own culture and the contexts in which it was (or was not).

In general, the reflective steps of the CPPs were favorably received by the students. A student from Greenview School explained, "You only really think about your culture if something really *weird* happens? And you think, oh, *we* don't normally do that?" The reflection sheets were a mediating tool, serving as a catalyst for regular comparison of the target culture with the student's own. In retrospect, though, more could have been done to maximize the opportunity for critical self-awareness. The reflection involved was, at times, superficial, and it was not necessarily conducted critically or objectively; that is, students were not encouraged to consider their cultural stance from any other perspective. This was evident in a response from a Greenview School student researching secondary schooling in Germany who, under *similarities and differences* on his reflection sheet, wrote, "Teachers in NZ and Germany are both strict overall. But NZ teachers are friendly."

A greater degree of critical reflection was called for in the reformulation step. In talking to their parents, other teachers, the librarian, or class visitors and by searching the Internet, students were exposed to alternative perspectives within their own culture and beyond their own peer group. For most, the "borders between self and other" were explored, and for some, those borders were "problematized and redrawn" (Liddicoat, 2005, p. 33). For example, a Muirside School student researching the value of Christmas in France had reflected critically on her culture's emphasis on receiving Christmas gifts. A student from City School had initially hypothesized that German people were tolerant of different religions, based on the many religious holidays. But in objective reflection when testing her reformulated hypothesis, she was surprised by the wide range of Christian and non-Christian spiritual occasions celebrated by New Zealand.

Still, reflection was not critical in every case. Another Muirside student of French testing her reformulated hypothesis, *That New Zealand people are very formal*, revealed an absence of formal address terms in New Zealand English (cf. French *vous* and *tu*) and New Zealanders' propensity to be informal. However, there was no evidence of objective consideration of alternative viewpoints on the New Zealand approach—Is informality ever rude or disrespectful? Is formality expressed in other ways? Is formality influenced by context? Why are New Zealanders informal? and so on.

7.4.2.3 Teachers' Cognitions on Reflection Post-CPPs

Helene specified "the learning of your own culture" as a particularly valuable aspect of the CPPs. Of the three teachers, Helene was most familiar with an ILT approach at the outset. Nevertheless, through the CPPs, she had become conscious that she needed to reflect more in her classes, and she was motivated to redress that in future classes.

Craig specified reflection as the most interesting or beneficial aspect of the CPPs. He saw value in the students thinking critically about what they had found and relating it to themselves. He was astonished that it was only in reflection that his students had come to realize things about their culture he assumed they would already know. This revelation led to a reflective moment for Craig, too, as he realized the extent to which he made assumptions about his students' awareness of their own cultures. Despite New Zealand having multiple traditions from a variety of contributing cultures, these students were more capable of recognizing complexity in the target culture than in their own. In Craig's opinion, the reflection elements of the CPPs mitigated this. By facilitating their students' reflection, teachers can gain a better understanding of their students as individuals, their levels of comprehension, their background knowledge, and the constraints and affordances they experience in language learning. In SCT terms, reflection allows the teacher to ascertain the student's zone of proximal development.

When asked whether her involvement in the CPPs had revealed value in reflection, Ada said it had allowed her class to see that there were multiple perspectives within their own culture and that not everyone will think the same or agree with their interpretation. She believed they might not otherwise consider other people's perspectives because "they're teenagers so y'know it all revolves around them." Interestingly, the CPP work had led her to a similar realization, learning that there were different perspectives within her own culture, as apparent in the following excerpt from her interview:

> *Ada*: I found it very interesting I mean I had to. . .hold back a little bit. . .I wasn't gonna put my opinion on them, um, because I think sometimes what they found on the 'net or even talking to other people might have been slightly different to what I would've said? but again that was very interesting for *me* to see that even other German natives see things completely different.

Initially seeing reflection as a hindrance, Ada's view had changed at the conclusion of the project. She indicated she would use the CPPs again; in fact, she was already doing so in two other German classes. Evaluating the reformulation of the hypotheses step, she said, "The one thing that surprised me. . .was the flipping it. . .that was a step I wouldn't [normally] have taken." She said her future applications of the CPPs would include "the looking at it from your perspective. . .doing the native speaker or the native input and then flipping it. I think those three main steps." That is encouraging, but it remains unclear the depth of value that Ada saw in reflection as mediating the construction of knowledge of both cultures, that is, the target culture and her own culture, internalization of that knowledge, and mediating the development of ICC. In Ada's view, the reflection sheets were most useful for recording associated words from the target language, and she said that in future use, "I wouldn't probably call it a reflection." This evaluation might indicate a lack of appreciation of the function of reflection, but it could equally signify the need to further develop the sheet's role in reflection.

7.5 Discussion

With the assistance of SCT, the results and findings of the two phases of the study can be interpreted to respond to the research questions. Each question serves as a section heading.

RQ1: To what extent do participants value reflection in the language classroom?

The majority of participants held cognitions that saw worth in reflection in language teaching. Questionnaire participants' scores suggested that they believed language education should include development of a reflective understanding of one's own culture (the sixth highest scoring of the 29 cognition statements) and contribute to students' understanding of their cultural identities. However, in an apparent inconsistency, they valued less the importance of deepening students' knowledge of their own culture. This was apparent in Phase 2, specifically in Ada's opinion. That is, spending time on reflection was unnecessary and potentially a hindrance. In general, participants recognized that comparing languages and cultures could draw students' attention to their own invisible cultures—something also particularly valued by Phase 2 participant, Helene—but they were less convinced that comparison was useful for understanding the target culture. By its very nature, comparison must include a reflective element.

When it came to practices, questionnaire participants reported being aware of their own culture when teaching (the third highest scoring practice statement, of 20), irrespective of whether it was their own culture that they were teaching. Also commonly reported was the teacher talking about their own experiences of the target culture, but they rarely critically analyzed their own cultural perspective. Despite most participants supporting cognition statements that valued students' reflection, a smaller proportion reported providing opportunities for students to make connections with their own cultural backgrounds and experiences, and even fewer were inclined to create opportunities for students to reflect on their own culture through the eyes of others. Reporting on the extent to which they practiced reflection-oriented ILT activities, the highest score was for an activity that involved teachers modeling reflection, *I talk to students about my own experiences in the culture*, rated second highest frequency of practice of the 17 ILT activities. Asking students about *their* experiences about the target culture, though, was less common, and asking students to describe an aspect of their own culture in the target language was rare, being one of the least frequently practiced activities.

On first consideration, these findings appear confusing, conflicting, and inconsistent. There is a series of apparent mismatches: between beliefs that reflection is valuable for self-development and beliefs that reflection does not assist language learning; between beliefs that value reflection in language education but an absence of reflection-based practices in the classroom; and between teachers practicing reflection but not encouraging it in their students. Critical and objective reflection is virtually absent.

One explanation for these inconsistencies is conflict between the participants' "subsets of beliefs" (Birello, 2012, p. 91). The teachers recognized reflection as influencing self-development and cultural identity and helping to reveal one's own invisible culture. However, reflection and relativization of own culture are often not explicitly promoted in education policy, curricula, and training programs as assisting language learning per se (Castro et al., 2004; Scarino, 2014). These concepts are, therefore, less likely to form a part of the teacher's own educational and teaching experiences. As such, reflection retains the position of an abstract belief, which yields to the concrete beliefs that have been experienced, tested, and found to be true in the reality of the classroom (Birello, 2012; Feryok & Oranje, 2015; Mangubhai et al., 2005).

Inconsistency between beliefs and practices can similarly result from competition between the abstract and the concrete. Teachers reported cognitions that valued reflection in language education, but reflective activities were practiced to a lesser extent in the classroom. This suggests conflict between theoretical ideas and practical context. Despite seeing value in reflection and reflective activities, the teacher participants appeared to feel unable to exercise these ideas (or personal ideals) because of the realities (real or perceived) of the classroom (Feryok & Oranje, 2015; Mangubhai et al., 2005). These included the perception that assessment focuses on the language dimension (Roskvist et al., 2011), and actual or perceived limitations on time (Sercu et al., 2005), resources (Larzén-Östermark, 2008; Moeller & Osborn, 2014), and policy and curricula support (Castro et al., 2004; Scarino, 2014). These aspects were bound up in Ada's concerns that taking time to reflect could hinder the learning of the necessary language content. These contextual constraints suggest that teachers valued reflection as something "nice to do" rather than a necessity for effective language learning and that beliefs that valued reflection in theory yielded, in practice, to concrete beliefs that considered reflection impractical or unsupportable.

Teachers were more inclined to model reflection—albeit without criticality—than to teach their students the skill of reflection. This suggests a lack of recognition of the role of reflection in language learning, either developmentally, as assisting with internalization of new material, or interculturally, as supporting self-awareness and open-mindedness and avoiding ethnocentricity. According to SCT, the process of internalization, through which learning occurs, provides the individual with the opportunity to reflect on, question, and develop the external information before it is accepted and internally controlled (Vygotsky, 1978). Applying this to acquisition of additional languages, reflection assists the learner in recognizing alternative cultural meanings which can then be internalized and subsequently serve to mediate their thoughts and behaviors in communication (Lantolf & Thorne, 2006).

The low levels of reflection demonstrated by the teachers in this study mean that ILT is not being practiced. Put another way, the absence of reflection may be the primary factor in keeping teachers from otherwise practicing ILT. The teachers in this study demonstrated many cognitions and reported practices that aligned with ILT, and all were employed in an educational system that promoted ILT (effectively or otherwise). Since teachers were not appreciating for themselves the value of reflection, it must be that they are undereducated in ILT. These findings must be considered in light of the results relating to awareness of ILT. With two-thirds of Phase 1 participants reporting a lack of familiarity with ILT, the obvious remedy is to increase education in the approach with an emphasis on teaching and modeling the skill of reflection. The CPPs in this study achieved that to some degree, as discussed next.

RQ2. How does the practice of an intercultural activity—cultural portfolio projects—mediate teachers' understanding of the value of reflection in language education?

The CPPs used in this study were designed to be consistent with ILT. Of particular value was the transparent demonstration of the fundamental elements of ILT through the project's emphasis on exploration, reflection, and comparison. The CPPs were shown to serve as a mediational tool in four key ways.

Firstly, the step-by-step nature of the CPPs mediated teachers' understanding of ILT by undertaking the key elements as distinct stages of the activity. In this way, the CPPs served as praxis or theory in practice.

Secondly, the CPPs raised the teachers' consciousness of the reflection elements, effectively giving them access to a new tool for language teaching and learning: reflection as both a strategy and a goal of ICC (Blasco, 2012). The teachers were given the opportunity to see and test reflective activities in the social interactions between themselves and their students and between themselves and the researcher. All three teachers specified the development of reflective abilities (in themselves and/or in their students) to have been a valuable outcome of the CPPs. The new information was therefore internalized and could be controlled in future applications (Vygotsky, 1978), and thus, the teachers' ILT understanding developed.

Thirdly, the CPPs reduced the conflict among the various subsets of beliefs (Birello, 2012; Feryok & Oranje, 2015; Mangubhai et al., 2005). The outcomes of the CPPs provided evidence that ILT can be enacted without compromising beliefs held. The release of these tensions assisted in aligning teachers' cognitions and practices. Limitations, real or otherwise, on time, resources, and support, did not restrict the practice of an ILT approach and, by implication, of reflection. The reflection steps allowed teachers to learn about their students and rectify assumptions they made about the students' existing knowledge or likely practices. Reflection also allowed the teachers to learn about themselves: Craig became aware of the extent to which he made assumptions about his students, and Ada recognized that her view as a native speaker was not representative of all native speakers.

Fourthly, the mediational value of the CPPs extended to supporting the participants toward achieving the values of the New Zealand school curriculum of developing in students an "actively reflective disposition" (Ministry of Education, 2016, "What's new or different," sect. 6, para 6). Through participation in the CPP interactions, an initial view that dedicating time to reflect impeded language teaching was transformed to an acknowledgment that students are unlikely to reflect without encouragement. CPP participation allowed teachers to ascertain that students recognized complexity in the target culture, but not in their own culture. Having gained this information, teachers could direct their support, so course content was within the students' grasp to aid internalization. Even teachers with some experience of ILT came to realize that reflection had not been prominent in their teaching.

With changes, the CPPs could further enhance the value of the reflective steps. Improving the reflection sheet's role in critical cultural awareness would enhance the students' practice of ILT techniques and illuminate the extent to which their own cultures shaped their viewpoint.

7.6 Conclusions

7.6.1 Reflection Is Not Valued

Research Question 1 asked the extent to which participants value reflection in the language classroom. This chapter has demonstrated that the teachers' practices are currently insufficient in terms of modeling, teaching, and supporting reflection on one's own cultural viewpoint. It has argued that a lack of reflection is a defining feature of teachers who do not take an intercultural approach to language teaching, even if they report cognitions that support ILT. The study's participants appeared not to value reflection in their language classroom as it seemed to them not to be useful for target language learning.

7.6.2 CPPs Revealed the Value of Reflection

The primary remedy is to improve teacher education in ILT with an emphasis on reflection. In seeking a means to develop teachers' awareness of ILT, and the role of reflection particularly, the second research question asked how the practice of CPPs mediated teachers' understanding of the value of reflection in language education. This chapter identified that the CPPs made a contribution to such professional development by serving as praxis, as a kind of in-house teacher education. ILT theory was demonstrated in practice without generating conflict among teachers' subsets of beliefs and obviating inconsistency between cognitions and practices. Participating in the CPPs informed teachers on the practicalities of the implementation of the projects, the ways in which language and culture could be integrated, and the ease with which ILT could be accommodated within the limited timeframes of a school program. This newfound or advanced knowledge enabled the teachers to see ways in which their usual class activities could be adapted to an intercultural approach, and all expressed the intention of doing just that.

7.6.3 Implications and Applications in Real Language Teaching and Learning Contexts

This study's participants were generally "favorably disposed" toward teaching methods that aligned with ILT (Sercu et al., 2005, p. 10), but common across the phases of this study, and across teachers' cognitions and practices, was a lack of emphasis on the role of critical reflection in language learning. Although the "borders between self and other" were often explored, they were rarely "problematized and redrawn" (Liddicoat, 2005, p. 33) or "interrogated" from the perspectives of other cultures (Bagnall, 2005, p. 107). Such is the level of critical self-awareness expected for ICC, necessary to influence learners' knowledge, attitudes, and skills, and the extent to which they undergo personal transformation (Byram, 1997). It is impossible to compare the target cultures with one's own without critical self-awareness and an appreciation of how one's culture might be perceived by others. Without reflection, comparison activities tend to focus on differences, not similarities, and without reflection, any discoveries about the target culture remain external to the learner as a feature of "the other" (Liddicoat, 2005). In the absence of explicit teaching and modeling of objective and critical reflective practices, the teacher is operating with a cultural, not intercultural, orientation, without the goal of ICC, and with emphasis on fluency of oral performance rather than an understanding of covert meaning-making elements of interactions (Forsman, 2012; Stapleton, 2000). The CPPs considered here were a means of introducing reflection into the language classroom, although scope remains for enhancing the criticality of that reflection.

The findings of this study have contributed to language education theory by identifying CPPs as serving as praxis; exposing teachers to the method of ILT, its benefits, and its logistics; as well as enhancing teachers' understanding of the role of reflection. With this knowledge, teachers are better able to align their intercultural cognitions with their classroom practices, thereby removing mismatches noted by Byram (2014), Sercu et al. (2005), Peiser and Jones (2013), Moeller and Osborn (2014), Scarino (2014), and many others.

The application of these findings extends to teacher education and to practicing teachers. Teacher educators can introduce CPPs to student teachers as a practical means of applying a recommended theory of language development. Practicing teachers can use CPPs in their classroom. In doing so, they will benefit from exposure to clear exemplification of ILT, and their students will benefit from the opportunities to explore the target culture and reflect on their own cultures, key attributes of intercultural communicative competence.

Acknowledgments I thank Dr. Anne Feryok for reviewing and providing feedback on the initial draft of this chapter.

References

Allen, L. Q. (2004). Implementing a culture portfolio project within a constructivist paradigm. *Foreign Language Annals, 37*(2), 232–239.

Bagnall, N. (2005). Teacher cultural reflection and cultural action learning: Researching a cultural dimension in teacher education. *Ethnography and Education: European Review, 4*, 101–116.

Barrett, M. (2007). *Children's knowledge, beliefs and feelings about nations and national groups.* Hove, UK: Psychology Press.

Birello, M. (2012). Teacher cognition and language teacher education: Beliefs and practice. A conversation with Simon Borg. *Bellaterra Journal of Teaching & Learning Languages & Literature, 5*(2), 88–94.

Blasco, M. (2012). On reflection: Is reflexivity necessarily beneficial in intercultural education? 1. *Intercultural Education, 23*(6), 475–489. https://doi.org/10.1080/14675986.2012.736750.

Borg, S. (2003). Teacher cognition in language teaching: A review of research on what language teachers think, know, believe, and do. *Language Teaching, 36*, 81–109.

Byon, A. S. (2007). Use of culture portfolio project in a Korean culture classroom: Evaluating stereotypes and enhancing cross-cultural awareness. *Language, Culture and Curriculum, 20,* 1), 1–1),19.

Byram, M. (1997). *Teaching and assessing intercultural communicative competence.* Clevedon, UK: Multilingual Matters.

Byram, M. (2014). Twenty-five years on - from cultural studies to intercultural citizenship. *Language, Culture and Curriculum, 27*(3), 209–225.

Byram, M., & Risager, K. (1999). *Language teachers, politics, and cultures.* Clevedon, UK: Multilingual Matters.

Castro, P., Sercu, L., & Méndez-García, M. C. (2004). Integrating language-and-culture teaching: An investigation of Spanish teachers' perceptions of the objectives of foreign language education. *Intercultural Education, 15*(1), 91–104.

Dörnyei, Z., & Csizér, K. (2012). How to design and analyze surveys in second language acquisition research. In A. Mackey & S. M. Gass (Eds.), *Research methods in second language acquisition: A practical guide* (pp. 74–94). Chichester, England: Wiley-Blackwell.

East, M., & Scott, A. (2011). Assessing the foreign language proficiency of high school students in New Zealand: From the traditional to the innovative. *Language Assessment Quarterly, 8*(2), 179–189.

Feryok, A., & Oranje, J. (2015). Adopting a cultural portfolio project in teaching German as a foreign language: Language teacher cognition as a dynamic system. *Modern Language Journal, 99*(3). https://doi.org/10.1111/modl.12243.

Forsman, L. (2012). Investigating the cultural dimension in foreign language education – From transmission of facts to dialogical uptake. *Educational Action Research, 20*(4), 483–496. https://doi.org/10.1080/09650792.2012.727602.

Han, X., & Song, L. (2011). Teacher cognition of intercultural communicative competence in Chinese ELT context. *Intercultural Communication Studies, XX*(1), 175–192.

Jedynak, M. (2011). The attitudes of English teachers towards developing intercultural communicative competence. In J. Arabski & A. Wojtaszek (Eds.), *Aspects of culture in second language acquisition and foreign language learning* (pp. 63–73). Berlin, Germany: Springer.

Lantolf, J. P., & Thorne, S. L. (2006). *Sociocultural theory and the genesis of second language development.* Oxford, UK: Oxford University Press.

Larzén-Östermark, E. (2008). The intercultural dimension in EFL-teaching: A study of conceptions among Finland-Swedish comprehensive school teachers. *Scandinavian Journal of Educational Research, 52*(5), 527–547. https://doi.org/10.1080/00313830802346405.

Liddicoat, A. J. (2005). Culture for language learning in Australian language-in-education policy. *Australian Review of Applied Linguistics, 28*(2), 28–43.

Liddicoat, A. J. (2011). Language teaching and learning from an intercultural perspective. In E. Hinkel (Ed.), *Handbook of research in second language teaching and learning* (Vol. II, pp. 837–855). New York: Routledge.

Mangubhai, F., Marland, P., Dashwood, A., & Son, J. (2005). Similarities and differences in teachers' and researchers' conceptions of communicative language teaching: Does the use of an educational model cast a better light? *Language Teaching Research, 9*(1), 31–66.

Ministry of Education. (2007). *The New Zealand curriculum.* Wellington, New Zealand: Published for the Ministry of Education by Learning Media.

Ministry of Education. (2016). *Learning languages*. Retrieved June 12, 2016, from http://seniorsecondary.tki.org.nz/Learning-languages

Moeller, A. J., & Osborn, S. R. (2014). A pragmatist perspective on building intercultural communicative competency: From theory to classroom practice. *Foreign Language Annals, 47*(4), 669–683.

Newton, J., Yates, E., Shearn, S., & Nowitzki, W. (2010). *Intercultural communicative language teaching: Implications for effective teaching and learning. (Rep.)*. Wellington, New Zealand: Ministry of Education.

Packer, M. J., & Goicoechea, J. (2000). Sociocultural and constructivist theories of learning: Ontology, not just epistemology. *Educational Psychologist, 35*(4), 227–241.

Peiser, G., & Jones, M. (2013). The influence of teachers' interests, personalities and life experiences in intercultural languages teaching. *Teachers and Teaching: Theory and Practice, 20*(3), 375–390. https://doi.org/10.1080/13540602.2013.848525.

Rokeach, M. (1968). *Beliefs, attitudes, and values: A theory of organization and change*. San Francisco: Jossey-Bass.

Roskvist, A., Corder, D., Harvey, S., & Stacey, K. (2011). Developing language teaching capability through immersion programmes and the impact on student language learning: Cultural knowledge and intercultural competence. In A. Witte & T. Harden (Eds.), *Intercultural competence: Concepts, challenges, evaluations* (pp. 209–224). Oxford: Peter Lang.

Scarino, A. (2014). Learning as reciprocal, interpretive meaning-making: A view from collaborative research into the professional learning of teachers of languages. *The Modern Language Journal, 98*(1), 386–401.

Scarino, A., & Liddicoat, A. (2009). *Teaching and learning languages: A guide*. Carlton South, Australia: Curriculum Corporation.

Sercu, L., Bandura, E., Castro, P., Davcheva, L., Laskaridou, C., Lundgren, U., & Ryan, P. (2005). *Foreign language teachers and intercultural competence: An international investigation*. Clevedon, UK: Multilingual Matters.

Stapleton, P. (2000). Culture's role in TEFL: An attitude survey in Japan. *Language, Culture and Curriculum, 13*(3), 291–305.

Su, Y. (2011). The effects of the cultural portfolio project on cultural and EFL learning in Taiwan's EFL college classes. *Language Teaching Research, 15*(2), 230–252. https://doi.org/10.1177/1362168810388721.

Swain, M., Kinnear, P., & Steinman, L. (2011). *Sociocultural theory in second language education: An introduction through narratives*. Bristol, England: Multilingual Matters.

Vygotsky, L. S. (1978). In M. Cole, V. John-Steiner, S. Scribner, & E. Souberman (Eds.), *Mind in society: The development of higher psychological processes*. Cambridge, UK, Harvard University Press.

Wertsch, J. V., Del Río, P., & Álvarez, A. (1995). Sociocultural studies: History, action, and mediation. In J. V. Wertsch, P. Del Río, & A. Álvarez (Eds.), *Sociocultural studies of mind* (pp. 1–34). Cambridge, UK: Cambridge University Press.

Part II
Forging the Future

Chapter 8
Attitudes Toward English as a Lingua Franca Among Prospective EFL Teachers in Spain

Rubén Chacón-Beltrán

8.1 Introduction

Lingua francas have played a crucial role throughout history on the development of civilization by facilitating communication among people of different cultures for different purposes. There have been, and there are, many instances of such "tools" for intercultural communication, but if there is a lingua franca that is playing a prominent role in the world at the moment, it is English. More than 375 million people speak English as a first language, and one-quarter of the world's population (375 million) speak it as a second or foreign language (Crystal, 2012).

Lingua francas have existed for centuries, as it is the case of Sabir in the Mediterranean, which dated back to the Middle Ages. A more recent example is English, which in the last 300 years has become a widespread means of communication for speakers not sharing a common first language. There are lots of definitions of *English as a* Lingua Franca (ELF) as it has become an area of interest not only in the fields of dialectology and intercultural communication but also because of its connections and interest for the areas of Foreign/Second Language Teaching and Foreign/Second Language Learning/Acquisition. A recent definition of ELF is "a vehicular language spoken by people who do not share a native language" (Mauranen, 2003, p. 513), a straightforward definition that emphasizes its instrumental nature and excludes the so-called native speaker of the language as part of the communication process. In a similar vein, Kecskes (2013) defines ELF as the use of English as a means of communication by speakers whose first language is not English. Some other broader definitions center on the eligibility of the language as a means of communication including the so-called native speakers of the language,

R. Chacón-Beltrán (✉)
Universidad Nacional de Educación a Distancia (UNED), Madrid, Spain
e-mail: rchacon@flog.uned.es

© Springer Nature Singapore Pte Ltd. 2021
M. D. López-Jiménez, J. Sánchez-Torres (eds.), *Intercultural Competence Past, Present and Future*, Intercultural Communication and Language Education, https://doi.org/10.1007/978-981-15-8245-5_8

for instance, "any use of English among speakers of different first languages for whom English is the communicative medium of choice, and often the only option" (Seidlhofer, 2011, p. 7).

Kecskes (2015) uses the term "intracultural communication" to define interactions between members of a relatively definable speech community who share conventions of language and conventions of usage. By contrast, "intercultural communication" is defined as "[. . .] interactions between speakers who have different first languages, communicate in a common language, and, usually, represent different cultures" (Kecskes, 2015, p. 175). He refers to these two terms not as absolute ones but as related ones that are situated at two ends of a continuum, and communication situations are closer or farther away from each end depending on a range of factors.

In the last few decades, many studies have analyzed ELF by paying particular attention to linguistic features such as syntax, phonology, and pragmatics (Björkman, 2011; Jenkins, 2000; McGroarty, 2006; Prodromou, 2008) or aspects like intelligibility (Berns, 2008; Mauranen, 2006; Pickering, 2006; van Mulken & Hendriks, 2015) or sociolinguistic features (Berns, 2009; House, 2003; Seidlhofer, 2013). More recent approaches have moved into the field of interculturality by analyzing ideas like "the projection of cultural identity, the promotion of solidarity, the sharing of humor" (Jenkins, Cogo, & Dewey, 2011, p. 296). Holmes and Dervin (2016) expand on this intercultural approach, exploring a number of aspects of research that are often understated or ignored but which account for the complexity of the intercultural communication process. They explore:

> [. . .] how languages are shaped and constructed in interactions and intercultural encounters as well as how the (inter)subjectivities of individuals' multiple realities and identities inevitably influence how and why people engage with one another, and their understandings of those encounters. Using and understanding language in communication thus goes beyond static, reified, normative and discrete forms of language and interaction to account for individuals' (inter)subjectivities, which in turn are influenced by history, geography, languages, culture, religion, multiple identities, social class, economics, power, belonging, etc. Reference to this aspect of research on interculturality is often absent from studies of ELF. (Holmes & Dervin, 2016, p. 2)

The truth is that at the beginning of the twenty-first century, English as a Lingua Franca has become "the global lingua franca" and one of the distinctive features of our time, together with other social phenomena like globalization, the Internet, networking, and a globalized economy. Mauranen (2009) signals that English is currently perceived as a vehicle of efficiency, both in business and science. An opposing view of the role of English in the world is held by those authors who consider the expansion of English a threat for multilingualism (House, 2003; Phillipson, 2006).

The vivid debate about the nature of language as a communicative tool and its relationship to wider culture continues among academics. As indicated by Holmes and Dervin (2016), the existing literature could usefully be extended by relating the discussions surrounding language and culture specifically to ELF. The work reported in this chapter extends the literature through the contribution of empirical evidence based on a survey of teachers.

8.2 ELF in Foreign Language Teaching and Learning

Mauranen (2009) describes how ELF has been hotly debated but relatively little studied. Therefore, research should probably focus on the elaboration of new learner and non-native corpora (generated by so-called non-native speakers) to characterize and identify distinctive features in the use of ELF. This way, we will better understand ELF and its relationship to English Language Teaching and Learning (ELT) and open up fresh avenues for research. In this sense, big improvements have been made, thanks to the establishment of projects like the ELFA corpus in Helsinki (www.eng.helsinki.fi/elfa) in 2008 and VOICE corpus in Vienna in 2009 (www.univie.ac.at/voice).

In terms of the increasing interest in researching ELF in ELT, Baker (2016) details current research on ELF and ELT spanning teachers and students' attitudes (Jenkins, 2009), teacher training (Dewey, 2012), materials (Baker, 2012a, 2012b), motivation (Csizér & Kontra, 2012), writing (Horner, 2011), English for specific purposes (Mauranen & Hynninen, 2010), English medium instruction in higher education (Jenkins, 2014), phonology (Walker, 2010), online communication (Guth & Helm, 2012), and grounding conceptual understandings could be added (Bjørge, 2016; Jenks, 2016; Kaur, 2016).

There remains an important contradiction at the moment with regard to the English language in ELT from a sociolinguistic perspective. Despite the widespread acceptance of the role of English as an international language that can be used as a lingua franca for intercultural communication, there seems to be a widespread resistance to welcoming its use in the area of ELT. This is perhaps caused by a rather ethnocentric perspective in the field of ELT, which, as an important worldwide industry, recognizes just two or three dominant varieties of English as linguistic and cultural models and referents; on the other hand, it may have to do with identity issues related to the preservation and expansion of certain varieties of language. The causes of the resistance are still widely discussed. Comparing the views of Sowden (2012) and Cogo (2012) serves to provide a sense of the character of the general debate. Sowden (2012) questions ELF models and corpus-based research, whereas Cogo (2012) is in favor of exploring naturally occurring real ELF data and considers that research should describe and make sense of the processes involved in lingua franca talk and the strategies used by its speakers. In this chapter, the focus will be placed on the attitudes toward ELF in ELT contexts.

8.3   The Study

In the current context of Spanish primary and secondary education, both within the public and private school systems, there is growing interest in the implementation of bilingual education programs. This tends to be in the form of the so-called CLIL (Content and Language Integrated Learning) programs, by means of which part of the curriculum is taught in a foreign language. Therefore, within this program, some content subjects are taught in English, often by teachers with a certain command of English whose first language is not English. The English proficiency level required from teachers is determined by local institutional regulations as regional governments in Spain are responsible for education. These teachers of various "content" subjects very often have not received extensive training in ELT and often have undergone only limited training in language use and linguistics. As a result, English teachers in schools, apart from teaching EFL (English as a Foreign Language), act as coordinators and assessors for these bilingual programs. This means English teachers hold a core position for both the implementation of the programs and as a reference and language consultant for content teachers.

Given the crucial role of English teachers in these educational programs and the fact that their first language tends to be Spanish rather than English, the current chapter intersects with an ongoing debate about the advantages and disadvantages of so-called "native" and "non-native" teachers. This debate was discussed extensively a couple of decades ago, making reference to EFL teachers (Árva & Medgyes, 2000; Chacón-Beltrán, 2000; Medgyes, 1994), but has recently returned onto the scene with the implementation of CLIL programs. More recently, some studies have analyzed linguistic differences in language use and discourse between so-called native and non-native teachers (Dafouz, Nunez, & Sancho, 2007; Llinares-García & Romero-Trillo, 2008). Analysis of their definition, classification, relative advantages and disadvantages of the teachers concerned, and more contentious issues related to discrimination is beyond the scope of this chapter. The wider debate is highlighted in this chapter to prompt researchers and teachers to start thinking about the issue of what variety of English, if any, should be taught in the classroom or, indeed, is currently being taught. In one sense, in a context where English is mainly taught by teachers whose first language is not the target language, as is the case with CLIL, the English being taught will depend on the particular training that each teacher has received. In this case, the most likely situation is that of teaching ELF for international and intercultural communication. The author of this chapter is unaware of any research analyzing this sociolinguistic aspect of the CLIL programs in Spain. Bearing these ideas in mind, there is a clear need for some appraisal and analysis of the attitudes toward ELF among prospective teachers at different stages in their training and compare those with qualified, serving teachers.

Three areas of interest were put forward in order to investigate the attitudes in each of the four groups of informants under analysis:

(a) The knowledge and awareness of ELF of prospective teachers of English
(b) The underlying reasons for attitudes toward ELF

(c) Individual respondents' beliefs, both as language learners and also as future teachers who will eventually be spreading a specific linguistic model among their students.

8.3.1 Research Questions

In the light of the above, the following research questions were raised:

1. Can prospective non-native teachers of English in a Spanish context identify varieties of English and provide examples? Do they show preferences for one variety over another? Does this perception change over time during their training, and how does it compare to professional teachers?
2. Are these prospective teachers aware of the idea of ELF and identify a correct definition? What do they know about the role of culture in the EFL classroom?
3. Do they think their use of English (both in speaking and writing) can change due to a long stay in an English-speaking country?
4. Do they think they will have more opportunities in life to speak to native speakers or to non-native speakers both on personal and professional grounds?

In answering these questions, we hope to provide insight into the perceptions, beliefs, and attitudes of prospective teachers of English in Spain and also analyze the impact these attitudes may have on their students.

8.4 Data Collection Procedure

An online questionnaire (see Appendix) was distributed among non-native speakers of English studying and working in Spain and being trained as prospective English as a Foreign Language teachers. A total of 175 informants took part in this study and completed a questionnaire containing three parts:

a. Demographic data, including age, gender, experience/s in English-speaking countries, and self-rating level of English
b. Checking their understanding of ELF and self-perception of the variety of English they speak
c. Analysis of attitudes toward ELF and implications for EFL

Both quantitative and qualitative data were gathered through the questionnaire and subsequently contrasted within and across groups.

8.4.1   Target Groups

Four target groups (TG1, TG2, TG3, and TG4) were chosen for this study with common features according to their linguistic and cultural background and professional interests. These four target groups were progressive in terms of their linguistic competence, and they were graded starting at CEFR level B2 (TG1) up to level C2 (TG4). With regard to their knowledge and understanding of the English-speaking culture, they also had increasing knowledge: the first group was composed of second year university students taking a degree in English language, linguistics, literature, and culture, and the top group comprised teachers being trained in CLIL and/or with teaching experience in the methodology. The four target groups also shared some common features. For example, they were all Spanish speakers of English as a Foreign Language, and they were based in Spain and surrounded by Spanish culture. They were familiar with both the Spanish education system and English a Foreign Language, and finally, they were all being trained following a distance education model particularly conceived for adult learning and based on the use of new technologies, that is, virtual courses. Here follows a more detailed description of the four aforementioned groups:

TG1 These were second year students taking a degree in English Studies who would eventually become EFL teachers. As part of their degree, they needed to take subjects related to language, linguistics, literature, and culture, all in a distance teaching/learning university which entailed distance teaching/learning methodology. The informants were asked to take part in the study on a voluntary and anonymous basis and were recruited from an English language course which aimed, by the end of the academic year, to help them to attain a B2 level of English according to the CEFR.

TG2 These were third year students taking a degree in English Studies who would eventually become EFL teachers. Being 1 year ahead of the informants in TG1 in the same degree, they were taking a subject in Applied Sociolinguistics; this covered the basic concepts and terminology related to the field of sociolinguistics as well as sociolinguistic aspects of bilingualism and bilingual education. The informants were again asked to take part in the study on a voluntary and anonymous basis, and at the end of the academic year, they were expected to be at C1 level of English according to the CEFR.

TG3 These were fourth year students enrolled in the same degree in English Studies as TG1 and TG2, but they had completed the subject in Applied Sociolinguistics and were therefore familiar with the concepts and terminology related to bilingualism and bilingual education. Their level of English was higher as they were in their next to last semester of study. Their level of English was then C1+, and they had a profound knowledge of the culture and literature from the English-speaking world.

TG4 Finally, the last group of informants was composed of practicing teachers of English, having completed a degree in English language and literature, as well as some teachers of different subjects (Maths, PE, Science, etc.) taking part in an online yearlong teacher training program on CLIL. Their level of English ranged from C1+ to C2, and they had a broad knowledge of the English language and culture as they had also often travelled to English-speaking countries.

8.5   Data Analysis and Results

A total of 175 informants took part in the study with the following distribution: TG1, n = 55 (31.4%); TG2, n = 82 (46.9%); TG3, n = 28 (16%); and TG4, n = 10 (5.7%). With regard to the demographic data, that is, age, gender, experience/s in English-speaking countries, self-rating level of English, specialized training, and professional preferences, the following data was gathered.

There was an unbalanced representation of males and females in the target groups as can be seen in Table 8.1. Roughly one-fourth of the informants were male, and three-fourths were female. This imbalance, however, closely corresponds to the percentage of students in Philology studies at the university level in Spain and consequently in the teaching profession more generally.

In terms of age, it is interesting to notice that, as illustrated in Table 8.2, most informants were in the age group comprising between 21 and 50. It should be remembered that the study was carried out in the context of a distance teaching university in Spain, namely, UNED (Universidad Nacional de Educación a Distancia). That is the reason why TG1, TG2, and TG3 are students with a higher mean age than usual in many conventional university settings.

As the aim of this study was to analyze the participants' attitude toward a foreign language, their background, in terms of time spent abroad as well as the specific location of their stays, is relevant as it may have an effect on these attitudes.

Table 8.1   Males and females taking part in this study in each of the four target groups

TG1			TG2			TG3			TG4		
Female	40	72.7%	Female	57	72.2%	Female	21	75%	Female	7	70%
Male	14	25.5%	Male	21	26%	Male	7	25%	Male	3	30%
N/A	1	1.8%	N/A	1	1.3%	N/A	0	0%	N/A	0	0%

Table 8.2   Age of informants taking part in this study in each of the four target groups

TG1			TG2			TG3			TG4		
−20	0	0%	−20	0	0%	−20	0	0%	−20	0	0%
21–30	18	32.7%	21–30	23	29.1%	21–30	9	32.1%	21–30	2	20%
31–40	18	32.7%	31–40	28	35.4%	31–40	13	46.4%	31–40	5	50%
41–50	17	30.9%	41–50	19	24.1%	41–50	3	10.7%	41–50	3	30%
51–60	2	3.6%	51–60	6	7.6%	51–60	3	10.7%	51–60	0	0%
+60	0	0%	+60	3	3.8%	+60	0	0%	+60	0	0%

Table 8.3 Length of stays abroad of the informants taking part in this study in each of the four target groups

TG1			TG2			TG3			TG4		
Yes	51	92.7%	Yes	69	87.3%	Yes	22	78.6%	Yes	8	80%
No	4	7.3%	No	10	12.7%	No	6	21.4%	No	2	20%
UK	47	92.2%	UK	65	95.6%	UK	20	90.9%	UK	8	100%
Irl	13	25.5%	Irl	25	36.8%	Irl	5	22.7%	Irl	4	50%
USA	18	35.3%	USA	26	38.2%	USA	11	50%	USA	5	62.5%
Aus/NZ	3	5.9%	Aus/NZ	7	10.3%	Aus/NZ	1	4.5%	Aus/NZ	0	0%
Other	5	9.8%	Other	8	11.8%	Other	1	4.5%	Other	0	0%
< 10d	5	9.8%	< 10d	9	13%	< 10d	4	18.2%	< 10d	1	12.5%
11 – 20d	8	15.7%	11 – 20d	7	10.1%	11 – 20d	2	9.1%	11 – 20d	0	0%
21d – 3 m	20	39.2%	21d – 3 m	14	20.3%	21d – 3 m	4	18.2%	21d – 3 m	1	12.5%
3 – 6 m	5	9.8%	3 – 6 m	15	21.7%	3 – 6 m	2	9.1%	3 – 6 m	0	0%
6 – 12 m	4	7.8%	6 – 12 m	8	11.6%	6 – 12 m	4	18.2%	6 – 12 m	0	0%
1 – 3y	5	9.8%	1 – 3y	11	15.9%	1 – 3y	4	18.2%	1 – 3y	5	62.5%
+ 3y	4	7.8%	+ 3 y	5	7.2%	+ 3y	2	9.1%	+ 3y	1	12.5%

Table 8.4 Self-rating of informants' overall level of English

TG1			TG2			TG3			TG4		
(A2)	1	1.8%	(A2)	0	0%	(A2)	0	0%	(A2)	0	0%
(B1)	11	20%	(B1)	2	2.5%	(B1)	1	3.6%	(B1)	2	20%
(B2)	20	36.4%	(B2)	15	19%	(B2)	4	14.3%	(B2)	2	20%
(C1)	16	29.1%	(C1)	40	50.6%	(C1)	13	46.4%	(C1)	2	20%
(C2)	5	9.1%	(C2)	18	22.8%	(C2)	9	32.1%	(C2)	4	40%
Native-like	2	3.6%	Native-like	4	5.1%	Native-like	1	3.6%	Native-like	0	0%

The following table (Table 8.3) shows that over 78% of participants had spent some time abroad; in the case of TG1, which corresponded to second year university students, an overwhelming 92% of participants had spent time abroad. It is interesting to see that TG1 and TG2 showed higher rates of stays abroad, and in very diverse places, compared to TG3 and TG4. This may indicate that younger generations are travelling more. With regard to the places visited, informants in TG4 correspond to an older age group, and that may explain why higher percentages have been obtained for each location.

As we can see in Table 8.4, self-rating level of English varies considerably, but rating at level B2 and below stands as TG1, 58.2%; TG2, 21.5%; TG3, 17.9%; and TG4, 40%, whereas self-rating at level C1 and above is TG1, 41.8%; TG2, 78.5%; TG3, 82.1%; and TG4, 60%. This data indicates that except for TG1, most informants report a level above C1, which entails a good command of English. The fact

Table 8.5 Informants' intention to become teachers

TG1			TG2			TG3		
Yes	29	52.7%	Yes	44	56.4%	Yes	15	53.6%
No	15	27.3%	No	13	16.7%	No	6	21.4%
N/A	11	20%	N/A	21	26.9%	N/A	7	25%

Table 8.6 Years of experience as teachers for TG4

TG4		
None	0	0%
< 1 year	1	10%
1 – 2y	1	10%
2 – 5y	2	20%
5 – 8y	1	10%
8 – 15y	4	40%
+ 15y	1	10%

Table 8.7 Informants' self-identification with a specific variety of English in speaking

TG1	TG2	TG3	TG4
Yes: 25 45.5% No: 30 54.5%	Yes: 37 46.8% No: 42 53.2%	Yes: 10 35.7% No: 18 64.3%	Yes: 5 50% No: 5 50%

that a higher percentage of TG1 participants report a level up to B2 just indicates that second year students at the university level are relatively aware of their level of English according to the CEFR as B2 is precisely the level they are aiming at in TG1.

The following question asked whether the informants intended to become teachers. Just over half of participants still in training were clear in their intention to embrace the teaching profession; about half as many in each group did not intend to become teachers. Notably, about a quarter of the informants did not answer the question which suggests that they were still undecided (Table 8.5).

With regard to TG4, a group which had already been trained as teachers, the results indicate that over 80% had more than 2 years of experience and 60% more than 5 years of experience, which shows that they were well immersed in the teaching profession (Table 8.6).

The next part of the questionnaire distributed to the informants consisted of a set of questions designed to analyze their understanding of what English as a Lingua Franca is. They were requested to provide instances of varieties of English they knew. They were also tested to see if they could identify a proper definition of ELF in a multiple-choice format. It was revealed that in absolute terms, 98.8% of the informants could identify the proper definition; interestingly, those who had not, or not recently, taken the course in *Applied Sociolinguistics*—TG1 and TG4—scored higher than TG2 and TG3, who were taking or had recently taken the subject *which* covers this content.

Next, informants needed to specify whether they identified themselves with a specific variety of English in speaking and writing (Table 8.7). It was revealing to

Table 8.8 Informants' self-identification with a specific variety of English in writing

TG1	TG2	TG3	TG4
Yes: 24 44.4%	Yes: 42 53.2%	Yes: 9 32.1%	Yes: 2 20%
No: 30 54.6%	No: 37 46.8%	No: 19 67.9%	No: 8 80%

Table 8.9 Informants' anticipation of a possible change in the variety of English they use over time

TG1	TG2	TG3	TG4
Fixed: 5 9.1%	Fixed: 9 11.3%	Fixed: 1 3.6%	Fixed: 5 50%
Changing: 50 90.9%	Changing: 71 88.8%	Changing: 27 96.4%	Changing: 5 50%

see how a majority of informants did not identify themselves with any particular variety in speaking. This is perhaps surprising given that many informants had travelled a lot and even lived for some time in an English-speaking country where they could be expected to have adopted a local variety; indeed, for this reason, the researcher had anticipated that most respondents would identify with a specific variety. As a matter of fact, the reasons provided by those who identified themselves with a specific variety to explain why they had adopted it supported this hypothesis (e.g., "Because I'm living in Cambridge at the moment," "Because I have lived in London," etc.), and it was just that less participants than expected reported having spent an extended period of time exposed to the same variety. These results were relatively consistent across the four TGs.

The absence of self-identification with a certain variety in speaking was consistent with responses about writing; overall, even more participants identified with no particular variety in writing than in speaking (Table 8.8).

Participants were asked whether they thought the variety of English they used would change over time. Their answers are summarized in Table 8.9.

There follow some sample reasons provided by participants explaining why they felt that their variety of English would not change:

Spending long periods of time in a place where that specific variety is spoken. (My translation)

Above all, living in an English-speaking country where a variety is spoken. (My translation)

Living in English-speaking areas. (My translation)

Spending a long time in an English-speaking country and acquiring features associated to that variety. (My translation)

The main aim of this study was to analyze the attitudes of teachers and prospective teachers toward the teaching of both English as a Foreign Language or content subjects (in CLIL programs) while adhering to either a specific variety of English or ELF. Table 8.10 shows how higher percentages of informants prefer to teach ELF rather than a specific variety in all TGs. This preference is especially conspicuous in TG3, with a higher experience and training in ELF as they are close to finish their university studies, and clearer still in TG4 composed of practicing teachers. It is also

Table 8.10 Percentages of informants who would rather teach a particular variety of English or ELF

TG1	TG2	TG3	TG4
Var: 23 41.8%	Var: 36 45.6%	Var: 7 25.9%	Var: 1 10%
ELF: 32 58.2%	ELF: 43 54.4%	ELF: 20 74.1%	ELF: 9 90%

Note: Var stands for "teaching a specific variety," and ELF stands for "teaching ELF."

Table 8.11 Scores in a multiple-choice test to identify the correct definition of ELF

TG1	TG2	TG3	TG4
100%	98.8%	96.4%	100%

Table 8.12 Percentages of informants who felt that teaching a language requires knowledge of the culture or could just be taught as a lingua franca

TG1	TG2	TG3	TG4
Cult: 43 78.2%	Cult: 56 71.8%	Cult: 12 42.9%	Cult: 4 40%
ELF: 12 21.8%	ELF: 22 28.2%	ELF: 16 57.1%	ELF: 6 60%

Table 8.13 Percentages of informants who, according to a 6-item Likert scale, felt that in professional contexts they will have more opportunity to use English to interact with non-native (1 on the scale) or native (6) speakers of English

TG1	TG2	TG3	TG4
1 1 1.8%	1 7 8.5%	1 0 0%	1 0 0%
2 7 12.7%	2 11 13.4%	2 2 7.1%	2 2 20%
3 7 12.7%	3 11 13.4%	3 2 7.1%	3 1 10%
4 7 12.7%	4 23 28%	4 11 39.3%	4 1 10%
5 20 36.4%	5 15 18.3%	5 9 32.1%	5 2 20%
6 13 23.6%	6 15 18.3%	6 4 14.3%	6 4 40%

Table 8.14 Percentages of informants who, according to a 6-item Likert scale, felt that in personal contexts they will have more opportunity to use English to interact with non-native (1 on the scale) or native (6) speakers of English

TG1	TG2	TG3	TG4
1 2 3.6%	1 5 6.1%	1 1 3.6%	1 2 20%
2 7 12.7%	2 16 19.5%	2 0 0%	2 1 10%
3 11 20%	3 12 14.6%	3 9 32.1%	3 1 10%
4 9 16.4%	4 20 24.4%	4 10 35.7%	4 3 30%
5 17 30.9%	5 17 20.7%	5 3 10.7%	5 1 10%
6 9 16.4%	6 12 14.6%	6 5 17.9%	6 2 20%

worth mentioning that these percentages are higher than those pertaining to informants' self-identification with a certain variety (see Tables 8.11 and 8.7).

Table 8.10 reflects how the different TGs perceived the relationship between dissociated and the teaching of English as a "neutral" instrument of communication with others in the form of an ELF.

Participants were asked whether they thought that English could be taught and learned purely as an instrument of communication (a lingua franca) or whether they felt that it constitutes an inextricable part of a cultural system which must be included, to a greater or lesser extent, in the teaching process (Table 8.12).

Finally, the four target groups were asked the extent to which they thought they would have more opportunity to use English to interact with native speakers of English or non-native speakers of English (see Appendix for the questions). It was found out that in professional contexts, a high percentage of informants felt that, on the whole, they would interact more with non-native speakers than native speakers: 4–6 on the 6-level Likert scale (TG1 72.7%; TG2 59.6%; TG3 85.7%; TG4 70%) (Table 8.13).

In personal contexts (i.e., holidays), the results showed increases in anticipated interaction with native speakers though there was still a majority of interaction with non-natives (see Table 8.14).

Some qualitative analysis of the issue was also considered relevant. Therefore, a few open answers in the questionnaires aimed at identifying the informants' feelings and perceptions in favor or against learning ELF. Here follow some comments of both groups:

General comments *in favor* of teaching and learning ELF:

You can be in Prague talking to a Frenchman in absolutely comprehensible international English. . .but you will probably won't understand (or at least not so easily) an Englishman from Bristol sitting next to you. (My translation)

Talking in English with a native speaker requires knowing of and participating in his culture. If we speak English as a Lingua Franca, it is a completely different context. In this case, the most important thing is communication, and cultural aspects can be considered separately. (My translation)

I worked for a few months in the Council of Europe that has English and French as official languages. That was a melting pot. Only the English people spoke English properly. Pronunciation was poor, language skills were rather scarce, but everyone could communicate adequately, both civil servants and politicians. That made me think. . .Why then should we learn "proper" British English? (My translation)

General comments *against* teaching and learning ELF:

Even if English is used as a lingua franca, we should not forget that it is also a mother tongue for many people and that the language is closely linked to culture and some patterns of behavior that we should also take into account and that we should learn and teach.

In order to teach English as a Lingua Franca, it is not necessary to know in depth the British, Irish, Australian, or North American culture. It is very important, however, to know the origins of the language, the cultural background, etc.

8.6 Conclusions

This research engaged teachers and prospective teachers of English to identify their preferences and attitudes toward ELF and other varieties of English. This work is based on the premise that understanding (prospective) teachers' knowledge and attitudes, based on their experiences, could shed some fresh light on a debate among linguists and language educators that often overlooks teachers. The fact that non-native teachers have such a central role in the spread of English for intercultural communication places them in an influential position. As Mauranen (2009) mentions, ELF needs to be researched further, and in view of the analysis presented in this chapter, it seems that both linguistic and educational perspectives should be researched together.

The data presented in this study shows that teachers, both training and practicing, are aware of the existence of many varieties of English. They tend to identify these as geographical varieties, and they often coincide with national boundaries, that is, countries rather than regions or cities within a country. In the same vein, informants of all four groups could provide clear examples of varieties they were aware of, or were familiar with, and they also showed personal preferences which were very often influenced by having spent some time where that variety was used. It was interesting to see how there was a distinction in their self-identification with a specific variety of English with regard to writing and speaking. In writing, there was a progression from teachers in initial stages of their training to in-service teachers in terms of detachment from one specific variety as they progressed in their training. This evolution was less commonly expressed in terms of speaking, which seems to indicate that they tend to find geographical features more present, or more conspicuous, in speaking than in writing. It was also evident from their responses to the open questions that even if they thought their use of both spoken and written English was closer to a specific variety of English, they did not consider themselves "speakers of that variety." Rather, they considered themselves speakers of an English which we have labelled *English as a* Lingua Franca.

The analysis of the data also confirmed how teachers and teachers in training can identify a correct definition of ELF and are well aware of its existence. It was also interesting to see an evolution from teachers in the early stages of their training, who mostly thought that learning the language had to be undoubtedly linked to the learning of the culture generally associated with the target language, to practicing teachers who tended to feel that the language can be learned for instrumental purposes without close association to culture. Teachers in CLIL teaching contexts do not generally focus on one variety of English unless they have spent an extended period of time in a given country, which is often not the case. Conversely, teachers, and prospective teachers, tend to teach a neutral variety of English, which contains features from different varieties, in essence, *English as a* Lingua Franca. This is probably so as a consequence of their training, with exposure to different varieties, and their personal experience in travelling or being in contact with native speakers from different English-speaking countries.

All four groups agreed that a stay abroad in an English-speaking country can have an effect on the variety of English used by the learner, but in their responses to open questions, some of them demonstrated that this effect may not be fixed. The most important thing for them is language for intercultural communication; the variety of English they use, both in speaking and writing, may change over the course of their lives.

The results also indicate that they consider that they and their students will have more opportunities to speak English with non-native speakers of the language than with native speakers, in both professional and personal contexts. This implies that they perceive the advantages of learning English for intercultural communication but not necessarily with native speakers of the target language, in this case English, but with native speakers of other mother tongues that use ELF.

In a world where intercultural communication is growing steadily, and where teachers and students more and more frequently have the chance to travel abroad with exchange programs, there seem to be more awareness of the importance of learning English as a language for wider communication.

This research has identified that (prospective) English teachers are generally aware of ELF and have a positive attitude toward it, mainly because they feel that they are likely to more often use English to communicate with non-native speakers over the course of their lives. This suggests that the wider debate surrounding so-called "native" and "non-native" teachers mentioned at the start of this chapter deserves consideration. In this sense, the value of teaching ELF seems to be recognized, bringing with it an increasing acceptance of the teaching of ELF in the classroom, at least among this sample. However, this study is just one piece of the puzzle in need of replication and extension. Work is needed to replicate this analysis with a larger cohort of participants and perhaps contrast these results with other contexts, such as teachers with a multilingual rather than a bilingual background.

Appendix

Online questionnaire used to gather information. This questionnaire was distributed in Spanish to the informants, and they were also requested to answer in Spanish.

Please answer this questionnaire which is part of a research project that is currently being carried out at the *Universidad Nacional de Educación a Distancia* (UNED), Madrid, in order to better understand teachers' attitudes toward teaching English. In this questionnaire, there are no "right" or "wrong" answers. All the personal information will be kept confidential. We are just interested in knowing your sincere opinion. Thanks for your cooperation.

Section 1

1. E-mail
2. Gender: female/male/NA
3. Specify your age: −20/21 to 30/31 to 40/41 to 50/51 to 60/+60
4. Apart for having completed or being taking a degree in English Studies, have you completed any other university studies? Please specify.
5. Have you ever been to an English-speaking country?

5.1. If your answer is yes, please specify: United Kingdom, Ireland, United States, Australia/New Zealand, others (specify).

5.2. In general terms, for how long have you been in an English-speaking country? Less than 10 days/Between 11 and 20 days/Between 21 days and 3 months/Between 3 and 6 months/Between 6 and 12 months/Between 1 and 3 years/More than 3 years.

6. What's your overall proficiency in English? (Check the highest option): Basic (A1)/Beginner (A2)/Lower-intermediate (B1)/Upper-intermediate/First Certificate (B2)/Lower-advanced/Advanced (C1)/Upper-advanced/Proficiency (C2)/ Native-like
7. Once you have finished your degree in English Studies, would you like to become an English teacher? Yes/No/NA

Section 2

Please answer the following questions without checking for information on the Internet or other references. We are interested in your opinion and what you remember.

8. English is a global language that is present in many parts of the world and has many varieties. Please specify six varieties of English you are aware of, for instance, American English.
9. What is *English as an International Language* or *English as a* Lingua Franca? Choose the right answer.

   (a) It's the use of English among people who speak English as a mother tongue but who are based in a country where English is not spoken widely.
   (b) It's the use of English as a medium of communication among people from different countries and with different cultures, who speak different languages and use English as a common language.
   (c) It's the English spoken in international institutions, such as the European Union, the UNO, but only if it is spoken by native speakers of English.

10. Do you think your SPOKEN use of English...

    10.1. Adheres to a specific geographical variety (for instance, American English)?

10.1.1. My SPOKEN English can be identified with the following geographical variety:

10.1.2. Why? For instance, because you have lived in a specific place for a long time, because it is your own decision, etc.

10.1.3. Can you provide some instances of SPOKEN use of that variety you adhere to?

10.2. Does not adhere to any specific geographical variety? Is it *English as an International Language* or *English as a* Lingua Franca?

10.2.1. Why? For instance, because you have lived in a specific place for a long time, because it is your own decision, etc.

11. Do you think your WRITTEN use of English. . .

11.1. Adheres to a specific geographical variety (for instance, American English)?

11.1.1. My WRITTEN English can be identified with the following geographical variety:

11.1.2. Why? For instance, because you have lived in a specific place for a long time, because it is your own decision, etc.

11.1.3. Can you provide some instances of WRITTEN use of that variety you adhere to?

11.2. Does not adhere to any specific geographical variety? Is it *English as an International Language* or *English as a* Lingua Franca?

11.2.1. Why? For instance, because you have lived in a specific place for a long time, because it is your own decision, etc.

12. Your use of English, whether it is a specific variety of English or an unmarked use of English as a lingua franca, do you think it may change at some point?

12.1. No, it is a fixed use of English.

12.2. Yes, it may change at some point.

12.2.1. If you think it may change, why do you think this might happen?

Section 3

Please read the following sentences, and provide an answer in relation to your own attitudes toward the English language. Make use of the following scale: 1 = strongly disagree; 2 = disagree; 3 = partially disagree; 4 = partially agree; 5 = agree; 6 = strongly agree

13. To what extent do you agree with the following statements? These statements are related to your own use and learning of English. Remember that there are no right or wrong answers, but try to provide accurate answers.

In PROFESSIONAL terms, I will have, or I think I will have, more opportunity to use English to communicate with people for whom English is not their native language (e.g., Germans or Japanese) than with people who speak English as their native language.

In PERSONAL terms, I will have, or I think I will have, more opportunity to use English to communicate with people for whom English is not their native language (e.g., Germans or Japanese) than with people who speak English as their native language.

14. As someone that has learned and is learning English, please order the following learning aspects according to their importance for you (1 for less important to 9 for more important). Each number must be used only once: Vocabulary/Grammar/Pronunciation/Listening comprehension/Reading comprehension/Speaking/Writing/Rules for language use (pragmatic aspects)/Sociocultural aspects

15. Please choose one of the two options shown below:

As a future teacher with specific training in English, I am interested in teaching a specific geographical variety of English as well as the cultural aspects associated with that variety.

As a future teacher with specific training in English, I am interested in teaching an international variety of English with no specific features that can be associated with a geographical area, with no specific linguistic features or cultural aspects associated with a geographical area.

16. Please select the option you agree the most.

Learning a language implies getting to know the culture of the country where that language is used.

Learning a language can have a purely functional purpose. That is, the language can be used as a lingua franca for intercultural communication without the need to know the culture and the traditions associated to that language.

17. Please add any comment related to English as an international language or as a lingua franca for intercultural communication.

References

Árva, V., & Medgyes, P. (2000). Native and non-native teachers in the classroom. *System, 28*(3), 355–372.

Baker, W. (2012a). From cultural awareness to intercultural awareness: Culture in ELT. *ELT Journal, 66*(1), 62–70.

Baker, W. (2012b). *Using online learning objects to develop intercultural awareness in ELT: A critical examination in a Thai higher education setting* (British Council Teacher Development Research Papers). Retrieved from http://www.teachingenglish.org.uk/publications.

Baker, W. (2016). Culture and language in intercultural communication, English as a lingua franca and English language teaching: Points of convergence and conflict. In P. Holmes & F. Dervin (Eds.), *The cultural and intercultural dimensions of English as a Lingua Franca* (pp. 70–89). Bristol, England: Multilingual Matters.

Berns, M. (2008). World Englishes, English as a lingua franca, and intelligibility. *World Englishes, 27*(3–4), 327–334.

Berns, M. (2009). English as lingua franca and English in Europe. *World Englishes, 28*, 192–199.

Bjørge, A. K. (2016). Conflict talk and ELF communities of practice. In P. Holmes & F. Dervin (Eds.), *The cultural and intercultural dimensions of English as a Lingua Franca* (pp. 114–133). Bristol, England: Multilingual Matters.

Björkman, B. (2011). Pragmatic strategies in English as an academic lingua franca: Ways of achieving communicative effectiveness? *Journal of Pragmatics, 43*, 950–964.

Chacón-Beltrán, R. (2000). El "hablante nativo" de la lengua meta: ¿qué importancia tiene para la enseñanza de la L2? *ELIA, 1*, 9–21.

Cogo, A. (2012). English as a lingua franca: Concepts, use, and implications. *ELT Journal, 66*(1), 97–105.

Crystal, D. (2012). *English as a global language* (2nd ed.). Cambridge, UK: Cambridge University Press.

Csizér, K., & Kontra, E. H. (2012). ELF, ESP, ENL and their effect on students' aims and beliefs: A structural equation model. *System, 40*(1), 1–10.

Dafouz, E., Nunez, B., & Sancho, C. (2007). Analysing stance in a CLIL university context: Non-native speaker use of personal pronouns and modal verbs. *International Journal of Bilingual Education and Bilingualism, 10*(5), 647–662.

Dewey, M. (2012). Towards a post-normative approach: Learning the pedagogy of ELF. *Journal of English as a Lingua Franca, 1*(1), 141–170.

Guth, S., & Helm, F. (2012). Developing multiliteracies in ELT through telecollaboration. *ELT Journal, 66*(1), 42–51.

Holmes, P., & Dervin, F. (2016). *The cultural and intercultural dimensions of English as lingua franca*. Bristol, England: Multilingual Matters.

Horner, B. (2011). Writing English as a lingua franca. In A. Archibald & C. Cogo (Eds.), *Latest trends in ELF research* (pp. 299–311). Newcastle upon Tyne, England: Cambridge Scholars.

House, J. (2003). English as a lingua franca: A threat to multilingualism? *Journal of SocioLinguistics, 7*, 556–578.

Jenkins, J. (2000). *The phonology of English as an international language*. Oxford, UK: Oxford University Press.

Jenkins, J. (2009). English as a lingua franca: Interpretations and attitudes. *World Englishes, 28*(2), 200–207.

Jenkins, J. (2014). *English as a lingua franca in the international university: The politics of academic English language policy*. London: Routledge.

Jenkins, J., Cogo, A., & Dewey, M. (2011). Review of developments in research into English as a lingua franca. *Language Teaching, 44*(3), 281–315.

Jenks, C. (2016). Talking cultural identities into being in ELF interactions: An investigation of international postgraduate students in the United Kingdom. In P. Holmes & F. Dervin (Eds.), *The cultural and intercultural dimensions of English as a lingua franca* (pp. 93–113). Bristol, England: Multilingual Matters.

Kaur, J. (2016). Intercultural misunderstanding revisited: Cultural difference as a (non) source of misunderstanding in ELF communication. In P. Holmes & F. Dervin (Eds.), *The cultural and intercultural dimensions of English as a lingua Franca* (pp. 134–156). Bristol, England: Multilingual Matters.

Kecskes, I. (2013). Why do we say what we say the way we say it? *Journal of Pragmatics, 48*(1), 71–83.

Kecskes, I. (2015). Intracultural communication and intercultural communication: Are they different? *International Review of Pragmatics, 7*(2), 171–194.

Llinares-García, A., & Romero-Trillo, J. (2008). Discourse markers and the pragmatics of native and non-native teachers in a CLIL corpus. *Pragmatics and Corpus Linguistics: A Mutualistic Entente, 2*, 191.

Mauranen, A. (2003). Academic English as lingua franca-a corpus approach. *TESOL Quarterly, 37* (3), 513–527.

Mauranen, A. (2006). Signaling and preventing misunderstanding in English as lingua franca communication. *International Journal of the Sociology of Language, 177*, 123–150.

Mauranen, A., & Hynninen, N. (2010). English as a lingua franca: Introduction. *Helsinki English Studies, 6*, 1–5.

McGroarty, M. E. (2006). *Lingua franca languages.* Cambridge, UK: Cambridge University Press.

Medgyes, P. (1994). *The non-native teacher.* London: Macmillan.

Phillipson, R. (2006). English, a cuckoo in the European higher education nest of languages? *European Journal of English Studies, 10*(1), 13–32.

Pickering, L. (2006). Current research on intelligibility in English as a lingua franca. *Annual Review of Applied Linguistics, 26*, 219–233. https://doi.org/10.1017/S0267190506000110.

Prodromou, L. (2008). *English as a lingua franca: A corpus-based analysis.* London: Continuum.

Seidlhofer, B. (2011). Conceptualizing English for a multilingual Europe. In A. De Houwer & A. Wilton (Eds.), *English in Europe today: Sociocultural and educational perspectives* (pp. 133–146). Amsterdam, The Netherlands: John Benjamins Publishing group.

Seidlhofer, B. (2013). *Oxford applied linguistics: Understanding English as a lingua franca.* Oxford, UK: Oxford University Press.

Sowden, C. (2012). ELF on a mushroom: The overnight growth in English as a lingua Franca. *ELT Journal, 66*(1), 89–96.

van Mulken, M., & Hendriks, B. (2015). Your language or mine? Or English as a lingua franca? Comparing effectiveness in English as a lingua franca and L1–L2 interactions: Implications for corporate language policies. *Journal of Multilingual and Multicultural Development, 36*(4), 404–422.

Walker, R. (2010). *Teaching the pronunciation of English as a lingua franca.* Oxford, UK: Oxford University Press.

Chapter 9
How Critical Has Intercultural Learning and Teaching Become? A Diachronic and Synchronic View of "Critical Cultural Awareness" in Language Education

Manuela Guilherme and Mark Sawyer

9.1 Introduction

This chapter has the wider aim of introducing new debates on "critical cultural awareness" in intercultural learning and teaching. Among those debates, there will be a discussion on the indiscriminate use of terminologies related to the idea of "intercultural encounters" within the scope of a critical pedagogy and a discussion on the limits of the concept of intercultural competence. This chapter then undertakes a diachronic comparative analysis of two studies investigating secondary-level English language teachers in Portugal, the former by Guilherme (2000a) and the latter in Japan by Sawyer (2013), which replicated some aspects of the first study. The chapter will also feature a synchronic analysis between the Portuguese data and some new corresponding data from Japanese teachers of English. In these contexts, the primary aim of these studies is to reveal the orientations of teachers toward promoting "critical cultural awareness" among their students. More specifically, it assesses the teachers' general view of the role of culture in the L2 classroom, their understandings of a critical approach to culture, and various facets of their implementation of this approach. Additionally, the chapter will also briefly refer to two other projects, one on the intercultural dimension of citizenship education carried out with secondary school teachers of various subjects in Portugal and the other about English teaching and learning in higher education in Brazil. The case studies mentioned above have different levels of contextual representativeness, although

M. Guilherme (✉)
Centro de Estudos Sociais, Universidade de Coimbra, Coimbra, Portugal
e-mail: mariaguilherme@ces.uc.pt

M. Sawyer (✉)
School of Policy Studies, Kwansei Gakuin University, Hyogo, Japan
e-mail: mark02@kwansei.ac.jp

© Springer Nature Singapore Pte Ltd. 2021
M. D. López-Jiménez, J. Sánchez-Torres (eds.), *Intercultural Competence Past, Present and Future*, Intercultural Communication and Language Education,
https://doi.org/10.1007/978-981-15-8245-5_9

none is nationally representative. Nevertheless, they may contribute to conceptual and practical reflection on the criticality of intercultural learning and teaching.

9.2   Literature Review: Theoretical Considerations for Foreign Language Education

9.2.1   The Incompleteness of the Concept of Intercultural Competence

Toward equipping young students and adult citizens for leading their lives in increasingly diverse societies and as mobile citizens in a globalizing world, academics and policy-makers have proposed many terms, definitions and descriptions, and usable models to fit the development of the most needed capacities. Unfortunately, they are often handled as if they were understood in consensual ways by everyone in whichever position or of whichever origin, and the term intercultural competence (IC) is no exception. Byram (2013) is explicit in countering this view: "'Intercultural competence' is a phrase best used when describing a person's abilities in context." In addition, Guilherme's (2000b–2013) attempts to define it, over a span of 13 years (Byram, 2000; Byram & Hu, 2013), well express that, in her view, no matter how condensed definitions should be for encyclopedia readers, the more researchers dig into this area, the more complexity they find. Despite attempts to provide practitioners with hands-on models that compartmentalize and organize elements assumed to foster IC, misunderstandings, doubts, and, above all, misleading certainties remain. Not every methodology, pedagogy, policy, or philosophy suits IC or vice versa. Among the best attempts to provide clarification, critique and proposals are some that have appeared in the *Routledge Encyclopedia of Language Teaching and Learning* (Byram [Ed.], 2000; Byram & Hu [Eds.], 2013), *The SAGE handbook of Intercultural Competence* (Deardorff [Ed.], 2009a), and *The SAGE Encyclopedia of Intercultural Competence* (Bennett [Ed.], 2015).

In the former, the first edition of the *Routledge Encyclopedia of Language Teaching and Learning*, IC was briefly defined as "…the ability to interact effectively with people from cultures that we recognize as different from our own" (Guilherme, 2000b, p. 297), while in the second edition, the same author reformulated the definition into a "general capacity…[that] combines notions of communication and interaction across languages and cultures by focusing on the readiness to establish fluid relationships at the interstices of different and multiply-determined identities whilst having a purpose or task in mind" (Guilherme, 2013, p. 346). There is almost a world between them, not that they are incompatible but that the latter expands the former exponentially and eventually leads the idea of intercultural competencies into the concept of "intercultural responsibility," aiming to "grasp the sociological, political and ethical intersections of a critical cosmopolitan society" (Guilherme, 2013, p. 349). Intercultural responsibility moves beyond the functionality of IC into the need of including language education into a larger scope of critical cosmopolitan citizenship education. A fundamental element that pushes IC into intercultural responsibility is *critical cultural awareness*. While Byram (1997) introduced this concept, also labeled *"savoir s'engager,"* among other "savoirs" for the *bildung* of "intercultural communicative competence," Guilherme (2000a, 2002) posited a more central role for "critical cultural awareness." Not that the other "savoirs" should be discarded but that, while focusing on intercultural communication and interaction, the development of "critical cultural awareness" is paramount in order to explore IC's intercultural component, which indeed means to get down to the "nitty gritty" of this issue, to be discussed below.

Regarding both *the intercultural* and the *competence* of IC, *The SAGE Handbook of Intercultural Competence* (Deardorff [Ed.], 2009a) includes several theoretical reflections based on empirical studies raising important issues on both concepts. Although competence seems to be the one term calling for more "objectivity," in the scientific sense, Spitzberg and Chagnon (2009) appropriately highlight that "no particular skill or ability is likely to ever be universally 'competent'" (p. 6), especially when dealing with difference in relation. As far as the concept *intercultural* is concerned, most authors in this book add elements in order to disentangle its intricacy, although it remains dense and perplexing largely due to its deep historical and cultural backgrounds, which also bring more variety and richness to the concept. Kim (2009) concentrates on the "identity factor in IC," by combining the individual and the collective dimensions, and defines ". . .intercultural competence as an individual's overall capacity to engage in behaviors and activities that foster cooperative relationships. . ." (pp. 61–62). In this same collection, well-known scholars in the field single out and examine different elements such as "the implications of trust in intercultural competence" within "the notion of a moral circle as key to intercultural competence" (Hofstede, 2009, pp. 96–98) and "intercultural conflict competence" for which "mindfulness" is a main component, according to Ting-Toomey (2009), which "means attending to one's internal communication assumptions, cognitions, and emotions" (pp. 103–104). In addition, Bennett (2009) brings in the idea of IC as a "positioning tool" through which we find some orientation "at the *interface*" between "differing culture maps" (p. 126).

The authors above have managed to push the concept of IC beyond a mere functional tool to deal with difference in such a way that the term itself now falls short of the needs of its own meaning. Therefore, it is not by coincidence that the *SAGE Encyclopedia of Intercultural Competence* (Bennett [Ed.], 2015) includes entries such as cosmopolitanism, social responsibility, critical theory, and critical pedagogy, as *The Encyclopedia of Applied Linguistics* (Chapelle [Ed.], 2013) also includes an entry on critical pedagogy.

In step with the researchers cited above, language teachers around the world have become more deeply aware that their students' future success in communication with cultural others depends on much more than functional language proficiency. In consequence, those teachers begin to search more earnestly for theoretical frameworks and pedagogical suggestions for understanding and promoting IC. Recently, such frameworks and suggestions have proliferated, providing an abundance, perhaps overabundance, of attractive ideas; some examples were presented above. There are at least three important issues that have added to teachers' confusion in trying to provide the most useful curriculum for their students. The first is that in the search for what constitutes IC and how it can best be fostered, many researchers have used terminology without sufficient care to how it relates to other researchers' work. Therefore, it is not uncommon for different researchers to use the same terms for different concepts and different words for the same concepts. Sinicrope, Norris, and Watanabe (2007), Deardorff (2009b), and most recently, Guilherme and Dietz (2015) are among the scholars who are making efforts to clarify the similarities and differences among proposals regarding IC and the concept of interculturality. Guilherme and Dietz (2015) expand previous work (e.g., Dietz & Mateos Cortés, 2012; Guilherme, 2014; Mateos Cortés, 2009; Medina-López-Portillo & Sinningen, 2009) on the meanings of interculturality. The word *intercultural*, academically speaking, is recent and generally traced back to Hall's (1959) work on intercultural relations in the 1950s. However, the EC-funded project "INTERACT: The intercultural dimension of citizenship education" (http://www.ces.uc.pt/interact/documents/final_activity_report.pdf) showed that as late as the early 2000s, the word was virtually unknown to secondary school teachers in England and Denmark who were involved in a citizenship education and project. While they preferred the word *multicultural,* their peers in Portugal and Spain were well familiar with *intercultural*. In fact, the term *intercultural* corresponds to a different idea of social diversity structure, familiar in the Portuguese/Spanish languages and originating in colonial matrices different from that of England, based as they were in miscegenation and hybridization rather than segregation. Therefore, the fact that *interculturality* in English is much less clear than *multiculturalism* results from the lack of ontological, epistemological, and sociopolitical roots of *interculturalidad(e)* such as those present in Portuguese and Spanish.

A second issue, also highlighted by Deardorff (2009b), is that there is not likely to be any single model of IC that can respond adequately and equally to every intercultural situation. This means, for example, that foreign language teachers either in Portugal, Brazil, or Japan may rightly choose different models of IC and pedagogical means to develop it. Although scholarship in IC has been dominated by northern European and North American approaches, successful intercultural communication involving people from the "South" or "East" will clearly need to be informed by perspectives from these areas. In a very useful discussion focusing on IC in Asia, Parmenter (2003) pointed out how cultural differences in viewing basic identity, and the importance of considering relationships, roles, and face in most interactions, present severe challenges for a universal model of IC. On a view from the South, the curriculum development analysis undertaken by Guilherme in three federal universities in Brazil (http://www.ces.uc.pt/projectos/glocademics/), with respect to English, Portuguese, and Spanish undergraduate education (Guilherme, 2019), gives abundant evidence of a critical and postcolonial approach to language education, although a neoliberal, hegemonic, and acritical version of English as lingua franca is still prevalent. Although English as lingua franca assumes that it is giving voice to non-native speakers, it bases its arguments on a native-speakerism that is outdated, fictional, and still considered as central; that is, the issue is wrongly put and constructed upon scientifically fragile foundations. However, this discussion shall not be included here. On the theoretical support for such postcolonial approaches, it is fundamental to give account of Santos' (1999, 2010, 2014) work, considered as a main reference in Brazil.

A third issue is the adequacy of IC as the ultimate goal of foreign language education. Just as foreign language teachers came to question the adequacy of communicative competence as the goal of language teaching in the 1990s, many teachers in the twenty-first century have likewise come to view IC as a too limited goal. Many conceptions of IC bear some resemblance to that of Spitzberg and Chagnon's (2009, p. 7) concept, which refers to "the effective and appropriate management of interaction between people who, to some degree, represent divergent affective, cognitive, and behavioral orientations to the world." While effective and appropriate communication with perceived others is clearly a worthy goal of foreign language education, it fails to make reference to the critical development of relationships much less the cooperative working together toward a society that is more just and respectful to diversity. Thus, Byram and colleagues (e.g., Alred, Byram, & Fleming, 2006; Sawyer, 2014a, b) have been working on a higher-level goal of intercultural citizenship, while Guilherme (e.g., 2013) has been developing the concept of intercultural responsibility, which expands the concept of intercultural competence, as mentioned above (Guilherme, 2012a, 2012b; Guilherme, Keating, & Hoppe, 2010).

9.2.2   More Than Ever, a Pressing Need to Get Back to "Critical Cultural Awareness"

Considering the three issues above, the research reported in this chapter focuses on the mid-level concept of "critical cultural awareness." As will be shown below, it is definitionally precise, theoretically grounded, pedagogically practical, and eminently worthwhile as a goal for self- and societal improvement.

Critical cultural awareness (CCA) is a concept first introduced by Byram (1997) who defined it as "an ability to evaluate critically on the basis of explicit criteria perspectives, practices, and products of one's own and other cultures and countries" (p. 53). He, at first, equated it with *savoir de engager*, one of the five *savoirs* that comprise his model of intercultural communicative competence. However, CCA is related to but transcends intercultural communicative competence because, for one thing, it involves rethinking and reexperiencing the concept of cultural identity itself. When students examine deeply their own multiple cultural identities, as well as the multiple cultural identities of members of other cultural groups with whom they have an opportunity or need to relate, they are able to understand, and eventually to feel, not only the overlap of identities between themselves and other groups but also the non-unitary, non-fixed nature of identity. The flexibility and openness to additional identities that result make it possible to feel real membership in diverse multicultural working groups, which have been normal in many parts of the world for a long time but until recently unusual in some other parts. Education for CCA involves helping students reach the point of appreciating deeply that all cultures and people are not separate, but interrelated, and not static, but constantly changing. With such an appreciation, a student is prepared to live and work comfortably with diverse groups of people and can get things done by working and negotiating skillfully and democratically with diverse others whose ideas, judgments, and values will certainly clash on many occasions.

The need to "evaluate critically" in Byram's (1997) definition of CCA is not so much to express criticism as it is to bring unconscious assumptions to the level of awareness, that is, to ask oneself "why?" about things that one has previously taken for granted. At the most basic level, this involves fundamental questions to oneself about how one's identities, values, and practices have developed (reflection), as well as curiosity, speculation, and inquiry about the corresponding items for cultural others (exploration). This process not only makes visible areas of commonality with diverse others but also allows deeper understanding of the nature of conflicts when they occur. Byram's specification of "explicit criteria" for evaluation allows the transcendence of a general disapproval of and/or unexamined annoyance with cultural others' statements, positions, approaches, practices, etc. Equally important, it gives multicultural group members the ability to pinpoint and articulate difference, such that conflicts can more likely be resolved with minimum misunderstanding, wasted time, and negative emotion.

Based on Byram's lead, Guilherme's (2002) definition of CCA is as follows: "A reflective, exploratory, dialogical, and active stance toward cultural knowledge and life that allows for dissonance, contradiction, and conflict as well as for consensus, concurrence, and transformation. It is a cognitive and emotional endeavor that aims at individual and collective emancipation, social justice, and political commitment" (p. 219). She completes the definition by adding that its development is cyclical rather than linear. She also later proposes specific cognitive/affective operations that can drive the cycle forward.

There is nothing in Guilherme's (2002) definition contradictory to the one of Byram (1997). However, there are at least two important differences. Firstly, Guilherme's definition is more specific in implicating classroom practices that will actually foster CCA. For example, whereas Byram (1997) suggests "an ability to evaluate critically," Guilherme specifies more particular qualities and actions that will lead to that ability, that is, reflection, exploration, dialogue, and proactiveness. She also warns that the process will necessarily involve some discomfort, in the form of dissonance, contradiction, and conflict, along with the hoped-for consensus, concurrence, and transformation. She makes it explicit that developing CCA is not solely a cognitive endeavor but also involves emotions, as indicated by the inclusion of dissonance, etc., in her articulation of the appropriate aims of CCA. She also shows its connection with responsible democratic citizenship, whether at local, national, or supranational levels. Keeping these elements in mind, ways to work toward CCA with adjustments to already existing classroom practices become readily apparent. Moreover, though Guilherme's (2002) intended domain is foreign language education, the components can serve as a potential template for all forms of citizenship education.

A second difference that distinguishes Guilherme's (2002) elaboration of CCA from Byram's (1997) definition is its groundedness in philosophy and political theory. Although Byram's discussions of his axiological model make reference to its political nature, Guilherme (2000a) goes much further in showing how her model of CCA is derived from and supported by several solid foundations of theory. The most pervasive influence is the critical pedagogy of Freire (1970) and his successors such as Giroux (1997). As philosophical underpinnings of CCA, Guilherme also draws on the Frankfurt School scholars of critical theory (Horkheimer, Adorno, Marcuse), Habermas, and the postmodern theorists Lyotard, Derrida, Foucault, and Baudrillard. In applying critical pedagogy to foreign language education, she connects her ideas not only to the approaches to intercultural communicative competence of Byram (1997) and Kramsch (1993) but also to the postcolonial language education suggestions of Pennycook (1994) and Canagarajah (2013), among others, and the progressive curriculum documents *The Common European Framework for Languages* (Council of Europe, 1996) and *Standards for Foreign Language Learning* (American Council on the Teaching of Foreign Languages, 1996). In developing her ideas on CCA since 2000, Santos's (2014) theory of the epistemologies of the South has provided productive interconnections, as have the work of scholars such Mignolo, Walsh, Canclini, and Bhabha, among others.

The above discussion has hopefully shown that CCA is a compellingly worthwhile goal for students of foreign languages in the twenty-first century, which is both theoretically sound and pedagogically practical. Although alternative proposals with overlapping aims and/or content have proliferated in recent years, none have surpassed CCA in preparing students with personal and societal visions for thriving in the conflicted but promising intercultural world. The insightful vision of Byram provided the foundation to language/culture educators to the end of the past century and inspired additional work by the beginning of this century. The apparent slowing down of such an emancipatory energy has to some extent eclipsed the concept of CCA, unfortunately pervading global educational systems with what Phipps (2010) calls "quick fix solutions." In an indispensable text about the risks involved in intercultural education and training, Phipps (2010) elaborates:

> intercultural encounter is a volatile, tricky and messy process which, like the learning of other languages to which it is inherently allied, changes the bedrock of the self and of self-understanding. In such a context there is no room for an immediately "satisfying" critical outcome, other than a performance of critical transformation in stated understandings about difference and culture and "the way things are always going to be." (p. 64)

Generating CCA in language/culture education is clearly challenging; therefore, it may be tempting to avoid the challenge, settling for more superficial and easily affordable goals. However, this is exactly the reason why maintaining the focus is essential until achieving the *inédito viável* proposed by Freire (1970), a concept which is as difficult to translate into English as *saudade* or *interculturalidade*. 'The feasible unknown' may capture it best, although Freire's translator Myra Ramas translated it as "untested feasibility" (Freire, 1993, p. 75) which is close. Nevertheless, Freire's (1970) work provides us with ample clarification of what he meant, for example, "*Consciousness of* and *action* upon reality are, therefore, inseparable constituents of the transforming act by which men become beings of relation" (Freire, 1970, p. 453). Phipps' (2010) quote above is highly consonant with Freire's (1970) idea, and together, they reinforce the need for not settling for less than CCA.

In focusing on CCA in foreign language education, it is clear that there is good conceptual and theoretical justification. The following sections will examine empirically the extent to which teachers in Portugal and Japan are also in agreement with this focus.

9.3 Methodology

The data on which this chapter is based comes from the following sources: (1) Guilherme's (2000a) empirical study with secondary school teachers of English in various regions of continental Portugal carried out for her PhD dissertation at the University of Durham[1] and is also inspired by two of her subsequent international research projects, namely, INTERACT (2004–2007)[2] on the intercultural dimension of citizenship education, also with secondary school teachers of diverse subjects and in different regions of continental Portugal (https://www.ces.uc.pt/interact/index. htm), and her just-completed study, at a few Brazilian public universities, about English curriculum development in higher education, within the scope of her Marie Skłodowska Curie project GLOCADEMICS (http://www.ces.uc.pt/projectos/ glocademics/)[3], both funded by the European Commission; (2) Sawyer's (2013) follow-up study of Portuguese teachers of English; and (3) his extension/replication of the research agenda to Japanese teachers of English. Each of the three sets of data will be described in the section below.

---

[1]This study was funded by the Fundação para a Ciência e Tecnologia, Portugal.

[2]This study was funded by the European Commission, FP6 Framework Programme Project CIT2-CT2003–506023.

[3]The research leading to these results has received funding from the People Programme (Marie Curie Actions) of the European Union's Seventh Framework Programme (FP7/2007–2013) under REA grant agreement n° 625,396.

9.3.1 Guilherme's (2000a) Dissertation

9.3.1.1 Aim of the Study

This study aimed to find out if, why, and how Portuguese teachers of English approach culture critically, how they define critical cultural awareness, and what sort of development models would help them improve their professional performance.

9.3.1.2 Data Collection Tools

The data consist of both questionnaire responses for quantitative analysis and transcribed focus group interviews as well as a few individual interviews for qualitative analysis. The questionnaire consists of six sections totaling 63 questions with predetermined alternatives.

9.3.1.3 Participants

The questionnaire was completed by 149 participants. The focus groups took place at seven schools, each with five to eight participants, and were the main and an especially valuable source of data due to the synergy and spontaneity that this methodology afforded the groups of participants. Additional data came from interviews with a Ministry of Education administrator, an English textbook author, and one of the authors of the national syllabus for foreign language teaching.

9.3.1.4 Data Analysis

In this chapter, the data are reanalyzed according to four categories: (1) the role of culture in foreign language education, (2) conceptions of critical cultural awareness, (3) student responses to critical culture in the classroom, and (4) experience and action in developing critical cultural awareness.

9.3.2 Sawyer's (2013) Follow-up Data Collection in Portugal

9.3.2.1 Aim of the Study

This study revisited the aims of Guilherme's (2000a) project but with a complementary methodology, and an eye to a diachronic comparison, to discover what, if anything, had changed in the intervening years.

9.3.2.2 Data Collection Tools

Individual interviews were conducted with a protocol consisting of 15 questions. The questions were developed jointly with the first author in an attempt to match the aims and scope of the earlier study. The interviews were between 45 minutes and 1 hour in length and were conducted in English, recorded, and transcribed. Although conducting the interviews in the participants' second language could potentially be a limitation, it turned out that without exception, the teachers were enthusiastic about having an opportunity to discuss their English teaching beliefs and practices in English. In that sense, the mood created was especially conducive to obtaining interesting material, parallel to the advantages that Alasuutari (1995) argues for focus groups.

9.3.2.3 Participants

Twelve Portuguese secondary teachers of English (seven in Lisbon, two in Oporto, and one in Setúbal) were invited to participate in the interviews. Two of the interviewees had participated in the previous study focus group interviews.

9.3.2.4 Data Analysis

The present chapter features the analyses of 10 of the 15 questions, those that bear specifically on the four categories mentioned above: (1) the role of culture in foreign language education, (2) conceptions of critical cultural awareness, (3) student responses to critical culture in the classroom, and (4) experience and action in developing critical cultural awareness.

9.3.3 Sawyer's (2016–2019) Ongoing Data Collection in Japan

9.3.3.1 Aim of the Study

This study's aim was to assess the orientation and level of awareness toward critical cultural awareness in Japan for the purpose of a synchronic comparison between teachers in very different geographical and cultural contexts.

9.3.3.2 Data Collection Tools

The data collection consisted of the exact same interview protocol of 15 questions that was specified in 3.2.2 above.

9.3.3.3 Participants

Four teachers have been interviewed so far (two in Osaka, two in Kobe). Although the number of informants is still small, the Japanese teachers have been equally as enthusiastic about sharing their beliefs and practices as the Portuguese teachers, and several interesting systematic differences with the Portuguese teachers are already evident.

9.3.3.4 Data Analysis

As specified in 3.2.4 above, the present chapter features the analyses of 10 of the 15 questions, those that bear specifically on the four categories mentioned above: (1) the role of culture in foreign language education, (2) conceptions of critical cultural awareness, (3) student responses to critical culture in the classroom, and (4) experience and action in developing critical cultural awareness. A different part of the comparative interview analysis, outside of the four categories analyzed for this chapter, can be found in Sawyer and Matos (2015).

9.4 Transversal Data Analysis Results

9.4.1 The Role of Culture in Foreign Language Education

Times were still special in Portugal when the first study was carried out with secondary school teachers of English in Guilherme's study (2000a). It was 25 years after the military coup. The democratic state was becoming stable, but the democratic society was still vibrant. Massification of all levels of education was at full speed, and school population diversity had grown exponentially with immigrants from Africa, East Timor, China, and eastern European countries. English had definitely replaced French supremacy, and above all, Portugal had recently joined the European Union and had just been one of the first to enthusiastically endorse the euro. Democracy, critique, debate, and citizenship were keywords in the massive teacher development programs. The Portuguese Ministry of Education had issued new national subject curricula following recommendations and joining projects emanating from the European Commission and the Council of Europe. In the following decades, the steam could not but lose pressure, but here is the context from where this diachronic and synchronic narrative begins.

In the English national syllabus in place when Guilherme's (2000a) study was carried out, a critical approach was a dominant perspective in the cultural component, and it also pervaded the sociolinguistic component, already inspired in the preparation activities of the Common European Framework for Languages. The national syllabus was one of the outcomes of a nationwide teacher trainer development program, coordinated by the Ministry of Education, which was based on authentic materials and innovative and critical development. Guilherme was one of the participants along with all the syllabus authors. One of the syllabus authors explained:

> E, portanto, nós tentámos dar, de facto, um enfoque muito grande para que os professores percebessem que a aula de língua estrangeira, neste caso o Inglês, para já não é uma entidade franca, quando estás a estudar uma língua estás a estudar uma cultura, ela transmite padrões culturais... (And, therefore, we actually tried to put a strong focus on the need for teachers to understand that in a foreign language class, in this case it is English which is not a franca entity in itself, when you are learning a language you are studying a culture, it conveys cultural patterns).

This message echoed the enthusiastic endorsement of the teachers participating in Guilherme's (2000a) data collection. That is, they did not view English as a lingua franca, and they understood their mission as teaching a dominant language that, at the same time, provided a vehicle for the opening up of cultural identities, international experience, and knowledge acquisition, and therefore deserved being handled in a way that developed the qualities of CCA. In sum, Portuguese teachers believed that they were forming active European citizens who were critically aware of the different dimensions of their citizenship commitment, not only Portuguese and European but also regional (both Iberian and intranational), global (mainly lusophone [Portuguese-speaking]), local, and their various mixed individual identities.

Quantitative data displayed that a great majority of respondents agreed with the view that "European and global identities of the pupil/citizen should be fostered in foreign language/culture classes" (85.2%) and that "learning about a foreign culture can change the pupil's attitude towards [their] own culture" (84.7%) but not at the cost of the students' loss of cultural identity. They also agreed that "the most important goal in learning about a foreign culture is to develop a critical attitude towards both target and native cultures" (70.5%).

The Ministry of Education administrator interviewed focused particularly on the importance of learning foreign languages/cultures, especially English, for enabling one to fulfil membership of European and global spheres. From the administrator's point of view, English teaching was at a crossroads because, on the one hand, it had become a language for global communication, "*Inglês para a comunicação global,*" and for global knowledge, "*língua de conhecimento global,*" but, on the other hand, it is not a lingua franca in its exact terms because it is always conveying some kind of culture. Therefore, it can be used as a means of communication among diverse so-called native speakers, who may be culturally very different, between so-called native speakers and so-called non-native speakers, and among so-called non-native speakers. Because language always carries culture with it, each situation implies complexity and negotiation. If you are a so-called non-native speaker, you have to "*exprimir a tua própria cultura noutra língua*" (express your own culture in another language) and, moreover, "*com os falantes nativos tem que ser negociado*" (it has to be negotiated with the so-called native speakers) wherever they come from, whether it be Scotland, New Zealand, or South Africa.

Most participants shared the fact that they sometimes included contemporary texts about Australia, New Zealand, South Africa, and India, although not frequently. One, for example, was even more vehement in condemning a Westernized perspective and criticized the excessive focus of the syllabus on the United States while disregarding South Africa; for example, when dealing with racism, "*estamos a dar voz, voz, voz, a quem já fala alto*" (we are giving voice, voice, voice, to those whose voices are already loud enough) they said.

In Sawyer's (2013) follow-up with interview data of Guilherme's (2000a) dissertation study, he found that Portuguese secondary teachers of English 14 years later maintained the enthusiasm of the teachers in 1999, but not until being asked about culture directly, and then with diverse ideas of what the culture in ELT should consist of. When asked in general about their pedagogical priorities, four teachers referred to some aspect of communication and two teachers prioritized motivation and two more classroom management. Only one teacher spontaneously specified culture ("because language is culture"), and one teacher specified national/world citizenship responsibilities, which implicitly invokes the kind of critical culture that motivated this study.

When asked specifically about the appropriate role for culture in ELT, the teachers' responses diverged into five distinct categories ranging from the intrinsic inseparability of language and culture to ambivalence based on its difficulty and Portuguese students' perceived unwillingness to read. In between were three approaches invoking the cultures of native English-speaking (NES) countries: (1) how particular aspects of language encoding depend on cultures (e.g., politeness systems), (2) contrasting cultural habits (e.g., eating habits, homework, school uniforms), and (3) the experience of "high" culture associated with NES countries (e.g., in painting, music). Finally, one teacher construed culture as including the reasons for the spread of English as a global language and the features of this global variety.

Unlike the teachers in Guilherme's earlier study (2000a), the teachers in Sawyer's 2013 study did not specifically refer to the national syllabus' emphasis on cultural content. However, several mentioned both the syllabus and the prescribed textbooks in favorable terms due to their allowance for and inclusion of cultural content. On the other hand, multiple teachers criticized the cultural content in the textbooks for being out of date and cited problems associated with supplementing the textbook with handouts.

When the same questions were asked in Japan, three of the four Japanese teachers of English were less oriented toward a role for culture than were the Portuguese teachers. When first asked generally about their priorities, three answered in terms of particular skills (reading, vocabulary, and balance among the four skills, respectively) in stark contrast to the fourth, who offered "engaging students to become good language users through interculturality." When the Japanese teachers were asked specifically about culture's role, two mentioned the interest that it creates in the students, and one had trouble finding an answer but eventually hit upon the idea of enhancing comprehension by exposure to different varieties of English. The teacher who had brought up interculturality suggested the value of teachers in sharing intercultural experiences through their own interpretations and then giving students opportunities to develop their own interpretations.

9.4.2 Conceptions of Critical Cultural Awareness

Although the Portuguese teachers in Guilherme's (2000a) study did not consider their own academic preparation in interdisciplinary terms, an idea which pervaded most focus groups was that being critical was an interdisciplinary capability, that is, which was part of the student's general education, "*faz parte do desenvolvimento global do aluno ... porque também é fundamental para a vida deles no futuro, porque se tornam cidadãos mais válidos*" (it is part of the student's global development...because it is also fundamental for their future. It makes them better citizens), as one teacher put it. Apart from a few exceptions, the definition of "critical" with respect to teaching/learning a foreign culture remained within a domain taken for granted among researchers, policy-makers, and teachers. Participants in focus group interviews did not make any reference to theoretical sources on this matter either. According to one of the authors of the syllabus, the reason why it was not included was "*porque se achou que uma posição crítica toda a gente sabe o que é*" (because we thought that everybody knew what taking a critical perspective meant).

On a superficial level, teachers' descriptions of a critical approach to foreign cultures did coincide, to some extent, in some common features such as adopting a comparative/contrasting point of view, understanding, accepting, questioning, and assuming an objective/detached view of the other. Reflecting upon and justifying one's positions were also considered important elements. The questioning stance and the political nature of teaching/learning a foreign culture generated much discussion. It was evident from the study that the participants did have ideas about the political implications of their role since approximately two-thirds of the questionnaire respondents endorsed the option put forward in the questionnaire that "having a political attitude toward the teaching about a foreign culture means establishing the relationship between its power structure and forms of cultural production" (69.9%). This was reinforced by some participants in the group discussions who clearly viewed teaching as a political act in the sense that, as one remarked, "*qualquer acto educativo é um acto político*" (any educational act is a political act). However, this seems to remain mostly in the rhetorical domain because participants did not view themselves, or their students, as politically active in any practical way other than by voting or by expressing informed opinions.

The data collected on this matter, a critical pedagogy of cultural content, can be divided into three main areas: (a) resources, both material and human; (b) the interaction among human resources, teachers and students, and the target cultures; and (c) the procedures used to teach/learn foreign cultures that best develop CCA. As far as material resources are concerned, participants in group discussions most frequently referred to the organization of schools and of the curricula. In general, participants in group discussions revealed that the topics included in the syllabus could increase or decrease the possibility of taking a critical approach toward the target cultures. Others expressed the feeling that the informational content included in the syllabus is so dominant that it does not leave enough time to approach it critically. Finally, the fact that a critical approach had not been considered in the final/national exams was also pointed out by group participants as a major impediment for teachers to focus on the development of CCA.

Similar to the teachers studied 14 years before, the Portuguese teachers in 2013 revealed approaches reflecting their own personalities and contexts and following more the general idea of critical thinking elaborated by Bloom (1956) than the more specific ideas of criticality developed later by Freire, Giroux, Byram, etc. The responses fell into four related categories, emphasizing respectively: (1) deeper questioning (for reasons), (2) skepticism (doubting), (3) knowledge (for justifying beliefs), and (4) observation and reflection (resisting first perceptions). When asked about scholars who had shaped their views, they yielded a startling array of scholars from wide-ranging fields as well as literary figures, but in terms of scholars producing work on the culture/pedagogy interface, only the names of Raymond Williams, James Banks, Lev Vygotsky, and Jerome Bruner came up once each, whereas, for example, Freire, Giroux, Byram, Kramsch, Pennycook, and Canagarajah were not mentioned at all.

The Portuguese teachers in 2013 all affirmed that they were in fact implementing their conceptions of a critical approach to culture in their ELT classrooms. One teacher lamented that adopting a critical approach was "very difficult because Portuguese students are really narrow-minded," also claiming to have always tried to provoke the students with "bizarre scenarios," to make them analyze things and develop broader minds. The rest of the teachers were unambivalent and articulate about their versions of a critical pedagogy. Most of these involved getting students to question reading materials, TV shows and movies, and stereotypes about groups and cultures, but none of them mentioned encouraging engagement beyond the classroom.

Three of the four Japanese teachers were unfamiliar with the concept of a critical approach to culture but speculated that it had to do with opening students' minds to different cultural practices while suspending judgment. The fourth (interculturality-oriented) teacher associated criticality with having students interpret cultural phenomena and connected this with the work of Pennycook and Philipson on resisting cultural invasion. While the latter teacher claimed to adopt this conception consistently in the classroom, and one more believed that he/she used a critical approach frequently in terms of showing/eliciting rationales for cultural practices different from Japanese practices, two teachers did not consciously use a critical approach at all.

9.4.3   Student Responses to Critical Culture in the Classroom

On the one hand, some of the 2000a Portuguese participants in the group discussions showed their concern about their students' attitude toward other cultures, one of them having said that "*a atitude crítica deles é sempre uma atitude destrutiva em relação aos outros e sobrevalorizando a nossa cultura*" (their critical attitude is always destructive toward other cultures and overvaluing our own). On the other hand, a few teachers expressed the feeling that when stimulated, their students had a good sense of critique. "*Têm o espírito crítico bem apurado*" (they have a refined sense of critique) according to one, while another added that their students' sense of critique was even more refined than their own had been at the same age, "*eles têm um sentido crítico até mais apurado do que quando eu fiz o liceu.*" Still another pointed out that students' sense of critique is only dormant: "*A sociedade em que estamos integrados não desenvolve muito essa capacidade nos nossos alunos, eles estão um bocado adormecidos, então a escola, para mim, deve exercer essa função de fazê-los pensar sobre as coisas, serem críticos e prepará-los para o futuro*" (our society does not develop that capacity very much. They are a little half asleep so, in my view, the school should fulfil that task and make them think about things, be critical and prepare them for the future).

Participants in both phases of the study—the questionnaire and the focus group interviews—were almost unanimous in recognizing the positive outcomes of the development of CCA in foreign language/culture classes. Both the questionnaire and the focus group discussions focused on two main sets of objectives, the first with regard to the individual and the second to the society in general. However, participants revealed that they feel constrained by school organization of time and space which prevents them from opening up the foreign language/culture classroom. They also brought up the point that the contents of the syllabus are not determinant of the adoption of a critical attitude, although some topics may increase/decrease the possibility of taking a critical approach. They also downplayed the textbook role. Human resources, namely, teachers and students, were considered as highly important in determining the implementation of a critical approach. Cultures were viewed as constantly changing, and thus, up-to-date cultural knowledge was considered fundamental.

When the 2013 Portuguese teachers were asked about the indications they had that their students had increased their critical cultural awareness, they offered a variety of ways that students had demonstrated development of CCA. Even the two teachers who claimed that such evidence was difficult to detect went on to say that they could detect changes in students' attitudes in compositions or presentations. Several of the teachers claimed confidently that change was clearly evident in how students expressed themselves, and several others had received direct feedback that the students had appreciated the cultural materials and tasks that the teachers had provided. One teacher saved student tasks so that they could see for themselves the following year how their ideas and attitudes had evolved. Another teacher was able to see the enhanced CCA of the students by having them rewrite the endings of stories they had read in class. Although all these forms of evidence do not imply that the students will apply their CCA outside the school environment, one teacher spoke about how many students, upon hearing a guest lecture about a project to redistribute wasted restaurant food, expressed eagerness to join the project as volunteers.

Associated with the indications of CCA development that the teachers observed, they perceived a range of benefits of their versions of critical culture teaching. Many teachers mentioned general developmental benefits to students, such as to "build their own personality"; "break the shell that they are in"; "think for themselves, to have their ideas, and be active in this society"; "grow a little bit psychologically and in terms of citizenship"; "get to develop a critical sense and open their minds and be more tolerant toward difference"; and "grow up and learn to respect other people, other cultures, and improve themselves as individuals." Two teachers made specific reference to the benefits of cultural comparison: "The more you learn about others, the better judge you are of yourself," and "students can learn the similarities and more about Portugal and being Portuguese." Four others cited the ability to make good free choices and remain committed to those choices: "In order to be a happy citizen, you have to choose to decide your way to be happy, the way to feel it"; "You have to fight, but you have to be right to fight, because the other thing is to respect values and to respect the society"; "[Students become] free to think and follow their own ideas, not as outsiders"; and "[One alumnus student] said it's what taught her to be responsible and committed and true to her commitments."

The most common difficulty that teachers perceived in implementing a critical approach to culture was overcoming student resistance, for example, "Sometimes, I find some difficulties in finding ways to [open minds]"; "It is the label 'culture is boring' for many of them"; "Sometimes, they believe that not only teachers or parents but adults in general came from a distant planet, inside a strange ship, and they spoke a different language that they could not understand"; and "I'm fighting against powers that are beyond my control—the [mindless] media." A variation on this theme was teachers' self-perceived inadequacy for this task: "We don't know how to do that. We don't have any support. We don't talk to anyone. We should work together but we don't." Finally, three teachers mentioned the challenge of finding time to promote CCA while dealing with all the other demands of the syllabus and textbook.

For three of the four Japanese teachers, it was not easy for them to offer indications of their students' enhanced CCA, given that the teachers were just developing their own understandings during the interviews, but two mentioned students giving positive feedback about the opportunities that they had had to analyze different cultural events and practices. One more said that students had revealed their increased cultural awareness through spontaneous humorous remarks. All of the Japanese teachers had thoughts about the general benefits of raising cultural awareness, including the ability to withhold judgment, to communicate successfully with people, to make implicit cultural ideas explicit, and to overcome confusion in communication in a foreign country. The difficulties that the Japanese teachers pointed out included the student attitudinal problems also mentioned by Portuguese teachers, that is, ethnocentricity and an unwillingness to listen, and the time management problem also cited by two Portuguese teachers—too many things to teach in too little time. The fourth teacher mentioned the expectation of evaluation based purely on linguistic development, a difficulty which is much more severe in Japan than in Portugal.

9.4.4 Experience and Action in Developing Critical Cultural Awareness

One of the Portuguese teachers in Guilherme's study (2000a) mentioned the importance of the student's search for knowledge about the cultures they are learning about in order to attain a critical perspective, "*se houver uma pesquisa e uma procura do saber por parte do aluno ele vai conseguir chegar a essa postura crítica mesmo que não tenha ido ao país ...*" (if the student does some research and searches for knowledge, they will reach such a critical perspective even though they have not been to the target country before). It was also a general belief that enabling students to give, justify, and maintain their opinions was an essential element of a critical approach. This tendency was confirmed by the group discussions where only one participant identified action as a purpose for the development of CCA: "*Para adquirirem cada vez mais direitos e combaterem quando se sentem discriminados ou sentem que outras pessoas são discriminadas, lutarem por elas e pelos direitos que todos temos*" (in order to gain more and more rights and to fight when they feel discriminated against or when they feel that others are discriminated against so that they fight for them and for the rights we all have).

Although participating teachers suggested that students in general ignore everything that is not contemporary or shown in their favorite programs or films, they conceded that the fact that their students have some background knowledge, no matter how distorted, makes it easier to work with them critically. One participant shared, "*Nós estamos influenciados como os alunos, no fundo, pelo que vemos na televisão, pelo que ouvimos, pelo que lemos*" (like our students, we are, in the end, influenced by what we watch on television, what we listen to, what we read). In other words, a critical approach has to depart from students' lives and background knowledge and stimulate their intellectual curiosity and emotional involvement in order to lead them to further their knowledge about alternatives found in different cultural frames.

The Portuguese teachers in Sawyer's (2013) study on the whole did not express a strong sense of the importance of outside experience and action for developing CCA. Multiple teachers attributed this to the difficult economic realities that Portugal has been facing. Several mentioned the value of field trips, especially international ones, if and when feasible, and those teachers invariably added that what was important was for the students to reflect on aspects of such experiences and communicate their ideas to schoolmates who could not participate. Two teachers cited the enrichment that is possible when some class members come from different backgrounds or with different experiences that they can share in class. Two other teachers expected that their students would eventually have individual intercultural experiences, so what was important was the advance preparation provided by what they were doing inside the classroom. In terms of more specific ways of facilitating CCA-relevant experience outside the classroom, two teachers mentioned simply trying to interact with their students outside the classroom to deepen understanding and trust. Others mentioned the importance of making students aware of cultural events such as concerts, plays, and valuable media programs. Museums were brought up by multiple teachers. Reading was mentioned several times as an effective and inexpensive way to promote CCA. One teacher's school featured various forms of cultural exchange, including American Field Service, Comenius projects with the European Union, the European Club, and a Moon Conference in Slovakia, but these resources were apparently not easily accessible in most of the other teachers' schools.

All four of the Japanese teachers had had extensive overseas experience themselves, and all felt that intercultural experience outside the classroom was very important. One teacher emphasized that self-initiated (not group or programmatic) study abroad, even if quite short, leads to dramatic changes. All of the Japanese teachers' schools featured official study abroad programs, though the number and scope varied largely with the economic level of the student population. In one school, all students had the opportunity to travel as a class to Singapore and Malaysia for 3 days, with various projects and presentations to complete upon return. Each of the schools also featured the participation of non-Japanese Assistant Language Teachers (ALTs), who took on various roles in the classroom with various periodicity and who were also sometimes available to interact informally with during break periods. Two of the schools also accommodated substantial numbers of international students for various periods of time. Finally, the teacher at the least affluent school also mentioned inviting university students with extensive overseas experiences to give guest lectures about their cultural experience.

9.5   Discussion

Finally, the discussion below will highlight some of the salient similarities and differences that were revealed in the two groups of Portuguese teachers diachronically across a gap of 14 years between 1999 (Guilherme, 2000a) and 2013 (Sawyer, 2013) and synchronically between the latter group and Japanese teachers who were interviewed just a few months later.

9.5.1 Diachronic Findings

Although the slightly different methodologies lent prominence to different aspects of the Portuguese teachers' beliefs and practices, they were by and large quite similar at the two points in time. Perhaps the most salient difference over time was the relative backgrounding of the syllabus and foregrounding of textbooks, in both positive and negative ways. On the positive side, multiple teachers in 2013 made comments suggesting that their textbooks were helpful in allowing them both to implement the national syllabus and meet their students' overall needs. On the negative side, some teachers felt too tied to the textbook content and/or that the content too quickly became obsolete. Also, whereas many of the teachers in 1999 felt energized by the idealistic national syllabus, that energy was not evident in the 2013 data. Thus, there was a diachronic move from the reference to the national syllabus toward the focus on the textbook, supplemented by authentic and updated materials selected by the individual teacher.

An important reason for this move was that the Portuguese national syllabus in 1999 was more innovative, challenging, and inspiring to teachers, due to cultural content playing a prominent role within a critical approach. In turn, this approach fit within a compelling contextualization of language education in a wider scope of renewed national intercultural citizenship education, together with the development of intercultural democratic citizenship at European and additional levels. The 2013 data show how teachers are adapting toward new syllabuses where technology is the focus, and European and global citizenship are viewed from a more entrepreneurial perspective. Although many teachers maintained their interest for cultural content, their focus on the development of CCA had clearly lost some of its vigor. In this respect, the two Portuguese national syllabi reflect an evolution that has been unfolding in educational policies in general as well as in research priorities.

9.5.2 Synchronic Findings

In general, the Japanese teachers had much lower consciousness than the Portuguese teachers regarding both culture and criticality. This reflects the overall state of foreign language teaching in Japan, where the overwhelming majority of students, after 8 years of English instruction in secondary schools and university, typically reach the proficiency level of "false beginner." The main direct reason for this situation is the implicit priority of secondary English teachers for their students' success on high-stakes university entrance exams, which continue to feature obscure grammar and often decontextualized vocabulary in discrete-point format. Then, once admitted to university, most students do not maintain a high expectation or need for improving their foreign language ability. In the background is the Japanese ambivalence toward foreign language ability, which is still often perceived as a threat to Japanese identity (Seargeant, 2007). This contrasts with the situation in Portugal, where efforts on many levels continue to promote integration into European and global identities, despite priorities having changed to more immediate and functional goals. Either way, the traditional Japanese protection of national identity, or the recent Portuguese focus on functionality, will likely prove counterproductive in the long term, both to high-level career expectations at the individual level and to committed participatory democracy at the societal level.

Regarding criticality, an additional constraint on Japanese teachers is the East Asian value of protecting the other's face in interaction (Parmenter, 2003). Since all disagreements are potentially face threatening in Japan, the care needed to handle them in a foreign language is understandably daunting for students and likewise so for teachers to try to integrate in low-proficiency language courses. Furthermore, the Japanese teachers reported that neither culture nor criticality have any role in current Japanese teacher education. Again, in the background, in contrast to the efforts in Portugal and throughout Europe to develop supranational identities, the Japanese government and media still promote improving international relations while maintaining a strong Japanese identity.

9.6   Conclusion

It was the researchers' intention in this chapter to alert language education professionals to the path which dominant language education policies, research, and teaching/learning have been taking, where the "thick" has given way to the "quick." Teachers are given insufficient time to think, even less to deepen and mature their ideas, as they are lured by the surface of things, by the brightness of the new, as they relinquish important ideals that they have not explored sufficiently but which will prove to be indispensable. Regarding this exploration, one important theoretical contribution of this chapter was the demonstration that the conceptual, historical, political, and cultural wealth of terms in use needs to be fully considered. Such consideration entails that ethnic and cultural complexities are not oversimplified, and it opens the way to maintaining a strong commitment in language/culture education toward social and epistemological justice, contributing to critical intercultural democratic citizenship. For such purpose, technologies are very important as a medium but not as a goal. Enhancing what is common is as important as respecting what is different, in reciprocity, not pretending that what appears consensual has not been somehow imposed. Researchers must be encouraged to cross the reductive boundaries of limiting terms, and teachers must act on their urge to look beyond imposed routines. Both are open to challenging their creativity and criticality, but often the pressure of entrepreneurial management and policies of educational institutions suffocate professional initiative. The development of CCA in depth promotes reflection and critique about the composition, negotiation, and conflicting views in diverse societies and about the various levels of citizenship. It generates hope and energy for the improvement of the self and social life. It gives teachers and students the dignity of having the "ability to evaluate critically on the basis of explicit criteria" (Byram,

1997, p. 53) every culture; to suspend judgment long enough to allow cultures, individuals, and societies to keep changing; to nurture intercultural encounters; and to create opportunities for mutual learning.

9.6.1 Teaching Implications and Applications

The implications and applications of this chapter for teachers in real language teaching contexts are somewhat different in the Portuguese context from in the Japanese context. In the Portuguese context, the teachers show some awareness of the importance of CCA and have ideas of how to develop it, but as suggested in the previous paragraph, they need to try even harder to resist the neoliberal forces that tend to vitiate their idealistic efforts. In the Japanese context, teachers need support for developing their incipient ideas about CCA into serious pedagogical goals that can compete with the currently dominant examination-oriented goals. It is a severe challenge because language teachers in Japan have traditionally not been encouraged to reflect deeply on their goals. However, there is growing realization in Japan that current language practices are not meeting the complexifying social needs of the twenty-first century, so the time is ripe for the substantial reorientation that CCA represents.

References

Alasuutari, P. (1995). *Researching culture: Qualitative method and cultural studies*. London: Sage Publications.

Alred, G., Byram, M., & Fleming, M. (Eds.). (2006). *Education for intercultural citizenship: Concepts and comparisons*. Clevedon, UK: Multilingual Matters.

American Council on the Teaching of Foreign Languages. (1996). National Standards in foreign language education.. Retrieved from http://www.actfl.org/sites/default/files/pdfs/public/StandardsforFLLexecsumm_rev.pdf.

Bennett, J. M. (2009). Cultivating intercultural competence: A process perspective. In D. K. Deardorff (Ed.), *The Sage handbook of intercultural competence* (pp. 121–140). Thousand Oaks, CA: Sage Publications.

Bennett, J. M. (Ed.). (2015). *The SAGE encyclopedia of intercultural competence*. Thousand Oaks, CA: Sage Publications.

Bloom, B. S. (1956). *Taxonomy of educational objectives: The classification of educational goals*. New York: Longman.

Byram, M. (1997). *Teaching and assessing intercultural communicative competence*. Clevedon, UK/Philadelphia, PA: Multilingual Matters.

Byram, M. (Ed.). (2000). *Routledge encyclopedia of language teaching and learning*. London: Routledge.

Byram, M. (2013). Intercultural competence. In C. Chapelle (Ed.), *The encyclopedia of applied linguistics*. Wiley-Blackwell: Chichester, West Sussex, UK. Retrieved from http://onlinelibrary.wiley.com.

Byram, M., & Hu, A. (Eds.). (2013). *Routledge encyclopedia of language teaching and learning* (2nd ed.). New York: Routledge.

Canagarajah, A. S. (2013). *Translingual practice: Global Englishes and cosmopolitan relations.* Abingdon, UK: Routledge.

Chapelle, C. (Ed.). (2013). *The encyclopedia of applied linguistics.* Chichester, West Sussex, UK: Wiley-Blackwell.

Council of Europe. (1996). *The common European framework for languages.* Strasbourg, France: Council of Europe.

Deardorff, D. K. (Ed.). (2009a). *The SAGE handbook of intercultural competence.* Thousand Oaks, CA: Sage Publications.

Deardorff, D. K. (2009b). Synthesizing conceptualizations of intercultural competence. In *The SAGE handbook of intercultural competence* (pp. 264–269). Thousand Oaks, CA: Sage Publications.

Dietz, G., & Mateos Cortés, L. S. (2012). The need for comparison in intercultural education. *Intercultural Education, 23,* 411–424.

Freire, P. (1970). *Pedagogy of the oppressed.* New York: Herder and Herder.

Freire, P. (1993). Notas. In Pedagogia da Esperança: Um reencontro com a Pedagogia do oprimido. [*Pedagogy of hope: A reencounter with the pedagogy of the oppressed*]. São Paulo, Brazil: Paz e Terra.

Giroux, H. A. (1997). *Pedagogy and the politics of hope: Theory, culture, and schooling: A critical reader.* Boulder, CO: WestviewPress.

Guilherme, M. (2000a). *Critical cultural awareness: The critical dimension in foreign culture education.* (Ph.D. Ph.D.), University of Durham.

Guilherme, M. (2000b). Intercultural competence. In M. Byram (Ed.), *Encyclopaedia of language teaching and learning* (pp. 297–300). London: Routledge.

Guilherme, M. (2002). *Critical citizens for an intercultural world: Foreign language education as cultural politics.* Clevedon, UK: Multilingual Matters.

Guilherme, M. (2012a). Critical language and intercultural communication pedagogy. In J. Jackson (Ed.), *The Routledge handbook of intercultural communication* (pp. 357–371). London: Routledge.

Guilherme, M. (2012b). A critical pedagogy of language and culture. In C. A. Chapelle (Ed.), *The encyclopaedia of applied linguistics.* Oxford: Blackwell. Retrieved from http://onlinelibrary. wiley.com/doi/10.1002/9781405198431.wbeal0283/full.

Guilherme, M. (2013). Intercultural competence. In M. Byram & A. Hu (Eds.), *Encyclopaedia of language teaching and learning* (2nd ed., pp. 346–349). London: Routledge.

Guilherme, M. (2014). 'Glocal' languages and north-south epistemologies: Plurilingual and intercultural relationships. In A. Teodoro & M. Guilherme (Eds.), *European and Latin American higher education between mirrors: Conceptual framework and policies of equity and social cohesion* (pp. 55–72). Rotterdam, The Netherlands: Sense Publishers.

Guilherme, M. (2019). Glocal languages beyond postcolonialism: The metaphorical north and the south in the geographical north and south. In M. Guilherme & L. M. T. M. Souza (Eds.), *Glocal languages and critical intercultural awareness: The south answers back* (pp. 42–64). London/New York: Routledge.

Guilherme, M., & Dietz, G. (2015). Difference in diversity: Multiple perspectives on multi-, inter-, and trans-cultural conceptual complexities. *Journal of Multicultural Discourses, 10,* 1–21.

Guilherme, M., Keating, C., & Hoppe, D. (2010). Intercultural responsibility: Power and ethics in intercultural dialogue and interaction. In M. Guilherme, E. Glaser, & M. C. Mendez-Garcia (Eds.), *Intercultural dynamics of multicultural working* (pp. 77–94). Bristol, UK: Multilingual Matters.

Hall, S. (1959). *The silent language.* New York: Doubleday.

Hofstede, G. H. (2009). The moral circle in intercultural competence: Trust across cultures. In D. K. Deardorff (Ed.), *The Sage handbook of intercultural competence* (pp. 85–99). Thousand Oaks, CA: Sage Publications.

Kim, Y. Y. (2009). The identity factor in intercultural competence. In D. K. Deardorff (Ed.), *The Sage handbook of intercultural competence* (pp. 53–65). Thousand Oaks, CA: Sage Publications.

Kramsch, C. J. (1993). *Context and culture in language teaching.* Oxford, UK: Oxford University Press.

Mateos Cortés, L. S. (2009). The transnational migration of the discourse of interculturality: Towards a comparative analysis of its appropriation by academic and political actors in the state of Veracruz - the *universidad veracruzana intercultural* and the secretary of education. *Intercultural Education, 20,* 27–37.

Medina-López-Portillo, A., & Sinningen, J. H. (2009). Interculturality versus intercultural competencies in latin America. In D. K. Deardorff (Ed.), *The Sage handbook of intercultural competence* (pp. 249–263). Thousand Oaks, CA: Sage Publications.

Parmenter, L. (2003). Describing and defining intercultural communicative competence–international perspectives. In G. Neuner, M. Byram, & Council of Europe. Directorate general IV–education culture youth and sport environment. In *Intercultural competence* (pp. 119–147). Strasbourg, France: Council of Europe Publishing.

Pennycook, A. (1994). *The cultural politics of English as an international language.* New York: Longman.

Phipps, A. (2010). Training and intercultural communication: The danger in "good citizenship". In M. Guilherme, E. Glaser, & M. D. C. M. García (Eds.), *The intercultural dynamics of multicultural working* (pp. 50–73). Bristol, UK: Multilingual Matters.

Santos, B. S. (1999). Towards a multicultural conception of human rights. In M. Featherstone (Ed.), *Spaces of culture: City, nation, world* (pp. 214–229). London: Sage.

Santos, B. S. (2010). Refundación del Estado en América Latina. Perspectivas desde una epistemología del Sur. [*A reconceptualization of the state in Latin America: Perspectives from an epistemology of the South*]. Lima, Peru: Instituto Internacional de Derecho y Sociedad.

Santos, B. S. (2014). *Epistemologies of the south. Justice against epistemicide.* Boulder - London: Paradigm Publishers.

Sawyer, M. (2013). *Foreign language teaching in Portuguese secondary schools: What is the role of culture?* Paper presented at the Universidade Lusófona de Humanidades e Tecnologia, Lisbon.

Sawyer, M. (2014a). Intercultural competence in Asian contexts: Toward integrating Asiacentricity and intercultural citizenship. In G.-M. Chen & X.-D. Dai (Eds.), *Intercultural communication competence: Conceptualization and its development in cultural contexts and interactions* (pp. 170–189). Cambridge, UK: Cambridge Scholars Publishing.

Sawyer, M. (2014b). Intercultural citizenship as the ultimate goal of foreign language education: The role of critical cultural awareness. *Journal of Policy Studies, 47,* 1–9.

Sawyer, M., & Matos, A. G. (2015). The intercultural role of literature in foreign language teaching: A comparative study (Portugal and Japan). *Gengo to Bunka* [Language and Culture], 14, 55–74.

Seargeant, P. (2007). *The idea of English in Japan: Ideology and the evolution of a global language.* Buffalo, NY: Multilingual Matters.

Sinicrope, C., Norris, J., & Watanabe, Y. (2007). Understanding and assessing intercultural competence: A summary of theory, research, and practice (technical report for the foreign language program evaluation project). *Second language Studies, 26,* 1–58.

Spitzberg, B. H., & Chagnon. (2009). Conceptualizing intercultural competence. In D. K. Deardorff (Ed.), *The Sage handbook of intercultural competence* (pp. 2–52). Thousand Oaks, CA: Sage Publications.

Ting-Toomey, S. (2009). Intercultural conflict competence as a facet of intercultural competence development: Multiple conceptual approaches. In D. K. Deardorff (Ed.), *The Sage handbook of intercultural competence* (pp. 101–120). Thousand Oaks, CA: Sage Publications.

Chapter 10
Building an Online Community to Contest Stereotyping and Otherization During Study Abroad

Jane Jackson

10.1 Introduction

Recent study abroad research challenges the "immersion myth," points to the need for interventions to foster language and intercultural learning, and promote a deeper level of engagement in the host environment (Jackson, 2012, 2016, 2018a; Jackson & Oguro, 2018; Lou & Bosley, 2012; Paige & Vande Berg, 2012). Centering on a fully online pedagogical intervention, this chapter examines the use of an asynchronous forum (discussion board) to foster the intercultural sensitivity and engagement of university students who were taking part in an international exchange programme.

Within the context of study abroad, eLearning platforms are now making it possible to offer blended and fully online intercultural communication courses to support and extend the learning of students at all stages: pre-sojourn, sojourn, and post-sojourn (e.g., Jackson, 2012, 2018b; Vande Berg, Paige, & Lou, 2012; Vande Berg, Quinn, & Menyhart, 2012). These developments are creating exciting affordances for the promotion of interculturality and language enhancement in student sojourners. It is incumbent on educators to record and share their experiences with various forms of online interventions.

At a university in Hong Kong, a fully online intercultural communication course has been designed to enhance the language and intercultural learning and adjustment of international exchange students while they are in the host environment (Jackson, 2016, 2018b, 2019). This chapter centers on the role that the weekly asynchronous forum (discussion board) played in the intercultural development of one of the cohorts. To this end, the threaded, full-class discussion that focused on stereotypes and Otherization was subjected to qualitative content analysis to identify patterns

J. Jackson (✉)
The Chinese University of Hong Kong, Shatin, Hong Kong
e-mail: jjackson@cuhk.edu.hk

© Springer Nature Singapore Pte Ltd. 2021   209
M. D. López-Jiménez, J. Sánchez-Torres (eds.), *Intercultural Competence Past, Present and Future*, Intercultural Communication and Language Education,
https://doi.org/10.1007/978-981-15-8245-5_10

and facilitate interpretations of the participants' evolving understanding of the negative consequences of essentialism and social categorization (Bazeley & Jackson, 2013; Grbich, 2012; Miles, Huberman, & Saldana, 2014).

In the literature review, the theoretical underpinning of the online course is explained, drawing attention to the rationale for the use of threaded discussions to promote intercultural learning and engagement in the host environment. After describing the core elements in the course, the design of the evaluative case study of the selected cohort is outlined, and a detailed profile of the participants is presented. Next, data excerpts from the threaded asynchronous discussion that centered on stereotyping and Otherization are presented and analyzed. Finally, the lessons learned are reviewed, and the chapter ends with a discussion of broader implications for the use of online forums to deepen the intercultural learning of student sojourners.

10.2   Literature Review

Relevant to the forum under study are notions of social categorization, Otherization, essentialism, and stereotyping, as well as contemporary approaches to intercultural education (e.g., guided critical reflection, intercultural mentoring) and online pedagogy (e.g., a social constructivist approach).

10.2.1   The Negative Consequence of Otherization

Social categorization refers to the way individuals group people into conceptual categories based on their current understandings, perceptions, and experience (Allport, 1954; Bar-Tal, 1989; Jandt, 2016). Interculturalists have drawn attention to the negative consequences of Otherization or Othering and outdated conceptions of culture as static and unitary (e.g., Dervin, 2012; Scollon, Scollon, & Jones, 2011). Basically, Otherization is a form of social representation or categorization that entails the objectification of another human being or group (Holliday, Hyde, & Kullman, 2010). When people engage in Otherization, they largely ignore the complexity and diversity of individuals who have a different cultural background from them (Dervin, 2012; Holliday, 2011). As an ideology, the process of essentialism rests on the following faulty assumptions: (1) that cultural groups can be clearly delineated and (2) that individuals who are perceived to be group members are more or less the same (Bucholtz, 2003; Holliday, 2011).

While people routinely make use of social categories to make sense of the complex world in which we live, essentialism and Otherization can be very detrimental to intercultural relations and promote polarizing "us versus them" stances. Holmes (2012, p. 468) explains:

...the cognitive activities of categorization and generalization that occur normally in the human brain are an important way of making sense of the world around us. Although such categorizations are useful as sense-making strategies for human behavior, if unchecked, they can lead to more extreme understandings of cultural difference, such as ethnocentrism, stereotyping, and prejudice—the roots of racism.

There are many definitions of stereotypes. Most often, they are depicted as preconceived ideas that attribute certain characteristics (e.g., intelligence, personality traits), intentions, and/or behaviors to all perceived members of a particular social class or group (Allport, 1954; Holliday, 2011). Pennington (1986, p. 90), for example, defines stereotypes as "grossly oversimplified and overgeneralized abstractions about groups of people that are usually highly inaccurate, although they may contain a grain of truth." When people stereotype, they impose their assumptions on others, usually drawing on commonly held beliefs (e.g., ideas presented in the media). In contrast, a generalization is a starting point, and interculturally sensitive individuals recognize that much more information is needed to determine if their ideas or perceptions apply to a particular individual.

Stereotypes often portray individuals or groups in a negative light, but even if these preconceived notions emphasize what are generally regarded as positive characteristics (e.g., advanced linguistic ability, musicality, high academic achievement), they can still be harmful to the person being stereotyped. As Spencer-Oatey and Franklin (2009) explain, stereotyping can easily lead to essentialism:

One of the major problems with stereotypes is that they easily take on an essentialist character, with the result that group members are treated as having certain invariable and fixed properties, and as being essentially different from members of other groups. (p. 142–43)

To push past stereotyping and Otherization, a growing number of international educators advocate research-driven interventions that actively promote interculturality and raise awareness of the harmful effects of an essential notion of culture.

10.2.2 Promoting Interculturality Through Guided Critical Reflection

Educators are now designing innovative intercultural communication courses that strive to enhance knowledge of (inter)cultural concepts while simultaneously promoting the acquisition of intercultural communication skills (Jackson, 2018a; Jackson & Oguro, 2018). Many contemporary interculturalists maintain that it is possible for students to develop mindfulness (Ting-Toomey, 2012) and a more open, intercultural worldview through guided, critical reflection and experiential learning (Hammer, 2012, 2013; Passarelli & Kolb, 2012). The reflection process can help learners make sense of their experiences (e.g., intercultural, international) and foster a deeper level of self-awareness, which is a core element in intercultural competence. For learners, engaging in the act of purposeful reflection entails:

> understanding the context of learning and the particular issues that may arise; understanding their own contribution to that context, including past experiences, values/philosophies and knowledge; drawing on other evidence or explanation from the literature or relevant theories to explain why these experiences have played out or what could be different; and using all of this knowledge to re-imagine and ultimately improve future experience. (Ryan & Ryan, 2015, p. 16)

Guided, intercultural reflection in the form of intercultural mentoring is now employed in intercultural education programs to help provide direction for individualized or group-oriented feedback (Hammer, 2013; Jackson, 2016, 2018a; Paige, 2013). In this approach, facilitators develop detailed profiles of the learners, usually by gathering data through multiple means (e.g., reflective essays, intercultural journals, sojourn diaries, in-depth interviews, portfolios, survey questionnaires) (Deardorff, 2015; Paige, 2013). In this intercultural pedagogy, the mentor then draws on this data to offer feedback and encouragement that is appropriate to the participants' level of intercultural awareness and sensitivity. The facilitator strives to "support students through intentional mentoring and guidance that is designed to help them learn to reflect on themselves as cultural beings, and to become aware of the ways that they characteristically respond to and make meaning within different cultural contexts" (Lou, Vande Berg, & Paige, 2012, p. 415). As a reflective mindset is crucial in the mentoring process, the facilitator or mentor continuously prompts the participants to think more deeply and critically about their intercultural attitudes and actions and encourages them to set realistic goals for future intercultural interactions.

10.2.3 A Social Constructivist Approach to Online Pedagogy

With advances in communication technology and social media (e.g., eLearning platforms, Facebook, Skype), it is now possible for intercultural educators to mentor students online. Following a social constructivist orientation to online pedagogy, learners may share intercultural experiences in a forum and receive feedback from a mentor as well as their peers (Jackson, 2018b, 2019). This approach is based on the belief that intercultural learning can be enriched through collaborative scaffolding and guided critical reflection (Bryant & Bates, 2015; Harasim, 2012; Lee, 2009). Social constructivists maintain that peer comments can spur the intercultural development and engagement of course participants. Thus, as students share ideas and experiences online, they are expected to learn from each other as well as the course facilitator.

Forums may be synchronous or asynchronous. In contrast with real-time computer-mediated communication (e.g., audio-video conferencing, Web chat, synchronous forums), in asynchronous forums, the participants are online at different times, allowing more opportunity for reflection and thoughtful responses. This can be helpful in intercultural communication courses that call upon the participants to disclose and discuss very personal subject matter (e.g., intercultural conflict situations, stereotyping). In fully online intercultural communication courses, it is therefore incumbent on the facilitator to create a supportive online community which encourages open, respectful dialogue among all participants.

While many studies have examined tandem intercultural communication courses, whereby learners interact with partners in another country, only a handful of researchers are systematically investigating fully online courses for international exchange students. Consequently, we know relatively little about the impact of asynchronous threaded discussions on the intercultural learning of this population.

10.3   Methodology

10.3.1   Course Description, Aims, and Components

At a university in Hong Kong, a fully online, credit-bearing, elective course was designed to introduce international exchange students to core elements in intercultural communication. By creating a supportive, interactive online community, the facilitator aimed to encourage the participants to discuss course concepts and share their intercultural experiences in the host environment. Ultimately, it was hoped that this intervention would propel the students to a higher level of intercultural competence and engagement during their sojourn.

The planning of *Intercultural communication and engagement abroad* drew on multiple theories and constructs: mentoring as an intercultural pedagogy (Hammer, 2013; Jackson, 2016, 2018b, 2019; Paige, 2013), experiential learning and guided critical reflection (Jackson, 2015a, b; Moon, 2000, 2006; Passarelli & Kolb, 2012; Ryan & Ryan, 2015), post-structuralist notions of identity expansion and interculturality (Block, 2007; Dervin, 2012; Jackson, 2018a), and a social constructivist orientation toward online pedagogy (Bryant & Bates, 2015; Lee, 2011).

In this 13-week course, Blackboard served as the eLearning platform (Web-based course management system). The course activities included a full-group forum (30%), related fieldwork in the host environment (40%), and reflective essays (30%). Each week, the students were required to complete readings in the core text (Jackson, 2014b), view related PowerPoint files and YouTube clips, and actively participate in our online community.

10.3.2   The Weekly Asynchronous Forum

The weekly asynchronous forum, a central component in the course, counted for 30% of the grade (see Appendix A for guidelines for posts). The weekly themes, which were related to the content in the core text (Jackson, 2014b), are presented in

Appendix B. To give the students a clear idea about what was expected in the forum and provide constructive feedback on their contributions, a rubric was developed and posted on Blackboard at the beginning of the semester.

10.3.3   Objectives

To gain a better sense of the impact of the course on student learning and facilitate the revision process, an evaluative case study of the present offering was carried out, drawing on the qualitative and quantitative data that was collected before, during, and after the course (Jackson, 2016, 2018a). While all course elements have been scrutinized, the remainder of this chapter focuses on the forum. Particular attention is paid to the participants' emergent understanding of the harmful effects of stereotyping and Otherization on intercultural relations. For this phase of the case study, the following questions guided this enquiry:

1. How do the participants perceive stereotyping and Otherization before, during, and after the course?
2. To what extent does the asynchronous forum foster collaborative learning, critical reflection, and intercultural learning in relation to stereotyping and Otherization?

10.3.4   Participants

In the offering of the course under study, there were 22 international exchange students: 18 (81.8%) females and 4 (18.2%) males. In this cohort, 17 (77.3%) spoke Cantonese as a first language, 3 (13.6%) Putonghua (Mandarin), and 1 (4.5%) Korean, and 1 (4.5%) grew up in a bilingual household and spoke both Putonghua and Cantonese at home. The majority (16, 72.7%) had spent their formative years in Hong Kong, while 6 (27.3%) had grown up in either Mainland China (5) or Korea (1). The average score on the IELTS was 7.34 (TOEFL 101–102 equivalent).

Among the 22 students, 2 (9.1%) were in their second year of undergraduate studies, and 20 (90.9%) were in their third year. Nine (40.9%) were from the Faculty of Arts (Chinese, English, Japanese studies, music, and translation majors), eight (36.4%) from the Faculty of Business Administration (international business, international finance, hotel and tourism management, and professional accountancy majors), two (9.1%) from the Faculty of Education (English language education majors), one (4.5%) from the Faculty of Medicine (a public health administration major), one (4.5%) from the Faculty of Science (a biochemistry major), and one (4.5%) from the Faculty of Social Science (an economics major).

In this cohort, 17 (77.3%) had prior travel abroad experience. Only 3 (13.6%) had previous study abroad experience (e.g., a summer language immersion program). Out of the 22 students, 16 (72.7%) had never taken a course in intercultural communication; 6 (27.3%) had studied modules on intercultural communication (e.g., an international business course). When the present course got underway, 2 (9.1%) had no intercultural friends; 12 (54.5%) had a few intercultural acquaintances. Only 8 (36.4%) indicated that they had several intercultural friends. In a pre-sojourn questionnaire, the participants assessed their ability to communicate appropriately and effectively with people who had a different cultural background. At this stage, only 3 (13.6%) rated their degree of intercultural competence as "excellent." Six (27.3%) rated it as "very good," 11 (50.0%) as "good," and 2 (9.1%) as "fair." None rated their intercultural skills as "poor." With regard to their openness to other cultures, in the pre-sojourn questionnaire, 4 (18.2%) rated it as "excellent," 9 (40.9%) as "very good," 7 (31.8%) as "good," and 2 (9.1%) as "fair." None rated their degree of openness as "poor."

In this cohort, 12 (54.5%) were taking part in a yearlong international exchange program, while 10 (45.5%) were semester-long sojourners. Only 1 (4.5%), a Japanese major, was required to participate in an international exchange program (in Japan) as part of her program of study. During the course, the participants studied in the following host countries: 5 (22.7%) Canada, 4 (18.2%) the United States, 3 (13.6%) Japan, 2 (9.09%) Australia, 1 (4.5%) Belgium, 1 (4.5%) Finland, 1 (4.5%) Germany, 1 (4.5%) Ireland, 1 (4.5%) the Netherlands, 1 (4.5%) Singapore, 1 (4.5%) South Africa, and 1 (4.5%) the United Kingdom. Except for the students who went to Japan and Germany, the primary language of instruction in nearly all of their courses was English, a second language for all of the participants.

10.3.5   Instrumentation and Data Collection

NVivo, a software program that aids the collection, organization, and analysis of mixed-method data, is especially useful for the processing of unstructured, qualitative data such as interview transcripts and online posts (Bazeley & Jackson, 2013). To facilitate the preparation of a full-group profile and enable the tracking of the developmental trajectories of each course participant, an NVivo10 database was set up before the course got underway. As soon as data was collected, it was entered into the database. Following the research ethics review procedures at my institution, the permission of the participants was obtained before the material was coded, triangulated, and analyzed. Anonymity was guaranteed and assurances were given that (non)participation would not impact grades.

The NVivo database consisted of varied types of qualitative and quantitative data that was gathered before, during, and after the course: pre- and post-course interview transcripts, hypermedia forum and fieldwork posts, questionnaire surveys (pre-course, mid-course, post-course), reflective essays (middle and end of course), and my field notes. The in-depth semi-structured interviews took place in Cantonese, Putonghua, or English, depending on the preference of the interviewee.

10.3.6   Data Analysis

With the assistance of the qualitative software program NVivo 10, all of the data for the case study was subjected to triangulation and open, thematic coding (Bazeley & Jackson, 2013; Grbich, 2012; Miles et al., 2014). A review of the triangulated, coded material helped understand the impact of various course element (e.g., the full-class, weekly forum) on the participants' evolving intercultural awareness and sensitivity.

10.4   Results and Discussion

Due to space limitations, this section focuses on the analysis of student posts in the asynchronous threaded discussion which centered on generalizations, stereotypes, and Otherization. As many contributions in the sixth forum were quite long, only a small percentage of the data can be presented, with a focus on student comments. The headings that were posted with the entries are included with all excerpts, and the comments are as in the original.

10.4.1   Analysis of Forum Posts

10.4.1.1   Awareness of the Difference Between Generalizations and Stereotypes (and Why It Matters)

The assigned reading for the sixth forum (Chapter 7 in Jackson, 2014b) included definitions and examples of generalizations and stereotypes. Early in the discussion, the students were prompted to debate the differences between these constructs and reflect on possible implications for intercultural communication. Interestingly, in the following exchange, S19 kept the tone friendly when responded to S12's post but also managed to offer a deeper level of analysis and a message.

> Thread: *Inevitable stereotyping, but there are other ways to go!*
> As we are primarily socialized by our parents, teachers, and society, I think that we learn that there is a "proper" way to decide what is correct and incorrect. We start to categorize and generalize people into different groups as if all individuals are the same as the group. When we see a person who comes from another group, it is easy to stereotype the person based on our generalization and beliefs. What do you think? (S12)

> Thanks for your sharing! I reckon that a generalization is a gateway for us to dig deeper into the complex cultures within one nation, while stereotyping is a misleading concept implanted in our heads which might be contradictory to the reality. Generalizations are perceived common trends within a nation. Yet, if these generalizations are not dealt with in a proper way or not considered together with individual differences, stereotyping might occur. (S19)

10.4.1.2   Unpacking the "Culture as Nation" Perspective

In the assigned PowerPoint file and related chapter, essentialism and the "culture as nation" perspective (Holliday, 2012; Jackson, 2014b) were explained in detail. In the forum, the course participants were asked to consider how an essentialist orientation can hinder constructive intercultural dialogue.

Thread: *"Culture as nation"*
 The "Culture as nation" perspective means others may think people from the same country may have a similar set of behaviors, mindset, norms, and beliefs. For instance, people may think that French people have a slow speed of living, like having dinner for more than two hours. And Japanese are polite and disciplinary. Being late is the taboo of Japanese. The danger of this is that you may have bias towards a person before you get to know more about him/her and it is certainly a barrier to communication. (S5)

Thread: *Breaking the frame*
 The "Culture as nation" perspective refers to the categorization and perception of people in the basis of nations, believing that people from the same nation share the same culture, such as their characteristics and behaviors. For example, "Finns love drinking" is a "culture as nation" perspective. Though it makes things simpler when you try to identify a particular culture, it is dangerous as you may be overgeneralizing the people within, regardless of their individual differences, and this leads to stereotyping. (S10)

Thread: *Avoidable stereotypes*
 To me, "culture as nation" perspective means people sharing the same culture come from the same nation. For example, Indians come with the strong curry smell. While stereotypes give us a first impression on others' culture and values, such approach is dangerous, because we perceive them as a group that is homogenous, instead of seeing them as unique entities. Individuals may not carry all the stereotypes and there may be a wide range of varieties within a culture, which may easily lead to misunderstanding and conflicts. (S17)

In their posts, many students included multiple examples that demonstrated their understanding of essentialism and Otherization. The following comments pointed to their growing awareness of the potentially harmful consequences of this way of thinking (e.g., discrimination, stereotyping, racism, xenophobia).

Thread: *Thinking out of the box*
 Assuming that all individuals from the same nation are identical hinders our genuine understanding of the traits (and more importantly the diversity) of the people in a nation. It might also lead to discriminatory practices, especially when the stereotyping process involves negative emotional attachment and behavioral reactions (e.g., using certain derogatory labels or offensive items in language, or just as simple as ignoring the people from a perceivably negative nation). Discrimination, racism and xenophobia are the worst repercussions. (S19)

Thread: *Barriers to intercultural communication*
 "Culture as nation" is defined as "a view of peoples within national boundaries as essentially homogeneous, possessing certain core characteristics. . ." (Martin, Nakayama, & Carbaugh, 2012, p. 18). In this theory, the nations and communities are viewed as homogeneous and the diversity among individuals is overlooked and "culture" is presented as "shared" by all nation members. This is closely linked to "essentialism," which indicates that group members are more or less alike. For instance, people from China are always

defined as nonaggressive, quiet, passive, and good at mathematics. People from Britain are viewed as ladies and gentleman, who are very polite but also reserved and a bit arrogant. People from Russia are categorized to be all alcoholics. French people are romantic but not very reliable. All of these examples can be seen as "culture as nation." Grouping and describing characteristics of people only in terms of nation can be quite misleading. It overlooks the difference among individuals and overgeneralizes the similarities. It will also lead to ethnocentrism and stereotyping. (S22)

10.4.1.3 Recognizing the Roots of Stereotyping and the One's Own Tendency to Put People into Boxes

In the forum, the students were also prompted to discuss the reasons why people engage in stereotyping. In their estimation, individuals, including themselves, most often resort to this form of reductionism to save time and simplify their life. The following comments were typical:

Thread: *Stereotyping as first impression*
I think I engage in stereotyping because it can quickly give me an impression of the new people and situation that I meet. I can have a simplified assumption on others. Then I may not be too surprised when I meet someone new. For example, when I see the American girls playing crazily in a party, I won't be shocked. (S6)

Thread: *Why we have to discriminate others?*
More or less, I think I have engaged in stereotyping. This is because we all rely on limited clues to guess or preview a person's personality to "know" a new friend. Just as we may trust in horoscopes, stereotyping is the way we find "tips" about a new person. Although it does not make any logical sense, people tend to trust these ideas. (S15)

An English education major who was participating in a semester-long exchange program in Ireland posted a longer entry, which revealed a higher level of reflection. In his post, he attributed stereotyping to a range of factors.

Thread: *Thinking out of the box*
Even though culture is a very complex construct, it might be simplified out of convenience or because of socialization, previous experiences, ethnocentrism, and so on. This might result in a "culture as nation" perspective, in which people from a nation are thought to share similar features physically (e.g., physical attributes), behaviorally (e.g., ways of behavior or communication including accents/language), and psychologically (e.g., beliefs, values, religions and so on). For example, Irish people are generally commented as with a strong accent and always a glass of whisky. Scottish people are depicted as humorous but can sometimes be quite critical and mean. Thais are generalized to be very devout just because many temples and different gods and goddesses can be found in their country. (S19)

Some of the students cited ignorance and fear as driving forces behind this phenomenon, including their own tendency to stereotype. Their posts were candid and suggested that they were actively engaged in the process of critical self-reflection.

Thread: *Breaking the frame*
Undoubtedly, I engage in stereotyping, and I think everyone does in reality.... I agree with the textbook that "a generalization is a starting point and...much more information is

needed to determine if your ideas or perceptions apply to a particular individual. . . ." I think that most of my stereotypes come from my ignorance and fear. (S10)

Thread: *Don't judge too quickly*
    It's really difficult to avoid engaging in stereotyping and I am no exception. I have fear towards people from Middle East. I felt quite unsafe meeting someone from the Middle East, as I thought they would be radical and aggressive, behaving violently. This may be due to a narrow way of seeing the world. I haven't met many people from the area and was influenced greatly by the media. Media only gives us a narrow view of the world. We need to experience the world ourselves to come to a reliable conclusion. I try to take more initiative to meet some friends from the Middle East, knowing more about them by myself instead of the media. I found many of them were really nice and warm. I thought it was unfair and offended to judge people according to their nationality without knowing what he actually is. If everyone just engages in stereotyping, people would just group together according to their nationality and fail to discover the true beauty of different people. (S14)

Many course participants noted that it is common to rely on the media or the perceptions of in-group members if you have limited information about people who are associated with a particular culture. An English major from China who sojourned in the United States also remarked that the degree of cultural distance can play an influential role in stereotyping. Her post suggests that she believed that stereotyping might diminish with meaningful intercultural contact.

Thread: *Stereotyping*
    According to chapter 7, people mostly stereotype for the sake of simplifying their life, making predictions about others, and so on. In my opinion, cultural distance does make a difference here, as when a culture is not that familiar and close to you, it is just harder to perceive the differences and individuality within that group and you thus tend to perceive the group as a whole. (S21)

10.4.1.4 Stereotyping: A Difficult Habit to Break

When discussing the reasons why individuals resort to stereotyping, some of the course participants attempted to explain why misconceptions persist even after personal experience suggests that these ideas are faulty. As noted by a business major who sojourned in Japan, people may simply choose to ignore information that does not fit with preconceived notions.

Thread: *Generalizations and stereotypes: What's the harm?*
    When we categorize people, we tend to find more information and proofs to prove they are who we think, at the same time, neglecting other information counter to proving these characteristics. This is why this kind of categorizing is rather difficult to reduce. (S15)

10.4.1.5 Heightened Awareness of the Dangers of Stereotyping and Otherization

By this stage of the course, many of the students were demonstrating much more awareness and understanding of the negative consequences of stereotyping and

Otherization. In the sixth forum, there was a notable reduction in "us versus them" discourse. Further, when prompted to discuss ways to combat stereotyping, in this forum, many participants resolved to pay more attention to their tendency to quickly "put people into boxes" based on scant information. They recognized the merits of refraining from making snap judgments and reaffirmed their desire to initiate and grow "genuine intercultural friendships."

Thread: *Otherization*

   Otherization means characterizing people into "our group" and "the others" based on their culture instead of their individual differences. This limits the development of genuine intercultural friendships because you tend to stick with your ingroup members and keep a social distance with the outgroup members. For instance, when I first arrived here, I always stuck with my Hong Kong roommate and dared not talk to other flat mates. This reduced my chance to make friends with them. Also, when you group a person by his/her culture instead of individual characteristics, you may impose a wrong image on him/her. As you need to know a person well enough to develop true friendship, when you have a wrong supposition on him/her, you may misunderstand what he/she wants to express and this hinders your communication. For example, in the university café, I met a guy who was half Finnish and half Indian. I have some prejudice against Indians (due to fear) and I ignored him at first. But after some talking I realized that he just wanted to make friends with people from other countries and had no bad intentions. Otherization blocks you from seeing the true personalities of the person that you are interacting with and restricts your intercultural communication with him or her. It limits the development of genuine intercultural friendships. (S10)

10.4.1.6   Challenging Peers to Move Beyond Stereotyping

Midway through the discussion, some of the students began to encourage each other to break the cycle of stereotyping and dig deeper into what lies behind this habit. In the following exchange, S16 responded with humor to S17's post but also challenged him to reflect on his own prejudicial thoughts and judgments.

Thread: *Breaking the frame*

   Hi! In Singapore there are quite a lot of Blacks and many Indians here. It seems that they are incompatible with the Singaporean Chinese as you seldom see any interracial group sitting together to have a chat or tea in a restaurant or canteen. I also discriminate against the Indians, since I do always smell a strong and stinky odor whenever they come across me. Although many times I tell myself not to view them in that way, I cannot stop myself from avoiding them. I think I need to be braver to come across that smell of spicy. (S17)

Thread: *Why we have to discriminate others?*

   Dear X, I guess we can think in another way. While we can smell their strong curry smell, they can also smell our Chinese smell that we may not be able to smell ourselves. Our smell should consist of garlic and ginger. . .ha ha. (S16)

10.4.1.7   Efforts to Reduce Stereotyping and Cultivate an Intercultural Mindset

The assigned reading also offered suggestions for ways to reduce the tendency to stereotype. Near the end of the forum, the students reflected on their own experiences and attitudes and shared ideas about ways to combat prejudice. Many cited the importance of gaining firsthand intercultural experience and the need to make an effort to cultivate an open, empathetic mindset.

> Thread: *The world is not that simple*
> As stereotyping is due to ignorance, meeting friends from different ethnic backgrounds is the best way to avoid it. Through interacting with people from different cultural backgrounds, we can know how people from different countries actually are. Moreover, we need to think ethnorelatively when we communicate with people from different cultures and try to put ourselves into others' shoes. These are important steps to prevent discrimination and racism. To make our world more peaceful and harmonious, we need to stop stereotyping. (S3)

> Thread: *Don't judge too quickly!*
> You have to realize that what you learn from the media may not be true so do spare some time and efforts collecting more information. Then, make an objective judgment. (S14)

> Thread: *Stereotyping*
> We have to overcome stereotyping. It is for the sake of treating others equally and fairly, and discovering real personalities of others, which is essential to develop more meaningful communications. This can also help to open our mind broader, and think more critically and reasonably. (S21)

While some of the students offered general advice, others thought more deeply about why they stereotype and described the steps that they were taking or planned to take to push past this habit. The following participants, for example, aimed to suspend judgment and talk with international friends when they encountered unfamiliar ways of being. They reminded themselves to view people as individuals rather than mere representatives of a particular culture.

> Thread: *Stereotyping as first impression*
> A stereotype overgeneralizes people and ignores the diversity in a nation. It also acts as a barrier to successful intercultural communication. . . . When I have ideas like this in my head I talk with my international friends and ask them questions. With their clarification, I can truly know the diversity of a nation and appreciate foreign cultures. I can learn to understand more about the differences and be open-minded to accept the new culture. (S6)

> Thread: *Unavoidable stereotypes*
> Even though stereotypes are something ingrained in ourselves, it is important to remove them in order to build meaningful and long-lasting intercultural relationships. I need to remind myself to see international students as individuals rather than as representation of a particular cultural group. Stereotypes are hard to break but let's try to do so and change our world! (S17)

In many of the posts, in line with messages conveyed by the assigned reading and the course facilitator, the students emphasized the importance of reflexivity, respect, open-mindedness, and appreciation to overcome essentialist tendencies and develop meaningful intercultural relationships.

> Thread: *Try to reduce stereotyping!*
> When I react negatively to someone, I need to reflect on what may be the source of my discomfort. That would be a good way to reduce the tendency of putting people into a box. I should be more open-minded to intercultural contacts. If a friend from Africa greets me with

a light punch or hug, I would not consider this as a rude act, but a way of expressing friendliness. Putting aside the cultural bias would definitely help eliminate stereotyping. To build a genuine relationship with others, I need to try to push beyond this habit so that I can truly understand and appreciate the way they are. (S8)

Thread: *Why do we have to discriminate others?*

To reduce stereotyping, I think it is the best to remind myself: Is it that all Chinese/Hong Kongers possess some core personalities? If not, I do not have the right to stereotype others. Moreover, I will ask myself: How do I feel when I am stereotyped? I feel I am not respected when people act as if they know who I am because they know something about the Chinese. As we are all different individuals, we should respect each person as a distinctive person. This is very important as stereotyping will affect the way we treat a person. (S15)

Thread: *Thinking out of the box*

I cannot promise not to stereotype others since all images about different nationals have been implanted in my mind for a long time under socialization. However, there are still ways to think out of the boxes. The first step is to really accept that cultures are diverse, and, from now on, let me try to put away the pessimistic labels and put on an optimistic face to get to learn more about the reality of cultures. If I do not take the initiative to apprehend, accept, and adjust why should other people react to me in a respectful way? (S19)

When compared with the posts in the first half of the course, the threaded discussions in the sixth forum offered much more evidence of intercultural awareness and understanding, enhanced knowledge about potential ways to cultivate an ethnorelative mindset, and demonstrate respect for individuals who have a different cultural background from them. Their comments suggested that many had understood and internalized the ideas conveyed in the assigned reading and comments posted by the course facilitator and teaching assistant. The findings were encouraging.

10.5   Summary and Conclusions

Drawing on an evaluative case study of the online course *Intercultural communication and engagement abroad*, this chapter reported on the participants' evolving understanding of what lies behind the practice of stereotyping and the negative consequences of social categorization. More specifically, the following research questions were addressed in this phase of the study:

- How do the participants perceive stereotyping and Otherization before, during, and after the course?
- To what extent does the asynchronous forum foster collaborative learning, critical reflection, and intercultural learning in relation to stereotyping and Otherization?

With regard to the first research question, by the end of the semester, most of the course participants had become more sensitive to the ways in which rigid social categorization and reductionism can hamper the development of constructive intercultural relations and potentially lead to prejudicial, racist behavior, if unchecked (Holmes, 2012; Spencer-Oatey & Franklin, 2009). The analysis of the forum posts provided compelling evidence that the intercultural intervention (e.g., related reading and YouTube clip, asynchronous discussion, facilitator/peer mentoring, guided critical reflection) had helped the course participants become more cognizant of the ways in which stereotyping and Otherization can affect their perception of and interaction with people who have a different linguistic and cultural background. As they became more aware of the complexity of the notion of culture and sensitive to diversity within cultural groups, including their own, they began to move beyond polarizing "us versus them" orientations. This, in turn, helped them to create more possibilities for meaningful intercultural dialogue in the host environment.

The second research question was concerned with the impact of the asynchronous forum on intercultural learning, especially with regard to the course participants' understanding of the harmful effects of stereotyping and Otherization. The building of a supportive online community, the careful selection and sequencing of multimodal learning materials to scaffold discussions, and guided critical reflection in the weekly forum propelled the participants to higher levels of mindfulness and intercultural awareness. A systematic content analysis of the threaded discussions and a review of other related course materials (e.g., post-course interviews and survey questionnaires, the reflective essays) offered valuable insight into the social categorization process employed by the students and their evolving understanding of essentialism. A review of the data revealed that the participants generally became much more sensitive to the harmful effects of stereotyping and Otherization and more aware of strategies to employ to develop meaningful intercultural relationships. For many of the course participants, there was a noticeable shift in their attitudes toward individuals who have a different cultural background; by the end of the semester, they were making more of an effort to get to know people as individuals rather than seeing them as mere representatives of a particular culture or national group. Significantly, a review of their online posts indicated that most were gradually eschewing the "culture as nation" orientation toward cultural difference (Holliday, 2012; Jackson, 2014b).

10.6 Implications and Applications

The analysis of the rich qualitative data amassed in the case study pointed to the benefits of social constructivism in intercultural e-pedagogy, contributing to both theoretical and practical understandings of this approach to teaching and learning in an online environment. Intercultural mentorship (both teacher and peer feedback) and the "unpacking" of ideas and experiences in a fully online course have the potential to bring about a range of rewards for international exchange students. In particular, intercultural interventions of this nature can help the participants develop a deeper awareness and understanding of elements that can impact the nature and quality of intercultural communication. Through the process of reflecting on assigned readings and the comments of their facilitator/teaching assistant, sharing ideas and experiences with peers online, and responding to probes that prompt them to dig deeper, students can reap multiple rewards: enhance their critical self-awareness, heighten their sensitivity to the dangers of stereotyping and Otherization, cultivate a more positive attitude toward cultural difference, and become more willing to initiate intercultural/second language interactions in the host environment (and elsewhere) and pushing past preconceived notions. All of these developments facilitate the building of healthy intercultural relationships. With encouragement and ongoing support, the intercultural communication skills and mindset nurtured in the host environment may then be employed by returnees in their home setting. Intercultural development entails lifelong learning.

This interactive, learner-centered, online course was developed in Hong Kong with outbound Asian international exchange students in mind; however, the peda-gogy (e.g., intercultural mentoring, online debriefings) and the findings of the case study that is the focus of this chapter are apt to be relevant for intercultural educators and study abroad professionals in other contexts who seek to promote interculturality, contest stereotyping and Otherization, and stimulate meaningful engagement in the host environment. To further advance the field of intercultural education, in addition to basic annual reviews of intercultural communication courses, it is important for educators to periodically conduct more thorough, detailed investigations of their pedagogical interventions, including specific course elements (e.g., online forums). The lessons learned can enrich theoretical understandings (e.g., the social categorization process, the tenets of social constructivism) and, on a practical level, inform subsequent revisions, further enhancing the quality of intercultural teaching and learning. Finally, the sharing of evaluative case studies like this through conference presentations and publications is essential so that a much greater number of students and intercultural educators can benefit.

Acknowledgments The development and refinement of the online course was supported by a Teaching Development Grant (#4170416) and an eLearning grant (#3210760) from the Chinese University of Hong Kong. General Research Fund project #4440713, which was funded by the University Research Grants Committee of Hong Kong, provided additional information about course participants. The Hong Kong Research Grants Council (RGC) Prestigious Fellowship under the Humanities and Social Science Panel (HSSPFS) (#34000616)) facilitated a systematic evaluation of the online course.

Appendices

Appendix A: Full-Class Forum

In an atmosphere of mutual respect and sharing, everyone will post comments in the forum each week. Before posting comments, it is important to read the assigned readings and view the related PPT files (and video or YouTube links). Our online discussion aims to facilitate the exchange of ideas, deepen your understanding of intercultural communication, help you make sense of your international experience, and enhance your intercultural competence. In the forum, we will be developing a community of internationally minded explorers who share a love of travel, intercultural interaction, and diversity. If you come across websites/readings/films/ videos (e.g., YouTube posts, study abroad sites) related to our weekly theme (or international/intercultural experience, more broadly), please tell us in the forum and provide a link (along with a few comments about the content/usefulness of the material). Bring your own international/intercultural experiences into the discussion, as well as your developing understanding of intercultural communication theories and concepts. The aim is to share and grow so that everyone benefits! Please submit your primary post on time so that others have time to read it and respond.

Appendix B: Forum Weekly Themes

1. Introductions: Getting to know each other better
2. Language and culture shock and adjustment
3. Elements of culture; language and culture
4. Language, gender, communication, culture, and power/communication style
5. Language, culture, and identity
6. *Generalizations, stereotypes, and Otherization*
7. Intercultural transitions: Adjusting to differing "cultures of learning"
8. Multicultural friendship/romance; relationship-building
9. Intercultural conflict and mediation
10. Global citizenship and intercultural competence
11. Taking stock and preparing to return home

References

Allport, G. (1954). *The nature of prejudice*. Reading, MA: Addison-Wesley.
Bar-Tal, D. (1989). Delegitimization: The extreme case of stereo-typing and prejudice. In D. Bar-Tal, C. Graumann, A. W. Kruglanski, & W. Stroebe (Eds.), *Stereotypes and prejudice: Changing conceptions* (pp. 169–182). New York: Springer-Verlag.
Bazeley, P., & Jackson, K. (2013). *Qualitative data analysis with NVivo* (2nd ed.). Thousand Oaks, CA: Sage.
Block, D. (2007). *Second language identities*. London: Continuum.
Bolen, N. (Ed.). (2007). *A guide to outcomes assessment in education abroad*. Carlisle, PA: Forum on Education Abroad.
Bryant, J., & Bates, A. (2015). Creating a constructivist online instructional environment. *TechTrends, 59*(2), 17–22.
Bucholtz, M. (2003). Sociolinguistic nostalgia and the authentication of identity. *Journal of Sociolinguistics, 7*(3), 398–416. https://doi.org/10.1111/1467-9481.00232.
Deardorff, D. K. (2015). *Demystifying outcomes assessment for international educators: A practical approach*. Sterling, VA: Stylus.

Dervin, F. (2012). Cultural identity, representation and othering. In J. Jackson (Ed.), *The Routledge handbook of language and intercultural communication* (pp. 181–194). London: Routledge.

Grbich, C. (2012). *Qualitative data analysis* (2nd ed.). Thousand Oaks, CA: Sage.

Hammer, M. R. (2012). The intercultural development inventory: A new frontier in assessment and development of intercultural competence. In M. Vande Berg, R. M. Paige, & K. H. Lou (Eds.), *Student learning abroad: What our students are learning, what they're not, and what we can do about it* (pp. 115–136). Sterling, VA: Stylus.

Hammer, M. R. (2013). *A resource guide for effectively using the intercultural development inventory (IDI)*. Berlin, MD: IDI, LLC.

Harasim, L. (2012). *Learning theory and online technologies*. New York: Routledge.

Holliday, A. (2011). *Intercultural communication and ideology*. London: Sage.

Holliday, A. (2012). Culture, communication, context and power. In J. Jackson (Ed.), *The Routledge handbook of language and intercultural communication* (pp. 37–51). Abingdon, UK: Routledge.

Holliday, A., Hyde, M., & Kullman, M. (2010). *Intercultural communication: An advanced resource book for students* (2nd ed.). London and New York: Routledge.

Holmes, P. (2012). Business and management education. In J. Jackson (Ed.), *The Routledge handbook of language and intercultural communication* (pp. 464–480). London: Routledge.

Jackson, J. (2012). Education abroad. In J. Jackson (Ed.), *The Routledge handbook of language and intercultural communication* (pp. 449–463). London: Routledge.

Jackson, J. (2014a). The process of becoming reflexive and intercultural: Navigating study abroad and reentry experience. In J. Byrd Clarke & F. Dervin (Eds.), *Reflexivity and multimodality in language education: Rethinking multilingualism and interculturality in accelerating, complex and transnational spaces* (pp. 94–126). London: Routledge.

Jackson, J. (2014b). *Introducing language and intercultural communication*. London and New York: Routledge.

Jackson, J. (2015a). "Unpacking" international experience through blended intercultural praxis. In R. D. Williams & A. Lee (Eds.), *Internationalizing higher education: Critical collaborations across the curriculum* (pp. 231–252). Rotterdam, The Netherlands: Sense Publishers.

Jackson, J. (2015b). Becoming interculturally competent: Theory to practice in international education. *International Journal of Intercultural Relations, 48*, 91–107. https://doi.org/10.1016/j.ijintrel.2015.03.012.

Jackson, J. (2016, April). *Optimizing intercultural learning and engagement abroad through online mentoring*. Keynote address, Intercultural learning through study abroad colloquium co-hosted by the University of Bern and the University of Technology Sydney, Bern, Switzerland.

Jackson, J. (2018a). *Interculturality in international education*. London and New York: Routledge.

Jackson, J. (2018b). Optimizing intercultural learning and engagement abroad through online mentoring. In J. Jackson & S. Oguro (Eds.), *Intercultural interventions in study abroad*. New York: Routledge.

Jackson, J., & Oguro, S. (2018). Introduction: Enhancing and extending study abroad learning through intercultural interventions. In J. Jackson & S. Oguro (Eds.), *Intercultural interventions in study abroad* (pp. 1–17). New York: Routledge.

Jackson, J. (2019). *Online intercultural education and study abroad: Theory into practice*. London and New York: Routledge.

Jandt, F. (2016). *An introduction to intercultural communication: Identities in a global community*. Thousand Oaks, CA: Sage.

Lee, L. (2009). Scaffolding collaborative exchanges between expert and novice language teachers in threaded discussions. *Foreign Language Annals, 42*(2), 212–228. https://doi.org/10.1111/j.1944-9720.2009.01018.x.

Lee, L. (2011). Blogging: Promoting learner autonomy and intercultural competence through study abroad. *Language, Learning and Technology, 15*(3), 87–109.

Lou, K., & Bosley, G. W. (2012). Facilitating intercultural learning abroad: The intentional, targeted intervention model. In M. Vande Berg, R. M. Paige, & K. H. Lou (Eds.), *Student learning abroad: What our students are learning, what they're not, and what we can do about it* (pp. 335–359). Sterling, VA: Stylus.

Lou, K., Vande Berg, M., & Paige, R. M. (2012). Intervening in study learning abroad: Closing insights. In M. Vande Berg, R. M. Paige, & K. H. Lou (Eds.), *Student learning abroad: What our students are learning, what they're not, and what we can do about it* (pp. 411–419). Sterling, VA: Stylus.

Martin, J. N., Nakayama, T. K., & Carbaugh, D. (2012). The history and development of the study of intercultural communication and applied linguistics. In J. Jackson (Ed.), *The Routledge handbook of language and intercultural communication* (pp. 17–36). Abingdon, UK: Routledge.

Miles, M. B., Huberman, A. M., & Saldana, J. (2014). *Qualitative data analysis: A methods sourcebook* (3rd ed.). Thousand Oaks, CA: Sage.

Moon, J. A. (2000). *Reflection in learning and professional development: Theory and practice*. London: Routledge.

Moon, J. A. (2006). *A handbook of reflective and experiential learning: Theory and practice*. New York, NY: Routledge.

Paige, R. M. (2013). *Factors impacting intercultural development in study abroad*. Paper presented at Elon University, 16 August 2013.

Paige, R. M., & Vande Berg, M. (2012). Why students are and are not learning abroad. In M. Vande Berg, R. M. Paige, & K. H. Lou (Eds.), *Student learning abroad: What our students are learning, what they're not and what we can do about it* (pp. 29–59). Sterling, VA: Stylus.

Passarelli, A. M., & Kolb, D. A. (2012). Using experiential learning theory to promote student learning and development in programs of education abroad. In M. Vande Berg, R. M. Paige, & K. H. Lou (Eds.), *Student learning abroad: What our students are learning, what they're not and what we can do about it* (pp. 137–161). Sterling, VA: Stylus.

Pennington, D. C. (1986). *Essential social psychology*. London: Edward Arnold.

Ryan, M., & Ryan, M. (2015). A model for reflection in the pedagogic field of higher education. In M. E. Ryan (Ed.), *Teaching reflective learning in higher education: A systematic approach using pedagogic patterns* (pp. 15–27). New York: Springer.

Savicki, V., & Brewer, E. (2015). Introduction: Issues in assessing study abroad. In W. Savicki & E. Brewer (Eds.), *Assessing study abroad: Theory, tools, and practice* (pp. 1–12). Sterling, VA: Stylus.

Scollon, R., Scollon, S. W., & Jones, R. (2011). *Intercultural communication: A discourse approach*. Oxford, UK: Blackwell.

Spencer-Oatey, H., & Franklin, P. (2009). *Intercultural interaction: A multidisciplinary approach to intercultural communication*. Basingstoke, UK: Palgrave Macmillan.

Ting-Toomey, S. (2012). Understanding intercultural conflict competence: Multiple theoretical insights. In J. Jackson (Ed.), *The Routledge handbook of language and intercultural communication* (pp. 279–295). London: Routledge.

Vande Berg, M., Paige, R. M., & Lou, K. H. (2012). Student learning abroad: Paradigms and assumptions. In M. Vande Berg, R. M. Paige, & K. H. Lou (Eds.), *Student learning abroad: What our students are learning, what they're not and what we can do about it* (pp. 3–28). Sterling, VA: Stylus.

Vande Berg, M., Quinn, M., & Menyhart, C. (2012). An experiment in developmental teaching and learning: The Council on International Educational Exchange's seminar on living and learning abroad. In M. Vande Berg, R. M. Paige, & K. H. Lou (Eds.), *Student learning abroad: What our students are learning, what they're not, and what we can do about it* (pp. 383–407). Sterling, VA: Stylus.

Chapter 11
Promoting Intercultural and Visual Media Competence in the Foreign Language Classroom with the *Autobiography of Intercultural Encounters Through Visual Media*

María-del-Carmen Méndez-García and Rachel Lindner

11.1 Introduction

"It is because pictures say nothing in words that so much can be said in words about them." This quote from the introduction to *The Mind's Eye: Using Pictures Creatively in Language Learning* (Maley, Duff, & Grellet, 1980) neatly summarizes why communicative approaches to foreign language education (FLE) have a history of using visual aids in the classroom. Beyond the common use of images as prompts for language production or to support reading and listening in the second language, educationalists in the field (e.g., Goldstein, 2008; Hecke & Surkamp, 2010) have more recently seen a role for FLE in fostering visual media literacy,[1] which, according to Averginou and Ericson (1997), Eilam (2012), and Stokes (2002), involves developing in students the cognitive skills needed to engage critically

---

[1] In the literature on multiliteracies education, visual literacy and media literacy are sometimes referred to separately, sometimes – in more recent years – together as "visual media literacy" or "visual and media literacy." In this chapter, except when citing specific authors, the term "visual media literacy" is used, in line with the authors of the *AIEVM*. Visual media are understood to be any context in which image is used. This could be a photograph or a painting seen in a book, at an exhibition, or in outdoor advertising; it could equally be a moving image seen on television, at the cinema, or on the Internet. Also in line with the authors of the *AIEVM*, the terms "intercultural and visual media competence" and "intercultural and media literacy competence" are used interchangeably as an extension of intercultural competence to incorporate visual media literacy.

M.-C. Méndez-García (✉)
Universidad de Jaén, Jaén, Spain
e-mail: cmendez@ujaen.es

R. Lindner (✉)
Universität Paderborn, Paderborn, Germany
e-mail: rachel.lindner@uni-paderborn.de

© Springer Nature Singapore Pte Ltd. 2021
M. D. López-Jiménez, J. Sánchez-Torres (eds.), *Intercultural Competence Past, Present and Future*, Intercultural Communication and Language Education,
https://doi.org/10.1007/978-981-15-8245-5_11

with the myriad of print and digital images from all over the world with which they are confronted daily.

In view of the encounters with otherness that take place through these globally transmitted images, the authors of this chapter propose that language learners need not only visual media literacy but also intercultural competence to engage with images and articulate their reactions to them. Specifically, the authors of this chapter report on insights for teaching gained from using the Council of Europe's *Images of Others: An Autobiography of Intercultural Encounters Through Visual Media* (*AIEVM*) (Barrett, Byram, Ipgrave, & Seurrat, 2013a) in an online intercultural exchange (OIE) that was conducted between preservice teachers of English at Dortmund University (Germany) and Jaén University (Spain). In this exchange, the *AIEVM* served as the central instrument around which activities were developed to help students reflect on the way cultural "otherness" is represented in and interpreted through images. An analysis of students' work during the exchange and post-exchange feedback suggests that the OIE learning environment enriched the experience of working with the *AIEVM* and helped in particular to heighten critical cultural awareness of visual media.

The chapter opens with a brief overview of the role of visual media literacy in education, then considers more specifically the use of visuals in FLE. It is argued that, although visuals are widely used in FLE teaching materials today, visual media literacy generally and intercultural and visual media competence in particular are rarely promoted. The chapter then presents the *AIEVM* and the theoretical framework that underpins it. It shows how this educational tool is designed to encourage structured reflection on intercultural encounters through image, which in turn can activate intercultural and visual media competence to help users deconstruct images of "others" and "otherness" in relation to their own sociocultural context(s) (Barrett et al., 2013a; Barrett, Byram, Ipgrave, & Seurrat, 2013b). The chapter explains the rationale for using the *AIEVM* in the FLE classroom and in language teacher training and then goes on to outline how it was implemented in the online exchange mentioned above. In the discussion of this learning scenario, excerpts from students' work and feedback are included to illustrate the learning opportunities afforded by the *AIEVM* in a multiliteracies approach to FLE.

11.2 Literature Review

11.2.1 Visual Media Literacy in Education

The term "visual literacy" is often ascribed to Debes (1969), who referred to the visually literate person as someone who can "discriminate and interpret the visible actions, objects, symbols, natural or man-made, that he encounters in his environment. Through the creative use of these competences, he is able to communicate with others" (Debes, 1969, p. 27). It is this ability to "discriminate" and "interpret" visuals, on the one hand, and the "creative use" for the purpose of communication, on the other, that is central to visual media literacy, a conceptualization that is underscored by Ausburn and Ausburn (1978, p. 291) in the notion of "using visuals for *intentionally* communicating with others" (authors' italics). Visual media literacy is perceived here as a two-way process that, like text literacy, involves not only passive understanding but also active production. If we use visuals to communicate with others in this way, then we might say that (a) images, like text, possess a vocabulary and grammar through which meaning-making can take place and (b) a visually literate person is able to "read" and "write" this visual language, that is, they are able to decode (describe, analyze, interpret) and encode (compose, produce) meaningful images themselves.

Neither Debes (1969) nor Ausburn and Ausburn (1978) could have anticipated the manner and speed with which new technologies would transform our visual environment, making what Mitchell (1995) terms the "pictorial turn" so central to communication, and prompting Kress and van Leeuwen (2006, p. 17) to argue that visual communication should be treated as seriously as linguistic communication in education. Indeed, the proliferation of images and the ways in which they are used through multiple media channels to capture or visualize experience on an everyday basis means that visual media literacy has become inseparable from media literacy in many contexts, and equally as important as text literacy for obtaining and filtering information, evaluating it critically, and constructing knowledge in both educational and professional environments.

Obinger and Obinger (2005, 2.4) point out the significance of this development in producing a generation of visual learners – so-called digital natives who are "intuitive visual communicators." Yet these "digital natives" often require pedagogical guidance to activate the higher-order cognitive skills needed for *critical* engagement with images (Averginou & Ericson, 1997; Eilam, 2012; Stokes, 2002). This presupposes that teachers themselves are at the very least aware of the role of visuals in learning and have ideally been trained in facilitating visual media literacy (Eilam, 2012). Taking the concept of literacy a step further, the New London Group (2000, p. 9) argues that, in order to meet the learning needs of the twenty-first century, the concept of literacy must move beyond reading and writing "formalised, monolingual, monocultural, and rule-governed forms of language." Instead, literacy pedagogy today has to take into account a "multiplicity of discourses." It should do so firstly with regard to our culturally and linguistically diverse and at the same time globalized, networked societies. Secondly, literacy skills are needed to cope with multimodality and multimediality – that is, the "burgeoning variety of text forms associated with information and multimedia technologies" as well as the "proliferation of communication channels and media [which] supports and extends cultural and subcultural diversity" (New London Group, 2000, p. 9). A "pedagogy of multiliteracies" is therefore required in all educational spheres, including FLE, as has been cogently argued by Hampel and Hauck (2006). The role of FLE in promoting the acquisition of multiliteracies, in particular the acquisition of intercultural and visual media competence, is discussed in the next section.

11.2.2 Visual Media Literacy and (Inter)Cultural Learning in FLE

Since the introduction of more communicative forms of language teaching, visuals have been a common feature of the second language classroom. They have been used, for example, to convey lexical and grammatical concepts that had formerly been taught through translation, as prompts for language production, as clues in information gap activities, or to provide sociocultural cues for reading and listening. In recent years, the use of both still and moving image has increased significantly, reflecting the ubiquity of visuals on the Internet and the ease for both teachers and students of retrieving, editing, creating, and posting them. Yet despite this development, the authors agree with Goldstein (2008, p. I), who suggests that images seem to remain peripheral to the main activity of teaching and practicing the language.

If this is the case, how might image be foregrounded in FLE? For a start, inspiration can be found in Kress and van Leeuwen's (1996) seminal book on "reading images," which shows how visual communication works in comparison to linguistic communication. They argue that critical discourse analysis, an approach to language learning that is used to develop students' awareness of how social relations, identity, knowledge, and power are constructed through written and spoken texts, should be extended to visual communication. This would help students analyze and reproduce the "complex interplay of written text, images, and other graphic elements ...[which] combine together into visual designs, by means of layout" (Kress & van Leeuwen, 1996, p. 15). In other words, images must be understood as socially and culturally constructed products. Their interpretation or *de*construction, however, depends on the cultural makeup of the person viewing the image.

It is this socially and culturally constructed-deconstructed dimension of visuals that is of particular interest to the authors of this chapter because it has hitherto received relatively little attention in FLE, despite significant developments in the field that foreground the (inter)cultural dimension of communicative competence (e.g., Byram & Zarate, 1997; Byram, Gribkova, & Starkey, 2002). Exceptions include Corbett's (2003) application of Kress and van Leeuwen's (1996) work on "reading" visuals to intercultural awareness raising activities in FLE. Pegrum (2008) shows how moving images (i.e., film) can be used in the foreign language classroom for the critical exploration of visual media literacy from an intercultural perspective. In their teaching materials and techniques to help students understand images, Stenglin and Iedema (2001) make the link between visual media literacy and the cultural perceptions that are at play in multimodal FLE learning environments. Similarly, Royce (2007) provides examples of multimodal classroom activities – for example, text together with still or moving image in different media channels – that aim to foster visual media literacy. He argues that images used in the foreign language classroom must be understood as "culturally bound" because their interpretation depends on the cultural perspectives from which they are viewed. Furthermore, approaches to FLE that include such multimodal activities may provide a "doorway" to the target culture (Royce, 2007, pp. 366–367).

Perhaps the most obvious multimodal doorway to the target culture is the Internet. One way in which language teachers are increasingly using this doorway is in online intercultural exchange (OIE), an activity for "engaging language learners in interaction and collaborative project work with partners from other cultures through the use of online communication tools" (O'Dowd, 2007, p. 4). OIE originally became popular within a communicative approach to FLE because of the opportunities it provides for authentic interaction with so-called native speakers of the language. Parallel to developments in the field toward a more *intercultural* communicative approach to FLE, many accounts have been published of institutionalized online exchanges between student groups in different countries who work together on scaffolded tasks with cultural themes aimed in particular at developing intercultural competence (e.g., Belz, 2002; Furstenberg, Levet, English, & Maillet, 2001; Müller-Hartmann, 2000; O'Dowd, 2003; Woodin, 2001).

Some of the exchanges reported on refer to the use of visuals in the tasks completed by participants. The Cultura Project (Furstenberg et al., 2001), for example, which established a framework for OIE that has been adopted by many teachers in secondary and tertiary education, includes an "images module" which is designed to help students "discover how to communicate their own culture with images" and "to compare their respective cultural realities and reflect about the meaning and impact of visual information" (Cultura website: https://cultura.mit.edu/educators-guide/images-module). Students might choose images to illustrate a concept, an aspect of their lives, or product advertising. They reflect on the chosen images on their own, in their home classes, and then in intercultural dialogue with their exchange partners before finally discussing in their home groups the cultural insights they gained from comparing and discussing images with their exchange partners.

The pedagogical notion behind the Cultura methodology is that iterative reflection on different media (images, film, text, etc.) in different constellations draws on multiple perspectives which may, under teacher guidance, encourage students to construct and refine their understanding of both their own culture and that of the exchange interlocutor (Furstenberg et al., 2001). Language learning is intrinsic to this process because students are in continual authentic dialogue with one another, sharing, comparing and reflecting, accessing, and working with "raw materials" from the web as well as materials that are prepared by the teachers.

Although the Cultura website does not explicitly mention the development of multiliteracies, in many respects, it paves the way for a current trend in OIE, which sees its potential for facilitating the development of a wider range of literacies in the acquisition of a second language (e.g., Guth & Helm, 2010; Hauck, 2010; Helm, 2014; Lindner, 2011). The authors of this chapter, both of whom work in the field of FLE and were involved in the development of the Council of Europe's *Images of Others: An Autobiography of Intercultural Encounters Through Visual Media* (*AIEVM*) (Barrett et al., 2013a), were interested in harnessing this potential by using the *AIEVM* in an online exchange between preservice teachers of English in Germany and Spain. The next section of this chapter discusses the *AIEVM* and the theoretical framework of intercultural and visual media competence that underpins it.

11.2.3   The AIEVM

The *AIEVM* (Barrett et al., 2013a, http://www.coe.int/t/dg4/autobiography/default_ en.asp), like its sister tool the *Autobiography of Intercultural Encounters* (*AIE*, Byram, Barrett, Ipgrave, Jackson, & Méndez García, 2009a, http://www.coe.int/t/ dg4/autobiography/default_en.asp), was designed under the auspices of the Council of Europe to help the user develop intercultural competence. The Council considers that a process of structured and repeated reflection on individual encounters with otherness – whether face-to-face (as addressed by the *AIE*) or mediated through images (as in the *AIEVM*) – can be instrumental in fostering the intercultural competences required for living together in culturally diverse societies (Barrett, Byram, Lázár, Mompoint-Gaillard, & Philippou, 2014).

Intercultural encounters, as defined in both the *AIE* and the *AIEVM*, occur when people with significantly different cultural identities meet. Perceived "significant difference" may stem from different affiliations, for example, national, ethnic, regional, religious, linguistic, gender, class, sexuality, political, generational, workplace, and so on. The user of the *AIE(VM)* is asked to select one such personal encounter, which may have made either a positive or a negative impact on them, and to analyze it systematically by answering questions that draw on a framework of intercultural competence. This theoretical framework encompasses four "subsets."[2]

Subset 1 addresses the *attitudes* required by the interculturally competent person, including respect for otherness, empathy, acknowledgment of identities, and tolerance of ambiguity.

Subset 2 describes the *skills* that the interculturally competent person demonstrates – communicative skills (especially in a foreign language), skills of interaction in knowledge discovery, skills of interpreting and relating, behavioral flexibility in new situations, and the evaluative skill of critical cultural awareness.

Subset 3, action orientation, refers to the willingness to undertake positive action either as a result of the intercultural encounter itself or as a result of reflection on the encounter (e.g., through working with the *AIEVM*).

Subset 4 is concerned with the *knowledge* of a culture (e.g., about social processes and their products), and specifically in the *AIEVM* with *visual media knowledge in an intercultural context*. This aspect of intercultural competence involves

---

[2]A detailed description of the theoretical framework underpinning the *AIEVM* can be found in the *AIE*'s explanatory context, concepts, and theories document (Byram, Barrett, Ipgrave, Jackson, & Méndez García, 2009b, pp. 23–25) and in the *AIEVM*'s facilitators' notes, both of which are available on the Council of Europe's website at https://www.coe.int/t/dg4/autobiography/default_ en.asp

understanding implicit messages about people from other cultures that are transmitted through visual media, whether print or digital, still or moving. Having knowledge of the media requires awareness of how images are produced and portrayed and possessing an understanding of media discourse. It involves being able to analyze both the intended audience(s) of the image and one's own cultural and social background and the expectations that these bring to bear on the intercultural encounter through the image (Barrett et al., 2013b, p. 5).

Similar to other models for structuring reflection (e.g., Gibbs, 1988, or Bain, Ballantyne, Packer, & Mills, 1999), the *AIEVM* follows a specific sequence. A series of questions progressively scaffolds the user's thinking about the image and the person they encountered in that image, from description to evaluation to analysis and finally to action. Before answering the questions, the user is invited to define themselves in terms of their own identity (e.g., in terms age, gender, nationality, ethnic group, country, region, community, religion, or languages), interpersonal relationships (son/daughter, brother/sister, best friend, etc.), or membership of local groups (school student, member of a club). By completing this self-defining *Who I am* task before working through the questions on the image, users focus their gaze on themselves and their own cultural positioning, against which the person or people in the image can be compared. After engaging with some or all of the questions, users can return to their initial description of themselves and revise it if reflection on their encounter prompts them to perceive themselves in a different light. Thus, similar to the Cultura Project methodology outlined above, the learner may refine their understanding of their own cultural identity in relation to their "interlocutor" (i.e., here the person or people in the image). In the process of working through the *AIEVM*, the user is engaged in reflection on themselves and the person or people in the image in all their cultural complexity. Iterative reflection of this kind may inform the critical and culturally sensitive appreciation and creation of images. It may also help the user avoid manipulation through the media.

Although it is not specifically designed as a tool for FLE, there are both ethical and pedagogical reasons that support the *AIEVM*'s implementation in the language classroom. The pedagogical rationale for using the *AIEVM* within a multiliteracies approach to FLE has already been outlined in the previous sections. The process of describing, interpreting, and analyzing intercultural encounters through image by systematically answering the questions in the *AIEVM* either in written or oral form provides ample language, intercultural, and visual media literacy learning opportunities. The ethical consideration lies in the importance the Council of Europe attaches to intercultural dialogue as the key to promoting tolerance, preventing conflict, enhancing societal cohesion, and thus supporting the core principles of human rights, democracy, and rule of law on which the Council of Europe was founded (Barrett et al., 2014; Council of Europe, 2008). The Council specifically acknowledges the role of language educators in supporting this purpose since intercultural dialogue is so intrinsically linked to language. The educational tools that the Council has therefore created, such as the *AIEVM,* and the learning methodologies that the Council supports, such as OIE, are intended to facilitate the development of intercultural competence both in and beyond the language class-room. However, teachers must also acquire the knowledge and skills necessary for working with these tools and methodologies. It therefore makes sense to incorporate them into language teacher training.

As the piloting of the *AIEVM* had been conducted in face-to-face environments only, the authors of this chapter, both of whom are active in FLE teacher training, decided to make it the main task of an OIE. The next section describes the exchange context and the phases of the exchange, shows how the *AIEVM* was used, and provides excerpts from students' work and post-exchange feedback to illustrate their response.

11.3   Methodology

11.3.1   Exchange Context and Participants

The online exchange took place between preservice teachers of English from the Universities of Jaén (Spain) and Dortmund (Germany). Although some of the German students spoke Spanish, English was used as the lingua franca of the exchange. All students had approximately C1 proficiency, so the authors anticipated no significant problems regarding linguistic communication and the ability to work with the English version of the *AIEVM*. For the Dortmund students, the exchange was a mandatory aspect of a course they were all taking on teaching and learning with educational technology. The exchange partners from the University of Jaén were participating on a voluntary basis. There were 23 students in total: 11 from Dortmund University and 12 from Jaén University (tandem 1 included 3 members, 2 from the University of Jaén, as one of these students was perceptibly weaker and the researchers estimated that, in this particular case, a group of three would benefit all its members). There were 18 women and 5 men from 19 to 30, 22 being the average age (J.W., in tandem 11, did not indicate her age). Table 11.1 shows the coding used to denote students (their initials), their age, gender, university, and their tandem partner.

11.3.2   Research Questions

The authors of this chapter were interested in finding out whether an OIE could enhance the potential of the *AIEVM* for developing intercultural and visual media competence. The research questions were:

1. Does working with the *AIEVM* benefit from online exchange in which it is framed within a wider analysis of images?

Table 11.1 Participants

	Students from Dortmund University			Students from Jaén University		
Tandem number	Initials	Age	Gender	Initials	Age	Gender
Tandem 1	S.W.	30	W	M.J./M.C.	19/22	W/W
Tandem 2	V.P.	23	W	I.C.	20	W
Tandem 3	J.S.	20	W	N.M.	27	W
Tandem 4	K.G.	25	W	M.A.	19	W
Tandem 5	L.P.	21	W	A.T.	19	M
Tandem 6	C.P.	20	W	J.B.J.	19	W
Tandem 7	S.G.	22	W	M.T.	19	W
Tandem 8	J.G.	20	W	C.H.	19	W
Tandem 9	M.M.	22	M	R.D.	19	M
Tandem 10	A.K.	22	W	M.A.	19	M
Tandem 11	J.W.		W	J.B.	19	M

2. In what ways does using the *AIEVM* impact on intercultural and visual media competence in online exchange?

11.3.3 Telecollaboration Framework

In a series of blended-learning task phases considered effective for telecollaboration (Dooley, 2008; Müller-Hartmann, 2000), students were invited to reflect on visuals and how they represent the image of the other over a four-week period. The exchange was conducted in a Wikispaces wiki (https://www.wikispaces.com/), which allowed both facilitators and participants to upload, compose, and edit multimodal text, incorporating image, film, and links, and to conduct discussions either in the wiki pages themselves or using the forum facility. For data collection purposes, the students were asked to conduct their exchanges within the wiki and not to move to other communication tools. In the initial phase of the exchange, participants were introduced to the purpose of the exchange in the home classes. In the first online week, participants worked in plenary with more intensive teacher moderation; the second online week involved tandem discussion of the *AIEVM*. Before, during, and post exchange, the participants in the respective cohorts at Jaén and Dortmund universities discussed procedural, conceptual, and experiential issues relating to the exchange.

Barrett et al. (2013b) note that some learners may find using the *AIEVM* difficult if they have not paid enough prior attention to encounters with otherness in the visual media. Therefore, working in plenary, students completed two preliminary tasks that aimed to sensitize them to the underlying cultural meaning that may be intentionally "written" into an image by the image's creator or "read" into the image by the viewer. For the first task, the facilitators selected two images, the first portraying an Australian farmer on his farm (http://theshaker.com.au/briefing/fair-go-farmers), the second portraying an Australian Indigenous person in front of Ayers Rock (http://

www.australiangeographic.com.au/blogs/on-this-day/2010/10/on-this-day-aborigi
nal-australians-get-uluru-back).

No contextual information was given, the caption beneath the former image only
stating "This is my land," whereas the second picture was given the caption "This
land is me." By juxtaposing the images in this way, the teachers purposefully
suggested an underlying stereotypical assumption that the students were challenged
to deconstruct.

For the second task, photographs from a blog post entitled "Muslim rage" linked
images of people from other cultures to media stereotypes. Students were first asked
to predict what the blog post might be about before following the link (http://gawker.
com/5943828/13-powerful-images-of-muslim-rage) and exchanging their thoughts
on the photographs. The photographs echo *Newsweek's* report on violent anti-
American protests, with the common image of angry Muslim men on the cover
page. The blog images, on the other hand, are ironically entitled "Muslim rage"
because they represent Muslims engaged in everyday peaceful activities. For example, the image of an Egyptian man sitting by the door of his shop reading a
newspaper is said to be "Filled to the brim with Muslim rage." Students were thereby
encouraged in this task to reflect on the potential bias of media reportage, which may
manipulate readers by repeatedly showing a particular kind of image so that, over
time, people associate certain concepts with certain images in their mind's eye.

The experience of decoding images in cultural terms in these initial plenary tasks
fed into the main task or phase of the exchange. Students were introduced to the
AIEVM and asked to complete it on their own, engaging in individual reflection on
an image of their choice. In their home classes, they compared and discussed the
images they had chosen and their reflection on those images. Students from the two
participating classes were then assigned tandem partners with whom they shared
their *AIEVM* and worked together to explore similarities and differences in the
interpretation of each other's images from their different cultural perspectives.
Finally, tandems wrote a joint reflection in the wiki about the insights they had
gained from working with the *AIEVM* in this way. In the final phase, debriefing took
place in the home groups by discussing and presenting tandem insights and evaluating the exchange with a Google Docs survey.

11.3.4   Data Collection and Analysis

Data were gathered from the initial plenary discussions in the wiki forums, the
AIEVM completed by each student and uploaded to the wiki, the eleven online
tandem discussions in the wiki on how the *AIEVM* can be used to facilitate
intercultural and visual media competence, the Google Docs survey which was
completed anonymously by the exchange participants, and the authors' notes on
the in-class debriefing conducted at each institution. The questions in the survey that
were particularly revealing were those about students' experience of working in the
OIE environment, their reflection on intercultural learning through completing the

AIEVM on their own, and their reflection on intercultural learning through discussing their *AIEVM* with their tandem partner.

Grounded theory, also referred to as constant comparison (Mackey & Gass, 2005) or thematic analysis (Braun & Clarke, 2006), was the methodology used for data analysis as it allows for qualitative analysis without following pre-established categories. Emerging categories were identified through the stages of familiarization with the data, searching for indicators of categories or themes, labelling and coding categories, reviewing and comparing codes to find similarities and differences, and locating central categories. The data were analyzed, marked, and assigned to categories by both authors independently and then through comparison of independent results in order to arrive at a joint understanding of the findings.

11.4   Project Outcomes and Discussion

This section discusses the impact of framing the *AIEVM* within a wider analysis of images and the development of intercultural and visual media competence through working with the *AIEVM* in online intercultural exchange. Although this was a small-scale study, there is some evidence that students were indeed critically engaged with the images, that the project facilitated the exploration of visual media literacy from an intercultural perspective, and that the scaffolded tasks triggered intercultural reflection and learning. The structure of the project – as outlined above in the previous section – may in itself have played a significant role in the learning process.

11.4.1   Framing the AIEVM Within a Wider Analysis of Images

Preliminary task phases in an OIE are recommended to ease students into dialogue with one another and to sensitize participants to aspects of learning addressed by the exchange. The pre-*AIEVM* tasks "This is my land – this land is me" and "Muslim rage" (outlined in the previous section) were intended to raise students' awareness to issues involved in the portrayal of culture in media images to prepare them for the main exchange task of working with the *AIEVM*. The following findings are drawn from data from the plenary wiki discussions on these tasks and are analyzed under three subthemes: firstly, the relevance of prior knowledge and critical cultural awareness to analyze visuals; secondly, the necessity to suspend belief about the media; and thirdly, the significance of personal experience to comprehend the messages conveyed by the media.

11.4.1.1 Using Prior Knowledge and Critical Cultural Awareness to Analyze Captions, Color Schemes, and Layout

Plenary discussions on the task "This is my land – This land is me" show that participants were initially influenced by the captions. Their comments draw on prior knowledge about Australian history, culture, and society and center on white man's eagerness to possess land compared to the Aborigine's symbiotic relationship with nature. Both men are considered to be proud of their land, but their views on what "the land" means vary depending on whether "man" possesses or is at one with it (J.V. and V.P.[3]), and this leads students to question whether these mindsets, which seem to contribute to social and cultural misunderstandings in Australia, can be reconciled (J.S). Student contributions that illustrate this point are as follows:

They seem to have a different opinion or perception of "possessing land." (J.V.)
The captions may tell us about the possessive attitude versus the notion of identification with the land. (V.P.)
The two pictures mean a demonstration of social and cultural misunderstanding. (J.S.)

Other comments, however, indicate that students' thinking goes beyond the captions and that they are able to grasp the underlying cultural assumptions that they perceive to be intentionally "written" into an image by the image's creator. J.B., for example, notes that there are different ways of feeling attached to the land and different ways of showing respect to it.

It may seem that the tribal attitude is more acceptable than the farmer one, yet I don't agree. They both respect the land and feel dependent on it. (J.B.)

Once students start thinking beyond the captions, they also note the composition of the images and how the viewer's interpretation is affected by the color scheme and layout. The tonality of the first photograph ("This is my land") is contrasted with the bright colors of the second image, in which the Indigenous person is perceived as blending in with the background (I.C.). The color scheme is considered an indicator of an intentionally positive message about aboriginal culture on the part of the photographer. On the other hand, reflecting on the layout, the elements foregrounded, and the positioning of the men, students come to the conclusion that the subjects are posing for a professional photographer and that the image of the farmer is probably closer to reality. The second picture is therefore considered stereotypical of western perceptions of nature-bound cultures (S.G.), which is far from the reality of thousands of disadvantaged Indigenous peoples who have become "the other" in their own land (V.P.). S.G. concludes that the illustrations were manipulated to create a particular reaction in the viewer.

In the first picture there are no vivid colours compared to the second picture where the sky is perfectly blue. (I.C.)

---

[3]The quotes extracted from plenary discussions are marked by the initials of the participant's name and surname.

The second image is not depicting the reality of aborigines in Australia – being the "Other" in Australia due to social problems such as drug abuse. (V.P.)

It displays a highly romanticised image which European people tend to have about nature-bound cultures. (S.G.)

While knowledge of a culture is a fundamental aspect of intercultural competence, it is important for students to be able to critically evaluate and reinterpret that knowledge "on the basis of explicit criteria, practices and products in one's own and other cultures and countries" (Byram et al., 2009b) and, in terms of intercultural and visual media competence, to apply this critical cultural awareness to the media landscape (Barrett et al., 2013b). The plenary exchange of perspectives on the first task seems to have helped students move from assumptions based on prior knowledge of the culture to a more nuanced, critical cultural awareness of the images themselves, of the intentions of the creators of the images, and how they may be interpreted from different cultural stances. This involves suspending belief about one's taken-for-granted assumptions and about the media.

11.4.1.2   Suspending Belief about the Media

The interplay between text and image is also the starting point for discussions about the "Muslim rage" task. V.P. writes about her anger concerning the way the media combines language and image to manipulate people's cultural associations, and S.G. notes her own susceptibility to such manipulation:

The term makes me very angry. It shows the power of language and how quickly such terms go viral through the media. (V.P.)

I got to recognise that I had a very similar image in mind about the term Muslim rage. (S.G.)

At the same time, students are intrigued by the effect of irony in the accompanying captions (V.P.), which engenders a desire to investigate the phenomenon more objectively (A.K.):

The whole idea desperately needs to be ridiculed in order to make the term lose its power to produce wrong images of Muslims, unnecessary fear, and prejudice. (V.P.)

These pictures made me want to learn more about it. (A.K.)

J.S. reflects on sensationalism as a criterion for news selection. Some events tend to be brought to the fore and emphasized by the media, even though they may only be carried out by a very small percentage of the population and do not represent, as sometimes seems to be implied, the group reported on. This may lead to overgeneralization and the "stigmatization" of particular groups (V.P.):

As long as people don't think about what they are told, or maybe research some facts, media can cause an incredibly far reaching damage! Only 0.001–0.007% of Muslim population are actually taking part in these violent protests the media hypes. (J.S.)

The danger of stigmatization is great and "Muslim Rage" just reinforces prejudices. Christians would feel terribly offended if they were considered abusers and rapists because Catholic priests have misused their power. (V.P.)

When encountering otherness through media images, it is therefore necessary to arrive at an informed understanding of what these images portray by asking questions (J.S.) and contrasting the information that appears in different sources (A.K. and J.S. above and J.B. below):

> People should dare to question "given" facts. (J.S.)
>   We should try to compare different newspapers. (J.B.)

In these comments, students demonstrate intercultural and visual media competence as defined by Barrett et al. (2013b) in various ways. Firstly, they show awareness of how the media uses language and image to manipulate perceptions of cultures, and they recognize the need to suspend belief about what is seen in the media and the need to acquire knowledge of a culture from different sources before passing judgment. Students may have had this awareness prior to the exchange, or it might also have been gained through the previous "This is my land" task, but they demonstrate their ability to apply this awareness to the new task. Secondly, students are able to relate the misunderstandings and misinterpretations of the "Muslim rage" example to other cultures or situations, as demonstrated by V.P.'s comment on the risk of stigmatization above, and J.B.'s account below of the *New York Times*'s misrepresentation of how the economic crisis affected Spain, which in turn had a negative effect on the Spanish stock market and the global perception of Spain:

> The New York's Time published an appalling article about the crisis in Spain and added a set of 15 gloomy and dismal photos (http://www.nytimes.com/2012/09/25/world/europe/hunger-on-the-rise-in-spain.html?pagewanted=all). The image of Spain was gravely affected. The USA and therefore most of the world kept these images in their minds. As well as in the "Muslim Rage," the damage is already done. (J.B.)

In this forum contribution, J.B. demonstrates the skill of interpreting an event from a culture and explaining and relating it to events in his own culture (Byram et al., 2009b). In the OIE learning scenario, J.B.'s contribution also gave the German participants a new take on Spanish society and culture.

11.4.1.3 Questioning the Messages Conveyed by the Media on the Basis of Personal Experience

The discussion of the "Muslim rage" images led students to analyze how stereotypical assumptions about a culture engendered by media images may disappear when a personal relationship is established. For example, N.M. asserts that the media negatively influenced her impression of Eastern Europeans until she met people from there:

> The image I had about people from Eastern countries was not good. I met people from these countries and had the opportunity to know about them. I became aware of how big mass media can influence people. (N.M.)

Similarly, other students comment on experiences, such as meeting or sharing a flat with somebody as a turning point in their impressions of a culture, which had previously been negatively influenced by media images. Through these examples, participants show a positive change in what is referred to in the *AIEVM* framework of intercultural competence as "attitudes," such as respect for otherness and acknowledging the identities of others, as well as behavioral flexibility, that is, the ability to "adjust and adapt your behavior to new situations and knowledge as they emerge in interaction with others" (Barrett et al., 2013b). These examples may also be related to Allport's Contact Hypothesis (1954), the theory that personal contact (as opposed to mediated contact) with a culture minimizes conflict. What participants seem to ignore, however, is that face-to-face encounters are only effective under certain conditions, such as the need for cooperation, a similar status (real or perceived), or sharing a common goal (Allport, 1954).

These findings suggest that the plenary discussion of images selected by teachers may start an awareness-raising process in which students are not only sensitized to the cultural agenda of the makers of images but also to how their own cultural assumptions influence their interpretation of images. Plenary exchange of this kind between all students participating in an OIE may therefore improve subsequent work with the *AIEVM*.

11.4.2 Intercultural and Visual Media Competence through Working with the AIEVM in an Online Intercultural Exchange

This section considers the ways working with the *AIEVM* in the online exchange impacted on learners' intercultural and visual media competence. It is organized into four categories: students' image of the other; critical thinking and knowledge discovery; considerations of identity, self-awareness, and perspective-taking; and finally students' views of the impact of the OIE context on working with the *AIEVM*.

11.4.2.1 Students' Image of the Other

When working with the *AIEVM*, students are invited to select an image which, for them, represents a meaningful intercultural encounter. An analysis of the images chosen by the OIE participants for their *AIEVM* reveals noteworthy underlying patterns, with six major categories emerging:

(a) Social exclusion in the western world is portrayed in the image of a homeless man and his dog (TD6).[4]

---

[4]SR stands for survey response, and TD means tandem discussion. Both abbreviations are followed by a number indicating the number of tandem discussion or the number of the survey response.

(b) Famine in the third world is represented in the photograph of a vulture watching a black child in the savannah (TD1) plus a photograph contrasting a black child suffering from malnutrition (probably in Africa) with a dog eating out of a full bowl in a western setting (TD8).

(c) Tenderness and affection are the major emotions in a photograph of Gandhi kissing a baby (TD1) and an image from the film "Blood diamonds," which shows a child and his father walking leisurely while the father is holding and looking at his son tenderly.

(d) Cultural traditions of Africa and New Zealand are present in the illustration of a Mursi woman with the traditional lip plate (TD3, TD6) and two Indigenous people in New Zealand performing the hongi or nose-pressing greeting (TD5).

(e) Political persecution, protest, and violence are the most prominent themes. The provocative YouTube image of the Chinese artist Ai Wei Wei, "F*** you, motherland," provides the background for reflecting on political persecution (TD2). Interestingly, war is ridiculed in two images: "The war and the guitarist," which in the context of struggles between despotic governments and rebels, portrays a guitarist next to people fighting with firearms, and "The man with the power to convince," which, against the backdrop of hostilities between Tunisian protesters and armed policemen, shows a demonstrator holding a baguette as if it were a weapon (TD3). A completely different view of war is expressed by two well-known photographs: children (some naked) fleeing a devastated area in the Vietnam War (TD9) and a western female soldier holding a leash attached to a prisoner's neck in the Iraqi prison of Abu Ghraib (TD4).

(f) Race and intercultural relationships constitute another key theme. Interracial tension is demonstrated in "Don't bring home a white boy," which features a white boy kissing a black girl's smiling face in spite of her family's disapproval (TD4). A further element emerges in "Bride market for Asian girls," an advert for western men looking for Asian brides (TD7). A more positive view of interracial relationships emerges in the picture of a white woman in her western wedding dress marrying a Massai in his homeland (from the film "The White Massai," TD11) and an image from a Spanish TV program portraying a white man shaking hands with a black man surrounded by members of his tribe[5] (TD5).

Despite learners' common European background and the teachers' emphasis on the fact that cultural difference can be expressed in many ways (e.g., sociocultural status, gender, or regional variation), most images – with the exception of the "homeless" – portray otherness far away from Europe (e.g., in Africa or New Zealand). Students therefore seem to perceive the "other" as somebody remote, sometimes "exotic" (e.g., the Mursi lip plate), somebody desperately needing western help (pictures of famine), somebody fighting for social justice and human rights

---

[5]"*Perdidos en la tribu*" ("Lost in the tribe") put members of Spanish families in contact with members of tribes in different countries so that the Spanish family can spend some time in the tribe and vice versa.

(represented by the Chinese artist Ai Wei Wei), or somebody who has suffered war and violence in a distant location. One pattern in these photographs is the link between this distant other and the violence against them committed by the western world – the students' world – as portrayed in the images of Vietnam or Abu Ghraib. The same pattern underlies the violation of dignity and rights in the image of a bride market for Asian girls. Notably, then, students focus on the remote, not the local encounter with otherness, with images ranging from stills to moving image, usually sourced on the web, in film, or in social media, where such images are easily accessible and equally easily brought into the OIE context.

Students' engagement with the "remote other" may be an indication of how they are touched by global problems or of how they are developing global, international (Fantini, Arias-Galicia, & Guay, 2001), and intercultural competences (Soria & Troisi, 2014). Indeed, the encounter with intercultural remoteness in some cases triggers empathy that draws on real-life experience. For example, "Don't bring home a white boy" had a special emotional significance for the participant whose friend had experienced similar interracial relationship problems. It is, however, also possible that the frequency of emotive images of the "remote other" selected by students was influenced by the discussion in the equally emotive "Muslim rage" task and that the selected images of the Arab world depicted in various contexts continued students' engagement with issues addressed in this task. It is also possible that the "This is my land – This land is me" task, with its emphasis on indigenous life and values, inspired the selection of the Mursi lip plate or the Hongi greeting images. Furthermore, the ironic tone of the "Muslim rage" blog post to address serious intercultural topics is echoed in some participants' selection of similarly ironic images of violence, war, and protest (e.g., the guitarist or the man holding a baguette). The choice of images for plenary discussion in the pre-*AIEVM* tasks therefore seems to determine, to a certain extent, students' choice of image when working with the *AIEVM*. In this study, "the other" mainly remains remote, exotic, and often somehow sensationalized by the media. On the other hand, it may simply be the case that more sensational images are those that remain in our minds or intrigue us most and therefore represent, for many people, the most meaningful intercultural encounters through visual media. What becomes clear to students after completing their *AIEVM* tandem discussions, however, is that not all images are equally useful for intercultural learning:

> The result of the *AIEVM* is strongly determined by the image/encounter it deals with. (TD9)

It might therefore be worth investing more input time into clarifying in pre-*AIEVM* activities what an intercultural encounter through visual media is, perhaps through discussion of images that are less commonly associated with cultural difference or media manipulation. Concurrent with research outlined in the literature review that suggests a surprising lack of visual literacy on the part of so-called digital natives, it might also be necessary to provide students with more guidance in selecting *AIEVM* images to ensure fruitful exchange on the image.

11.4.2.2   Critical Thinking and Knowledge Discovery

Referring specifically to the *AIEVM*, students note that the inventory of questions that make up the *AIEVM* sharpened their intercultural and visual media competence by prompting them to reflect in depth on different cultural contexts (SR8, TD2, and TD9). Consequently, the *AIEVM* is perceived as an effective framework for critical analysis of images as it guides the user's stream of thought, helping them transfer partially formed impressions of an image into a logical and coherently organized written document (TD11):

> Through working with the *AIEVM* I sharpened the way of "reading" and regarding different pictures that show people from different cultural backgrounds. (SR8)
>   The *AIEVM* inspires you to think critically. (TD2)
>   Some abstract or complex questions are hard to answer or you must think about it considerably. (TD9)
>   It helps to give certain order to one's ideas. It somehow scaffolds the development of ideas from our messy stream of thoughts. (TD11)

As a result, students noted gains in detecting implicit or "hidden" information in the image (SR6) and were inspired to conduct further research into the background of the image (TD2 and TD3), thereby activating the intercultural competences of knowledge discovery and action orientation (Byram et al., 2009b).

> Some hidden things can be discovered when you answer the questions. (SR6)
>   The *AIEVM* offers a great opportunity to "look behind" a given image, investigate further. (TD2)
>   I just tried to find out more about Mursi in order to avoid prejudices. I sat nearly an hour on the Internet. (*AIEVM*, TD3)

In answer to the *AIEVM* question whether working with the *AIEVM* had changed their way of thinking about images, some respondents did not believe that the *AIEVM* makes any difference while others observed significant gains beyond the image itself.

> First, I can see now differently and deeply any pictures, films, or books. Secondly, it also reinforced my way of seeing and thinking about the world. Thirdly, it has been quite useful to re-analyse myself, to find out things which I had without firm reasons or justifications. (*AIEVM*, TD9)

This comment suggests that the *AIEVM* has the potential to help the user depart from the image and employ it as an opportunity to reflect on or research cultural issues that they had not considered before, activating their critical thinking. Furthermore, the *AIEVM* also invites individuals to ponder different perspectives that may cause them to reexamine their points of view, hence paving the way to perspective-taking and self-awareness.

11.4.2.3 Considerations of Identity, Self-Awareness, and Perspective-Taking

The tandem exchange enabled students to view their images from multiple perspectives, with a constant shift from the personal perspective to the perspective of the tandem partner and to the imagined perspective of the people portrayed in the images. TDs and SRs show that shifts in perspective helped them consider identity, their own cultural affiliations, and worldviews in more depth (TD9 and SR1), all of which are paramount for intercultural competence in terms of self-awareness (Glaser, Guilherme, Méndez García, & Mughan, 2007), cultural knowledge, and critical cultural awareness (Byram et al., 2009b; Barrett et al., 2013b). The tandem partner's interpretation of the image in comparison with the culture-bound perspective and personal experiences of the student who originally selected a particular image led to self-reflection on how human beings become what they are through socialization (Berger & Luckmann, 1966). In this scenario, self-awareness is a basic intercultural competence that does not surface until one person is confronted with the other (Glaser et al., 2007) as the students state:

> The *AIEVM* not only made me think about the image, but also about myself and my relation to the culture I was raised in. (TD9)
> I became aware of why I am the way I am. Through the *AIEVM* one had to automatically reflect and [understand] how far the cultural background influences one's way of thinking and acting. (SR1)
> To learn about and to understand "the other" one should be aware of oneself. The questions in the tool are a good guideline to ask questions about one's own biography and culture. They help to understand where our individual points of view come from. (SR4)
> Through empathizing myself with the people in the image I got a better understanding of their situation. (SR9)

Self-awareness is facilitated by working with the *AIEVM* and is recognized as a prerequisite for understanding or empathizing with the other. It encourages retrospection and reflection on the influence of an individual's own cultural background on their attitude and behavior toward others.

11.4.2.4 Students' Views of the Impact of the OIE Context on Working with the AIEVM

Students generally see the potential of an exchange of perspectives on images, even though a similar degree of commitment is needed on the part of both members of the tandem to exploit the *AIEVM*, as this SR emphasizes:

> My tandem exchange partner did not answer my messages. I was really curious about her opinion of the image I selected. If she had answered me I would have learned more. (SR3)

Nevertheless, participants generally report on the positive effects of working with the *AIEVM* in the online exchange because it balanced individual reflection and collaborative learning (SR1), providing a learning environment beyond the regular classroom in which students had new opportunities to question or even reinforce their views (SR3a), the intercultural competence of unlearning and relearning (Glaser et al., 2007).

> Answering the questions on your own and then sharing it with your partners guides the direction of the discussion/project and leaves enough freedom for individual thinking. (SR1)
> This kind of activity helps you to realize how different people's ideas can be, and it also makes you either question or reinforce yours. In my experience with German students, ideologies are not that different and the impressions on images have been quite alike. (SR3a)

Despite differences in their cultural backgrounds, students discovered that there are many commonalities in feelings, ideals, and opinions when discussing their images (SR3b and SR8):

> German and Spanish culture differ so much, yet the kind of ideals and opinions are mostly shared (SR3b)
> We both had chosen completely different pictures but our feelings were nearly the same. (SR8)

From a different perspective, students note that the exchange contributed to improving their language skills and to acquiring cultural knowledge (both through their tandem partners and through the tasks), two of the intercultural competences in the *AIEVM* framework: communication skills and cultural knowledge.

> It has been a good opportunity for me to improve my English and to know new things about other cultures. (SR6)

The scaffolding of the project in the wiki, with pre-*AIEVM* tasks followed by the completion of the *AIEVM* and the post-*AIEVM* tandem discussion, is perceived as being essential to the success of the exchange (TD9).

> We have gone through from the most basic and simplest elements to the most complex or concrete parts, passing through different blocks of similar but at the same time different topics. We dealt with controversial issues. Finally, I liked the idea to work with a partner, since it favors cooperation. (TD9)

Finally, SR2 suggests that projects of this kind not only improve English skills but also foster respect for otherness and shape participants' attitudes and behavior toward others:

> I learnt that we can be quite understanding and receptive when we have to talk to people from different countries. And the most vital element, to respect one another. It does not only favour our use and level of English, but also our attitudes, behaviours or manners to the rest of people. (SR2)

Online exchange with the *AIEVM* therefore involves the development of communication skills on different levels. Linguistic and intercultural communication skills can be put into practice and enhanced at an initial level through respectful dialogue with the tandem partner. The act of collaborating on tasks focuses the dialogue and engages the tandem partners in their joint purpose. However, the use of a tool that is specifically designed to support the development of intercultural and media visual competence through structured, systematic reflection of intercultural encounters through image, namely, the *AIEVM*, significantly enriched the tandem exchange of perspectives and prompted several of the students to reexamine their own cultural position(s), to engage in further enquiry into the images, and ultimately to achieve a better understanding of the underlying cultural message(s).

The findings are therefore consistent with research in the field of FLE that suggests OIE can be used not only for fostering linguistic and intercultural communicative competence but also for a wider range of literacies. Taking as its starting point the premise that interculturally sensitive visual literacy is required to critically engage with the profusion of images that have become so central to communication in our networked society, the findings of this study suggest that the *AIEVM*, which is specifically designed to develop intercultural and visual media competence, can enhance OIE. At the same time, OIE provides a useful framework for multiperspectival reflection on and verbalization of encounters with otherness through images, thus enriching the learning experience of working with the *AIEVM* and heightening critical cultural awareness of visual media.

11.5 Teaching Implications and Applications

Diverse implications and applications for language teaching and learning contexts may be derived from this study. To complement the range of tasks and procedures of the OIE reported here, alternative courses of action are suggested below.

Firstly, this study showed that work with the *AIEVM* can benefit from preliminary tasks in which students consider and discuss images together. However, it was also found that the choice of image for *AIEVM* analysis was influenced in several cases by the choice of visuals used in preliminary tasks. Teachers could therefore use a wider range of images for initial discussion to demonstrate the breadth of possibilities of intercultural encounter as it is understood by the *AIEVM*. Exotic or sensationalized images of other cultures with which students are likely to be familiar may be discussed critically to draw attention to the role of the media in manipulating perceptions, but these might be compared with local images with people from different cultures to show that intercultural encounters can take place anywhere, or images of people from different social groups, different religious groups, different generations, or different social strata to broaden the concept of culture. Subsequent guidance in selecting the *AIEVM* images might ensure a more effective learning experience.

Secondly, when working with the *AIEVM*, tandem partners may be encouraged to agree on a single image (rather than selecting an image each) so that the same image is analyzed individually before proceeding to the comparison phase. Working with the *AIEVM* in OIE has the advantage that considerations of otherness can be discussed with "the other" (i.e., the tandem partner), which in turn entails examining different standpoints.

Intercultural dialogue and awareness of one's own and the other's culture may likewise be fostered by inviting learners to discuss images that would be considered appropriate and/or inappropriate in their culture, either these days and/or in the past.

By incorporating the notion of appropriateness into a historical perspective, learners need to explore and present their culture to their tandem partner within a wider framework, thereby heightening awareness both of their own and the target culture in the image.

By the same token, to promote awareness of self, one's own culture, and other people's cultures, it is possible to use the *AIEVM* to consider specific aspects of "otherness." For example, tandem partners may discuss their first experiences of otherness through images, how otherness may be portrayed in local images, or the most recent, the most impartial/partial, or the most thought-provoking image of otherness portrayed by visual media about a "distant or faraway other."

Both online during the exchange and in the debriefing conducted in the individual classes, participants in this study wondered whether their tandem partner expressed their own perspective or whether this perspective reflected a broader sociocultural stance. Partners may look into both the individual and the collective conception of otherness by filling in the *AIEVM* individually and then inviting family or friends to comment on their understanding of otherness as conveyed in their *AIEVM*. The ensuing tandem debate would thereby raise issues of individual versus collective interpretation of otherness in both partners' communities.

Finally, the benefit of OIE for developing intercultural and visual media competence depends to a large extent on engagement on the part of both tandem partners. To minimize the effects caused by one tandem partner's lack of involvement in the task, facilitators may wish to choose other groupings, such as four students, two from each culture, to facilitate small group discussions rather than tandem debates and to ensure the exchange of different perspectives.

11.6 Conclusion

This chapter started with the assertion that, despite the wide usage of visuals in FLE, visual literacy pedagogy as such is rarely properly incorporated in the teaching process. It proposed that, if images are understood as socioculturally constructed "messages," visual media pedagogy might be fruitfully integrated into intercultural learning at its intersection with FLE. The *AIEVM* was developed by the Council of Europe for precisely this purpose – that is, to facilitate the development of intercultural and visual media competence in educational contexts, particularly in FLE. The value of the *AIEVM* lies in its design (the sequence of sections, questions, and prompts) and in the theoretical framework of competence subsets that underpins the design. Structured narration of and reflection on intercultural encounters through image is meant to foster the development of intercultural and visual media competence; at the same time, the theoretical framework should enable FLE teachers using the *AIEVM* to guide and evaluate this aspect of their students' learning. Because the *AIEVM* had been piloted in face-to-face FLE, this study explored its efficacy for developing intercultural and visual media competence in online exchange and, vice versa, the affordances of OIE for enhancing the learning potential of the *AIEVM*.

With regard to the first research question, the findings provide evidence that the *AIEVM* benefits from online exchange in which it is framed within a wider analysis of images. Compared to working with the *AIEVM* individually or in the classroom as suggested in the *AIEVM's Notes for facilitators* (Barrett et al., 2013b), online exchange with students from another country provided further dimensions to learning. Multiperspectival opportunities for reflection, collaborating with tandem partners and sharing results in the wiki, motivated students not only to critically reflect on their own intercultural encounters through visual media and to consider other points of view but also to relate these experiences to other situations and to follow up on insights gained.

In the course of reflecting on self in relation to the mediated other – that is, the tandem partner mediated through the wiki or the person mediated through the image – students demonstrated a number of the competences on which the *AIEVM* draws, including media literacy as it pertains to empathy, respect for otherness, behavioral flexibility, knowledge of other cultures, skills of discovery and interaction, skills of interpreting and relating, critical cultural awareness, and action orientation. This process was supported by the initial activities in preparation for working with the *AIEVM,* with images chosen by the authors. However, as discussed in the previous section, the potential for such activities laying the foundations for subsequent work with the *AIEVM* may be exploited better through discussion of a wider range of images that helps to clarify what is meant by an intercultural encounter through image and to rehearse critical analysis of the image.

In relation to the second research question, the findings also provide evidence that a multiliteracies approach to OIE might be enhanced by using a theoretically grounded tool which is specifically designed to support the development of intercultural and media visual competence. Firstly, similar to the approach used in the Cultura Project, the design of the *AIEVM* helped students in this study to refine their understanding of their own culture in relation to others through iterative reflection on their own and with students in another country. The *AIEVM*'s sequence of questions fostered a process of engagement with images that progressed from describing to narrating, evaluating, and analyzing an encounter with otherness. This process prompted several participants to reexamine their own cultural position (s) and to undertake further enquiry into the images, thereby arriving at a better understanding of the underlying cultural message(s). Secondly, the robust theoretical framework of intercultural and visual media competence that informs the sequence of questions in the *AIEVM* proved effective in guiding, identifying, and evaluating the development of intercultural and visual media competence in the participating students. It might therefore provide valuable theoretical underpinning for other OIE projects aimed at developing multiliteracies.

Both the Council of Europe and other people working in the field of visual media literacy argue that there is a need for teachers, too, to acquire intercultural and visual media literacy. The *AIEVM* was therefore trialed in this study with preservice non-native teachers of English with at least C1 proficiency in the language. These participants seemed to have little difficulty in articulating their reflections. However, similar projects with less linguistically proficient students would require more specific language input and perhaps more focus on the communicative awareness aspect of the *AIEVM*'s theoretical framework.

Finally, although media awareness can inform the culturally sensitive creation of images, the current study did not exploit the multimodal affordances of the wiki for exploring the two-way process of decoding and encoding – reflecting on *and* creating image. Designing activities that support the move from reflection to production would therefore be a logical step in further developing a multiliteracies approach to OIE.

References

Allport, G. W. (1954). *The nature of prejudice*. Cambridge, MA: Addison-Wesley.

Ausburn, L., & Ausburn, F. (1978). Visual literacy: Background, theory and practice. *Programmed Learning and Educational Technology, 15*(4), 291–297.

Averginou, M., & Ericson, J. (1997). A review of the concept of literacy. *British Journal of Educational Technology, 28*(4), 280–291.

Bain, J., Ballantyne, R., Packer, J., & Mills, C. (1999). Using journal writing to enhance student teachers' reflectivity during field experience placements. *Teachers and Teaching: Theory and Practice, 5*(1), 51–73. Retrieved from http://www.tandfonline.com.

Barrett, M., Byram, M., Ipgrave, J., & Seurrat, A. (2013a). *Images of others: An autobiography of intercultural encounters through visual media*. Strasbourg: Council of Europe Publishing. Retrieved from http://www.coe.int/t/dg4/autobiography/default_en.asp.

Barrett, M., Byram, M., Ipgrave, J., & Seurrat, A. (2013b). *Images of others: An autobiography of intercultural encounters through visual media. Notes for facilitators*. Strasbourg: Council of Europe Publishing. Retrieved from http://www.coe.int/t/dg4/autobiography/default_en.asp.

Barrett, M., Byram, M., Lázár, I., Mompoint-Gaillard, P., & Philippou, S. (2014). *Developing intercultural competence through education* (Pestalozzi Series No. 3). Strasbourg: Council of Europe Publishing.

Belz, J. A. (2002). Social dimensions of telecollaborative language study. *Language Learning and Technology, 6*(1), 60–81.

Berger, P., & Luckmann, T. (1966). *The social construction of reality: A treatise in the sociology of knowledge*. Harmondsworth, UK: Penguin.

Braun, V., & Clarke, V. (2006). Using thematic analysis in psychology. *Qualitative Research in Psychology, 3*, 77–101.

Byram, M., Barrett, M., Ipgrave, J., Jackson, R., & Méndez García, M. C. (2009a). *Autobiography of intercultural encounters*. Strasbourg, France: Council of Europe Publishing. Retrieved from http://www.coe.int/t/dg4/autobiography/default_en.asp.

Byram, M., Barrett, M., Ipgrave, J., Jackson, R., & Méndez García, M. C. (2009b). *Autobiography of intercultural encounters. Context, concepts and theories*. Strasbourg, France: Council of Europe Publishing. Retrieved from http://www.coe.int/t/dg4/autobiography/default_en.asp.

Byram, M., Gribkova, B., & Starkey, H. (2002). *Developing the intercultural dimension in language teaching. A practical introduction for teachers*. Strasbourg, France: Council of Europe Publishing.

Byram, M., & Zarate, G. (1997). Defining and assessing intercultural competence: Some principles and proposals for the European context. *Language Teaching, 29*, 14–18.

Corbett, J. (2003). *An intercultural approach to language teaching*. Clevedon, UK: Multilingual Matters.

Council of Europe. (2008). *White paper on intercultural dialogue: 'Living together as equals in dignity.* Strasbourg, France: Council of Europe Publishing. Retrieved from http://www.coe.int/t/dg4/intercultural/Source/White%20Paper_final_revised_EN.pdf.

Debes, J. (1969). The loom of visual literacy: An overview. *Audiovisual Instruction, 14*(8), 25–27.

Dooley, M. (2008). *Telecollaborative language learning.* Bern, Switzerland: Peter Lang.

Eilam, B. (2012). *Teaching, learning and visual literacy.* Cambridge, UK: Cambridge University Press.

Fantini, A. E., Arias-Galicia, F., & Guay, D. (2001). *Globalization and 21st century competencies: Challenges for north American higher education. "Understanding the differences". A working paper series on higher education in Mexico, Canada, and the United States.* Boulder, CO: Western Interstate Commission for Higher Education.

Furstenberg, G., Levet, S., English, K., & Maillet, K. (2001). Giving a virtual voice to the silent language of culture: The culture project. *Language Learning and Technology, 5*(1), 55–102.

Gibbs, G. (1988). *Learning by doing: A guide to teaching and learning methods.* London: FEU.

Glaser, E., Guilherme, M., Méndez García, M. C., & Mughan, T. (2007). *Intercultural competence for professional mobility.* Graz, Austria: Council of Europe.

Goldstein, B. (2008). *Working with images. A resource book for the language classroom.* Cambridge, UK: Cambridge University Press.

Guth, S., & Helm, F. (Eds.). (2010). *Telecollaboration 2.0: Language, literacies and intercultural learning in the 21^{st}century.* Bern, Switzerland: Peter Lang.

Hampel, R., & Hauck, M. (2006). Computer-mediated language learning: Making meaning in multimodal virtual learning spaces. *The JALT CALL Journal, 2*(1), 3–18. Retrieved from journal.jaltcall.org/articles/2_2_Hampel.pdf.

Hauck, M. (2010). At the Interface between multimodal and intercultural communicative competence. In S. Guth & F. Helm (Eds.), *Telecollaboration 2.0: Language, literacies and intercultural learning in the 21^{st}century* (pp. 219–248). Bern, Switzerland: Peter Lang.

Hecke, C., & Surkamp, C. (Eds.). (2010). *Bilder im Fremdsprachenunterricht.* Tübingen, Germany: Gunter Narr Verlag.

Helm, F. (2014). Developing digital literacies through virtual exchange. *eLearning Papers, 38.* Retrieved from http://www.openeducationeuropa.eu/en/article/Developing-digital-literacies-through-virtual-exchange

Kress, G., & van Leeuwen, T. (1996). *Reading images: The grammar of visual design* (1st ed.). London: Routledge.

Kress, G., & van Leeuwen, T. (2006). *Reading images: The grammar of visual design* (2nd ed.). London: Routledge.

Lindner, R. (2011). ESAP students' perceptions of skills learning in computer-mediated intercultural collaboration. *International Journal of Computer Assisted Language Learning and Teaching, 1*(1), 25–42.

Mackey, A., & Gass, S. M. (2005). *Second language research. Methodology and design.* Mahwah, NJ: Lawrence Erlbaum Associates.

Maley, A., Duff, A., & Grellet, F. (1980). *The mind's eye: Using pictures creatively in language learning.* Cambridge, UK: Cambridge University Press.

Mitchell, W. J. T. (1995). *Picture theory.* Chicago: University of Chicago Press.

Müller-Hartmann, A. (2000). The role of tasks in promoting intercultural learning in electronic learning networks. *Language Learning and Technology, 5*(1), 55–102.

New London Group. (2000). A pedagogy of multiliteracies: Designing social futures. In B. Cope & M. Kalantzis (Eds.), *Multiliteracies: Literacies learning and the design of social futures* (pp. 9–37). London: Routledge.

O'Dowd, R. (2003). Understanding the 'other side': Intercultural learning in a Spanish-English email exchange. *Language Learning and Technology, 7*(2), 118–144.

O'Dowd, R. (Ed.). (2007). *Online intercultural exchange. An introduction for foreign language teachers.* Clevedon, UK: Multilingual Matters.

Obinger, D. G., & Obinger, J. L. (2005). *Educating the net generation*. Washington, DC: EDUCAUSE. Retrieved from www.educause.edu/educatingthenetgen/.

Pegrum, M. (2008). Film, culture and identity: Critical intercultural literacies for the language classroom. *Language and Intercultural Communication, 8*(2), 136–153.

Royce, T. D. (2007). Multimodal communicative competence in second language contexts. In T. D. Royce & W. L. Bowcher (Eds.), *New directions in the analysis of multimodal discourse* (pp. 361–390). Mahwah, NJ: Lawrence Erlbaum.

Soria, K. M., & Troisi, J. (2014). Internationalization at home alternatives to study abroad: Implications for students' development of global, international, and intercultural competencies. *Journal of Studies in International Education, 18*(3), 261–280.

Stenglin, M., & Iedema, R. (2001). How to analyse visual images. A guide for TESOL teachers. In A. Burns & C. Coffin (Eds.), *Analysing English in a global context* (pp. 194–208). London: Routledge.

Stokes, S. (2002). Visual literacy in teaching and learning: A literature perspective. *Electronic Journal for the Integration of Technology in Education, 1*(1), 10–19.

Woodin, J. (2001). Tandem learning as an intercultural activity. In M. Byram, A. Nichols, & D. Stevens (Eds.), *Developing intercultural competence in practice* (pp. 189–202). Clevedon, UK: Multilingual Matters.

Chapter 12
Intercultural Competence and Parsnip: Voices From Teachers of English in Australia

Thuy Ngoc Dinh and Fenty Lidya Siregar

12.1 Introduction

The globalized era together with demographic, geographical, and structural changes to English has reshaped the landscape of English language teaching (ELT) and emphasized the importance of preparing language learners for intercultural communication. Research has shown that without intercultural communication, academic success and life satisfaction are hard to achieve (Young, Sercombe, Sachdev, Naeb, & Schartner, 2013). However, in order to engage successfully in intercultural communication, language learners need intercultural competence. Intercultural competence (IC) is variously defined; however, here it refers to "being aware that cultures are relative. That is, being aware that there is no one 'normal' way of doing things, but that all behaviours are culturally variable" (Liddicoat & Scarino, 2013, p. 24). It is also understood as the ability to interact, communicate, and work effectively with people from various linguistic and cultural backgrounds both in local and international contexts (Sharifian, 2009).

Thus, IC has been highlighted as an appropriate goal for language learning (e.g., Byram, 1997, 2012; Liddicoat & Scarino, 2013). Despite this, intercultural teaching material is still rare (cf. Diaz, 2015). Textbooks which have always been part of foreign language teaching materials in many educational institutions have been of limited use in developing the aspects of intercultural understanding that help facilitate intercultural competence (Liddicoat & Scarino, 2013).

T. N. Dinh (✉)
Monash College, Monash University, Melbourne, Australia
e-mail: dinhngocthuy2111@gmail.com

F. L. Siregar (✉)
Maranatha Christian University, Bandung, Indonesia

© Springer Nature Singapore Pte Ltd. 2021
M. D. López-Jiménez, J. Sánchez-Torres (eds.), *Intercultural Competence Past, Present and Future*, Intercultural Communication and Language Education,
https://doi.org/10.1007/978-981-15-8245-5_12

Language teaching resources, as argued by Liddicoat and Scarino (2013), which incorporate topics related to gender, social class, ethnicity, region, religion, and political affiliation inherently include variability of cultures in any context and can be exploited to facilitate intercultural competence. Nonetheless, not all topics are represented in language materials for some may be culturally sensitive and are likely to provoke cultural conflicts if not pragmatically addressed in class (Gray, 2002). PARSNIP (*Pork, Alcohol, Religion, Sex, Narcotics, Ism,* and *Politics*) was coined by Gray (2002) to refer to the seven most observed taboo topics that have been widely avoided in ELT. Gray coined the concept to create "one size fits all" materials (Gray, 2002, p. 159). For publishers, the avoidance of these issues means their products can reach as many potential consumers across cultures as possible (Gray, 2002). However, debates surrounding whether or not these culturally sensitive topics should be represented in ELT materials and addressed in class remain controversial yet under-discussed. On the one hand, taboo topics can create conflicts and discourage consumers from purchasing materials when they find hard to cope with (Gray, 2002); on the other hand, a textbook which excludes thought-provoking issues and taboos is bland or boring (Leather, 2003).

This study aims to investigate teachers' voices regarding PARSNIP and intercultural competence within their existing curriculum. To be more specific, it addresses the responses of teachers of English in Australia to PARSNIP and the extent to which PARSNIP has been and should be incorporated in their teaching for the development of intercultural competence.

12.2 Theoretical Framework

12.2.1 ELT and Intercultural Competence in Australia

Australia is a country where "the multicultural fabric of the society has been well established" (Sharifian, 2014, p. 35). Due to the changing patterns of the Australian immigration, the ethnic, linguistic, religious, and cultural diversity is significant in the Australian primary and secondary schools (Collins & Reid, 2012), and many Australia's teachers in general come from non-English-speaking countries in Asia and Africa (Collins, 2012). Specifically, in ELT, Sharifian (2014) observes that many teachers of English in the country have different cultural linguistic backgrounds who have grown up and learned English in countries other than Australia.

Reflecting on its diversity, Australian schooling is attempting to cultivate interculturality and places emphasis on facilitating students' awareness and understanding of cultural differences and similarities to enhance their self-respect and appreciation for others' values, practice, and attitude (Harbon & Moloney, 2015). Furthermore, higher education in Australia accentuates that IC and critical thinking about culture should go hand in hand (Moloney & Hui, 2015). It is specifically suggested that teachers provide students with opportunities for critical observations of language and culture and for cultural meaning negotiation practice to develop intercultural competence (ibid).

In the field of ELT in Australia, regardless of the sociocultural diversity and intercultural learning goal, the presence of British English or American English rather than Australian English, as Sharifian (2014) notes, is obvious in ELT textbooks. In order to better address intercultural competence in language education, there are several suggestions, one of which is treating English as a pluricentric language, focusing on students' intercultural communication skills (Sharifian, 2014). In doing this, according to Diaz (2015), the development of teaching resources can be a starting point to move from information-oriented to IC-oriented practice in class. However, Diaz (2015), in her own study, found that selecting, adapting, and using interculturally oriented teaching resources remain challenging. The challenges lie in the availability, suitability, and teachers' readiness to develop and implement (inter)cultural materials and activities in order to develop IC. These facts highlight the need for teachers to receive professional development as to how personally engage in adapting available resources to make the most of teaching materials as well as teachers' potential to provide intercultural materials which suit their students' needs and context.

In Australia, ELICOS (English Language Intensive Courses for Overseas Students) focuses on EAP (English for Academic Purposes) and general English for international students, migrants, refugees, and tourists. As such, ELICOS prepares students with skills and proficiency in English for further education, business, and living both in a multicultural Australia and elsewhere. The reason is after completing their studies, students will return to their home or move to other countries. In other words, understanding linguistic and cultural diversity should be targeted in ELICOS (see, for more description of ELICOS, Hatoss, 2006) which implicitly or explicitly regards intercultural competence as one of the ultimate goals.

12.2.2 PARSNIP in ELT

Recently a group of teachers in Australia have created two series of activity book on PARSNIP. In the foreword of the first book entitled *Parsnips in ELT: Stepping Out of the Comfort Zone (Vol. 1)*, it is highlighted that what is considered controversial and untouchable varies across time as the world has become more homogenized (Smith, 2015). While it might be true that some "controversial" topics no longer are controversial as time goes by, it is certainly not due to the world which has become homogenized but rather due to "super-diversity" (Vertovec, 2007, p. 1024).

In this super-diverse world, classrooms are our students' social meeting interface where they can encounter and negotiate different cultures (Pratt, 1999). Classrooms are also connected to wider contexts which cannot be ignored. Thus, teachers, as intercultural mediators, need to prepare a space for students to begin this journey of negotiating different values embedded in an array of contexts and explore cultural diversity through many topics including PARSNIP. For intercultural language learning to take place, teachers can engage students by asking questions of "why" and "how" (How did I interpret the writer's/speaker's meaning? Why did I interpret this event/text in this way? How was the meaning different from what I expected? How did I respond and why?, etc.) and go beyond questions of "what" (What did I see? What did I think? What did I feel?, etc.) ("Module 2 - Exploring intercultural language teaching and learning," 2007).

Over the years PARSNIP has been considered as "taboo topics" (Gray, 2002) and extended differently in different contexts, which reveals its limitations, and that taboo topics are culturally and socially constructed. For example, Gray (2002) includes anarchy, AIDS, and Israel on the list of taboo topics in the ESL classroom. In a different Western context, Keturi and Lehmonen (2011) add suicide, violence, abortion, cursing, and smoking in an analysis of four series of EFL textbooks published in Finland by Finnish publishers for junior to senior high school English language learners. In a more comprehensive study, Keturi and Lehmonen (2012) investigated forty-four Finnish EFL textbook series for upper secondary school and interviewed two book authors. They found that there was an absence of topics such as incest, pedophilia, taboo language, sexual abuse, offending political opinions, or religious beliefs in the textbooks. They also observed that topics that both authors consider to be either taboo or borderline taboo include bodily effluvia, sex, and taboo language. They, however, have different opinions on these topics as they consider alcohol, tobacco, and body parts such as breasts and buttock as taboo topics and bullshit, asshole, hell, and menstruation as mild taboo language. Zaid (1999) elucidates 16 cultural values of non-Islamic societies which can be offensive to Muslims, namely, boyfriend/girlfriend, dating, beach/bikini wear, the consumption of wine and alcohol, dancing, hugging, a picture of an uncovered breast, fortune-tellers and predicting the future, a cross worn by a man subliminally conveys an advocacy of a Christian perspective, the Christian church, sexism, superstitions, guns, teen suicide, life after death, and birth control.

Gobert (2015) argues that although all of these listed topics above are taboo in Gulf Arab Muslim classrooms, they might not be in other Muslim or Arab contexts such as Pakistan or Lebanon. The use of PARSNIP as a filter to avoid culture clash is problematic. It unveils a generalization by publishers which may ultimately be just another example of stereotyping. Thus, language teachers should be more critical of and reflective on this practice since they are in a much better position to change this drawback. Moreover, Hook (2011) puts forth that "the unwillingness to approach teaching from a standpoint that includes awareness of race, sex, and class is often rooted in the fear that classrooms will be uncontrollable and that emotions and passions will not be contained" (p. 93). However, Mambu (2014) argues that

> although not all teachers have to include issues of PARSNIP in any ELT-related class [...] in an ever-pluralizing society of our time in this 21st century, it is crucial that English language teachers or teacher educators are better equipped with the ability to engage with, and reflect upon, such issues, especially spirituality and/or religion, in class. (p. 180)

After all, teachers play an important role in constructing a cultural environment through a range of work including selecting videos, collecting newspapers, planning seating, and setting tasks that are of social, cultural, and educational values (Duff & Uchida, 1997).

In short, avoiding PARSNIP in teaching does not prevent teachers from facing conflicts in classroom. Instead, it takes them to ignore potential learning opportunities which can be used to prompt students to develop skills, attitude, and awareness to manage their stereotypes and prejudice when facing controversial issues such as taboos. It is also important to locally interpret PARSNIP as language teachers need to reflect on their immediate and wider social, linguistic, and cultural context(s) and guide their students to do the same by engaging them to deal with complex or confronting issues in their learning. As Gray (2010) emphasizes, the cultural content should always be meaningful to the learners. The decision of what kind of cultural content might be appropriate is best reached locally by local teachers for whom English may have a range of meanings other than those determined for them by British ELT publishers. Thus, it is important to gain an insight into local teachers' voices on PARSNIP in the context of Australia.

12.3   Methodology

12.3.1   Context and Participants

This study collected data from five teachers of Australian (1), Iranian (1), Saudi Arabic (1), and Vietnamese (2) backgrounds who are currently involved in ELICOS in Melbourne, Australia. They volunteered to participate in the study, and all shared one feature: not having been informed of PARSNIP before. Below is a summary of their personal information together with the pseudonyms used in the study (Table 12.1).

They were teaching general English (intermediate level) to international students at the same language center that utilizes internationally marketed English textbooks in Melbourne.

12.3.2   Research Questions

The study aims to gain answers to the following research questions surrounding two main issues: teachers' response to PARSNIP and their integration of PARSNIP in practice.

Teachers' response to PARSNIP

1. To what extent do they believe PARSNIP should be addressed in ELT to facilitate intercultural competence?
2. What does PARSNIP mean to teachers of different cultural backgrounds?

Table 12.1 A summary of English teachers' personal information in the PARSNIP study

Name	Gender and age	Cultural backgrounds	Qualifications	TESOL experience outside Australia	TESOL experience in Australia
Helen	Female, 25	Australian	PhD candidate in Applied Linguistics	1 year in China	2 years in Australia
Marzieh	Female, 32	Iranian	PhD candidate in Applied Linguistics	9 years in Iran	2 years in Australia
Leila	Female, 36	Arabic	PhD candidate in TESOL	6 years in Saudi Arabia	4 years in Australia
Huy	Male, 31	Vietnamese	MATESOL	7 years in Vietnam	3 years in Australia
Thu	Female, 42	Vietnamese	PhD in TESOL	7 years in Vietnam	8 years in Australia

3. What issues, if any, have impacted teachers' decisions to avoid or address PARSNIP?
   Teachers' integration of PARSNIP in practice
4. To what extent do they address PARSNIP in class?

12.3.3 Data Collection Tools, Procedure, and Analysis

This study employed the NAR (narrative action reflection) workshop (Lorenzo, 2005) to gather data and the analysis procedure of the study followed the NAR workshop (Lorenzo, 2010) and complemented it with in-depth interviews. A snapshot of the research methodology is as follows (Table 12.2):

According to Lorenzo (2010), NAR workshops can be used as a data-gathering tool or data trigger. In this study, one of the researchers conducted a one-hour workshop on what is meant by PARSNIP, how it has been discussed in ELT, how it is relevant to intercultural competence, and which activities can be implemented in class. The teachers were also given materials on PARSNIP that outline some sample activities. They then were engaged in a small group discussion right after the workshop to share ideas on whether or not they believed PARSNIP should be avoided in ELT materials, what PARSNIP meant to them, whether they had addressed these "cultural taboo" topics in class so far, and to what extent they thought PARSNIP would help enhance intercultural competence.

The second small group discussion was conducted one week after the first workshop. It aimed to yield more data on how the PARSNIP materials and the workshop informed them of the tools for their current ELT materials evaluation and their teaching pedagogy as well as their concerns/issues regarding PARSNIP and intercultural competence in ELT. After that, an in-depth interview was conducted

Table 12.2 Research methodology

Data production			
Data generation	Data triggers	Facilitation techniques	Data-capturing method
Narrative telling reflection workshop on PARSNIP and intercultural competence	Materials on PARSNIP Sample activities on how to address PARSNIPS in class	Small group discussion Discussion 1: Right after the workshop Discussion 2: 1 week after the workshop	Audio recording
⬇			
Interviews			

with each teacher to clarify certain points they made at the workshops and elicit elaboration.

12.4 Results

The findings were grouped into four main sections elucidating teachers' responses to PARSNIP, which were collected during the workshop and discussion, and teachers' integration of PARSNIP in the followed-up discussion and interviews.

12.4.1 PARSNIP Across Teachers of English in Australia

During the first discussion, the teachers revealed variations in their interpretations of PARSNIP and added further taboo issues, from their own personal perspectives and the current curriculum (Table 12.3).

It is evident from the summary that not all elements in PARSNIP are considered offensive to teachers. Here are the teachers' key responses related to the different taboo topics of PARSNIP.

First, pork is, to all five participants, a non-taboo topic. They observed that pork and other types of meat such as beef and chicken are represented in ELT materials. However, there was a shift in addressing pork when teachers, Marzieh and Leila, moved to another context. In Iran and Saudi Arabia, according to them, topics related to pork and beef are strictly monitored and avoided as they are connected to taboos in the Islamic culture. Also, the ELT textbooks, which are mostly censored by the government and republished to suit the local cultures, have cut off those topics. Yet, in a completely different context, Australia, the two teachers found it normal to talk

Table 12.3 A summary of findings on taboo topics across teachers of English in Australia

Teachers	Which PARSNIP topics are taboos?	Reasons	Other taboos
Helen	S: Sex P: Politics R: Religion	Sex-related topics are private, personal and uncomfortable to discuss even with friends.	Topic Age -> It may single out some mature-aged students, and it is a taboo to many Australians.
			Disabilities
			Swearwords
			Nonverbal offensive behaviors
		Politics-related topics can be out of hand and off the focus easily.	Visuals Provocative visuals
		Religion: God, Jesus Christ, Allah as exclamation should be avoided in class on the part of the teachers.	
Marzieh	S: Sex	Sex-related topics are sensitive and do not promise engaged discussion.	Visuals: Bikinis, intimate images, and body figures
Leila	S: Sex R: Religion	Sex-related and gender topics are sensitive and personal	Topics and visuals Violence, dancing, and boys and girls in bars
		Religion-related topics might provoke a lot of explanation in the part of the teachers and do not engage students.	
Huy	P: Politics (communism and democracy)	The teacher has little knowledge in politics and the discussion might be out of hand.	Topics and visuals Age and poverty -> They might upset some students and relate to some specific countries.
Thu	S: Sex R: Religion P: Politics	These topics are sensitive and rarely addressed in textbooks.	Topic Gender (gay, lesbian) -> It may single out some individuals and create irritation if not approached appropriately.

about pork and beef. Huy elaborated on this element by suggesting the variation in the notion of meat. As Huy observed and experienced, pork is not a taboo to him, his colleagues, and many students in his teaching context and has not so far created any conflicts, but dog and cat meat have. Huy shared that

> in a country where dogs and cats are valued pets like Australia, I find it immoral to mention those types of meat though I know in some cultures where my international students come from, dog or cat meat is acceptable. Yet, I try to avoid as it may cause discomfort to both whether they approve or disapprove of the practice. (Discussion data)

Therefore, pork is not a universal taboo; instead, the types of meat considered as taboos are determined divergently across cultures. All the teachers in the discussion agreed that an understanding of students' cultural backgrounds is essential in the teaching process.

Second, alcohol is not a taboo to the teachers either. To them, the internationally marketed textbooks that they have used sometimes contain some images of beer and people holding champagne at a party. Even though alcohol is sensitive to some cultures/countries (e.g., Iran and Saudi Arabia), the teachers all found the topic about alcoholism, food, and drink educationally relevant. Thu demonstrated that some discussion questions about whether alcohol should be avoided at some parties or how alcoholism should be dealt with in Australia are of relevance to both speaking and writing tasks.

Third, religion is culturally sensitive to Helen, Leila, and Thu. These three teachers admitted that as students come from different cultures and teachers themselves do not have sufficient knowledge about different religions, they avoided it to prevent themselves from mentioning something that is unintentionally offensive to some students. Also, they were afraid that discussion about religion might be out of focus and control, posing difficulty to both teachers and students. While Helen, Leila, and Thu were reluctant to discussing religions, Huy strongly supported that religion has been and should be discussed in class to raise students' awareness of different worldviews, cultural values, and beliefs. He cited an example of Christmas which should not be taught as a mere feast when people party and exchange gifts but as a religious festival; hence, stories related to God, how Christ was born, and relevant facts about Christian teachings should be presented. He also added that occasionally, he reflected on the Bible teachings and his religious background as a Catholic to share educational lessons and provoked discussions surrounding lessons about religious diversity. For Leila and Marzieh, addressing religious topics was not actually a taboo at all as in their home cultures, Iran and Saudi Arabia, Islamic practices were explicitly represented across materials. In Australia, they felt comfortable talking about their religious backgrounds and festivals when asked by students and sometimes posed some reflective questions in class such as whether and how students celebrate Vesak, Christmas, or Ramadan in their own cultures. Nonetheless, Leila and Marzieh shared that no more in-depth discussion on religion was integrated for the fear of unintentionally touching on sensitive issues among different belief systems. They admitted that they did not feel comfortable talking deeply about or praising their religion as it may sound like promoting Muslim or provoke some controversial issues such as people's attitudes to Muslim and the association of Muslim and terrorism throughout the discussion.

Fourth, sex is the most fully agreed taboo topic across the participants except for Huy. In the discussion, the five teachers supported that the topic is not common among their friends and family, let alone in class. In addition, textbooks do not address sex, and this topic may bring about certain awkward atmosphere including negative feelings of discomfort, shyness, and offense and does not promise engaged discussion among students. Thu stated that

> sex is a personal and private issue that we rarely talk about in public and talking about it may cause some misunderstanding and our self-representation in public as well. Everyone has his/her own secret, so we can teach students that sex is among those secrets and they had

better avoid asking sensitive questions since they may cause offence or discomfort to the interlocutors. (Discussion data)

Huy, in contrast, was totally convinced that topics about abortion, cohabitation, same sex marriage, and sex education are common in language class. Huy believed that these topics will allow students to express their viewpoints about socially debatable issues for they may encounter these issues in reality. Thus, knowing how to express their opinions pragmatically should be taught at school. Another issue that emerged during the discussion is the selection of appropriate visuals in class. Sometimes the topic is not necessarily about sex or an overly romance but provocative images such as girls wearing bikinis and accentuated body figures that may evoke certain associations in students. These images should be carefully censored by teachers in class.

Fifth, narcotics are regarded as normal to all the participants. Being against narcotics does not mean the absolute avoidance of the topic as it can promise numerous discussions and lends itself to various educational values. Helen, for instance, suggested that teachers could create some discussion questions about how to educate people awareness of narcotics and how to deal with it in reality. Huy added that supplementary materials based on newspapers and other mass media could help enhance reading practice and convey educational messages about the use of drugs among youngsters.

Sixth, -ism was seen as a vague concept to the five teachers. They clarified that there were numerous -isms related to religions, politics, and certain social beliefs. Nevertheless, the pivotal issue is how comfortable teachers and their students are when discussing those topics. There were two -isms substantially discussed in the workshop: racism and terrorism. Four teachers, Helen, Thu, Leila, and Marzieh, confessed that they avoided the two issues as they may trigger reflection on past experiences, for example, the 2014 terrorist attack in Sydney, Australia, caused by an Islamic individual. As a result, stereotypes and unpleasant association between Muslim and terrorism may arise uncontrollably. With regard to racism, Helen encountered a situation when some of her students complained about being treated unfairly by local people as they were Chinese. According to her, this can lead to "hatredness to the current society" (interview data). In contrast, Huy believed racism should be taught in class, for example, posing a reflective question of what can be considered racism. He said that "sometimes students do not intend to be discriminatory [. . .] they may comment on one's accent and it can be racist" (interview data). Racism, to him, can occur, so it is advisable to develop students' awareness of racist acts and empathy as sometimes people do not mean to be racist. It is our interpretation that also counts.

Seventh, politics is controversial among the participants. While Helen, Huy, and Thu were reluctant to the topic, Marzieh and Leila found it normal. To Helen, politics is avoidable as it may easily trigger conflicts even within one culture let alone different cultures in her multicultural class. Huy and Thu were used to refraining themselves from discussing communist topics in Vietnam; hence, political topics were subconsciously considered to be taboo. This finding makes it clear that teachers' sociocultural backgrounds determine taboo and non-taboo issues in class. They have brought what they learned in Vietnam to Australia. Despite shifting the contexts, the teachers still feel reluctant to discussing an issue they believed to be avoided. In contrast, to Marzieh and Leila, politics is an ordinary topic which provides much space for discussion on the current local and international affairs.

12.4.2   PARSNIP, Teachers' Roles, and Intercultural Competence

In spite of viewing some of PARSNIP elements as culturally sensitive, all five teachers advocated that they should be addressed in class. To justify this argument, they reflected on their roles as teachers of English, the current sociocultural context, and the goal of teaching and learning English in a globalized era. Below is a summary of their rationale for the integration of PARSNIP in ELT for enhancing intercultural competence.

- *The roles of English teachers nowadays* include raising students' awareness of language and culture; cultivating manners and ethics through language education; widening students' worldviews; exposing them to linguistic and cultural diversity; educating them to become global citizens, respect diversity, and appreciate differences; and developing skills to deal with unexpected intercultural communication situations.
- *The sociocultural context* is signified by the advent of globalization, multilingualism, multiculturalism, and the popularity of online and offline communication across cultures.
- *The goal in ELT* entails intercultural competence (explicate one's own cultures, be aware of other cultures, avoid sensitive topics, negotiate cultural differences, and discuss different topics competently and pragmatically).

All five teachers emphasized that PARSNIP should be incorporated in ELT as the role of English teachers is not merely about teaching language. They acknowledged the need to raise students' awareness of diversity, in this case taboo variation across cultures. Students are expected to know that what is considered taboo to them might not be to others and vice versa. Thus, the ability to negotiate cultural differences and handle sensitive issues competently and appropriately is essential. Helen ascertained that "linguistic competence is insufficient, as teachers definitely do not want their students to be fluent fools – fluent in the language but do not know what to say in certain cultural situations." Here Helen's viewpoint echoes Bennett, Bennett, and Allen's (2003) observation of "the person who learns language without learning culture risks becoming a fluent fool" (p. 237). Agreeing with Helen, Leila added that "students at least need to know what topics are taboos when communicating with people of different cultures and how to explain themselves if miscommunication occurs." Huy highlighted that if teachers do not teach students how to handle these topics in English, then who will [?] They will face these issues in their real life anyway, and it is not wise to avoid them. The more we avoid, the more problems students will face later when they are not well prepared. (Interview data)

Overall, taboo topics are regarded as essential for intercultural communication as "successful communication should be learned from reflection on miscommunication and misunderstanding" (Helen, interview data). Another reason is the fact that their own current classrooms in particular and in Australia in general are multilingual and multicultural which pose both opportunities for intercultural understanding and challenges in cultural conflicts. Henceforth, misunderstandings and miscommunication regarding cultural taboo issues can occur if students are not aware and fully prepared.

In terms of teaching goals, all teachers stressed that teaching English should go beyond linguistic fluency and accuracy. Instead, it is the intercultural competence that needs to be addressed and emphasized as one of the participants, Helen, reiterated, "global citizenship is what both teachers and students aim at" (interview data). Even though some of the participants admitted that they did not implement this goal to the full in all classes, they needed to pursue it regarding the status of English as a global language and the interrelationship of English and multiple cultures.

12.4.3 PARSNIP and Classroom Decision-Making in Practice

The discussion also revolved around what issues and possible challenges impacted their decisions to integrate PARSNIP and other culturally sensitive topics in ELT classes. The teachers listed out the following issues as decisive factors:

- *Students' cultural backgrounds* (age, levels of proficiency, and ethnicity): A thorough understanding of students' cultural backgrounds plays a significant role. The teacher participants fully agreed that students' cultural backgrounds determine how teachers approach the topic, how language should be articulated when they address the topic, and which images can be shown in class. Moreover, students' age and level of English proficiency help decide whether it is appropriate to discuss controversial issues or not.
- *The aims of the whole course and specific lessons*: The decision to incorporate further topics depends on course objectives. For example, if the course is about grammar or IELTS, then teachers will have little room to explore cultural issues.
- *Relevancy to the currently used ELT materials*: The choice of illustrated images, supplementary materials, redesigned tasks, and elaboration on those topics should be tied to and based on the themes or subthemes of the lessons. Otherwise, students will be perplexed and fail to gain the most out of the materials and activities.

- *Class experience*: Reflection on past experiences with the class is an important factor. Leila, for instance, encountered an unpleasant experience with gender issues when she mentioned same-sex marriage. One of her students expressed discontentment and emotional outburst on talking about people's attitudes to gay people in some societies as the topic, to a large extent, triggered his personal experience. Therefore, she tried to avoid the topic in class. Other teachers agreed that teachers, in designing tasks, would have a prediction about the extent to which the tasks suit the students' needs and work well in their class.
- *Potential for productive and interesting activities*: Whether the topic lends itself to relevant, helpful, and interesting activities is of significant consideration.
- *Teachers' knowledge, confidence, and teaching strategies*: It is obvious that if the teachers know little about a certain topic or feel uncomfortable talking about it, it is unlikely that they will bring it to class. All five teachers consider "sex" to be an uncommon topic even in their daily life, so they avoid it in class or misunderstanding may arise. Similarly, if the teachers were not interested in "politics," they would avoid it as much as possible. Also, how confident teachers can be in dealing with challenging topics is of importance. As a result, teachers' preparation, experience, and teaching strategies when unexpected scenarios arise will decide the presence of those topics in their tasks.
- *The availability of existing supplementary resources*: The participants were concerned about the materials and sample activities around PARSNIP and beyond. According to them, searching supplementary materials and devising extra activities is time-consuming. Henceforth, more guidelines and resources are critically needed for a successful integration of PARSNIP and intercultural competence.

To sum up, the workshop discussion was fruitful in revealing teachers' interests in exploring and integrating PARSNIP, their awareness of their roles, ELT and intercultural competence, and their concerns about the possibility of addressing taboo topics in class.

12.4.4 Teachers' Integration of PARSNIP in Practice: Reflection and Orientation

After the workshop and first discussion, the teachers were given further materials, both printed and nonprinted, on PARSNIP for another discussion 1 week after. They were invited to talk about their reflection on the workshop, materials, and past experiences and their orientation for future practice.

The teachers reported that they actually had addressed the taboo topics of PARSNIP. Some examples are talking about Ramadan (Leila); citing Bible teaching and stories about God and Christmas (Huy); dating online, voting rights, immigration policy (Helen); and drug trafficking (Thu). They all had positive reactions from the students. For example, in Huy's lesson about Christmas, he talked about the role of religious festivals and beliefs in people's life and the history of God. On eliciting students' reflection and viewpoint, Huy perceived that students were engaged in the tasks and positive about expanding cultural knowledge.

The teachers also suggested different strategies and possible activities for their ELICOS classes. Each of the teacher participants shared their own activities that addressed PARSNIP and intercultural competence. They together discussed the pros and cons of the activities in relation to classroom context and lesson goal.

Below is a summary of strategies and example activities that the participants proposed (Table 12.4):

In addition to these activities, in the second workshop, the teachers discussed possible problems and proposed strategies to deal with potential conflicts or discontentment as far as culturally sensitive topics are concerned. Those include:

- Topic introduction – for example, "today we are going to discuss swearwords, is anyone not comfortable with the topic?" (Helen, discussion data).
- Clear explanation of the aim and rationale of the lesson and tasks – this helps make students convinced and aware of why and how they conduct the tasks.
- Attention to teachers' own choice of words and nonverbal behaviors on talking about sensitive topics.
- Acknowledgment of possible conflicts and offense – for instance, "this topic is quite sensitive, so if I unintentionally say something that might be inappropriate in your cultures, I apologize in advance" (Huy, discussion data).

The participants explicitly and implicitly advocated that taboo topics should be incorporated to develop students' intercultural competence in terms of awareness, attitude, knowledge, and communication skills. They also expressed their concerns over possible challenges including students' disengagement in the topics, discontentment at the teachers, and unmanageable discussion; as a result, several strategies outlined above can help minimize such challenges.

12.5   Discussion

The findings reveal that PARSNIP is, to the teachers, relatively reductionist and essentialist as there are further taboos that may be inappropriate in their teaching contexts. Those include age, disability, vulgar language, violence, poverty, and visual illustrations that provoke negative associations such as provocative body figures, bikinis, boys and girls in romance, and violent scenes.

The teachers decoded PARSNIP in terms of topics, language, and visuals, and at times, there is an inconsistency among the three. For instance, sex education can be a relevant discussion topic in class, but an explicit sex scene image is definitely a taboo. Some teachers' reluctance to exploring topics related to sex supports Hook's (2011) argument that teachers might be unwilling to address sex-related issues since they are afraid of not being able to control emotions and passions. Another example is a discussion on how people celebrate a Buddhist festival. Vesak is possible while

Table 12.4 Implementation of PARSNIP in activities by teachers

Strategies	Example topics	Example activities
Share self-culture with students	Culture Emails Politeness	List out some topics that are normally avoided in conversations in your own culture. Explain why.
Facilitate culture exchange		Talk about some festivals in your cultures.
		What are some activities people do in the festival? Do people dance? Drink wine?
Facilitate culture comparison		Do you find any similarities and differences between your and your friends' cultures?
Encourage culture understanding	Sex education Cohabitation Abortion Same-sex marriage	Should sex education be compulsory in high school education?
Elicit viewpoints		What are pros and cons of cohabitation?
Elicit speculations		Are you pro or against abortion? Justify your viewpoints.
		Is same-sex marriage accepted in your country? If yes, what is your view? If no, do you think it will be? Why or why not and what is your view? If you were the government of your home country, would you accept same-sex marriage?
Raise awareness of the functions of language and variations in seemingly offensive language use	Swearwords	What words or phrases seem offensive to you? How would you react if people used these words? Why do people swear? Do you swear? Does swearing show that you are bad people? What are the functions of swearwords?
Provoke thoughts on hypothesis/imagined scenarios		
Elicit self-reflection on language use		
Improve general knowledge	Cultural and religious festivals	What is the national religion in your country? Introduce to your class some religious festivals in your country. What are some festivals that you have attended in Australia? Do you celebrate them in your home country? If yes, is the way people celebrate it the same or different from that in Australia?

an image of Buddha beer can be offensive to Buddhist students (Thu). A quiz or supplementary reading about Jesus Christ and Christmas is interesting, but an overuse of such expressions as "oh my God" and "Jesus Christ" to convey certain emotional states can be inappropriate in class, at least on the part of teachers (Helen). Therefore, taboo needs to be broken down to language use, topic, content, image use, and nonverbal communication.

The data indicate that the five teachers viewed some of the elements within PARSNIP culturally sensitive resulting in their avoidance especially for the topic religion. While Huy overtly shared his belief and used materials related to his belief, other teachers chose to avoid the topic or only openly shared their religious affiliation but did not engage the students in in-depth discussion on religion. The findings reinforce Mambu's (2014) argument that teachers should be prepared to engage students to reflect on topics related to spirituality and/or religion in class. In addition, as Purgason (1994), as cited in Mambu (2014), suggests, when teachers discuss topics related to religion, "students will not hear what the teacher says as propaganda or proselytizing" if all ideas by students are "welcomed, encouraged, and appreciated" (p. 32). However, Mambu (2014) warns that teachers still need to be cautious of power that they exercise when they are in class, and they have to make sure students have equal opportunities to share their perspectives. Thus, it is crucial to prepare teachers to be able to ethically deal with questions about religion and be mindful of power relations between them and students and between students and students. The preparation will not only help them develop students' IC but also hinder them from forcing their religious values to their students.

The activities, topics, and strategies in Table 12.4 are relevant to intercultural competence as they invite students to reflect on their own cultures, exchange worldviews, discuss global issues, explore the functions of language use, and play different cultural roles to negotiate their ideas. Nonetheless, there is still room for improving these activities by modifying teachers' questions. For instance, the questions can encourage students to explore the fundamental values and beliefs underlying those cultural practices such as why people in a culture drink wine in a festival, what the roles of wine are, and why it is so. Furthermore, the questions need to raise students' awareness of diversity and how different cultures are in contact. To be specific, one recommendation/suggestion is that teachers could ask how their religion influences their cultural daily practice, how their living in Australia raises their awareness and understanding of other religions, and how religions impact their language use such as "may God find you in good health" or "God bless you" instead of or in addition to asking students what their country's national religion is. The findings support Diaz's (2015) observation that teachers' readiness to develop and implement (inter)cultural materials and activities remains a challenge.

Although the teachers admitted that it is their students' cultural backgrounds that determine whether or not these topics are better avoided in class, it can be seen that their own cultures do play a role since teachers normally rely on their cultural experiences as the compass of what to tackle or not in class. For instance, the religious affiliation and religious experiences of Huy, Marzieh, and Leila influence how they deal with topics related to religion. In a former study by Sercu (2005), it is stated that teachers' IC practices are shaped and influenced by "the social, psychological and environmental realities of the school and classroom" (p. 174). Nevertheless, what was found in this study indicates that besides these realities, the teachers' cultural backgrounds and identities also play a role in their enactment of IC through the application of PARSNIP. The findings are in line with the autoethnographic study by Siregar (2016) which demonstrated that the incorporation of teaching material related to PARSNIP was influenced by teachers' cultural backgrounds and identities.

12.6   Conclusions and Implications

The findings above answered the research questions in terms of the teachers' responses and interpretation of PARSNIP and their integration of PARSNIP activities as follows:

To what extent do they believe PARSNIP should be addressed in ELT to facilitate intercultural competence?

The teachers advocated that since taboo topics in general and PARSNIP in specific vary across cultures and are inevitable in everyday intercultural communication, addressing them in class is advantageous in multiple ways. Those include (i) raising students' awareness of culturally sensitive topics and variations in the notion of taboos across cultures and (ii) preparing them with strategies to deal with the topics appropriately and pragmatically to maintain harmonious relationship in intercultural exchange. In general, teachers are opposed to the avoidance of taboos in ELT as the more they are avoided, the more potential dangers students can encounter in reality due to a lack of preparation.

What does PARSNIP mean to teachers of different cultural backgrounds?

PARSNIP, despite being viewed as universal taboos (Gray, 2002), is interpreted differently across cultures and individuals. Teachers' varied responses on what is taboo reinforces the fact that taboo itself is a fluid, comprehensive and elusive concept as it is culturally specific and can be religious, dietary, or cultural. Some of the elements of PARSNIP are not taboos to the teachers while there are other elements that are considered potentially sensitive such as age, disabilities, violence, gender, and poverty. In their experience, not only topics but also the use of language and visuals should be handled with caution. Their reflection indicates that the interpretation of PARSNIP is context, culture, and individual specific.

What issues, if any, have impacted teachers' decisions to avoid or address PARSNIP?

As revealed by the five teachers, whether PARSNIP is addressed in their teaching or not does not lie in the fact that it is widely regarded as taboos but in a multitude of objective and subjective factors. They include the students' cultural backgrounds; the aims of the whole course and specific lessons; the relevancy to the currently used ELT materials; the class experience; the potential for productive and interesting activities; the teachers' knowledge, confidence, and teaching strategies; and the availability of existing supplementary resources.

To what extent do they address PARSNIP in class?

The teachers had addressed these culturally sensitive topics intentionally or unintentionally in class. There have been negative and positive experiences in doing so, but they supported that had they been well prepared for tackling with these issues, they would have turned discussion or activities in a more engaging manner.

The teachers believed that PARSNIP and beyond, if being addressed appropriately in class, would foster students' understanding of different cultures and develop their intercultural competence in terms of awareness, attitudes, knowledge, and strategies.

They also came up with a range of activities and strategies including eliciting self-reflection, encouraging critical observation, facilitating cultural exchange, and explication of cultural practice, as well as drawing attention to language use, visuals, and different negotiation strategies.

In brief, PARSNIP is not homogenously interpreted as taboos across teachers of English in Australia. The findings illuminate the expansion and implications of PARSNIP in the current and future ELT practice as teachers acknowledged the pros of addressing global and local taboo issues in class for the development of intercultural competence. They also become cognizant of factors determining their decisions on whether or not an issue should be addressed to develop students' intercultural competence. The findings emphasize that teachers' awareness of PARSNIP will inform their roles as English teachers in today's era and in the future. The awareness will increase teachers' readiness to discuss global issues and controversial topics competently and pragmatically in English. Hence, teachers have to keep developing their questioning skills so that they can engage students in any debatable topics and empower their students to take actions and negotiate when facing cultural conflicts. It is implied that there is a real need for material development and professional development courses which can give teachers learning opportunities to reflect on the limitations of PARSNIP as well as its potentials as debatable topics that can develop students' IC when handled critically and ethically. In other words, what has been found regarding cultural taboo topics in this study opens a dimension of discussion on addressing intercultural communication and cultural conflicts, one of the challenges in ELT in the globalized era.

As discussed above, the study offers an insight into IC and PARSNIP. However, the study was conducted on a small number of teachers in an institution in Melbourne, Australia. Thus, further research is needed to confirm and expand on the findings of this study by incorporating more teachers' voices from different institutions in Australia and elsewhere.

References

Bennett, J. M., Bennett, M. J., & Allen, W. (2003). Developing intercultural competence in the language classroom. In D. L. Lange & R. M. Paige (Eds.), *Culture as the core: Integrating culture into the language curriculum* (pp. 237–270). Greenwich, CT: Information Age Pub.

Byram, M. (1997). *Teaching and assessing intercultural communicative competence.* Clevedon, UK: Multilingual Matters.

Byram, M. (2012). Language awareness and (critical) cultural awareness-relationships, comparisons and contrasts. *Language Awareness, 21*(1–2), 5–13. Retrieved from https://doi.org/10. 1080/09658416.2011.639887

Collins, J. (2012). Integration and inclusion of immigrants in Australia. In J. Frideres & J. Biles (Eds.), *International perspectives: Integration and inclusion* (pp. 17–37). Montreal, Quebec: McGill- Queen's University Press.

Collins, J., & Reid, C. (2012). Immigrant teachers in Australia. *Cosmopolitan Civil Societies Journal, 14*(2), 38–61.

Diaz, A. R. (2015). Developing interculturally-oriented teaching resources in CFL: Meeting the challenge. In R. Moloney & L. X. Hui (Eds.), *Exploring innovative pedagogy in the teaching and learning of Chinese as a foreign language* (pp. 115–135). Singapore, Singapore: Springer.

Duff, P. A., & Uchida, Y. (1997). The negotiation of teachers' sociocultural identities and practices in postsecondary EFL classrooms. *TESOL Quarterly, 31*(3), 451–486. Retrieved from https:// doi.org/10.2307/3587834

Gobert, M. (2015). Taboo topics in the ESL/EFL classroom in the Gulf region. In R. Raddawi (Ed.), *Intercultural communication with Arabs: Studies in educational, professional and societal contexts* (pp. 109–124). Singapore, Singapore: Springer.

Gray, J. (2002). The global coursebook in English language teaching. In D. Block & D. Cameron (Eds.), *Globalization and language teaching* (pp. 151–167). London: Routledge.

Gray, J. (2010). *The construction of English: Culture, consumerism and promotion in the ELT global coursebook.* New York: Palgrave Macmillan.

Harbon, L., & Moloney, R. (2015). 'Intercultural' and 'multicultural', awkward companions: The case in schools in New South Wales, Australia. In H. Layne, V. Trémion, & F. Dervin (Eds.), *Making the most of intercultural education* (pp. 15–33). Newcastle upon Tyne, UK: Cambridge Scholars.

Hatoss, A. (2006). Globalisation, interculturality and culture teaching: International students' cultural learning needs in Australia. *Prospects, 21*(2), 47–69.

Hook, B. (2011). Transformative pedagogy and multiculturalism. In T. Perry & J. W. Fraser (Eds.), *Freedom's plow: Teaching in the multicultural classroom* (pp. 91–98). Abingdon, UK: Routledge.

Keturi, S., & Lehmonen, T. (2011). *Taboo or not taboo: A study of taboo content in Finnish EFL learning materials* (Thesis). University of Jyväskylä, Jyväskylä, Finland. Retrieved from http:// urn.fi/URN:NBN:fi:jyu-2011120911780

Keturi, S., & Lehmonen, T. (2012). *Thou shalt not write about. . .: A study of taboo content in Finnish EFL textbooks for upper secondary school* (Thesis). University of Jyväskylä, Jyväskylä, Finland. Retrieved from https://jyx.jyu.fi/dspace/bitstream/handle/123456789/37466/URN_ NBN_fi_jyu-201202291322.pdf?sequence=4

Leather, S. (2003). Taboos and issues. *ELT Journal, 57*(2), 205–206.

Liddicoat, A. J., & Scarino, A. (2013). *Intercultural language teaching and learning.* Retrieved from http://onlinelibrary.wiley.com.helicon.vuw.ac.nz/book/10.1002/9781118482070

Lorenzo, T. (2005). *We don't see ourselves as different: A web of possibilities for disabled women: How black disabled women in poor communities equalise opportunities for human development and social change* (Doctoral thesis). University of Cape Town, Cape Town, South Africa. Retrieved from https://open.uct.ac.za/handle/11427/9982

Lorenzo, T. (2010). The right to rehabilitation: From policy development to implementation. *South African Journal of Occupational Therapy, 40*(1), 1–1.

Mambu, J. E. (2014). *Negotiating the place of spirituality in English language teaching: A case study in an Indonesian EFL teacher education program* (Doctoral thesis). Arizona State University, Tempe, AZ. Retrieved from https://repository.asu.edu/attachments/143405/content/Mambu_asu_0010E_14422.pdf

Module 2- Exploring intercultural language teaching and learning. (2007). Retrieved from http://www.iltlp.unisa.edu.au/doclibmodules/iltlp_module2.pdf

Moloney, R., & Hui, L. X. (2015). The effects of language materials on the development of intercultural competence. In R. Moloney & L. X. Hui (Eds.), *Exploring innovative pedagogy in the teaching and learning of Chinese as a foreign language* (pp. 1–18). Singapore, Singapore: Springer.

Pratt, M. (1999). Arts and the contact zone. In D. Bartholomae & A. Petroksky (Eds.), *Ways of readings: An anthology for writers* (pp. 581–596). Boston: Bedford/St Martins.

Purgason, K. B. (1994). How to communicate values and truth in the context of teaching English as a second or foreign language. *Evangelical Missions Quarterly, 30*, 238–243.

Sercu, L. (2005). Foreign language teachers and the implementation of intercultural education: A comparative investigation of the professional self-concepts and teaching practices of Belgian teachers of English, French and German. *European Journal of Teacher Education, 28*(1), 87–105. Retrieved from https://doi.org/10.1080/02619760500040389

Sharifian, F. (2009). *English as an international language: Perspectives and pedagogical approaches*. Bristol, UK: Multilingual Matters.

Sharifian, F. (2014). Teaching English as an international language in multicultural contexts: Focus on Australia. In R. Marlina & R. A. Giri (Eds.), *The pedagogy of English as an international language: Perspectives from scholars, teachers, and students* (pp. 35–46). London: Springer.

Siregar, F. L. (2016). *In pursuit of intercultural communicative competence: An investigation of English language policy and practices at a private university in Indonesia*. Wellington, New Zealand: Victoria University of Wellington.

Smith, E. L. (2015). English as an International Auxiliary Language. Journal of English as a Lingua Franca, 4(1), 159–164.

Vertovec, S. (2007). Super-diversity and its implications. *Ethnic and Racial Studies, 30*(6), 1024–1054. Retrieved from https://doi.org/10.1080/01419870701599465

Young, T. J., Sercombe, P. G., Sachdev, I., Naeb, R., & Schartner, A. (2013). Success factors for international postgraduate students' adjustment: Exploring the roles of intercultural competence, language proficiency, social contact, and social support. *European Journal of Higher Education, 3*(2), 151–171.

Zaid, M. A. (1999). Cultural confrontation and cultural acquisition in the EFL classroom. *Review of Applied Linguistics, 37*(2), 111–126.

Epilogue

Darío Luis Banegas

Revisiting the Past and Present

While edited volumes are not usually intended to be read from beginning to end, a concluding chapter may help readers find connections between introductory paragraphs, contributors' chapters, and what this volume has left as it develops in the trajectory we imprint when reading it. The aim of this concluding chapter is to highlight the strengths the collection holds in understanding the past, present, and future regarding intercultural competence. It also aims to problematize ramifications and opportunities for further development across sociopolitical and geographical contexts.

In this volume, each contribution has been solid in depicting the origins and evolution of interculturality and intercultural competence mostly in the area of language learning and teaching. The volume leaves us with a stronger understanding of intercultural competence within a broad applied linguistics perspective. From this perspective, the past and the present have cemented the notion that language is a semiotic resource human beings have for creating and recreating social practices. In the field of language teaching, whether we refer to first or additional languages, understanding of language has translated from language as a system to language as discourse (McCarthy & Clancy, 2019).

On the one hand, this paradigmatic shift in language understanding can be explained by acknowledging the power and potency of the work in systematic functional linguistics (SFL). According to work in this branch, language is meaning and a resource for constructing and enacting socioculturally embedded experiences and practices (Chappell, 2020). On the other, and definitely more significant and meaningful across narratives and rhetorics in education, is the fact that viewing

D. L. Banegas
University of Strathclyde, Glasgow, UK
e-mail: dario.banegas@strath.ac.uk

© Springer Nature Singapore Pte Ltd. 2021
M. D. López-Jiménez, J. Sánchez-Torres (eds.), *Intercultural Competence Past, Present and Future*, Intercultural Communication and Language Education, https://doi.org/10.1007/978-981-15-8245-5

language as a semiotic resource places the school in a complex landscape. If language mediates schooling as a social practice, it follows that the main drive underpinning schooling is not instrumental but transformative and educational. If we transpolate this discussion to language education, this entails that language teaching cannot remain passive at the level of instrumentality (e.g., how to ask for directions); it is expected to include a stronger educational view, one which allows language learners to discuss issues such as identity or diversity across their linguistic repertoire.

Under this transformative paradigm, an interest in intercultural competence in language education has attracted the engagement of several educators around the globe. For example, from the Colombian context, Barletta Manjarrés (2009) calls for deeper understandings of culture and cultures in English language education. In her concluding remarks, she highlights:

> The importance of foreign language education then could lie in preparing citizens to have more flexible views of the Other and of the Self and in the attempt at having more mutually reinforcing encounters. This is especially true of Colombia, which is a multicultural country. This issue, however, is hardly tackled in day-to-day English classrooms. And instead, it is a superficial approach to the teaching of culture that prevails. (p. 154)

Based in Argentina, Porto (2019b) extends and revamps this discussion as follows:

> An acknowledgment of the political and ethical duties and responsibilities of foreign language education moved it beyond the goal of linguistic and communicative competence toward the goal of intercultural communicative competence (Byram, 1997; Liddicoat & Scarino, 2013). The model of intercultural competence (Byram, 1997) laid out the different dimensions of knowledge, skills, and attitudes, beyond the linguistic, that language education should address. In terms of knowledge or *savoirs*, intercultural competence comprises, for instance, knowledge of the ways of life in a given society or context including work, education, traditions, history, dress codes, and food, among others. Attitudes have a place and involve the attitudes of curiosity and inquisitiveness, or *savoir être*, which are complemented with the skills of interpreting and relating those *saviors*, or *savoir comprendre*, and the communicative skills of discovery and interaction, or *savoir apprendre/savoir faire*. Finally, critical cultural awareness, or *savoirs'engager*, is paramount in this model and involves not only critical thinking but also social transformation through critical self-reflection, intercultural dialogue, and action (Holmes, 2014; Houghton, 2012) by both learners and teachers. (p. 143)

These two quotes seem to anticipate the tones that intercultural competence has shown in the volume. Aspects such as heritage languages and motivation (Chaps. 1, 2, 4), attitudes towards English (Chap. 7), critical cultural awareness (Chap. 8), othering (Chap. 9), or the media (Chap. 10) reveal that intercultural competence has grown in association with a complex array of analytical frameworks not only from applied linguistics but also from psychology and sociology. In concomitance with such research frameworks and epistemologies, and by drawing on the various research contexts depicted in this volume, we come to learn that intercultural competence, and interculturality as a broader term, results from social concerns and practices that are channeled through formal educational practices for their exploration and understanding. Put differently, situated practices call for a post-structuralist perspective that organizes and supports reflection and criticality around the social, the political, and ideological forces that intersect and shape human experience, where humans are intercultural beings in the material and digital worlds.

In revisiting the past and the present in the study of intercultural competence, some research features found in this volume should be highlighted as through them we can trace how scholars in different settings have approached intercultural competence. For example, while intercultural competence cuts across all levels of education, the authors included in this volume have had children and teenagers (e.g., Chap. 1) as well as adults (e.g., Chaps. 2 and 5) as their participants. Participants in each chapter have a rich variety of cultural backgrounds, and while some chapters have focused on a few participants as case studies (Chap. 2), other chapters draw on data from more than 100 participants (e.g., Chap. 8). Perhaps, this focus on adult participants is an invitation for other scholars to examine intercultural competence with younger learners in different settings.

Regarding research methods, qualitative inquiry, usually materialized through the use of in-depth interviews (Chaps. 2, 11), and narrative inquiry (Chap. 11) help provide laser-focused understanding of how participants can navigate their identities, motivations, and multilingual practices. The same applies to Chap. 2, in which ethnography and case study perspectives were used to arrive at thick descriptions of a participant's understanding and biography. On the other hand, mixed methods, often in sequential mode, that is, quantitative instruments followed by qualitative tools, were employed to gain broader insights from larger research population, as it can be found in Chaps. 3 and 6, where in the latter we also have examples of group interviews. Quantitative data, mostly from questionnaires, became the backbone of Chaps. 4, 6, 7, and 8.

Two chapters stand out, given their more innovative research methods. In Chap. 9, data came from an ecological perspective (Edwards & Burns, 2016; van Lier, 2004), that is, from the immediate context in which it emerged: a classroom, before, during, and after the delivery of a course. This perspective puts forward worth considering pedagogical contours as it shows what may happen with the typical implications and suggestions included in academic articles on the issue of intercultural competence, in the case of Chap. 9, framed in a course. In Chap. 10, data collection delves into the territories of wiki forums and image-centered discussions. These two strategies reveal that the present is interested not only in the research of verbal representations, beliefs, and perceptions of participants but also in the investigation of multimodal affordances (Höllerer et al. 2019).

Future Directions

In view of the emerging themes, discussions, and implications traced in the volume, we can think of directions in terms of language learning, global citizenship, and their impact on curriculum and teacher development.

In terms of language learning, the research included in this volume indicates that a multilingual lens may necessitate from a conceptual framework which describes the multiplicity of language practices without disregarding the "messiness" in which they occur in the environment. In this regard, notions of plurilingualism and translanguaging may be incorporated in our understanding of intercultural competence.

In a recent article contextualized in Colombia, Ortega (2019) describes plurilingualism as follows:

> Plurilingualism refers to the number of languages or even variations of the same languages that coexist in the same society (Council of Europe, 2001). The concept behind plurilingualism implies that the languages we use for communication are not siloed or homogenous monolithic systems, but are elements of a dynamic multi-system that overlaps with other languages. (Wandruszka, 1979, as cited in Piccardo, 2013)
>
> [...]
>
> One of the highlights of plurilingualism is that it has assumed a subtle yet profound shift in perspective towards the use of multiple languages, in a manner that benefits individuals by negating the notion that it is essential to achieve linguistic perfection; this removes the stress of trying to achieve the fluency of a native speaker. (Coste, Moore, & Zarate, 2009, p. 157)

The quotes stress that the languages that a speaker (individual plurilingualism) may use are all part of a complex repertoire, and therefore they are not isolated from each other. By the same token, societal plurilingualism comes to describe how, in a given city, for example, the languages found in "immigrant" neighborhoods are not restricted to a specific neighborhood. They go beyond those borders and can be heard in different parts of the city in interaction with other languages. The fact that minority/immigrant languages are spoken regardless of geographical boundaries has shifted our understanding of how bilingual, in the broadest sense of the term, speakers engage in social practices through more than one language. Research has moved from the concept of code-switching to that of translanguaging. According to Garcia (2009), translanguaging refers to the multiple discursive practices in which bilinguals engage to make sense of their worlds; it is the only discursive practice that can include all family members. The author adds that in the classroom, translanguaging has the potential to explicitly valorize all models and practices along the continua of biliterate development. Drawing on this term, future studies on intercultural competence can center their micro-lens on individuals in context and understand how the multifarious cultural-mediated practices in which bilinguals develop are encoded in particular language practices and linguistic behavior.

With a stronger hold in the area of criticality in language education (Banegas & Villacañas de Castro, 2016), global citizenship/citizenship education appears to be the next informing source in the development of intercultural competence. The recognition, celebration, and awareness of the plurilingual and pluricultural world in which we live leads to the need to promote and develop intercultural competence, which in turn is sought to enable the social construction of peaceful and broader interpretations of how we live with others. This overarching aim greatly exceeds language education and even education, it is a sociopolitical program; yet, it needs to be built on the pillars of language education and education in general for its sustainable accomplishment.

Speaking from the Global South, Calle Diaz (2017) defines global citizenship education as

> an umbrella term that comprises earlier developments on education as the basis to achieve sustainable development, peace, values, civics, human rights, global education, intercultural awareness education, environmental education, education for social justice and equity, among others. (pp. 157-158)

In the merging of the concepts discussed so far, the term intercultural citizenship education appears as a critical amalgamation to work on. In the guest editorial to a special issue, Porto, Houghton, and Byram (2018) describe that

> intercultural citizenship education acknowledges the instrumental value of learning one or more languages but crucially focuses on its educational worth and potential. It is a development in which the role of foreign language education in citizenship and political and moral education is seen as an extension of the scope of citizenship education. (p. 485)

Thus, the future of research and practice in intercultural competence lies in interdisciplinary work that embraces institutions as catalysts for social change and social justice. In line with this premise, the literature has already shown connections between intercultural competence and citizenship with human rights education (e.g., Osler & Starkey, 2015; Porto, 2015, 2019a).

It seems crass to point out that the incorporation of working concepts such as translanguaging, intercultural citizenship or global citizenship education have direct implications for curriculum development and teacher education. As a socio-political organizer, a curriculum reflects wider and deeper ideologies, and therefore, for intercultural competence to develop with intercultural citizenship, policymakers are to be approached and become engaged in this innovative framework. Alongside curriculum development and developers, advances in how intercultural competence can be conceptualized and how it intersects with other interests and constructs, for example, human rights, need to be introduced in teacher education programs so that future teachers are formally prepared to enact a curriculum for action (Porto & Byram, 2015).

References

Banegas, D. L., & Villacañas de Castro, L. S. (2016). Criticality. *ELT Journal, 70*(4), 455–457.

Barletta Manjarrés, N. (2009). Intercultural competence: Another challenge. *Profile, 11*(1), 143–158.

Byram, M. (1997). *Teaching and assessing intercultural communicative competence*. Clevedon: Multilingual Matters.

Calle Díaz, L. (2017). Citizenship education and the EFL standards: A critical reflection. *Profile, 19* (1), 155–168.

Chappell, P. (2020). A functional model of language for language teacher education. In D. L. Banegas (Ed.), *Content knowledge in English language teacher education: International insights* (pp. 29–48). London/New York: Bloomsbury.

Coste, D., Moore, D., & Zarate, G. (2009). *Plurilingual and Pluricultural Competence: with a Foreword and Complementary Bibliography*. Strasbourg: Council of Europe.

Edwards, E., & Burns, A. (2016). Language teacher–researcher identity negotiation: An ecological perspective. *TESOL Quarterly, 50*(3), 735–745.

Garcia, O. (2009). *Bilingual education in the 21ˢᵗ century: A global perspective*. Malden/Oxford: Wiley-Blackwell.

Höllerer, M., van Leeuwen, T., Jancsary, D., Meyer, R., Andersen, T., & Vaara, E. (2019). *Visual and multimodal research in organization and management studies*. New York: Routledge.

Holmes, P. (2014). Business and management education. In J. Jackson (Ed.), *The Routledge handbook of language and intercultural communication* (pp. 464–480). London: Routledge.

Houghton, S. A. (2012). *Intercultural dialogue in practice: Managing value judgment in foreign language education*. Bristol: Multilingual Matters.

Liddicoat, A. J., & Scarino, A. (2013). *Intercultural language teaching and learning*. Retrieved from http://onlinelibrary.wiley.com.helicon.vuw.ac.nz/book/10.1002/9781118482070

McCarthy, M., & Clancy, B. (2019). From language as a system to language as discourse. In S. Walsh & S. Mann (Eds.), *The Routledge handbook of English language teacher education* (pp. 201–215). London/New York: Routledge.

Ortega, Y. (2019). "Teacher, ¿puedo hablar en español?" A reflection on plurilingualism and translanguaging practices in EFL. *Profile, 21*(2), 155–170.

Osler, A., & Starkey, H. (2015). Education for cosmopolitan citizenship: A framework for language learning. *Argentinian Journal of Applied Linguistics, 3*(2), 30–39.

Piccardo, E. (2013). Plurilingualism and curriculum design: Toward a synergic vision. *TESOL Quarterly, 47*(3), 600–614.

Porto, M. (2015). Beyond foreign language teaching: Intercultural citizenship and human rights education in practice. *Argentinian Journal of Applied Linguistics, 3*(2), 139–147.

Porto, M. (2019a). Affordances, complexities, and challenges of intercultural citizenship for foreign language teachers. *Foreign Language Annals, 52*(1), 141–164.

Porto, M. (2019b). Does education for intercultural citizenship lead to language learning? *Language, Culture and Curriculum, 32*(1), 16–33.

Porto, M., & Byram, M. (2015). A curriculum for action in the community and intercultural citizenship in higher education. *Language, Culture and Curriculum, 28*(3), 226–242.

Porto, M., Houghton, S., & Byram, M. (2018). Intercultural citizenship in the (foreign) language classroom. *Language Teaching Research, 22*(5), 484–498.

van Lier, L. (2004). *The ecology and semiotics of language learning: A sociocultural perspective*. Boston: Kluwer Academic.

Wandruszka, M. (1979). *Die Mehrsprachigkeit des Menschen* [The plurilingualism of the human being]. Stuttgart: Kohlhammer.

Printed by Books on Demand, Germany